WILFRID FREEMAN

The genius behind
Allied survival and air supremacy
1939 to 1945

Anthony Furse

WILFRID
FREEMAN

The genius behind Allied
survival and air supremacy
1939 to 1945

Foreword by the late
PROFESSOR R.V. JONES CH

SPELLMOUNT

STAPLEHURST

© 2000 Anthony Furse

British Library Cataloguing in Publication Data:
A catalogue record for this book is available
from the British Library.

ISBN 1-86227-079-1

Published in the UK in 1999 by
Spellmount Limited
The Old Rectory
Staplehurst
Kent TN12 0AZ

1 3 5 7 9 8 6 4 2

Set in Photina
Designed and produced by
Pardoe Blacker Publishing Limited
Lingfield · Surrey

Printed in Slovenia

Contents

AIRCRAFT NAMING POLICY
Production versions of World War II military aircraft were named differently by the
combatants. RAF aircraft are usually referred to by names alone, such as Spitfire,
Mosquito or Lancaster. American planes often had names as well as a numbered
category, thus B-17 Flying Fortress or P-47 Thunderbolt. Although German aircraft
are usually referred to by their maker's acronym and a number as He 177, Ju 88 or
FW 190, most histories, and the pages that follow, refer to aircraft designed by
Messerschmitt for the Bayerische Flugzuegwerke before the company was renamed in
1938, as the Me 109 or Me 110 rather than Bf 109 or Bf 110.

Foreword

by the late Professor R.V. Jones CH
(written in 1996)

LOOKING BACK on my memories of the wartime Air Staff in a lecture to the Royal Air Force Historical Society in 1986, I remarked that 'If I had to single out the senior Air Officer who has had least recognition from posterity for the magnitude of his contribution it would be Wilfrid Freeman'; and I hopefully suggested that no one deserved a biography more.

Here we now have it, thanks to the work of three successive authors. The original plan was that it should be written by Jeffrey Quill, whose outstanding contribution as a test pilot is evident from his book *Spitfire*. When illness prevented his proceeding, Sebastian Cox of the Air Historical Branch of the Ministry of Defence took over until he, too, had to hand the work on, this time to Anthony Furse, a nephew of Wilfrid Freeman himself. The task has been a substantial one, handicapped by the loss of all Freeman's personal papers and by the demise of many of those with first-hand memories of Freeman and his work, although eased perhaps by the mellowing of passions with time, and by the papers that have become available in the sixty years that have elapsed since Freeman, as Air Member for Research and Development, signed the production contract for the first 310 Spitfires.

Like many of the senior officers of the Royal Air Force in the Second World War, Freeman had also served in the First. There, the novel challenge of aerial warfare, demanding speed of personal reaction and skill in flying, along with a readiness to experiment with new techniques, could best be met by young men. And by the time the Royal Air Force was created out of the Royal Naval Air Service and the Royal Flying Corps in 1918, most of its outstanding officers were still young despite the intensity of their experiences. They thus formed a cadre whose members could naturally rise to the highest levels as the Royal Air Force entered the Second World War.

Among them the public became familiar with the names of Dowding, Portal, Joubert, Harris, Tedder, Leigh-Mallory, Park and others as the events of the war unfolded. The public rarely heard, though, the name of Wilfrid Freeman; but this biography will show what a debt we owed him for his unique contribution to the successes of both the Royal Air Force and of its American counterparts.

His Service experience had begun in 1908, when he joined the Manchester Regiment after two years at Sandhurst, following school at Rugby; but unexcited by life in the pre-Contemptible Little Army, he moved to the Royal Flying Corps in 1913, and was posted to No. 2 Squadron. By 9 September 1914 he was in France, and was soon flying to reconnoitre the advancing German forces.

At Neuve Chapelle in March 1915 he acted as 'spotter' to direct the fire of the British guns, and was awarded one of the first MCs gained by the RFC. In so doing he learnt the value of 'wireless' communication between aircraft and guns, and of the airborne camera as a major factor in reconnaissance. Posted then to Egypt, he proved as good an organiser as he was an airman, and in June 1916 he was recalled to England as a Lieutenant-Colonel to command a Training Wing.

The following year he was commanding a Wing in France, and proposing a method of blind bombing at night, using three vertically pointing search-lights placed in line with the intended target. If a pilot flying along the line defined by the lights were to continue on the same compass course after passing over the third light, this should bring him over the target regardless of wind, and he could estimate when to release his bombs from the time he took to cover the known distance between the second and third lights, and the distance of the target beyond the third light.

On the formation of the Royal Air Force in 1918, Freeman – now a Wing Commander – was posted by Trenchard to the Naval Staff College at Greenwich. And when the Royal Air Force set up its own Staff College at Andover in 1922, Freeman was appointed as a senior instructor with Sholto Douglas, Keith Park, Charles Portal and Richard Peirse among the students. In 1926 Freeman became Commandant of the Central Flying School, where he supported a special Aerobatic Flight for the 1927 air display at Hendon; its success was a step in the long tradition of precise aerobatics that led to the Red Arrows.

After further command and special appointments, including those of AOC Palestine and Commandant of the RAF Staff College, Freeman joined the Air Council in 1936 as Air Member for Research and Development in succession to Dowding who had become Commander-in-Chief, Fighter Command. Freeman's new appointment was crucial, for he, more than any other man, was to determine the choice of aircraft and equipment with which the RAF would fight the coming war.

His first assets were his own experience of air fighting and of command problems at all levels, combined with prescience, patience, and a selfless sense of fair play, principle and duty.

His further assets were the inventiveness, expertise and enthusiasm aroused among scientists, engineers and industrialists by the rise of the Nazi threat; and on these he could draw in fullest measure. Watson-Watt, for example, had already conceived radar, Mitchell the Spitfire, and Whittle the jet engine; and de Havilland were to follow with the Mosquito in 1939. But to select which concepts to back, and drive them with utmost urgency through all the stages of doubt, research and development, and then on to production was a task as challenging as any man of his time had to face.

No one else would have done it so admirably as Freeman did: Anthony Furse shows us how he did it, and some of the difficulties he countered on the way. 'I am making a background on which to paint the future' he told his daughter in 1936. And one of his achievements was so to shape that background that with his encouragement other men could best make their individual contributions. When R.J. Mitchell, the designer of the Spitfire, was dying he wrote to Freeman 'I have felt that my enthusiasm had quite a lot to do with your decision to place an order'. And when after Mitchell's death the film *The First of the Few* had its showing in London, Freeman found it too much of an ordeal to attend, so deeply did he feel Mitchell's loss.

Watson-Watt placed Freeman, 'sparkling but serious, cynical but constructive, frank but friendly', amongst his four champions of radar. Maurice Dean, who as a senior Civil Servant saw nearly all the senior air officers, wrote 'Among the achievements of Freeman's reign must be mentioned Lancasters, Spitfires, Mustangs, Mosquitoes, and Tempests. When one considers the technical disasters which beset the German Air Force despite German technical ability one realises the depth and scope of Freeman's achievements.' Freeman was a most attractive man. He was a bit of a rebel. His Air Marshal's cap was in fact adorned with golden oak leaves, but they were placed on the shiny black peak of a ranker's cap, not the cloth-covered peak of an officer's cap.

Many of us would agree with Maurice Dean's verdict that 'The Mosquito has claims to be considered the outstanding aircraft of the Royal Air Force... Its successful emergence as the only unarmed bomber of an air force in the Second World War was due to the brilliance of the conception and design backed by the wisdom and courage of Wilfrid Freeman.'

And yet the Mosquito had been cancelled by Portal in December 1940, and its bomber version by Portal and Harris in 1942. It was saved on both occasions by Freeman's intervention – he got round the second cancellation by ordering an extra 250 of the photo-reconnaissance version, knowing that these could readily be converted into bombers once both Harris and the Air Staff realised their value.

Freeman's subterfuge proved thoroughly justified. His enthusiasm had led to the Mosquito being dubbed 'Freeman's Folly'; but as the aircraft proved capable of carrying the guns to make it a formidable nightfighter, or a 4,000lb bomb, or an anti-tank gun, in addition to its superb capability for reconnaissance, de Havilland happily advertised its multi-role supremacy in an advertisement in *Flight*, showing a Mosquito spread-eagled as though it were an insect impaled on a pin like an entomologist's specimen, with the pseudo-zoological designation of 'Anopheles de Havillandus' – an insect with exceptional vision and vicious sting – with the further information that the female of the species 'lays large eggs'. By the end of the war nearly 7,000 Mosquitoes had been built, and another 1,000 before production ceased in 1950.

It was not only the speed of the Mosquito that gave it the advantage over German nightfighters. It could operate at heights they could not reach, whilst at the same time its height increased the range at which its navigators could pick up the pulses from ground stations in England transmitting Oboe signals, enabling them to mark targets in Germany with unrivalled precision. A small force of Mosquitoes could thus act as pathfinders to mark the targets for the main bomber force, and so emulate the success of their German counterparts, KampfGruppe 100.

Here again, Freeman's influence was critical. As Commander-in-Chief, Harris was emphatically opposed to the creation of a separate pathfinding force, and in this he had the support of some other senior officers. His arguments against the formation of a separate élite inside the Command were by no means negligible but Freeman intervened on the other side, having been convinced by the Deputy Director of Bomber Operations, Sydney Bufton. The result was that Portal summoned, and was convinced by, Bufton, who afterwards said that he had no doubt that it was the 'fortuitous intervention of Freeman' that pushed the formation of PFF against the shifting and evasive procrastination of Harris, and it was the united determination of Portal and Freeman that made Harris give way.

I myself knew Sydney Bufton; our relations had always been warm because it was his brother Hal (H.E.) who had been the pilot of the outstandingly competent and vital flight of 21/22 June 1940 which had demonstrated the existence of the Knickebein beams by the aid of which the Luftwaffe intended to bomb us in the Blitz. Anthony Furse has done history a service by reproducing Bufton's letter to Harris questioning the latter's opposition to the formation of the pathfinders. It must have been a difficult letter for a Group Captain to write to the most bombastic of Commanders-in-Chief, but it was as polite as it was brilliant: it should still be required reading for Staff Colleges. I only wish that I had seen more of Bufton.

In contrast with the Mosquito, some of the other aircraft for which Freeman felt responsible were not conspicuously successful. The first of the four-engined bombers, the Stirling, was one of these; but it was again characteristic of Freeman that he wanted to share the risks of the Stirling air crews by joining them in a flight over Germany. 'Going', he told his wife, 'would ease my conscience.' With his knowledge of Ultra and other defence secrets, it was out of the question for him to go, but Churchill for one would have understood his agony. Forced to renounce his intention to go with the Invasion Forces in the Normandy landings of 1944, Churchill wrote that 'A man taking, with the highest responsibility, grave and terrible decisions of war may need the refreshment of adventure. He may need also the comfort that when sending so many others to their deaths he may share in a small way their risks.'

But whilst Freeman could do little to improve the Stirling, it was otherwise with two other aircraft that he had ordered, the Lancaster and the Mustang. The Lancaster had started life as the Manchester with two Vulture engines, each of 2,000hp. But these were proving insufficiently reliable, and although some Manchesters were built and flown with success in operations, their future seemed doomed; but Chadwick, the Avro designer, tried the Manchester airframe with four Merlins, and with Freeman's support in August 1940 the Lancaster evolved. A year later Chadwick acknowledged Freeman's part: 'I am confident that the Lancaster will prove to be the outstanding aircraft of the war, and it is largely due to you that it has come into existence'.

All his efforts in the development and production of aircraft for the Royal Air Force were governed by his experience of 1914–1918 when he had known many pilots killed because they had been given inferior aircraft to fly. He was therefore determined that the aircraft for which he was responsible should be of the highest quality.

The Mustang was a further example where a mediocre aircraft was transformed into an outstanding one through Freeman's inspiration and support. Originally ordered by him from North American Aviation in America – a relatively small company not so far engaged in making combat aircraft – its early version proved to have only a moderate performance at height. But trials in England showed that its airframe and aerodynamics were remarkably efficient; and Freeman therefore arranged for its Allison engine to be replaced by a Merlin; the result was a fighter of such exceptional speed, agility, and range, that it transformed the American bombing campaign against Germany by providing the bombers with escorts that could outfly the defending German fighters. That might never have happened if the American aircraft industry had been left to itself. Anthony Furse tells the full story in Chapter 14.

The only German answer to the Mustang (and the Mosquito) would have been the jet fighter, the Messerschmitt 262, but fortunately its development as a fighter had been held back by Hitler's instructions, first to delay production and then to produce it as a 'Blitz Bomber' not a fighter. Coincidentally, development of the jet engine, which would naturally have come within Freeman's province, was also delayed: this was because of Whittle's reluctance to ally himself with, and perhaps be swamped by, a major engine manufacturer, which led him to choose the Rover car firm against Freeman's advice. Rover's progress was so ambulatory (I heard that its chairman had regarded the jet engine as a promising project to be pursued after the war) that as soon as he returned to MAP Freeman had to intervene and bring in Rolls-Royce. As a result the development of the jet engine was speeded up; but even so the Meteor had its first flight some time after the Me 262.

Besides the inspiration that Freeman gave to the development and production of the most outstanding aircraft and engines of the Second World War, and to the creation of the pathfinders, the thoroughness with which he tackled all his commitments ensured that the less glamorous aspects of organisation, such as the supply of spares and repair and maintenance, were equally well covered; and his tact in personal relations was vital in steering both Beaverbrook and Cripps (two of the Ministers of Aircraft Production under whom he worked) away from their wilder projects.

I myself encountered two examples of his tactful support.

Soon after I joined his staff in 1938, I had to report on a complaint from the outspoken editor of *The Aeroplane*, C.G. Grey, that the Air Ministry had rejected the offer of a new and secret infra-red detector based on ekacaesium.

Not only did this element not exist in nature, but I could prove that his device was no more than a conventional photocell, and that his claim was bogus. When my report went to Freeman, he summoned Grey to meet us.

Grey was so shaken to find that he had supported a charlatan that as I escorted him out ruefully said 'One day I should like to learn how someone like you ever came to be working in the Air Ministry'.

Among my treasures I have a letter from Freeman, the only one that he wrote to me. It is dated 22.1.41 and must have been written shortly after an attack of influenza, when he appeared to Diana Richmond as 'overworking to an idiotic degree, and is far from well...he looks extremely tired and white about the forehead and eyes'. It was the height of the Blitz, and I had written a report highly critical of our failure to jam the X-beams which the German pathfinders had been using to locate their targets. What I said was so unwelcome that some sections of the Air Staff had demanded that my report should be recalled. I was therefore most gratefully surprised to receive a handwritten letter from Freeman himself, which ran 'Last night I read your admirable report No. 10 with the greatest interest. A good deal of it is beyond me, but I hope to find time to go into it more thoroughly and so learn a lot more. Many thanks.'

Now, he was an Air Chief Marshal, and my equivalent rank would have been at most Squadron Leader, six rungs below him. Yet tired and ill as he was, and with the entire administration of the Royal Air Force on his shoulders, he could find time and patience to read through my report (it ran to some forty pages) and to write so generously. And more than a year later I found that he was intervening in the administrative background to help me find new staff.

I was indeed fortunate that he should have thought so well of my work and I am only sorry that I had so little chance to know him and to work directly for him. I would have cheered, for example, when he savaged with his own incisive prose the profusion of clichés in Air Staff reports on operations.

G.P. Bulman, who worked closely with him, spoke of his unusual panache, his piercing perception, and his cynical realism, with a faculty for comments that could be sparkling, wickedly mischievous, impish, generous and understanding. 'Impish' also occurs in Tedder's appreciation of Freeman whom he described as 'Very quiet but also shrewd, refreshing and inspiring urgency without panic, and with little time to waste on fools'. The Intelligence Service of the Luftwaffe was right on the mark when, in its March 1944 assessment of senior personalities in the Royal Air Force, its verdict was 'Freeman is regarded as an upright, honest, forthright, plain speaking, open character, with a special grasp of potential developments in technology and organisation. He is to be regarded as the driving force in the Ministry of Aircraft Production and Cripps' right-hand man.'

In all Freeman's actions his sense of loyalty and selflessness were supreme. He might well have resented, for example, Portal being preferred over him for the post of Chief of Air Staff; but he accepted Portal's request to become his Vice-Chief even though he would have preferred some other post. 'It is not for me' he told Beaverbrook on 4 November 1940 'to judge where I am most needed. My first duty must be to Portal... That by so doing I am taking a step down rather than up the ladder is a consideration that cannot count at such a time.'

In October 1941 he was sent out to the Mediterranean by Churchill and Portal to investigate Tedder's performance as Commander and, as ever, sent back an honest assessment. Portal then sent a signal asking whether he would be willing to take over from Tedder; this could have been an opportunity which would lead to the post of Deputy Supreme Commander of the Allied Forces for the Normandy landings. But Freeman's reply to the suggestion was sublimely characteristic: 'The role of Judas is one I cannot fill'.

Portal afterwards wrote of him 'His utter loyalty and conscientiousness, his shining intellectual insight and, almost above all, his happy wit and mischievous sense of humour combined to make him not only one of the greatest officers of his time but also the most lovable and dependable of friends'. Robert Burns was at his perceptive best when he wrote:

> The rank is but the guinea's stamp;
> The man's the gowd for a' that!

For Wilfred Freeman the stamp was exquisite and the gold twenty-four carat.

Preface

WILFRID FREEMAN died in May 1953. The fact that no one else has yet attempted to recount his magnificent services to his country and to the Royal Air Force and USAAF is no reflection on his almost unique importance to the activities of the Royal Air Force in the Second World War.

Well known authors like Denis Richards and John Terraine both refused because his papers had disappeared, and no professional author could afford the time to extract the vital needles of information from the great haystack of files in the Public Record Office and the other museums and archives.

Jeffrey Quill, the brilliant Spitfire test pilot, and most charming and modest of great men, embarked on the task in 1986, helped by Sebastian Cox from the Air Historical Branch of the RAF, who masterminded a comprehensive review of the most likely records, most of them in the PRO. This search was conducted with relentless precision by Sebastian Ritchie, a very young and able historian.

Failing health eventually obliged Quill to withdraw, after receiving much help on early chapters from Peter Pimblett. Cox also eventually found that he was unable to spare adequate time on the biography, due to the pressures of a family and a full time job. With characteristic generosity, he decided that his role would be to help me, which he has done with endless patience and the phenomenal depth of his background knowledge.

Freeman's achievements were such that all those who became involved over the past twelve years have been fascinated, and have given their time and help without stint. Sadly many of them have since died, including Quill who got the project going, but I am immensely grateful to him and to the others, particularly Air Vice-Marshal S.O. Bufton, Lords Nelson of Stafford, Cheshire and Kings Norton, Air Marshal Sir Denis Crowley-Milling, Sir John and Lady Richmond, Harald Penrose, Ronald Kerr-Muir and J.V. Connolly. To this list must be added, alas, Professor R.V. Jones, who has always looked forward to such a biography, and read early drafts, contributed personal letters and made vital comments and wrote the Foreword, and Betty Whitcombe who befriended Wilfrid and Elizabeth Richmond in Palestine, and filled in much about his personal life at that critical time.

Lord Plowden, Sir Alec Cairncross and Sir Peter Masefield, all of whom worked with Freeman at MAP, Sir Arthur Knight, a colleague at Courtaulds, Dr Alex Moulton and Peter Ware who assisted Roy Fedden at Bristol, Sir Robert Lickley of Hawker Siddeley, Dr Robert Feilden who worked under Frank Whittle during the war, Margaret Hitchcock, Tommy's widow and Air Chief Marshal Sir Kenneth Cross who served under Tedder in 1941–42, all gave valuable help.

My cousin Anne Beese, Freeman's much loved eldest daughter, kept all his letters to her, generously giving me access to them and, with her sisters Susan Malcolm and Joan Morgan-Grenville, to his fascinating letters to their mothers. The letters and family diaries have been a mine of information about their father and the Freeman family, and I am deeply grateful to them and Christopher Beese who helped to make it possible. Despite failing health his sister-in-law Eileen Freeman gave sparkling memories of Wilfrid and the Freeeman family with her usual, buoyant wit. Yet another Freeman cousin, Dr Mark Walker researched the early history of the amphetamine sulphate drug, Benzedrine.

Andrew Nahum at the Science Museum explained the problems of the aero-engines of the First World War, and Mike Evans and Dave Piggott of the Rolls-Royce Heritage Trust responded to much more detailed questions about the later Rolls-Royce engines in authoritative detail, helped by the expert drawings of Lyndon Jones. Robert and Donna Neal had all the facts about Packard Merlins, whilst Patrick Hassall, John Heaven and Peter Pavey talked or wrote about the problems and progress of the Bristol radials with great patience – a saga that was further explained by the discoveries of their Heritage librarian, Denis Hunt. The administrators of the Roosevelt Museum at Hyde Park, NY, which houses the Roosevelt, Hopkins and Winant archives, the RAF Museum at Hendon, the Imperial War Museum, the Royal Aeronautical Society and the Archivists of the Churchill and Portal papers all turned up documents which were vital to the story. I am most grateful to them and to the town librarians at Mold who went to endless trouble discovering rare and unusual books.

Jack Bruce and Stuart Leslie were a marvellous source of information and photographs of World War I aircraft and of the Royal Flying Corps.

The charming Anne Rowley-Williams, 'sheep-farmer's wife extraordinary', made sense of endless dictated drafts, and long tape-recorded interviews. My three sons taught me the basics of successive word-processors choosing and programming them, and staying calm and constructive when the 'frustrations of a computer illiterate' burst over the telephone. My wife endured six years of cluttered rooms, visits and visitors with exemplary patience.

Colonel Geoffrey Powell, Air Vice-Marshal Tony Mason, John Borron, Sarah Lush, William Goldie, Patrick Hassell and Anthony Price all made time to read drafts, and their encouragement at critical moments was heart warming. Dr Sebastian Ritchie deserves even greater thanks, for he diverted many hours of his spare time to the work of editing, contributing invaluable additions to chapters on aircraft production, and the Middle East and performing the essential surgery when the task of further editing seemed intolerable.

Finally my thanks and sincere admiration for Elwyn Blacker and his team at Pardoe Blacker. They instantly recognised the historic uniqueness of Freeman's achievements, and their composition, and expert contributions have made this somewhat technical tale more readable than I could have possibly expected.

Without this help I doubt whether that tangled web, those slivers of detailed information, would ever have been assembled into a story. Most of the advice and guidance has been superb, always touched by unreserved admiration for that remarkable man, and if, despite every care there are errors, or conclusions which later prove unjustified, the fault can only be mine.

Abbreviations

ACAS (I)	Assistant Chief of the Air Staff (intelligence)	{Senior assistants
ACAS (O)	Assistant Chief of the Air Staff (operations)	to Chief and Vice-
ACAS (P)	Assistant Chief of the Air Staff (policy)	Chief of Air Staff
ACAS (T)	Assistant Chief of the Air Staff (technical)	on special matters}
ADC	aide-de-camp	
AEI	Associated Electrical Industries Ltd	
AFDU	Air Fighting Development Unit	
AHB	Air Historical Branch, Royal Air Force	
AI	Airborne Interception; radar device to detect aircraft	
AMDP	Air Member for Development and Production	
AMSO	Air Member for Supply and Organisation	
AMRD	Air Member for Research and Development	
AMSR	Air Member for Supply and Research	
AMP	Air Member for Personnel	
AOA	Air Officer Administration	
AOC	Air Officer Commanding	
AOC-in-C	Air Officer Commanding in Chief	
ASR	Air Sea Rescue	
ASV	Air to Surface Vessel; radar device to detect ships	
BAC	British Air Commission; set up by Beaverbrook for MAP	
BPC	British Purchasing Commission; run by Arthur Purvis	
CAS	Chief of Air Staff	
CEO	Chief Executive Officer	
CFS	Central Flying School	
CIGS	Chief of the Imperial General Staff	
C-in-C	Commander-in-Chief	
CMDP	Civilian Member for Development and Production	
CMSO	Chief Maintenance and Supply Officer	
COS	Chiefs of Staff	
CRD	Civilian Repair Depots (1939–1940)	
CRD	Controller of Research and Development (1940–1945)	
CRO	Civilian Repair Organisation	
DAF	Desert Air Force	
DAP	Director of Armament Production	
DBO	Director of Bombing Operations (Air Ministry)	
DDBO	Deputy Director of Bombing Ops (Air Ministry)	
DCAS	Deputy Chief of the Air Staff – assistant to CAS/VCAS	
DDOI	Deputy Director of Operations and Intelligence	
DGAP	Director General of Aircraft Production	
DGM	Director General of Maintenance	
DGP	Director General of Production	
DMD	Director of Maintenance Design	
DNC	Director of Naval Construction	
D of P	Director of Plans	
DOR	Directorate of Operational Requirements	
DRM	Director of Repairs and Maintenance	
DSR	Directorate/Director of Scientific Research	
DTD	Directorate/Director of Technical Development	
DUS	Deputy Under-Secretary	
DWO	Department of War Organisation	

EL	Embodiment Loan equipment
FTS	Flying Training School
GAF	German Air Force
Gee	Radio-pulse aid to navigation
G-H	Airborne radar transmitter/receiver system for blind navigation (Oboe in reverse) – very accurate
GHQ	General Headquarters
GKN	Guest Keen and Nettlefolds Ltd
GOC	General Officer Commanding
GOC-in-C	General Officer Commander-in-Chief
H2S	airborne radar equipment which displayed an impression of the ground beneath the aircraft on a cathode-ray screen
Hendon	The Royal Air Force Museum, Hendon
ICI	Imperial Chemical Industries Ltd
IFF	Identification – Friend or Foe
IWM	Imperial War Museum
MAF	Metropolitan Air Force
MAP	Ministry of Aircraft Production
NAAFI	Navy, Army and Air Force Institute (Forces canteen)
Oboe	Precision radar method by which ground transmitters guided aircraft to the point of weapons release
ORC	Operational Requirements Committee
OTU	Operational Training Unit
PFF	Pathfinder Force
PR	Photographic Reconnaissance
PRO	Public Record Office, Kew.
PRU	Photographic Reconnaissance Unit
PUS	Permanent Under-Secretary
RAE	Royal Aircraft Establishment
RAF	Royal Air Force
RAFM	Royal Air Force Museum, Hendon
RDA	Aircraft Research and Development
RDE	Engine Research and Development
RDF	Radio Direction Finding – later renamed Radar
RFC	Royal Flying Corps
RNAS	Royal Naval Air Service
rpm	revolutions per minute
R-R/RR	Rolls-Royce
SASO	Senior Air Staff Officer
SBAC	Society of British Aircraft Constructors
S of S	Secretary of State
Tac-R	Tactical reconnaissance
TAF	Tactical Air Force
tpa	tons per annum
USAAF	US Army Air Force
USSBS	United States Strategic Bombing Survey
VAD	Voluntary Aid Detachment; nursing auxiliaries
VCAS	Vice-Chief of Air Staff
VCNS	Vice-Chief of Naval Staff
VHF	very high frequency (radio)
WAAF	Women's Auxiliary Air Force
WPB	The American 'War Production Board'

CHAPTER I

Family background

WILFRID RHODES FREEMAN was born on 18 July 1888. His father, William Freeman, was a partner in the civil engineering firm, Mowlem, Freeman & Burt, and his mother, Annie Dunn, the only daughter of a successful Aberdeen advocate. Both Freeman's parents therefore came from the new middle class created by the industrial revolution and made prosperous by the free-trade policies of Victorian governments. The comfort and stability of their circumstances gave him the best possible start in life for the career he was to choose.

The Freeman family came from Yorkshire. After diversifying from road building into civil engineering, and buying granite quarries in Cornwall, they began to supply stone to John Mowlem, a civil engineer who had started his business at Paddington Wharf in 1823 with contracts to pave some of London's streets. Mowlem and his old friend, George Burt, had married sisters, Susannah and Laetitia Manwell, and since the Mowlems were childless, Joseph Freeman, William's father and husband of Mowlem's niece, Elizabeth Burt, was taken into the partnership in 1840, together with her brother George. The young men obviously proved highly competent, for Mowlem retired in 1844, and for the next fifty years, for Freeman and Burt, the streets of London were indeed paved with gold.[1]

William left school when he was 14 and joined his father in the business. After marriage he and Anne settled near Paddington, like the Forsytes in Galsworthy's saga, whom they closely resembled. It may have been 'the wrong side of the Park' compared with more fashionable districts like Mayfair and Belgravia, but the five-storey houses were very comfortable, with columned porticoes, area steps down to the basement, and a mews behind for carriages and coachmen. The kitchens and staff rooms were in the basement, staff bedrooms in the attic, nurseries on the top floor, and the rest of the family in between. In such a comfortable and safe environment, William Freeman's family could enjoy to the full all the advantages and privileges which his wealth bestowed.

The Freeman children inherited much of the vigour and shrewdness that had helped to found that wealth, and many other good qualities besides. From his father, Wilfrid Freeman derived kindness, generosity, concern for the feelings of others, an immense capacity for detailed organisation, and a strong sense of duty; from his mother, wit, courage, and a rather sharp tongue; and from both, enormous personal charm. He grew up into an exceptionally intelligent young man, with sound judgement, bull-dog tenacity and a quick and intuitive perception which aptly equipped him for the many formidable challenges that lay ahead.

Wilfrid Freeman with six of his brothers and sisters: (from left to right) Wilfrid, Josephine, Sibyl, Ralph, Russell, Noël and Max.

Wilfrid was the fifth child and third son in a family of eight, the first six of whom were born within seven calendar years. Russell, born four years later, soon joined his older siblings, but Alan, the youngest, remained a loner, posting a weekly 'Hating List' on his bedroom door on Sunday evenings; Noël, the eldest, was always top. They formed an extraordinary united band: they were consistently loyal to one another all their lives, and much preferred their own company to that of outsiders. Cousins and school friends found visits to the Freemans an alarming experience.

Joseph Freeman died in 1895. After making handsome provisions for his daughters he left the residue of his estate to William and his younger brother John. They each received nearly £100,000, a considerable fortune in those days, and enough for William to retire from the family firm and devote himself to his wife and children, whom he adored. Christmas holidays were always in London: the children were taken to Bertram Mills' Circus, exhibitions, theatres, concerts, the latest Gilbert and Sullivan operas, and to the famous Royal Society lectures. At Easter there were rowing expeditions on the Thames, and sight-seeing visits to France and Belgium; in the summer the whole family migrated to Scotland, the highlight of the year.

Anne Freeman's parents owned the Murtle estate, six miles from Aberdeen, and loved having their only daughter and her family to stay. Murtle House, with its green copper dome, was large and very comfortable, and elegantly placed on a ridge above the Dee, enjoying a fine view along it. It had everything a young family could want. There was a beautiful walled garden with a stream running through it, woods, a long avenue, farms and mills; for sport there was archery, croquet, cycling, trout fishing and canoeing on the dams, and salmon-fishing on the river. Beyond the estate there were family expeditions all over Deeside by trap, carriage and wagonette; in the evening there were word-games, charades, cards and billiards. Murtle was a paradise for London children.

As his family grew, William realised that they would soon be too many for Murtle House, especially if they brought cousins and friends with them, so he built Murtle Den, another large house, nearby; he also started a golf course at Bieldside, and added tennis and shooting to the Murtle attractions. Murtle thus became the centre of the Freemans' world, and they returned there as often as possible.

Wilfrid Freeman was delicate as a child and because a heart weakness was suspected his doctors unwisely warned, in his presence, that he must not be allowed to cry. Family legend has it that he was left one day in the care of his Scottish grandmother, while everyone else went on an expedition. When the family returned, they found her crouched beneath the plush table cloth, with Wilfrid marching round it, threatening to cry if she came out. Despite his

Murtle Den from the upper dam.

Anne Freeman with her four eldest sons: (from left to right) Max, Ralph, Noël and Wilfrid. Noël, a major in the Royal Artillery, was killed in France in 1918 and, four months later, the fifth son Russell, an RFC pilot, was shot down and killed.

early medical problems he recovered well enough to follow his brothers to prep school, and Noël to Rugby, but under stress he was to be plagued with migraines and high temperatures for the rest of his life.

Freeman was not academically minded, and used to claim that the only benefit he obtained from Rugby was his life-long friendship with an older boy, Ainstie Williams, who instilled in him a love of poetry and a discriminating taste for good literature:[2] books were to be his passion in the years to come and he soon acquired a large library. While his brothers went on to university, therefore, he chose an Army career which allowed him to enter the real world sooner. After leaving Sandhurst in 1908 he joined the Manchester Regiment; he was gazetted Lieutenant in 1912.

He found peacetime soldiering boring, however; it cannot have helped that his regiment was stationed at Mullingar in Ireland, far from the lights of

London. As soon as the Royal Flying Corps (RFC) was formed, he decided to transfer to it. He was passionately interested in engines and was always consulted as 'the final authority' when someone in the family wished to buy a 'motor', so the new world of aeroplanes attracted him strongly.

Possession of an aviator's certificate was essential before he could apply for a transfer to the RFC, but if he obtained one and was accepted, he would be eligible for a bounty of £75 towards the cost of his training. So, in 1913, he obtained leave from his regiment, travelled to France at his own expense, and took a course at the Farman School of Flying, in a Maurice Farman biplane. At this early stage in the development of aviation, training was rudimentary and the science of flight imperfectly understood; aircraft were fragile and ungainly, engines unreliable. Nevertheless, Freeman found it all fascinating and liked the French villagers with whom he lodged.[3] He passed the course, was accepted by the RFC, and in January 1914 joined the Central Flying School at Upavon for further training, becoming a Flying Officer (not then a rank) in April, while still nominally in the Army.

During his years in the Army Freeman pursued a hectic social life whenever he could escape from Mullingar. Weekends with friends, nights out at the theatre, dances, and suppers with actresses were all faithfully recorded in his admiring father's diaries (the entry 'Wif at home, for a wonder' appears very seldom). It was an expensive way of life, and although his doting father periodically increased his allowance, Freeman was always in debt. His attempts to straighten out his affairs by betting on horses ended in disaster; again, his father came to the rescue.[4]

To the opposite sex, Freeman was both popular and susceptible, and he fell in and out of love several times a year. But in 1913 he 'formed a more lasting attachment' to Gladys (usually called 'G'), the daughter of John Mews, a rich

barrister who lived opposite the Freemans in Westbourne Terrace. The two families dined together occasionally and as early as 1911 William's diary records, 'Miss Mews, a good-looking and well-mannered girl, was a distinct feature in the entertainment'. Initially her father fiercely opposed her liaison with Wilfrid, for he thought little of an airman's career prospects, but Gladys, who was strong-willed as well as attractive, was keen to escape from her family's dull and rather strict household. The couple became engaged in 1914 and John Mews eventually agreed to an autumn wedding. The outbreak of war then intervened, delaying the marriage until June 1915.[5]

Gladys Freeman, known as 'G'.

CHAPTER 2

War service in the
Royal Flying Corps
1914–1918

BY AUGUST 1914 the Royal Flying Corps (RFC) had been active for two years and, despite the novelty of its role, a remarkably thorough organisation had been created comprising four squadrons, the Central Flying School (CFS) at Upavon, and the supporting Royal Aircraft Factory. The Corps was commanded by General Henderson, the War Office's Director of Military Aviation (DMA), and he insisted that everyone in his directorate must qualify as a pilot before the age of 40.[1] This wise measure kept control of the RFC in the hands of young men who understood its special needs, and ensured that it wasn't 'stuffed with military dugouts'.

In 1912, a public competition to select a standard aircraft for the RFC had been won by a box-kite machine entered by the former showman W.F. Cody, which had a speed range of 24mph.* This was large for the time, and a significant factor, given the inexperience of *all* pilots and the instability of most contemporary aircraft, since a single handling mistake could cause a stall, followed by a potentially fatal spin; a wide speed range gave a bigger margin of safety. The Government awarded Cody the prize, but wisely ordered the factory-made B.E.2, a simple tractor biplane designed by Geoffrey de Havilland, which would probably have won the competition had it been eligible to compete. Cody's machine later broke up in mid-air killing the pilot. By 1914 the improved B.E.2c version was both reliable and inherently stable.† It served the RFC well, until its lack of manoeuvrability and unsuitability as a weapon carrier were exposed by the first German fighters with fixed machine-guns in 1915–16.

After the outbreak of the First World War, the Royal Aircraft Factory ceased production of service aircraft. Its staff designed and made a whole series of prototype new aircraft, the best of which – and some of the worst! – were then produced in quantity by independent aircraft firms. An Aeronautics Inspection Department was added to the Factory's staff after a series of avoidable accidents caused by inexperienced constructors or bad maintenance. This significantly raised the private contractors' standards of work-manship, and the safety and strength of their designs.[2]

---

* Speed range: the difference between maximum and stalling speeds
† Such an aircraft resumes level flight if the controls are relaxed, unless in a spin.

Freeman joined No.5 (primary flying training) course at Upavon in January 1914, and learned to fly on a strange assortment of pusher and tractor training planes. On pusher aircraft, the engine and propeller were installed behind the crew; on tractor aeroplanes, the engine was in front. Flying training was very rudimentary: after a brief period of dual control instruction, pupils effectively taught themselves through experience, moving up to more advanced aircraft as they progressed. The quality of instruction was inevitably limited by the capabilities of the aircraft, and by the fact that there was no recognized way of recovering from a spin. There were many fatal accidents.

On qualifying Freeman was posted to No. 2 Squadron at Montrose; his formal appointment to the post of Flying Officer was dated 28 April 1914. The squadron was commanded by Major C.J. Burke, who Sir Sefton Brancker described as 'one of the most gallant and devoted soldiers I ever met, and the bravest bad pilot I have ever flown with'.[3] Equipped with B.E.2as, the squadron had already taken part in a series of realistic exercises, the most demanding of which was a long distance flight by five aircraft from Montrose to Farnborough in February 1913, which they all completed in thirteen days. In September the squadron participated in the Irish Command manoeuvres, which entailed outward and homeward journeys of more than 400 miles, and a double crossing of the Irish Sea. The aircraft were fitted with flotation bags

The Irish Command manoeuvres. Three B.E.2as and a Farman Longhorn of No. 2 Squadron fitted with flotation bags under the wings for the crossing of the Irish Sea.

under the wings, a magnetic compass of doubtful accuracy, and Ordnance Survey maps which were not designed with aerial navigation in mind.[4]

In June 1914 No. 2 Squadron flew down from Scotland to summer camp at Netheravon; one aircraft crashed on the way in fog. The concept of air fighting was discussed, and both the armed services agreed that the whole purpose of military aviation was reconnaissance.[5] As 'only the most wretched lodgings were to be had' near Netheravon,[6] Freeman persuaded his father to buy a second car (for Murtle), and to lend it to him for the period of the camp. This allowed him to live in London, and to take Gladys to dinners and parties. He realised the importance of being known to the senior officers of the RFC: on one occasion, after dining with General Henderson in London, he gave him a lift back to Farnborough.[7]

In July the Admiralty took control of the RFC's naval wing, renaming it the Royal Naval Air Service (RNAS) and placing it under a brilliant engineer from the Admiralty Air Department, Commodore Murray Sueter. This left the RFC with fewer than 100 aeroplanes and pilots: at least 200 of each – and a reserve of 100 – were needed to man the eight squadrons which it planned to create. Moreover, 'wastage' rates of at least 100 per cent per annum were expected. There were few British airframe makers, and even fewer aero-engine makers: all the Renault and Gnome engines then used by the RFC were made in France.[8] Three firms were therefore contracted to make French rotary engines*: Beardmore made the 120hp Austro-Daimler, while others built the 70 and 80hp V8 Renaults.[9] Sefton Brancker, who was in charge of equipment at the Directorate of Military Aviation, bought as many aircraft and engines as he could from France and scrambled together four squadrons, leaving enough aeroplanes to equip the reserve squadrons at Farnborough and the CFS, and then set about recruiting 1,100 of the best mechanics in England†. These men became the backbone of the RFC in the years ahead.[10]

Brancker and Sueter were worried that the Admiralty Air Department and the DMA would compete for engines and airframes from the limited number of UK producers, so they agreed to delineate the activities of the two departments. The RFC would only order engines of 100hp or less (the Austro-Daimler/Beardmore engine excepted), but would buy all the landplanes, while the RNAS would procure engines of more than 100hp and would concentrate on seaplanes.[11]

No. 2 Squadron started south from Montrose before 4 August, Freeman flying an elderly Farman down to Farnborough – taking three days against headwinds, but 'getting ovations' from the towns he overflew on his way south. He spent a few days at Farnborough learning to fly the new BE2a which had been allocated to his squadron. This gave his doting father time to pay a visit, and send him off with £25 in sovereigns‡ and the extra kit he needed for service in France.[12]

---

* In Britain, most Gnomes were made by Hookers, Le Rhônes by Allens, and Clergets by Gwynnes.

† They were to be paid ten shillings a day, which was a high wage in 1914.

‡ £25 represents at least £1,000 in 1990s currency.

He left on 11 August, losing his way between Farnborough and Dover, but joining his squadron in time to move with them up to Maubeuge, just before the battle of Mons. In the following weeks the British Expeditionary Force faced a formidable challenge from the advancing German forces, and Freeman's squadron retreated steadily south. After losing two aircraft in accidents by 1 September, Burke dispatched Freeman to collect a replacement B.E.2 from the central depot at Étampes. He rejoined the squadron at Melun on 9 September.[13]

Three days later, as he went to reconnoitre St Quentin with another pilot named Dawes, their aircraft began to rock and vibrate in the air, as if the tail was loose, and he had to make a forced landing in a wooded area behind German

Wilfrid Freeman: a 1914 portrait.

lines. On either side, barely 200 yards away, were large German columns. Taking only a biscuit and some tubes of beef extract, Freeman and Dawes hid in another wood close by. German cavalry searched for them for an hour and a half, but without success, and in the evening the two pilots were able to walk south towards the River Aisne, passing several German pickets on the way. They were lucky: at this early stage of the war the German Army was over-confident and the pickets made so much noise that the airmen managed to pass by unobserved. They finally reached the Aisne at 3am on 13 September. After three hours sleep they were awakened by gunfire and realised that they were in front of the German positions. Unobserved by German cavalry patrols, and unscathed by heavy shell fire from the British, they swam across the Aisne and its canal in broad daylight and at last reached a British cavalry unit. On rejoining their squadron they were reprimanded for ignoring the order that 'no two pilots should fly together in the same machine'.[14]

The minutiae of Freeman's meticulous reconnaissance work emerges from No. 2 Squadron's diary for 29 September 1914.[15] Once the front stabilised the superiority of the German heavy artillery became clear and all RFC work was focused on artillery spotting, making the best use of the Army's limited resources, by monitoring the shell-bursts and using lamp signals to correct the gunner's aim. Freeman was one of the two most active pilots in the squadron, always in the air, and in October, with J.T.C. Moore-Brabazon, he was given a coveted posting to No. 9 Squadron, the first to be equipped with wireless, and which Hugh Dowding now commanded. The squadron moved to St Omer in October, as part of a general shift of British forces to the northern end of the front, and this coincided with one of the more desperate offensives of 1914, a serious German attempt to break through at Ypres, which the BEF only just repelled. Freeman's base eventually came under artillery fire, and the squadron had to move again, Freeman flying a damaged aircraft back to depot.[16]

After a week's leave Freeman returned to France on 6 December and began to concentrate wholly on artillery observation work, once again one of the most active pilots in the squadron. Early in January 1915 extra wireless flights had to be formed as the squadron was regularly directing the fire of more than one battery. Freeman became more confident of his skills as a wireless operator and because the sets weighed 75lb he started flying alone, using new and simple two-digit clock-code signals, which could easily be sent by Morse. Towards the end of his first sortie on 5 February 1915 Freeman actually saw a German battery start firing; he therefore signalled his guns on to the target, and both German guns were quickly silenced. The squadron diary recorded:

> Lt W.R. Freeman in a Maurice Farman Shorthorn, with Lt Spence as observer, successfully co-operated with 112th and 113th batteries by means of wireless; they were shelled incessantly at 4,500–5,000ft, but were untouched.[17]

Freeman told Gladys: 'there were almost 60 shells ... but none of them hit me – and they were really close, but ... it is not good for my nerves.'[18] His

A Maurice Farman Shorthorn. The officer second from the right is Major (later Major-General Sir) Sefton Brancker in charge of equipment at the Directorate of Military Aviation. He is talking to Major Sykes, the OC of the Military Wing.

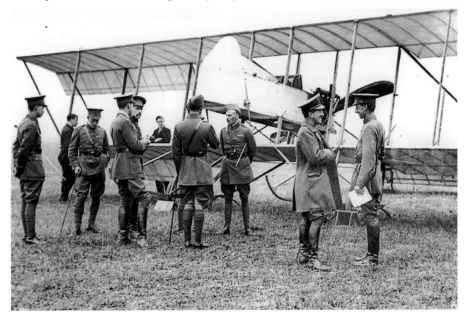

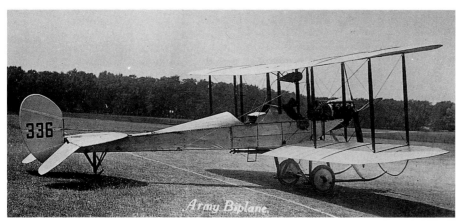

No. 9 Squadron was the first to be equipped with wireless. Wilfrid Freeman flew this wireless-equipped B.E.2a (No. 336) in March 1915.

brother, Max, watched such a sortie with an artillery general who was full of admiration for the pilot: 'By Jove! ... [he] deserves a VC'. Max was even more impressed by the casual way in which the pilot filed his report on landing, realising only then that the pilot was none other than Wilfrid.[19]

In March Freeman was appointed Flight Commander. Major H. Musgrave, the CO of 9 Squadron, wrote at this time:

> I consider Lt Freeman to be the best qualified [of my squadron] for promotion to Flight Commander and ... recommend that Lt Freeman be considered for the vacancy ... He is endowed with more sense of responsibility than is often found in officers of his age and is ... in all respects a very promising officer.[20]

Once the British and French armies had recovered from the first battle of Ypres, an attack was planned to capture the Aubers Ridge, near Neuve Chapelle. The RFC photographed all the German lines opposite the British front, enabling General French, the C-in-C, to select objectives and to provide detailed, up-to-date maps for his infantry.[21] Wireless aircraft flew continuously over the area of fighting during the battle, reporting the fall of shot to the gunners and using the innovations developed during the winter.[22] One grateful recipient of these reports was a gunner captain, Alan Brooke, later the CIGS, then serving with the Indian Cavalry Division.[23] Freeman was hit by a shell fragment on 13 March, but not hurt by it.

The Neuve Chapelle attack was a failure. Nevertheless, by providing photomosaic maps, wireless reports for the artillery, and weather reports from the battle area, the RFC was beginning to act as a tactical air arm. Freeman's contribution to this action over a period of three days was so continuous and effective, despite intensive shelling from the ground, that in June he received one of the first Military Crosses to be awarded to an RFC officer. He told Gladys about the MC as soon as he heard. 'You couldn't see the country ...

for shells', he wrote. 'All the streams were coloured yellow from the lyddite.'[24]
A week later he wrote again to say that he had paid for her [engagement] ring.

To cope with the pressure of wartime expansion, the DMA established new
RFC training schools almost as fast as new operational squadrons. Brancker
continued the army tradition of alternating periods of action by moving experienced pilots back to the training schools at regular intervals; they could then
pass on up-to-date, practical knowledge of warfare to the trainees. Freeman
was posted as an instructor at the new Flying Training School (FTS) at Shore-
ham in June 1915.

The techniques of flying training had hardly changed since Freeman's
time at the CFS: tractor B.E.2s and Avro 504s were coming into service, but
pupils still flew pusher Farmans and Vickers F.B.5s. Unable themselves to
recover from a spin, flying instructors still concentrated on teaching pupils
to control aircraft within safe flying speeds; 'stunting' was frowned on. Air-
to-air combat had not really started, and although good pilots could take
some liberties with aircraft, they were discouraged from doing so lest the
inexperienced be tempted into rash manoeuvres.

Freeman was a popular instructor. Sholto Douglas, then one of the pupils,
remembered him as 'a slim, dark, handsome man with an attractively quizzical
expression on his face: very intelligent, and with a nicely cynical sense of
humour ... I quickly formed a great liking for him.'[25] Six months away from
operations gave Freeman time to reflect on his experiences in France; he
realised that there was much more to air warfare than flying alone, and he
carefully studied every aspect of the new service, and its training schools,
while carrying out his instruction duties. He also used his period back in
England to marry Gladys, bringing a strong-willed wife into his close-knit,
critical family, but unaware of the extent to which the ordeal of his flying and
new responsibilities had changed his priorities, and brought out his innate
ability.

The RFC was a young and growing corps; promotion stemmed from both
the rapid rate of expansion and from aircrew losses, and Freeman was
fortunate in that his posting to flying training took him out of operations just
as air-to-air fighting was beginning. The lack of Allied aircraft fitted with
forward-firing machine-guns quickly placed British and French pilots at a
serious disadvantage, and casualty rates increased steadily. Freeman was
equally fortunate with his next posting, to Egypt, to command No. 14 Squadron,
part of the 'Arabian' Wing which was being developed under Colonel Geoffrey
Salmond. As late as 1916 the Germans sent very few aircraft to support the
Turks, and the elderly Farmans, B.E.2cs and D.H.1s that equipped his new
squadron faced little opposition. Between June 1915 and December, 1916
therefore, whilst Freeman's promotions continued, his absence from the
Western Front spared him the ordeal of air-to-air combat in which so many
of his contemporaries lost their lives. Indeed the high casualty rate, and the
further expansion of the RFC, created opportunities for promotion for more
experienced middle-ranking officers, such as Freeman himself.

Leaving Liverpool on the *Olympic* on 3 January 1916, Freeman enjoyed the voyage to Egypt and was in good spirits when he reached Mudros Harbour in the Aegean. He awoke to 'a magnificent sight of warships', the fleet of battleships which had been assembled for the abortive attempt to force the Dardanelles and which had remained to support the attack on Gallipoli.[26] Freeman disembarked at Alexandria on 16 January 1916, and discovered that No.14 Squadron, though officially based at Heliopolis, outside Cairo, was split into about five separate sections.[27] It had arrived in Egypt in November 1915 equipped with five Farmans and one aged B.E.2a, and after an initial spell at Ismailia in the Canal Zone, had moved to Heliopolis, where new aircraft, BE2cs, were being uncrated and assembled. Two aircraft from the squadron had been moved 250 miles westwards to Mersa Matruh in support of operations against the Muslim Senussi tribesmen, who were allied to Turkey; another detachment had been sent to Fayoum, and a third to the Sudan. Since most of the tribesmen had never seen an aeroplane, their mere appearance had a significant effect.[28]

Freeman was soon able to recall the detached flights from their frontier activities and, once re-equipped, the squadron moved back to Ismailia in the Canal Zone; a detached flight was located at Kantara.[29] The state of the RFC base at Ismailia was appalling and, in a whirlwind of activity, more than 3,000 empty petrol cans were cleared away, furniture was procured for the Mess, and a rat-hunt organised under the kitchens and in the Mess itself, which killed 60 rats.[30] The serviceability of Freeman's aircraft was of vital importance, and shortly after his arrival at Ismailia he flew first to Divisional HQ at Kantara and then to Port Said, to see those responsible for the provision of spares and equipment for engine maintenance: serviceability promptly improved.[31]

A **Martinsyde G100** of No. 14 Squadron. The heavy – it was nicknamed 'the elephant' – but reliable M100 was flown by Wilfrid and later Russell, Freeman.

Lieutenant Slessor (later Marshal of the Royal Air Force Sir John) preparing to take off in a B.E.2c of No. 14 Squadron to bomb the Turkish pumping station at Hassana.

When the rest of the Wing arrived at Ismailia on 9 February 1916 operational flying was intensified.[32] Regular early morning reconnaissance flights over Turkish outposts were launched to keep the army well informed of enemy troop movements. The most important operations were photo-reconnaissance missions over the British outposts along the coast road, and over Sinai, east of the Suez Canal; in 1915 a Turkish raid had passed through this region. The resulting pictures were used to prepare a map which was the first to be entirely constructed from photographs.[33] This achievement made an excellent impression on the commander of British forces in the Middle East, General Murray, and on Major-General Lynden-Bell, his Chief of Staff. Murray was particularly pleased with photographs of the Turkish inland roads, including Jifjaffa and Hassana: 'The work of the RFC was most actively and gallantly pursued, keeping enemy posts under close observation', Murray recorded.[34] A few weeks later an aircraft successfully bombed the Turkish pumping station at Hassana, removing a vital water source for the Turkish troops in that area.[35]

The direction of operational flying absorbed a considerable amount of Freeman's time, but a wide range of administrative tasks had also to be fulfilled. In March he was asked by Salmond for a report on the reorganisation of the RFC in Britain and on the Western Front, while in April and May he assisted Salmond in the preparation of a scheme to establish a flying training school in Egypt: this necessitated several long and tiring train journeys to Alexandria, where the school was to be based.[36] When Salmond was absent Freeman also administered the Wing, as well as his squadron.

Another important duty was public relations. The RFC station at Ismailia was often visited by war correspondents and naval officers: Ward, the King's messenger, was given a joy-ride, there were two visits from the Prince of Wales, and one from Murray, the Commander-in-Chief, who inspected the station and enjoyed a flying display.[37] They were all deeply interested in the station's work and intrigued by the young Major who was proving to be such a live wire.

Freeman had always suffered from migraines, which the hot weather exacerbated, and he often felt unwell, but these discomforts seldom kept him away from his work. He flew as often as he could, choosing a little Bristol Scout or a Martinsyde G100, rather than the B.Es; on 20 April he took a Bristol up in an attempt to catch a German Rumpler, but without success. There was much excitement when the first of six new de Havilland D.H.1As arrived. The 1A, a two-seater 'pusher' with a 120hp Beardmore engine, was a great improvement on the F.E.2bs then in service in France. Freeman flew the aircraft the day after its arrival without realising that several wing ribs had been broken in transit, but he landed safely.

As well as fulfilling the numerous tasks normally expected of a squadron commander, Freeman accepted a range of other responsibilities. For example, he organised courses on the wireless control of gunnery for the Army and the Navy, drawing on his experience in France. British naval gunnery during the first stage of the Dardanelles offensive had been poor.

The obsolete battleships deployed in the attack had proved unable to hit their targets when on the move, and the Navy's seaplanes could not reach an adequate altitude for observation. There was, therefore, an enthusiastic re-

No. 14 Squadron in Palestine was allocated six new D.H.1As, designed by Geoffrey de Havilland. Equipped with one machine-gun the D.H.1A had a top speed of 90mph.

sponse to Freeman's offer of training, and his courses culminated in active rehearsals in which the battleships' guns fired under wireless control.[38]

On 20 April, while at GHQ to plan a bombing raid on Beersheeba, he was informed by Lynden-Bell that he had been recommended for a DSO: 'Goodness only knows why', Freeman wrote in his diary. On the following day there was a champagne dinner at GHQ in celebration. He had, of course, achieved a great deal in the three months since he arrived in Egypt, taking a firm grip of the situation, assembling the scattered flights of his squadron, moving them to the Canal Zone, and keeping seven or eight aircraft serviceable to complete the photographic survey of the area, as well as the regular reconnaissance sorties and attempted interceptions. He had handled his publicity work well, run flying demonstrations, and had given lectures on, and demonstrations of, wireless control of gunnery to both the Army and the Navy. His report about the RFC's reorganisation in March, and the plan for a new flying school in Egypt in April, were also greatly to his credit.

All of this was achieved at a time when his personal life was causing him considerable anxiety. Letters from Gladys brought the news that she had quarrelled with the family friends with whom she had been living as a paying guest, and had moved.[39] They had apparently criticised the frequency with which she 'went out' with young officer friends, who were home on leave, and Gladys, now independent as a married woman, simply moved out and lived in a hotel.[40] Freeman asked Salmond to let her join him in Egypt, but at that time this was not permitted.

In fact, the whole question of allowing officers' wives to join them overseas was apparently under discussion at this time, and Salmond may have been unable to pre-empt a general decision by granting special permission to one of his subordinates. Freeman's disappointment was exacerbated by the arrival, on the very same day, of a 'beastly letter' from Gladys. 'I wish I had not read it at all', he wrote in his diary.[41]

On 22 April 1916 Salmond confided in Freeman that he was expecting a Turkish offensive: the attack, involving 2,500 troops and four guns, commenced on the following day and captured Quatiya. No. 14 Squadron responded by launching a low-level dawn raid on the camp, with bombs and machine-guns, causing heavy casualties and destroying the Turkish camp. Other Turkish forces were observed further east and attacked successfully the following day. Murray commented in his dispatch:

> 'I cannot speak too highly of the admirable work done by the 5th Wing RFC during these few days. The strain thrown on pilots and machines was very heavy and the former displayed the utmost gallantry and resource on all occasions. Chiefly through their efforts, the enemy was made to pay a very heavy price for his partially successful raid.[42]

Two days later the squadron made a successful dawn raid on the Turkish advanced base at El Arish, following a bombardment by the Navy and a raid by the RNAS; all six aircraft returned safely. However, when the raid was

Grant Dalton who rescued Van Rynefeld, a future leader of the South African Air Force, after he had been shot down in a raid by 14 Squadron on the Turkish base at El Arish.

repeated on 18 June, three of the twelve attacking aircraft were shot down, one of them landing in the sea, where the crew were rescued by the Navy, and two on land. One pilot was captured; the other, Van Rynefeld, a future leader of the South African Air Force, was rescued by Grant-Dalton, who not only landed in enemy territory but flew ninety miles home to Ismailia with two passengers.[43] Freeman spent the next two days arranging for the repair and replacement of aircraft. The day after the raid, Freeman's brother Russell arrived, and they talked late into the night, catching up on local and family news.[44] Russell had given up his medical studies to join the Army, and had been sent to the trenches in France, where life expectancy was particularly short. Deeply anxious, Noël and Max Freeman begged Wilfrid to arrange for Russell's transfer to the RFC, where his chances of survival would be better, and after he had been transferred and trained, Salmond organised his posting to Egypt.[45] Russell had always been the family favourite – the perfect younger brother – and Freeman was delighted to have him in his squadron.

At the end of June 1916 Freeman was clearly expecting to remain in Egypt for some time. Russell had arrived, but although Freeman confidently hoped

Russell Freeman in an elderly B.E.2c in 1916. Very few German aircraft supported the Turkish army, so it was possible for No. 14 Squadron to operate obsolete aircraft.

that Gladys would be able to join him in the near future, he suddenly asked for some leave, clearing this, in Salmond's absence, through Lyden-Bell, Murray's Chief of Staff*. He raced home, lunching his VAD sister at Boulogne on the way,[46] and discovered that, even before he arrived in Britain, the War Office had decided, on the strength of the many excellent accounts of his work in Egypt, to retain him in the UK to run a new flying school. On 18 July he was appointed to command No 4 Training Wing at Netheravon. On 25 July he was promoted to Temporary Lieutenant-Colonel, with effect from 5 July, and shortly afterwards he took command of No 7 Training Wing at Gosport.

Freeman's term at Gosport was short and uneventful. The British flying training system had hardly changed since the outbreak of the war, largely because standard procedures for spin-recovery were still unknown. Aircraft behaviour varied widely, some recovering easily from a stall and others quick to 'drop a wing' in an incipient spin. Until 'spin-recovery' became an essential part of a flying training course, instructors themselves studiously avoided the risks of spinning, and thus had no option but to play safe; indeed, they were compelled to do so by Central Flying School regulations. Flying training was in for a revolutionary change, however, by December 1916, for spin-recovery procedures had been finally established, but Freeman had moved on before

---

* Geoffrey Salmond was 'very stuffy' about the matter. It was out of character for Freeman to skip the proper channels in this way. If, however, Lyden-Bell had been confidentially forewarned about Freeman's posting by Brancker or Henderson, he may have secretly told Freeman, and been sympathetic when he asked to go home at once, to fit in some leave.

the flying schools were affected. He was, in fact, succeeded at Gosport by the pioneer of the modern flying training systems, the former CO of No. 60 Squadron, Smith-Barry, in December 1916.

OPERATIONS IN FRANCE, 1917–18

The nature of air warfare had changed considerably by the time Freeman returned to the Western Front in January, 1917. The development of forward-firing machine-guns had soon proved that in fast, manoeuvreable aircraft they gave a clear advantage in air fighting, and that the casualty rate of obsolete aircraft was becoming serious. Brancker, who was still in charge of aircraft supply, realised that aircraft with much higher performance, were now urgently needed by the RFC, but the new engines ordered by the 'technically literate' committee which advised him, were all, at first, disastrous failures.[47]* Luckily, the RNAS, under Sueter's able direction, had also ordered a series of new aero-engines, including the Rolls-Royce Eagle and Falcon, the Mayen Hispano-Suiza, and rotaries of Le Rhône, Clerget and Bentley designs.[48] With great prescience, Sueter had also ordered a whole range of light, manoeuvrable, land-based aircraft for the RNAS from Sopwith and, despite their comparatively low-powered engines, Sopwith's 1½ Strutter, Pup, Triplane and Camel designs all proved invaluable in their turn. The loan of RNAS squadrons or their equipment virtually rescued the RFC late in 1916 and early 1917, when manoeuvrable aircraft with much higher performance, were desperately needed and the RFC's new engines were not ready.[49]

As late as March 1917 the four squadrons in the 10th Army Wing, which Freeman now commanded, were No. 25 with a mixture of F.E.2bs and F.E.2ds, No. 40 with the slow and obsolete F.E.8s[50], No. 43 with the Sopwith 1½ Strutters, and No. 8 RNAS with nimble Sopwith Triplanes[51]. The German Air Force (GAF) however, had been re-equipped and retrained by 1917. New fighter groups were formed, and early in 1917 the formidable Albatros D.III entered service[52], giving the GAF a performance advantage which lasted until the British Camels, S.E.5as, and French Spads, came into operation in late summer.

The work of reconnaissance, observation and bombing for the British Army was normally undertaken by 'brigade squadrons' equipped with aircraft which were slower than those of the RFC Wings, but so many of their aircraft had been shot down in 1916 that they were forbidden to operate more than 4,000 yards behind the German lines. More distant sorties had therefore to be undertaken by the Wings.[53] Freeman's Wing spent two weeks reinforcing 1st Brigade RFC in January 1917, and a further week in March, but found its aircraft outclassed by the German opposition and, like the rest of the RFC, suffered heavy casualties. The worst disaster was on 9 March 1917, when 'an offensive patrol' of nine of the appalling F.E.8s from 40 Squadron, were slaughtered by a formation of Albatros fighters, led by Richtofen. Four were shot down, four were forced down on the British side of the lines in a

---

* The early Wolseley- and Brasier-made Hispano-Suizas, BHP, Sunbeam Arab and, worst of all, the ABC Dragonfly.

No. 8 RNAS Squadron, one of the four squadrons in Freeman's 10th Army Wing, was equipped with Sopwith Triplanes (*above*). With a single machine-gun the Triplane had a top speed of 112.5 mph at 6,500 feet and 106.5 mph at 10,000 feet. The German Air Force were equipped with the Albatros D.III (*below*) which had two machine-guns and a top speed of 108 mph.

One of the outclassed F.E.8s of 40 Squadron which were forced down behind enemy lines by a formation of Albatros fighters led by Richtofen on 9 March 1917.

damaged condition, and the pilot of the ninth was wounded, but managed to escape, although his aircraft caught fire.[54] No.40 Squadron was promptly re-equipped with Nieuport 17s.[55]* In the following month, with only 114 fighters available against 385 British fighters, the GAF shot down 151 British aircraft at a cost of only 66, and lost 119 aircrew against 316. Heavy air fighting continued in support of the various Flanders offensives later in the year, and British aircrew losses from April to October 1917 averaged 204 a month. It was a very difficult period and Freeman, who was sensitive to the aircrew casualties, must have dreaded the task of sending out aircrew in inferior machines.

The photographic work of the 9th Wing was undertaken by No. 25 Squadron, mostly equipped with F.E.2bs powered by the old 120hp Beardmore engine,[56] – aircraft which were extremely vulnerable by 1917. While the Canadian Corps were preparing for their successful attack on Vimy Ridge, they asked 10th Wing to carry out the difficult and dangerous task of taking 'oblique photographs of the Ridge from Givenchy to Farbus with the camera pointing in a north-westerly direction to show up the crest of the hills and ridges', and then for further areas to be the subject of 'bird's eye photographs'. Three days later, after 25 Squadron had taken panoramas of the ridge from both sides, they asked for a reconnaissance flight to discover 'if the new trench undergoing construction continues north of the Deule Canal'. Freeman's deep sensitivity to the dangers of photographic work emerges from the advice which he drily added: 'To obviate an after order for photographs, it would be as well if a camera is taken up and photographs taken of the area'.

* The Nieuport had a single machine-gun and a top speed of 104mph at 6,500ft.

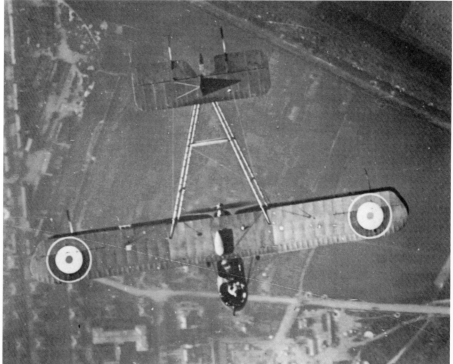

9th Wing, commanded by Freeman, undertook night bombing sorties in support of the offensive at Cambrai. The F.E.2bs (*top*) had V-strut undercarriages so that they could carry a single 230-lb bomb in addition to seven 25-lb bombs on underwing racks. The F.E.2d of 25 Squadron (*bottom*) is flying at 6,000 feet over the lines.

But the 10th Wing was not always on the receiving end, and Freeman personally organised an exceptionally successful attack early in May. Much German observation work was done from captive hydrogen balloons, which were well protected by anti-aircraft guns, but vulnerable to incendiary bullets. The Germans soon devised an ingenious way of lowering the balloons very quickly, by placing a pulley over the balloon cable, attached by a rope to a lorry. As soon as there was any sign of an enemy aircraft approaching, the lorry drove off down a prepared roadway, pulling down the balloon faster than any winch. Freeman worked out a way of defeating this with Tilney, the CO of No. 40 Squadron, which involved a low-level approach to the balloon site whilst a well-timed artillery barrage drowned the noise of the aircraft.[57] The squadron practised hard with their new Nieuports and, on 2nd May, taking advantage of ground cover wherever possible as they approached, they climbed rapidly to attack the balloons, damaging eight of them, and shooting down four, one in flames; all the Nieuports returned safely to base.[58] General Kiggell, Murray's successor as the Chief of Staff, drew Haig's attention to the exploit, drawing the comment:

> A very fine performance, please congratulate those who carried out the attack on the great success of their effort. Also please let me know the name of the officer who planned the attack. I admire his resourceful guile and initiative.[59]

As the year wore on, the more powerful aero-engines ordered by Sueter began to enter service. Installed in Bristol Fighters, D.H.4as, S.E.5s, Camels and Dolphins, their extra speed enabled the RFC to recover air superiority in most areas during the final year of the war.

Freeman took over the 9th Wing when Cyril Newall was appointed to command the new 'Independent Bomber Force' near Nancy, in October 1917. It was a coveted posting, for his new command was being re-armed with Bristol Fighters, and D.H.4s, the best of the RFC's new 2-seater aircraft.

The British offensive at Cambrai in the following month marked the beginning of a new era in military history, since, for the first time, the attack was led by a large number of tanks, after a very short artillery bombardment. The attacking forces successfully breached the Hindenberg Line, advancing three or four miles in some areas, though much of this territory was subsequently lost to German counter-attacks. The offensive was also one of the earliest for which the local RFC Corps squadrons were reinforced, on this occasion by the 9th Wing from HQ and four of the fighter squadrons were briefed to help the advance with bomb and machine-gun attacks on enemy airfields and other tactical ground targets.[60] Success was patchy due to the weather and communication difficulties, but the morale effect was significant, as the GAF proved when they counter-attacked. Heavily reinforced, the new German Air Force 'battle flights' were equally successful, despite heavy casualties.[61]

Two of the squadrons from 9th Wing undertook night bombing sorties in support of the offensive, and the problems they experienced gave Freeman a

The D.H.4 which first flew in August 1916, was one of the finest aircraft of the First World War. Universally praised for its handling qualities, wide speed range and high performance – at its best when fitted with a Rolls-Royce Eagle. When Freeman took over 9th Wing it was being re-equipped with DH4s and Bristol Fighters.

further opportunity to show how quickly he assimilated difficulties and proposed solutions. His Wing had been ordered to send six F.E.2bs to attack railway stations at Douai and Somaines, 50–60 miles behind the German lines, so as to delay the arrival of German reinforcements. Clearly these night raids proved difficult: in one of his later operational instructions, Freeman stated that 'should a machine land without finding its objective, another or the same machine will be sent up until twelve machines from each squadron have reached the objective for which they are detailed'[62].

A week after the Cambrai attack, having studied the difficulties of target recognition at night, Freeman suggested a way of improving both the accuracy of night bombing attacks and the safety of returning air crews.[63] He asked for the loan of three searchlights, mounted on lorries for mobility. When a raid was ordered he planned to position the lights exactly two or three miles apart, on the course that his aircraft would have to follow to their target. As soon as his bombers had climbed to their operating height, they were to fire Very lights, signalling that the searchlights should be switched on, pointing vertically upwards. Pilots would manoeuvre until the three were in line, and would then steer the compass course which kept them in line, verifying their ground speed by the time taken over the pre-determined distances between the lights. Freeman suggested that experienced pilots would go first and drop long-burning marker flares, on or near the target, to help the less experienced, and for star shells to be fired at regular intervals to 'home' the bombers back to Allied lines.

Given the technical limitations of the time, the scheme combined a remarkably practical navigational aid with a rudimentary target-marking system and a homing device for tired pilots. Although based on the technology of 1917,

Freeman's plan contains the essentials of a primitive 'Pathfinder' system, on the lines developed in the Second World War to guide bombers to their targets at night. In 1917 his ideas were rejected by the GOC; 25 years later, however, he would intervene decisively to insist on the creation of just such a force.[64]

John Salmond had succeeded Trenchard in command of the RFC in France on 18 January 1918, and he arranged for the RFC to run a series of Army courses on the problems of low-level co-operation with the Army, during the four months after the Cambrai offensive.[65] As the Fifth Army braced themselves to meet the German spring offensive in the Arras/Amiens area, Salmond decided to reinforce their air support by aircraft from HQ Wings, and 9th Wing was the obvious choice.[66] While the strength of the British Army in that sector had declined since 1917, German units had been heavily reinforced by troops released by the Russian peace treaty, and they held a substantial numerical advantage when the attack was finally launched. The RFC was also outnumbered, with only 579 serviceable aircraft (261 fighters) against the GAF's 730, (326 fighters).

Six of the 9th Wing's squadrons had been established at the southern end of the British front by the time the German offensive opened on 21 March, leaving only their night bomber squadrons on the northern sector.[67] The Germans penetrated nearly forty miles through the Fifth Army sector in the first week. But the front was never totally broken and the movement of German transport and reserves was severely hampered by British air attacks, which

The Sopwith Camel, with two Vickers machine-guns in the 'hump' before the pilot, entered squadron service in July 1917. Inexperienced pilots found its handling difficult but it could out-turn most German aircraft and destroyed more of them than any other Allied fighters.

played a vital part in halting the advance. On the fourth day the Germans attempted to break through on the crucial Third Army front, and Freeman's squadrons were switched to the northern end of the sector, where a deep penetration would be dangerous. Salmond ordered Freeman to:

> Send out your Scout Squadrons and those of 27, 25 and 62 that are available on the line. These Squadrons will bomb and shoot up everything they can see. Very low flying is essential, all risks to be taken.[68]

He reinforced them with ten additional squadrons, most of them RE8s despite their unsuitability for ground attack.[69]

The RFC pilots did indeed attack from very low altitudes: one German company commander who threw himself flat on the ground was actually touched by the wheel of a British fighter.* Their remarkable daring, commented on in many German regimental histories, exacted a mental toll from their opponents which was out of proportion to their moderate material impact[70].

Freeman inevitably had a hectic week, and after working around the clock for several days in succession he fell ill. He was only in hospital for 48 hours, however, before Salmond insisted that he was indispensable; he returned to duty the following day. 'I must be where I am most wanted', he told Gladys,

> That I am pleasing Salmond is all that matters – and to be indispensable is flattering. The Flying Corps has done magnificently and I have been jolly proud to have commanded such people – they have worked magnificently ... I have never had such a time in all my life.'[71]

It was to be the high spot of his career as an operational commander, for he was recalled for a Staff course in April, and had more important tasks in the Second World War.

The Freeman family suffered two tragic losses in 1918. Noël, Wilfrid's eldest brother, a major in the Royal Artillery, was killed by the tremendous barrage which opened the German offensive on 21 March. At his best Noel was exhilarating company, and Wilfrid and his brothers would come to him for advice rather than their generous, kindly, but rather ineffective father. Russell's death, exactly four months later, was an even more devastating blow. He had had a successful 'tour' with 14 Squadron, during which he made a five-hour, 350-mile flight in a Martinsyde to attack a bridge on the Hejaz railway,[72] and won an MC and a Croix de Guerre; he returned to Britain in June 1917, to become an instructor and Squadron Commander under Colonel Louis Strange at the Central Flying School. The instructors worked long hours, trying to raise the standard of the newly qualified pilots, and Russell was remembered as a very thorough and conscientious teacher, giving his pupils much longer hours of instruction than officially permitted at the time.

In the summer of 1918, however, after the death of a close friend, he insisted on returning to operations in France, to command 73 Squadron,

* The German Lieutenant Nocke, who was run over, was in the 8th Grenadier Regt.

equipped with Sopwith Camels, with the rank of Major. He was shot down and killed near West Belleau on his first operational sortie, by Lieutenant von Bulow of Jasta 36.

He had seen very little air fighting whilst with 14 Squadron, none at all at CFS, and Strange's attempts to dissuade him from returning to an operational squadron may have been for that reason. There is no record that Russell had to retrain on Sopwith Camels at an OTU before joining his new squadron, if such a policy was by then in force, but perhaps as a Major, he was too senior for this. Wilfrid Freeman would have known the facts however, and he was to exert great emphasis on thorough training in the next war.

THE FORMATION OF THE ROYAL AIR FORCE

The onset of daylight air-raids on London by German Gothas in June 1917 caused the Government to review the entire conduct of the air war, and in August the Cabinet decided to turn the RFC and the RNAS into a single, unified air force. Lloyd-George had lost confidence in both Jellicoe and Haig, and accepted the advice of General Smuts that the whole problem of aircraft supplies and control should be made independent of the other services.

The first wartime Staff College course at the Royal Naval College, Greenwich. Lieutenant-Colonel Freeman is third from the right in the back row. The other RAF officer (third from left, centre row) is Wing Commander (later Air Vice-Marshal) H. Cave-Brown-Cave. The second from the right in the middle row is Commander Tovey, later Admiral of the Fleet Lord Tovey.

The decision was made public in October, and in April 1918 the Royal Air Force (RAF) came into being, together with its own Department of State, the Air Ministry, and its supervisory body, the Air Council. On its creation, Freeman was attached to the RAF as a Lieutenant-Colonel, but the amalgamation of the two air services had little immediate effect at the operational level until the German offensive petered out. The formation of the new service and the establishment of a proper Air Staff meant, however, that thought had to be given to the training of potential senior officers, and Freeman was recalled from France on 21 April. He marked time on a training station, before being posted to the newly re-opened Royal Naval College at Greenwich on 3 June to attend the first wartime Staff College course.

The decision to send Freeman to the Staff College before he was 30 shows that he was already a marked man, one of the élite of young officers on whom the future of the RAF would depend. He had been brave and resourceful in operations, quick to understand and focus on the essentials of air warfare, wily and perceptive in planning raids, and ingenious and practical in thinking through operational problems and devising ways to improve the performance of the units under his command. He was a natural leader who earned the respect and admiration of his airmen, and he was held in equally high esteem by officers in the other armed services: he took great pains to cultivate his acquaintance with those who did not have exaggerated ideas of their own importance, and they in turn recognized the ruthless perfectionist behind Freeman's handsome, well-dressed façade. He was also a very capable administrator, resolved 'to fill the day with useful work', and his reports were memorable, succinct and thorough. He had a determination 'to do today what could have been put off until tomorrow', and the self-confidence both to take decisions and implement them.

He never forgot the agonizing experience of operating Wings in which some squadrons were equipped with obsolete aeroplanes, against enemy aircraft with better performance. The grim periods between 1916 and 1918 demonstrated that the operational capability of an air force was dependent on the quality of its equipment, and no one took this lesson to heart more completely than Freeman. Twenty years later, when he assumed responsibility for aircraft development and production, quality was his watchword; on the success of his pursuit of quality depended the future not only of Britain, but of democracy itself.

CHAPTER 3

The promotion ladder

REEMAN AND CAVE-BROWN-CAVE were the only RAF students on the twelve-month Naval Staff course, and when it was over Freeman, as a supernumerary Lieutenant-Colonel, marked time before his next posting at the RAF Air Pilotage School. He was offered a managerial job by William Morris at Cowley, and despite the family prejudice against 'trade', seriously considered the proposal, but ultimately refused.[1] On 1 August 1919 he accepted a permanent commission as a Wing Commander in the RAF and resigned his Army commission, moving to command No. 2 Flying Training School at Duxford until the Andover Staff College opened in 1922. Twenty years later, Lord Londonderry, a member of the Air Council in 1919, recalled that he and the CAS had at this time carefully identified officers likely to reach the top ranks of the new service.[2]

The RAF was drastically reduced in size as soon as the war ended: in November 1918 the Service comprised 280 squadrons, 20,000 aircraft, 27,500 officers and 264,000 other ranks; a year later, only 5,300 officers and 54,000 men remained, in 28 squadrons, 18 of them overseas. Trenchard, Chief of the Air Staff, recognized the need to create a proper career infrastructure to cope with the long-term needs of the new service and therefore established an Apprentice School at Halton, a Cadet College at Cranwell, a Flying Instructors School (the CFS), Schools of navigation, administration and photography, and a Staff College at Andover. All of these institutions were essential for the training of career servicemen for the RAF, the most technical of the three armed services.

Freeman's formal appointment as a senior instructor at the RAF Staff College at Andover was notified on 14 October 1921, before the College opened, but his actual posting, as No. 3 of the directing staff, came on 3 January 1922: the first course started on 4 April 1922. Other members of the staff included Brooke-Popham, the Commandant, Joubert de la Ferté and Bertine Sutton; among the students were Sholto Douglas, Keith Park, Charles Portal and Richard Peirse. The courses surveyed the principles of war, imperial strategy, the tactics and organisation of air, ground and naval forces, supply and communications, intelligence, domestic and foreign policy and the relationship of economics, commerce and science to RAF affairs. Basic staff duties, letters, reports and signals had to be mastered, and students were also taught how to organise formal receptions: Brooke-Popham understood the importance of setting high standards on social occasions.[3]

Courses lasted a year. There were aircraft to enable students to maintain flying practice, and bicycles on which they surveyed sites for airfields. Students had to consider a wide range of non-RAF matters: they visited the Navy, where some of them went out on a submarine, the London Docks, and a railway terminus.[4] There were also exchange visits to the Navy and Army Staff Colleges. Among the problems considered in the joint sessions with the Navy at Greenwich was the defence of Singapore, an exercise which became all too real for Brooke-Popham nineteen years later.[5]

Freeman found his work as an instructor at the Andover Staff College undemanding, for he was not really cut out to be a schoolmaster, and he told his nephew Richard Walker, Josephine's son, who cycled over to Andover from his school nearby, that it was a very dull job and that he was seriously wondering whether to stay in the Service.[6] Promoted to Group Captain in January 1923, he headed the directing staff for the third course and was then posted to command the CFS at Upavon, and to prepare it for a projected move to Wittering in 1925. Building on Smith-Barry's pioneering system, the CFS had achieved a world-wide reputation for its flying instruction since 1916, and most of its eleven-week courses had one or two overseas pupils. In the intervals between courses, instructors visited other flying schools to monitor standards.

During 1926 a de Havilland D.H.60G Moth with a light Genet radial engine was lent to the CFS to teach some Greek pupils who were used to the aircraft. It was such a delight to fly that Freeman persuaded the Air Ministry to buy six more of them to equip a special aerobatic flight for the 1927 Hendon Air Display.[7] The instructors team had some outstanding pilots, D'Arcy Greig, Dick

The RAF Staff College, Andover, 1922. In addition to Wilfrid Freeman (second from the left in the front row), five of the staff shown went on to become Air Chief Marshals: Brooke-Popham (front row, fourth from the left); Sholto Douglas (middle row, fourth from the right); and in the back row: Portal (second from the left); Pierse (third from the left); and Keith Park (second from the right).

Atcherley, Waghorn, and Stainforth, all future members of the High Speed Flight which won the Schneider Trophy. Their aerobatics were unique. Harald Penrose, the Westland test pilot, recorded that the 'outstanding event' of the display 'was the demonstration of close formation aerobatics by the five Genet-powered, scarlet-topped, de Havilland Moths from the Central Flying School . . . They looped in formation . . . rolled in formation, flew on their backs in formation . . . spun and recovered in formation . . . It was breathtaking.'[8]

The Central Flying School's special aerobatic flight of D.H.60G Genet Moths at the 1927 Hendon Air Display. The five aircraft in the team performed formation aerobatics in the hands of CFS instructors.

Freeman was remembered by his CFS staff as a brilliant officer. Although intolerant and incapable of suffering fools gladly, he had a quiet and reserved manner and a sense of humour that inspired affection and respect.[9] He was the ideal person to take over the CFS after the lax regime of 'Topsy' Holt, his predecessor, who allowed – indeed positively encouraged – all sorts of stunts by his instructors, many of which damaged the School's aircraft.[10] Freeman tightened up flying discipline without losing the support of his instructors, and under his control the School both enhanced its already famous reputation and further developed the concept of that most spectacular of all air displays, formation aerobatics.

After less than two years at the CFS, Freeman became Deputy Director of Operations and Intelligence (DDOI) at the Air Ministry, assuming his new post on 27 February 1927; he spent the next twenty-one months working closely with Trenchard. A number of short letters from Trenchard and Salmond survive, sympathising with illness, congratulating him on promotions and postings, and generally showing an intense personal interest in Freeman's progress. His wife had always refused to have a permanent home, although it was offered to her by her father, but there were no RAF quarters in London, so Wilfrid took a house in Sussex Gardens while he was working at the Air Ministry and could spend more time with his family. His eldest daughter Anne was born in 1920 and Keith Noel (named after his uncles) followed in 1923.

William Freeman died in 1925. His widow inherited the Murtle Estate and also kept on the Freemans' large house at 103 Westbourne Terrace, taking for granted the luxury of a full household staff and chauffeur; Freeman and his family treated the two houses as second homes. A large hamper of food came down by train from Murtle every week, with vegetables and fruit from the gardens, eggs and butter from the home farm, oatmeal for porridge and oatcakes, and game and salmon.

Freeman's youngest brother, Alan, and the much older Max, both confirmed bachelors, lived at Westbourne Terrace. Knowledgeable about wines, they built up a cellar, and persuaded their parents to engage an excellent cook and a butler, Rennie, to assist the rugged old Scots parlourmaid, Margaret Cults. There were housemaids, a chauffeur, and latterly a companion to Mrs Freeman, who was always known to the family by her surname, Chandler. Sibyl and her family, and Ralph, stayed there when home from Kenya; Jo and her children were also frequent visitors. They enjoyed being taken to the latest shows, and appreciated the new sophistication of the Freeman household. It was a sort of family *Hôtel particulier.*

Freeman had always been subject to migraines, but after 18 months in London, working long hours with the Air Staff under Trenchard, he was ill more frequently, suffering from an intermittent fever. Trenchard was contrite, and promised him[11] 'a more out of doors job',* with the result that after less than two years as DDOI, he was given command of the RAF station at Leuchars, near St Andrews in Scotland. Leuchars was an RAF airfield on which Naval pilots and RAF aircrew of the Fleet Air Arm were stationed and trained by the RAF. Four flights of Fairey III aircraft with Napier Lion engines operated from it, when not on aircraft carriers.

He was remembered as a strict but fair and generous Station Commander. One of his airmen, aircraftsman Martin, a 22-year-old from Halton, later recalled that when he was chosen for the station cricket team, Freeman quickly realised that he lacked a pair of white flannels. An aircraftsman's pay was only 24 shillings a week, so Martin could hardly have been expected to pay for a pair, and Freeman called him in and gave him one of his own. Hearing that he was a trumpeter, Freeman also bought an expensive new trumpet, officially for the station band but for Martin's exclusive use while he remained at Leuchars.[12] On another occasion, at one of the routine London meetings attended by Station Commanders, Freeman supported proposals for equipping NAAFIs with refrigerators, which were then new and revolutionary kitchen

---

* He added in his letter'... I cannot say how much I have appreciated your brain for the short time you have been with me ... get really well because you ought to aspire to high places in the Air Force, if you keep fit, with your energy, brain and tact.'

appliances. Freeman described how one of the sausages delivered to the NAAFI at RAF Duxford had been secretly marked, and its progress to the dining table carefully monitored. The meeting collapsed in laughter when he disclosed that the marked sausage had not been served up for three weeks.[13]

Three months after promotion to Air Commodore in July 1929, he was appointed Senior Air Staff Officer (SASO) of the UK Inland Area, a post which he held for a year before being transferred to Iraq as SASO to Ludlow-Hewitt, the Air Officer Commanding (AOC) Iraq. Less than two months later Freeman, aged 41 and still only an Air Commodore, was appointed AOC Transjordan and Palestine, his first important independent command.

At that time this was an immensely important post with considerable political responsibilities. The Middle East was a highly sensitive area: tensions were rising between the Arab and Jewish communities*, and serious rioting had broken out earlier in the year; the British Government's policy in the region seemed on the point of veering towards a pro-Arab position.[14] The RAF was the main military arm of British interests. Although Freeman could count on direct support from an RAF squadron at Amman and the Transjordan Frontier Force, he also had the full resources of the larger Iraq Command behind him.

The appointment reflected Freeman's outstanding ability and the recognition of his superiors† that he was an officer of exceptional ability; it was yet another positive step in his steady advance towards the top echelons of the RAF high command. And yet, at a personal level, there was a heavy price to pay, for the posting exposed irreconcilable tensions within his marriage to G. Years later, in a wartime letter to his second wife, Freeman wrote: I knew beforehand that doubt existed in my mind over my marriage to G. If I had been able to talk it over with Noel it would probably never have come off.[15]

Gladys had been restless and dissatisfied before she married. Unhappy and bored at home, resenting her rather strict parents, she was flattered by the attentions of Wilfrid and the Freeman family, who lived in the same street and came from much the same background. Marriage to her charming and amusing suitor promised greater freedom; indeed, she told him almost immediately after their wedding that she had only married him to get away from home.‡ His long absences during the First World War had been boring for

* Due to the Balfour declaration the Palestine Mandate was difficult to administer. Lord Plumer's period as High Commissioner had been peaceful, but Sir John Chancellor, who succeeded him in 1928, was a colourless figure, much influenced by his Chief Secretary, Sir Stephen Luke. Trouble began before Chancellor arrived, over access to the 'Wailing Wall', sacred to both Jews and Muslims, and because Chancellor encouraged the Arabs to suppose that a Legislative Assembly might be formed, allowing the Arab majority greater influence on policy, a decision which led to serious rioting in August 1929.

† Trenchard's influence was still dominant, but John Salmond his successor, would have agreed on an appointment so vital to Freeman's subsequent career.

‡ Richmond letters. Diana Galbraith, a school friend of Elizabeth Richmond, married Elizabeth's brother, John, in 1939, and came to live at Murtle Den, the family house owned by Wilfrid and Ralph Freeman, in 1940. Her weekly wartime letters to John in Egypt, have been a valuable contemporary source.

her, and she was not the first grass-widow to amuse herself with other friends. The children steadied the marriage, but they usually only saw their parents in the evenings and at weekends, and ate separately;[16] holidays at Murtle were therefore all the more welcome.

Until 1930 none of Freeman's postings had been overseas, and without the allowances and cheaper amenities which came with service abroad, he and G were unable to afford an active participation in English social events. This did not bother Freeman in the slightest, for he disliked such occasions, but G obviously resented the deprivation: it was one of a number of issues about which she frequently nagged him. The barbed wit and cynicism, which Freeman had found stimulating and amusing twenty years before – when they both enjoyed the endless round of parties, and G was a pretty girl – surrounded by mutually supporting friends, had palled and become corrosive from a clever but sardonic older woman, when her husband's successful career needed her unselfish support.

His appointment as AOC in Palestine, where the RAF was in charge of all the military aspects of the Mandate, and where he was therefore, *de facto*, Commander-in-Chief, brought matters to a head. The move from Britain and from the support of the Freeman family, 103 Westbourne Terrace and Murtle, involved a sharp contraction in their circle of friends and family and in their interests, and exacerbated many of the incompatibilities and irritations of what was now an unhappy partnership. The fact that Freeman detested the pompous formalities obligatory for an officer in his position whilst G apparently revelled in her exalted status as wife of the AOC, epitomised the problem. Moreover G not only perceived the failings of others, but mentioned them, thus failing the obligatory standards of diplomacy and tact essential for such a position. The precise circumstances of their final separation have long been forgotten, but in the autumn of 1931 it was decided that G should accompany the children when they went back to school in Britain. She left in October, and did not return.

Freeman made a success of his posting, getting on just as well with the Civil Servants from the Colonial Office and with the soldiers in the area as he did with his RAF colleagues. The Palestine mandate came under the Colonial Secretary, Philip Cunliffe-Lister, and Freeman's relations with him were so relaxed and friendly that he went so far as to ask his advice over his future Service career. Although Freeman found operational duties rewarding, much of his time as head of the armed forces in Palestine was absorbed by pompous service rituals, a seemingly endless round of long, formal dinner parties, luncheons, visits and inspections, which he detested. Cunliffe-Lister was a kindred spirit, but he persuaded Freeman to stay.[17]

Another firm friend was Colonel Charles Miller, who commanded the Transjordan Frontier Force while Freeman was in Palestine.[18]

Many, if not most, of the non-military residents of Jerusalem in the late 1920s and early 1930s were part of the civil and business administration of the Mandate. Among them were 'Eggs' Whitcombe, of Barclays, and his wife

Betty, daughter of Colonel Ainsworth from the Indian Medical Service, (who was then at the St Johns Opthalmic Hospital in Jerusalem), and Ernest Richmond, an architect, Curator of Antiquities. Richmond's younger daughter, Elizabeth, came out to Jerusalem at about this time, soon after leaving the good new girls school, Downe House.

There was the usual shortage of unattached girls in that rather limited expatriate society, and Elizabeth ('Liz' to friends and family) was immediately absorbed into the round of parties, tennis, picnics and expeditions: Freeman, who had an eye for a pretty girl, noticed her driving her family's Ford, and promptly asked her name. Dining with the High Commissioner at the Old Government House soon afterwards, he found himself sitting next to her: 'she was wearing a blue dress with a high collar at the back, with fur on it'.[19] Much to his amusement, when asked what she thought of such formal occasions, her inimitable, low-pitched reply was 'absolutely bloody'.[20]

Freeman was lonely: as usual he was working very hard, his forces were few, and although the unrest of the previous year had subsided, there were deep tensions between the Arabs and the Jewish settlers; much of the British community was sympathetic to the Arab cause. He liked young people, and Elizabeth was not embarrassed by his interest, so he saw her often, meeting her at the club and dancing with her at parties. As Government House was very near the Sports Club, she and her friends visited him when playing tennis; he went out of his way to be kind to them all, engaging Elizabeth's brother John to teach mathematics to RAF airmen working on their trade tests, and Whitcombe as an extra ADC.[21] Charles Strafford, a Squadron Leader

The Richmond family. Elizabeth is second from the right, next to her father.

serving under Freeman, often noted in his little pocket diary, 'AOC and Liz Richmond to tea before riding', and 'Edna [his wife] with AOC, Liz Richmond and I played tennis at Government House.'[22]

To a contemporary, Elizabeth was intelligent, very good looking, 'indeed almost beautiful in an austere way'[23], but she was not a warm person, and criticism came easily to her. Apart from holding a slightly pessimistic view of life, she had a rebellious streak, and she was often the first to defy or ignore rules and conventions at Downe. They were traits which owed much to a sense of insecurity engendered by her father's short temper, but not wholly unlike those which Freeman had found attractive in G 20 years earlier. Elizabeth was good company, and was always ready to 'have a go at something new', but she was not frivolous,[24] appreciating music and poetry, and loving her dogs and the pleasures of travelling: she both shared Freeman's interests and widened them. Although she rode well, she spared Freeman from that unshared enthusiasm, and whilst she enjoyed an argument, it was apt to get heated, unlike the practised, serene and witty Freemans.

During a cocktail party on her twenty-first birthday, Freeman realised that he had fallen deeply in love.[25] Elizabeth knew Freeman was married, but her rebelliousness enabled her easily to accept the wit and sparkling company of her charming and important admirer. She was lucky enough to be able to do so unobtrusively in the company of Betty Whitcombe and of Freeman's niece and god-child – Sibyl Walker, a former school friend – a pretty, laughing, dark-haired girl, with a bubbling sense of humour, who was staying with him at the time.

There were many picnics with the Whitcombes and others on the beach at Jaffa, and on one occasion the four of them went further north along the beach between Tyre and Sidon. Driving back along the beach, Freeman obviously thought he had been indiscreet, for Elizabeth was made to curl down on the back seat, covered in a blanket, with Betty upright beside her, apparently alone in the back of the car. It was not the only occasion when a blind eye was needed: Betty subsequently received a beautiful 'compact' from Freeman inscribed 'In memory of the Back', a tribute to her tact on these occasions.[26]

One evening, when the others were on the tennis court, Betty had the courage to ask Freeman, 'What are you going to do about Liz?' Her question brought a period of relaxed admiration sharply into focus, and inexorably triggered the next steps. Freeman and Elizabeth became secretly engaged on 18 May 1932,[27] when Elizabeth was twenty-one and he forty-three, and when he rejoined G and the children at Murtle in September he asked her for a divorce. It was agreed that their decision to part should initially be kept secret; the Freeman family was only told in April 1933. It was not until 17 April 1935, however, that Freeman married Elizabeth, after the dreary business of a 1930s divorce – including the obligatory deceits and separations – was over.

*   *   *

Elizabeth Richmond was twenty-one and Wilfrid Freeeman forty-three when they became secretly engaged in 1932.

Meanwhile both of them were under great strain. Writing to his sister Sibyl, after her visit in April 1933, Freeman admitted to being 'nervy' and depressed, described his life as 'utterly intolerable', and again admitted his inclination to quit the RAF:

> I feel now as if I could cut and run from everything and everyone and E[lizabeth] would come with me I know. That would be cowardly, but I feel it would avoid the united censure of my family . . .[28]

It was a great relief to him that Sibyl both accepted the overriding urgency of his love, and reassured him that the family would, in fact, be understanding and supportive.

Elizabeth had to face tremendous opposition once her family realised that Freeman's plans were serious. Ernest Richmond, her father, had been the Political Assistant Secretary in 1920–1, and Arab adviser to the Palestine Government from 1922–7, before becoming Director of Antiquities, and was very much a part of the local 'Arabist' establishment. He and the rest of his family had come to know an immensely charismatic and influential French Roman Catholic priest in Amman, and under his tuition and leadership, had become Catholics, leaving only Elizabeth defiantly Anglican. Happily, John Richmond, her brother, was not censorious, and treated the couple, in Freeman's words, 'as if we were human beings in that bad time'.[29] John Richmond's courtesy and sympathy earned him and his family Freeman's lifelong respect and affection, but opposition from the other Richmonds sadly deepened his innate prejudice against Roman Catholics to a degree of unreason; few who criticised his decision to divorce and remarry were ever readily forgiven.

Quite when Freeman disclosed his pending divorce to the Air Ministry is not certain, and he may well have said nothing until the first Divorce Court hearing early in 1934. It was almost certainly after his promotion to Air Vice-Marshal in July 1933 at the age of 44.* Divorce at that time was conditional upon there being no collusion, and this was supervised by the King's Proctor for the conditional period of twelve months. Freeman's Decree Absolute came through in May 1935, so application for a Decree Nisi need not have been made before April 1934. His posting to command the RAF Staff College on 2 January, 1934, was unaffected, but the social consequences of a divorce were still significant for a service career, and the leaders of the RAF were probably concerned that, as the junior service, they should not appear to be willing to overlook them. The fact that Freeman wrote to Charles Miller on 20 February 1935, 'I am preparing myself to leave the RAF in 1936',[30] almost certainly meant that he must have been warned that he would have to retire when his time as Commandant was over.†

He was a stimulating Staff College Commandant. Besides two students from the Army, the Navy, Canada and Australia, 22 from the RAF made up the 30 members of the 1934 course. They included Walter Dawson, who became an Assistant Chief of the Air Staff, and subsequently Air Member for Supply and Organisation after the war. Dawson later recalled how all the answers to Staff College questions and exercises had to be handwritten 'on the grounds that there would be occasions when staff officers had to write their instructions, and that it was important that they should be legible'. Most were returned with comments not only by the directing staff, but by the Commandant himself. Addressing the students, Freeman said that he had 'studied their work with interest and growing astonishment, and had come to the conclusion that they used their backsides for thinking and their feet for writing, and that it was his job to cure those tendencies.'[31]

He took a close interest in individual students. Dawson was invited into his Commandant's study to see if he could recognize any of the books which lined the walls. When he failed, Freeman said, 'It was just as I expected from studying your work; you have read far too much of the military stuff and nothing like enough of other subjects. . . . A Staff College graduate is a specialist . . . and a specialist without a broad background is a danger to himself and to

---

* Other promotions to equivalent rank in 1932–3 included Colonels A.P. Wavell (50) and Alan Brooke (53) to Major-General, and Commodore A.B.Cunningham (49) to Rear-Admiral.

† Such a warning, on a 'social' matter like divorce, was unlikely to have been decided upon by the Air Member for Personnel on his own. Freeman was one of Trenchard's 'high fliers', and it is more than likely that the decision to warn him that retirement loomed would have been taken after consultation with Londonderry, the Secretary of State, and the two 'éminences grises' of the RAF, Trenchard and Salmond.

everyone else.'[32] He then ordered Dawson to ignore certain recommended Staff College texts, and throughout the following year Freeman directed his reading in an attempt to broaden his knowledge and interests. 'I really did appreciate and profit from his personal help', Dawson later recorded.

As Commandant, Freeman was asked to attend Chiefs of Staff meetings, at which he did what he could to promote a better understanding with the other services. 'Here we all still breathe the spirit of inter-service co-operation', he told Charles Miller in February 1935. He found that the Navy tended to stand aside from the other armed forces, but saw more scope for working with the Army, describing himself as predominantly 'pro-Army', and even suggesting to the service chiefs the appointment of an Army officer to the Andover staff.[33]

There were many personal problems during his two years at Andover. The application for a divorce had to come from a reluctant G, who was only finally persuaded to apply by the intervention of Freeman's daughter Anne, then just fourteen.[34] G's lawyers drove a hard bargain on her behalf, which Freeman understood and ruefully accepted, but shortly before the hearing, they stunned him by bluntly demanding a fifty per cent increase on the settlement, threatening to withdraw her petition if he refused. 'I instantly agreed; the best decision I ever made', Freeman later recalled.*

Freeman's mother died in 1935, leaving the Murtle Estate in her will to the son, or otherwise the daughter, who would live there and maintain it for fifteen years. But no investments had been set aside to support the estate, which was not financially viable on its own,† and one by one all the Freemans refused it, to their unanimous regret. Max, the eldest, and an executor, was very ill, Alan had been killed in a car accident at about the same time as his mother's death, and Ralph was in Kenya, so it fell to Wilfrid to obtain his brothers' and sisters' agreement to a series of heart-rending decisions about their inheritance. The outcome was that Murtle House, its estate, and '103' were sold, and the proceeds divided among the Freeman family.

*   *   *

Hitler came to power in Germany in 1933, and on the advice of the Chiefs of Staff, Britain's National Government headed by Ramsay MacDonald abandoned the 'ten year rule' – the assumption that the Empire would not be engaged in a major war for the next ten years. A limited air rearmament programme was launched in 1934, entitled Scheme A, but in March 1935 Hitler untruthfully told Britain's Foreign Secretary, Sir John Simon, that the German air force had already attained numerical parity with the RAF, and would soon achieve parity with France.[35]

The Government promptly established a small sub-committee on air parity, chaired by Philip Cunliffe-Lister, to recommend steps to ensure that British air power would not be inferior to that of any country within striking distance,[36] and in two reports the sub-committee acknowledged that there was

---

* Freeman gave the author and his fiancée dinner in Scotland in 1952, and talked freely.
† The rates on the mansion house alone cost £500 pa, equivalent to £20,000 in 1997.

already a deficiency of first-line aircraft. Although this would be offset somewhat by the allegedly superior training and organisation of the RAF, the Luftwaffe's numerical advantage would increase if each side maintained its existing armaments programmes. The Government therefore accepted the inadequacy of the 1934 plans for an Air Force of 62 squadrons and in May 1935, in the midst of the Silver Jubilee celebrations, announced Scheme C, a rearmament plan designed to raise the strength of the RAF in Britain to 123 squadrons (1,500 first line aircraft).[37]

As international relations deteriorated, Freeman's career took a sudden and unexpected upturn. Stanley Baldwin succeeded MacDonald as Prime Minister on 7 June 1935, and promptly appointed Cunliffe-Lister, Secretary of State for Air, a crucial decision both for Britain and for Freeman's career, for Cunliffe-Lister, soon to be Viscount Swinton, was by then thoroughly familiar with the problems of air rearmament and knew exactly who he wanted to control the expansion of the RAF.

As Colonial Secretary, he had seen a great deal of Freeman and of Cyril Newall, during their Palestine and Iraq commands, and liked them both, finding them decisive and level-headed. As Commandant of the Staff College, Freeman had also attended meetings of Swinton's air parity sub-committee since its formation in April 1935. Faced with the formidable task of re-equipping the RAF with fast modern aircraft from a small and backward industrial base, the new Secretary of State for Air naturally wanted to work with senior officers he knew; men who were congenial to him, and on whose judgement the industry could rely; men with the personality and intelligence that was likely to earn the respect of the other services, and of the government departments involved. He realised that Freeman had technical, operational and administrative ability of a high order,[38] and did not hesitate to introduce him to his future tasks well before his term as Commandant was over.

Aircraft procurement had previously been controlled by the Air Member for Supply and Research (AMSR), Sir Hugh Dowding, but the responsibilities had been divided in 1934: Dowding became Air Member for Research and Development (AMRD) so that he could concentrate on the development of new aircraft technology, while Newall was appointed Air Member for Supply and Organisation (AMSO), with responsibility for production. At the beginning of 1936, Freeman was transferred to the Air Ministry to understudy Dowding's work before taking over as AMRD on 1 April. He was well prepared for his new position by his experience of the air parity sub-committee and his attendance at the Chiefs of Staff Committee, and was able to start taking decisions almost as soon as his appointment became effective.

CHAPTER 4

Air Member for Research and Development

REEMAN'S APPOINTMENT to the Air Council on 1 April 1936 was an astonishing change in his circumstances and career prospects. Three or four years before he had miserably contemplated the boredom of peacetime service life, the corrosive effects of his failed marriage, and the social complications of his divorce, and had seriously considered leaving the Service. Everything on which he had founded his life seemed to be crumbling: his marriage, his career, the trust of his children and the respect of his family. Beyond his career and his family, he had serious moral worries. As committed members of the Anglican Church, the Freeman family's Sunday observance rules had been those of a middle-class, half-Presbyterian, Scottish-Victorian family: books that could be read on Sundays were limited, cards and games were forbidden. The decision to seek a divorce, so as to re-marry, nagged at his conscience.

Yet he had single-mindedly accepted that his loveless marriage was at an end, and he was too decisive to compromise. The unlikely appearance of Elizabeth, and the blissful prospect of a second chance, led him to risk everything for the sake of his love for a very attractive, intelligent, if slightly immature, young woman. As with all his decisions, once it was taken he dismissed his doubts, and did not let them affect his selfless, dedicated commitment to the mountainous task ahead of him.

Trenchard, Salmond, and Londonderry had selected him years before as one of the high fliers of the RAF,[1] and his posting to command the Staff College at the age of 45 promised better things to come. Their warning that he must retire two years later, aged 47, obviously signified that his career was about to end under a cloud, but he was rescued by Swinton and German rearmament.

By the mid-30s the Third Reich was creating a new air force, and German military and naval forces were being rapidly rebuilt. In response the British Government committed itself to rearmament on an unprecedented scale, and gave top priority to the expansion of the RAF. The Air Ministry would require men of exceptional ability to direct rearmament, and outstanding officers like Freeman could not be wasted, whatever the official views on divorce.

THE AIR MINISTRY

The creation of the Luftwaffe in the early 1930s coincided with a technical revolution in aircraft design, involving the introduction of all-metal stressed-skin monoplanes with increasingly powerful aero-engines. Aluminium alloy 'monocoque' structures, retractable undercarriages, flaps and covered cockpits became virtually essential. By 1935 the contrast between the most advanced aircraft being made for the Luftwaffe, and the aircraft in service and being supplied to the RAF was very pronounced. The largest British engines developed only 600–700hp, the top speeds of bombers like the Heyford and Hendon were only 130–150mph, and of biplane fighters like the Gauntlet and the Fury, 220mph: none of them would have been of operational value in a European war. Just as the launch of HMS *Dreadnought* in 1906 rendered every existing battleship obsolete, so the general introduction of high-powered monoplanes by the world's air forces could not now be avoided. The task facing the RAF by the mid-1930s therefore involved not only expansion, but wholesale re-equipment with modern aircraft.

The specifications for new military aircraft issued after 1931, incorporated the modern technology of the metal monoplane, but until 1935, the Air Staff had failed to appreciate the sheer size and imminence of the threat posed by Germany. The RAF's aircraft procurement process remained slow and bureaucratic, and little was done to accelerate it until the first military monoplanes began to appear in Germany and the United States.

The RAF rearmament programme 'Scheme C', launched in Britain in 1935, under which 3,800 aircraft were to be produced by March 1937, was an interim measure. Apart from the fact that none of the new monoplane designs were ready for production, the British aircraft industry was so small and fragmented that it lacked the industrial capacity to re-equip the RAF in just two years. Throughout the 1920s and early 30s, RAF orders had been carefully rationed to keep alive the sixteen 'family' firms, and their design teams. Most of the companies were still run by men with experience of the production volumes of the First World War, but Hawker and Avro were the only two with recent experience of volume production of military aircraft, although de Havilland was building a lot of light civil aircraft. The scale of military aircraft purchases had been severely restricted during the depression years, and a number of firms had eked out a threadbare existence on an absolute minimum of aircraft work: the expansion of military aircraft production was certain to be a slow and laborious process.

The Air Ministry therefore had no alternative to giving firms production orders for obsolescent aircraft so that they could train and enlarge their workforces, and expand their factories. More advanced models were only ordered in small quantities, and the production of such designs was not expected to start before the summer of 1937. Scheme C was superseded however in February 1936, when Scheme F was approved, raising the target to 8,000 aircraft by 31 March 1939. Apart from creating a better balanced force with adequate reserves, Scheme F planned the creation of an air force largely equipped with reliable, high-performance, all-metal monoplanes which could easily be maintained in war.

Freeman's task when he joined the Air Council was to drive forward the development of such aircraft, and to draw up longer-term plans for their replacement by even more advanced types. The measures he took during the

The first Handley Page Heyford I was delivered in late 1933. The last of the RAF's biplane heavy bombers it had a maximum speed of 142 mph and a bomb load of 2,000 lb. It is shown here being 'attacked' by a Hawker Demon.

The Fairey Hendon, the RAF's first monoplane heavy bomber, entered service after Freeman became AMRD in April 1936.

The Handley Page Harrow, with relatively powerful Pegasus engines, had a speed of 200 mph and a maximum bomb load of 3,000 lb, but was already obsolescent when it entered service in 1937. It never saw active service as a bomber.

next two years, and his subsequent achievements in production planning, provided the fighters, the wireless control and the radar systems which won the Battle of Britain. Moreover, his forethought, then and later, kept air superiority for the Allies, almost throughout the war, and 'he, more than any other man, was responsible for building such aircraft as eventually enabled Bomber Command to become an effective arm of war'.[2]

As Air Member for Research and Development, Freeman was directly responsible to the Secretary of State for Air, Lord Swinton. He admired Swinton: 'a splendid man to work for, and that makes all the difference',[3] but not without reservations, fearing lest Swinton's egotism and ambition would mar his admirable hard work.[4] Freeman's other mentor was Lord Weir, a wealthy, laconic Scottish industrialist. Weir had rejoined the Air Council in 1935 as a part-time advisor on production (unpaid at his request), and was much more experienced than Swinton about practical production problems. An almost legendary figure in the history of the RAF, Weir had been Controller of Aeronautical Supplies and a contributor to the Smuts Report in 1917, and a member of the first Air Council; he had also served as Air Minister in 1918. He understood the long-term nature of all aeronautical programmes, the remorseless supply demands of active air warfare, and the need for prompt

Lord Swinton, the brilliant, hardworking Secretary of State for Air 1935–38. He rejected the political emphasis on numbers, and used the interval before the modern aircraft and engine designs were ready for mass production, to build the shadow factories in which to make them. Swinton's foresight, and the airfields and radar chain he ordered, ensured that the RAF was ready to defend Britain in 1940. Freeman found him 'a splendid man to work for'.

Viscount Weir, Controller of Aeronautical Supplies in 1917–18. Drawing freely on Weir's vast practical experience, Swinton and Freeman made few mistakes despite the huge technical challenge of rearmament.

decisions. He also recognized the acute problems facing the aircraft industry in the mid-1930s, and, from his experiences with national aircraft factories in 1918, that state control was not the answer.

Freeman's knowledge of the needs of the RAF, deftly presented in terse, clear memoranda, and backed by the wit and quick intelligence he showed at meetings and the superb political support he received from Swinton, soon established his ascendency on matters of quality at meetings of the Air Council. He readily accepted advice from Weir, mistakes were rare and, reassured by Freeman's decisiveness, his Civil Servants soon learned to work as a team.

Freeman was backed by a large and growing department staffed by a mixture of Air Force officers and technical Civil Servants. Dr Pye and W.S. Farren ran the Directorate of Scientific Research (DSR), Air Commodore R.H. Verney was Director of Technical Development (DTD), H. Grinstead headed Aircraft Research and Development (RDA), and G.P. Bulman and A.A. Ross Engine Research and Development (RDE). Mention should also be made of R.N. Liptrot,* whose ability to estimate the performance of a new design with accuracy, while it was 'on the drawing board' was exceptional and invaluable.

As the size of Freeman's task and the full range of his responsibilities became clearer, he began to recognize the host of uncertainties ahead. It was

* According to J.V. Connolly, he had the affectionate nick-name of 'Loopy'.

a time for decisiveness and patience, a time to choose, test and inspire his staff, a time to weigh up the quality of the aircraft industry's designers and development departments, to make his own assessments of his colleagues on the Air Council and in the Air Force, and above all to lead them with a confidence and courageousness that required enormous strength of character. The senior members of the aircraft industry found him responsive and friendly, but some of his Air Ministry staff 'thought him unreliable at first. They soon learned that behind his ready smile and quick mind was a highly independent thinker who sometimes had unexplained changes of mind.'[5] They were not used to working under Air Marshals who thought for themselves, and found that Freeman would often accept arguments made by designers whose views might differ considerably from those of the Directorate of Operational Requirements (DOR).

Bulman, responsible for aero-engines under both Dowding and Freeman, had found Dowding 'a magnificent leader', but found Freeman in a different class altogether...

> He ... was full of *élan* and the spirit of adventure, a visionary, but one who endeavoured to make his dreams effective; extremely handsome, rather like one's picture of Mercury; in many ways a cynic, because he was such a realist ... It was Freeman's job to say ... how Development could be driven to secure a maximum of advanced new aircraft ... to be produced in large quantity with the reliability and essential 'serviceability' appopriate to the Royal Air Force...
>
> As the early months of his posting passed, I think he realised that fate had picked him to oversee and inspire this great surge of unprecedented effort – if there were but time. Time. Two or three years at most perhaps. He put away the thought of his daunting task, to set about lighting up his staff with his own incandescence, with the ultimate criterion of 'Is it fit for war and vast production?' instead of the merely technically interesting experimental aircraft which had been too often sought.
>
> His outstanding personality and magnetism attracted the Industry and made them feel a sense of relief that there was now this key man at the Ministry, urging and pulling them along with an unusual panache; a man of piercing perception, ready to play for high stakes, to take instant decisions, by no means always on the advice of his Civil Servant staff or indeed of his Service colleagues. He was a man who walked alone, sometimes withdrawn into himself, apt to suffer from migraine, but generally sparkling, most penetrating in conversation, often delighting in playing the devil's advocate to see how one would respond; in my case often with fury, but ending in a mutual chuckle.
>
> He could be wickedly mischievous and impish in his comments, and as often most generous and understanding ... he was a wonderful Boss, though sometimes I could have killed him ... beyond doubt he was the most inspiring man I ever served.[6]

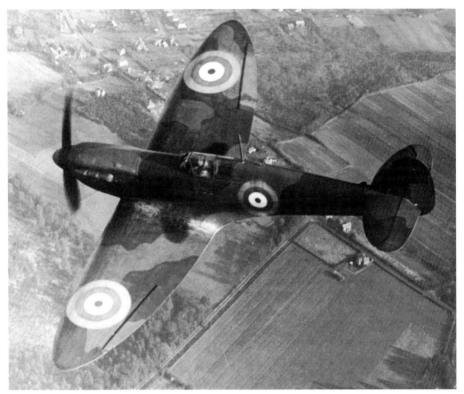

The prototype Spitfire, flown by Jeffrey Quill, chief test pilot of Supermarine. It was on Freeman's advice that the Air Council agreed to place the first order, for 310 Spitfires, if the prototype achieved a top speed of 350 mph.

Air Commodore J.C. Slessor, who worked alongside him as Director of Plans, and was a personal friend, confirmed that his personality and boundless energy inspired and challenged all who worked with him:

> He was as quick as lightning; the living antithesis of pomposity; a great lover of books and music, and a man of culture in the best sense . . . He was intensely human – critical but never unkind – with an impish, unpredictable humour and a capacity for selfless loyalty, that were at the same time the despair and delight of those to whom he gave his friendship.[7]

AIRCRAFT AND AERO-ENGINE DEVELOPMENT

As AMRD, Freeman was formally responsible for the technical quality of service aircraft. His authority extended from airframes to aircraft components, communications equipment and armament, but above all to the aero-engines which, more than any other item, were the absolutely crucial element of aircraft design, production and programming. In 1936 the Air Ministry's most important supplier was the engine division of the Bristol Aeroplane

Company, whose poppet-valve Mercury and Pegasus engines had already been in production for some years. Advised by Roy Fedden*, the head of their experimental engine division, Bristol had decided to cease development of these[8], and had concentrated on their new sleeve-valve designs, particularly the two-row Hercules and Taurus. Pressure for rearmament was such that large factories, stocked with expensive machine tools had to be set up to make them, and aircraft like the Beaufort, Beaufighter and Stirling, designed and put into production to use them, well before the technical problems of actually mass producing sleeve-valve engines were solved.

Apart from Bristol, the most important suppliers of the larger engines had been Rolls-Royce, Armstrong Siddeley and Napier, but de Havilland, Alvis, Fairey and the Nuffield group were all offering new designs. The official history of the flying services in the First World War had been completed in 1936 however, giving the true details of the lamentable failure of most of the new British aero-engines developed during that war, and cogent reasons for restricting orders to the established makers who had successful 'track records' and were capable of controlling the work of subcontractors.[9] Freeman was therefore selective, restricting Armstrong Siddeley's production to low-powered engines,[10] rejecting offers from Nuffield,[11] and Alvis,[12] and placing only an experimental order for big new engines from Fairey.[13]

Amongst the other firms, Rolls-Royce's development programme seemed to offer most promise. The aero-engine division of the Rolls-Royce Company was much smaller than that of the Bristol group in 1936, and the only engine they were producing in quantity was the 21-litre Kestrel, designed in 1927, which had limited future potential. Four new engines, the Merlin, Vulture, Peregrine and Exe (or Boreas) were under development however, but they were all still at the experimental stage, and as late as October 1937 none of them had passed their 100-hour tests.[†] Throughout that year the company wrestled with the formidable challenge of transferring production from the well known Kestrel to the new Merlin; production of the engine was repeatedly delayed, a cause of much anxiety to Freeman and his staff, and deliveries of production engines only began towards the end of 1937.

In the airframe sector, one of Freeman's earliest and most significant steps was to recommend the order of the first 310 Spitfires. Hawker had been supplying the RAF with fighters for some years, and the Air Council originally intended to order 900 Hurricanes for Scheme F. As soon as it became clear that Hawker would not be able to complete such a contract by 31 March 1939, Freeman proposed that Hawker's contract be limited to 600, and that 310 Spitfires be ordered from Supermarine. Supermarine had previously built only flying boats for the RAF, but their Chief Designer, R.J. Mitchell, had been responsible for the superb S5, S6 and S6B seaplanes which won the Schneider Trophy races in 1927, 1929 and 1931, and raised the world

---

* Roy Fedden, the world famous head of the Bristol Company's engine department, decided to use sleeve-valves in 1926, and began his first sleeve-valve radial in 1931.

† New engines had to be capable of running, non-stop, for 100 hours at high power.

speed record to 407mph. On Freeman's advice, the Air Council agreed to place the order, if the prototype achieved a top speed of 350mph.[14]

The normal acceptance routine for new RAF aircraft involved a week or ten days of ground inspections and trials at Martlesham Heath before the first flight*, but when the prototype Spitfire arrived there on 26 May 1936, Flt. Lt. Edwardes-Jones was told to fly the aircraft immediately, and then to telephone Freeman at the Air Ministry. He knew that Edwardes-Jones could give no detailed information about the aircraft after only one flight and explained that he was interested in only one question and wanted a straight answer. 'Was the aeroplane ... capable of being flown safely by the ordinary Service-trained fighter pilot, more particularly those emerging from the training courses being set up to meet the new expansion programme?' To his great credit, Edwardes-Jones answered: 'Yes ... provided they were adequately instructed in the use of retractable undercarriages, flaps and other systems, [pilots] would have no difficulty with the Spitfire, which was a delight to fly'.[15] The first Spitfire production contract was issued a week later.

Progress with most of the other aircraft produced under Freeman was less dramatic, but virtually all were monoplanes with retractable undercarriages, flaps, and closed cockpits; variable-pitch propellers were to be fitted later. A number had, of course, been selected before Freeman became AMRD, but he assumed responsibility for their development, including transitional designs like the Fairey Battle, the Hurricane single-engined fighter, the Bristol Blenheim light bomber, and the Whitley and Wellington medium bombers. Radial-engined fighter prototypes were ordered from Bristol and Gloster, powered by the elderly Mercury, but they were slower than the Merlin alternatives.

From the moment he became AMRD however, Freeman's influence over the selection of the subsequent generation of RAF aircraft was decisive. The models which he ordered, in prototype form, in this period included fighters such as the single-engined Hawker Typhoon and Tornado, the twin-engined Whirlwind and Beaufighter, and four new heavy bombers, the Short Stirling, the Supermarine B12/36, the Handley Page Halifax, and the Avro Manchester. He was also responsible for the selection and development of a wide-range of more specialised aircraft, such as torpedo bombers and fighters for the Fleet Air Arm, and flying-boats for Coastal Command.

Severe development difficulties were encountered with the majority of these aircraft; in some cases the problems were insuperable and the contracts for a number of models which went into production, like the unmanageable Saro Lerwick flying-boat and the disappointing Blackburn Botha torpedo bomber, were stopped.

The Halifax and the Manchester were designed to specification P13/36, and to use two 1,800hp, Rolls-Royce Vulture engines which were still being developed in 1937. Worried by the dependence on the Vulture, Freeman

---

* The airfield at Martlesham Heath in Suffolk was used by the RAF for testing all new aircraft. The site was too close to the Continent for safety, and the whole Experimental and Testing establishment was moved to Boscombe Down in Wiltshire, before the war started.

A Halifax Mk I. Whilst Handley Page was building the prototype, Freeman ordered them to redesign their P13/36 airframe to accept four Merlins rather than two Vultures. Handley Page installed the Merlins in nacelles of their own design.

considered employing four Taurus or Merlin engines instead, and when his staff estimated that no significant loss of performance would be involved, he hedged his risks, and told Handley Page to redesign their airframe for four Merlins, placing an order for 75 aircraft. Avro, despite distrusting the newer engine, had to continue work on their Manchester with two Vultures*.[16]

In selecting new aircraft, Freeman rarely relied entirely on the recommendations of his staff, or the optimistic promises of the Air Ministry's contractors. As they reached prototype stage, he travelled incessantly, mostly by air, passing judgement on the management, the quality of the new aircraft and their fitness for war, and on the development of suitable engines and armament. He visited Westland at Yeovil, Saunders Roe and Supermarine near Southampton, Bristol and Gloster, Avro and Rolls-Royce – 'the Rolls-Royce works were marvellous'[17] – and many more.

By accepting responsibility for compilation of the return of experimental aircraft and engines – on a quarterly basis – Freeman identified the firms that were capable of taking on additional development work,[18] and he always played the key role in selecting contractors for new projects. When Hill, his Director of Technical Development, endorsed a proposal for a twin-engined turret fighter, for the obsolete role of 'standing patrol', and asked to order two prototypes, Freeman refused on the basis of his knowledge of the company concerned. 'I am not only not satisfied that Parnall's could build this aircraft

* Chadwick, Avro's designer began work on a four-Merlin version in 1938.

...', he wrote, 'but I am certain that they will not achieve it in 18 to 24 months. The last machine they built ... was, I believe, such a failure that it was never delivered.'[19]

He was not always so dismissive. Indeed, there was a genuine humility about his respect for a number of the aircraft industry's chief designers but he reserved his greatest admiration for R.J. Mitchell of Supermarine. The Air Council had ordered two B12/36 heavy bomber prototypes from Supermarine, despite the news that Mitchell was dying of cancer, and when Mitchell had to withdraw from design work, Freeman wrote to reassure him:

> You must not worry yourself with thinking that you have let us down. You've never done that.
>
> Your illness has been a blow to the whole department, but the blow is not because you cannot get on with this aeroplane, it is only our grief at the illness of a personal and greatly respected friend.

Mitchell, deeply touched, replied: 'I shall always feel extremely grateful to you for the friendly sentiments expressed in your letter and I now feel very much happier about everything.'[20] Freeman later wrote that Mitchell was 'the best designer the industry ever produced ... He had the courage of a lion in his small body'.[21]

Until they resigned in 1938, Freeman had the best possible help and guidance from Swinton and Weir. Although he himself shouldered the main

R.J. Mitchell, chief designer of Supermarine, with the 1931 Schneider Trophy pilots. Freeman described Mitchell as 'the best designer the industry ever produced'.

responsibility for directing the Air Ministry's support for essential develop-ment work on new aircraft, their vast experience in dealing with Parlia-mentary critics, long-term planning, industrial problems and the formalities of Civil Service procedures was readily available to him and immensely helpful. When the political pressure for quantity at the expense of quality threatened to jeopardise the progress of future design projects, he fought hard to defend the work of his department, insisting that development should continue, that all firms should be given a quota of experimental aircraft for design staff to work on, and that such staff should not be diverted to work on production.[22] He refused to be bound by 'orthodox' Air Ministry views con-cerning the future development of aircraft technology, and personally pioneered a number of revolutionary new designs.

Of all the aircraft employed by the RAF in the Second World War, his name is most closely associated with the de Havilland Mosquito. The specification which produced the Mosquito was not officially approved until 1940, but the concept originated in a technical debate within the Air Ministry on the opera-tional utility of high-speed unarmed bombers which began in 1935. A pessi-mistic Air Staff paper, dated 22 June, maintained that:

> ... it was impossible to build a bomber with a useful range and load which was significantly faster than a two-seater fighter, and that such an aircraft 'will always be slower than a single seater'. A crew of two would be re-quired, for navigation and bomb aiming and, because the aircraft would be slower than fighters, and unarmed, it would be vulnerable to inter-ception, which would 'depress the morale of the crew'. Even if the bomber was faster than the fighter this superiority would not last, and the aircraft would then be useless. The aircraft might be more attractive, however, if it could be fitted with remotely controlled machine guns.[23]

The idea survived, but this ambivalence towards the unarmed bomber con-tinued for the next four years, revealing a significant gap between official RAF tactics, on the one hand, and the potential operational capabilities of modern aircraft on the other. Rumours that Heinkel was thinking of designing a two-seat, high-speed medium bomber, with no defensive armament, may have reached Freeman after representatives of Rolls-Royce visited the German firm in April 1936.[24] A year later, after suffering acute problems with the armament installations of the Hampden bomber, G.R.Volkert, Handley Page's designer, decided to challenge some of the orthodox RAF thinking. He questioned the value of attempting to fly in close formation, and stressed that by dispensing with gun turrets and extra crew to man them, a smaller, lighter, unarmed air-craft would have better aerodynamic form and would therefore be faster than a larger aircraft. A specially designed unarmed aircraft was needed.[25]

Both Liptrot, at the Air Ministry, and A.H. Hall, the Chief Superintendent of the RAE, now agreed that if size was irrelevant, a high-speed bomber was feasible. The Air Staff's Operational Requirements Committee (ORC) reluctantly agreed that performance, especially speed, would help protect attacking

The Whitley V (*above*). Changing the original Armstrong Whitworth Tiger engines for Merlin Xs transformed the Whitley performance to Wellington I standards.
Handley Page Hampdens (*below*). The light weight of the Hampden gave it a good performance and it was used for mine-laying after good service up to 1942.

aircraft from interception, but again displayed the ambivalence of official thinking by insisting that 'formation flying is an important tactical require-ment', and that defensive turrets would enable bomber formations to defend themselves when attacking strongly defended targets in fine weather.[26]

Freeman saw these papers and became keenly interested. Like Volkert, he was well aware of the technical difficulties of developing effective defensive armament for modern aircraft, but manpower considerations were also im-portant. Aircraft would be useless unless trained aircrew were available in sufficient numbers to man them, and Freeman knew that if the new large aircraft were ordered, huge numbers of aircrew would have to be recruited and trained to man them and their gun turrets. Sensing that they might be a 'blind alley', he asked his staff whether other developed countries had modern bombers with tail turrets; '... modern types with a cruising speed of more than 150mph,' and when told that there was only one prototype, in Italy,[27] he asked that a 'speed bomber' specification be prepared.

The concept was simple enough. Maximum performance was to be achieved by incorporating a significantly higher standard of streamlining than that attained by existing specifications, and this would call for simplicity of outline and for the elimination of all external imperfections. The principal advantages of such an aircraft would be its high speed, simplicity of construction and low cost, and its economy in trained personnel, equipment and maintenance.[28]

No such specification emerged for eighteen months, however, and the delay, and implied indecision, requires explanation. A long paper about a so-called 'ideal bomber' had been prepared for the Air Staff in March 1938, which reviewed the cost of delivering a given weight of bombers on Germany from British bases. It considered factors like the structural weight and labour cost of the airframe, the number of engines, the cost of training crews, and the number of servicing and maintenance men needed to keep aircraft opera-tional. If their vulnerability was disregarded, large twin-engined and four-engined aircraft showed huge savings, both in construction and operating costs, over smaller bombers.

Other considerations may also have caused Freeman to postpone the 'speed bomber' project. Quite apart from the uncertainty as to whether it was, in fact, possible to design a bomber which was faster than a fighter, there was the danger that if such an aircraft was designed, the Treasury might insist that it was ordered in place of expensive four-engined alternatives. Freeman may also have believed that it would be impossible to keep the project secret in peacetime and that, if the Germans learned about it, they would concentrate more research on a faster fighter.

Freeman's work as AMRD was by no means confined to aircraft. He was, for example, actively involved in the development of radar. Baldwin's gloomy forecast that 'the bomber will always get through'[29] had accurately reflected the almost impossible task of visually detecting high flying aircraft which might appear from any direction at any hour of day or night, but Watson-Watt's discovery of Radio Direction Finding (RDF), later called radar, offered

The fragile-looking 350-ft masts, of the Chain Home radar system needed high quality imported timber, but were difficult to damage by bombing.

a solution. An experimental station for testing the process had been set up immediately, and in June 1935 the Air Council made one of its most courageous decisions. Without waiting for the new invention to be properly tested and developed, it began planning a chain of radar stations around the south and east coasts of England, a defence force of high speed, heavily armed fighters, and a network of aerodromes from which to operate them.

Freeman was quick to endorse the project after his appointment to the Air Council, and Watson-Watt remembered him as the most supportive of the Air Marshals: 'He believed in my little team from the first and fought many of its battles for it'.[30] By June 1937 the first radar station was in satisfactory working order, but the specification of the 350ft-high wooden masts was still undecided. The special wood to build the masts had to be imported, and Freeman pressed for an immediate start on the 20 stations needed to cover the east coast as far as the Tyne, and for the extension of the chain as far as Scapa Flow. Authorisation for the additional stations was quickly obtained by Swinton,[31] and permission to extend them to Scapa Flow followed in August 1937. Although the early 'Chain Home' system could not detect low-flying aircraft, the full chain might not have been ready by 1940 if the decision to build it had been delayed.

AIRCRAFT PRODUCTION

Whilst only AMRD, Freeman had no formal responsibility for production matters, and between 1936 and 1938 he did not personally place production contracts or plan the expansion of factory capacity. Such jurisdiction was exercised by the Air Member for Supply and Organisation, (AMSO) although the ultimate responsibility for policy rested, of course, with the Secretary of State. However, at weekly Air Council 'Progress Meetings' which directed the rearmament programme, Freeman frequently spoke on production matters. By the end of 1937 he had formed very definite opinions concerning future production policy, and Swinton and Weir realised that he was the man to be given the new post of Air Member for Development and Production, the creation of which they strongly recommended in the summer of 1938.

There was a good example of Freeman's limited authority over production policy soon after he became AMRD. At the beginning of Scheme F, Swinton had decided to build the so-called 'shadow' factories,* which were to be managed by firms from outside the professional aircraft industry, so as to help with the rearmament programme. Five of the largest motor manufacturers were persuaded to co-operate to meet the need for aero-engines, and by October 1936 six engine shadow factories were being erected to make Bristol Mercury and Pegasus engines for the RAF, five of them to be managed by Austin, Daimler, Rootes, Rover and Standard, and the sixth by Bristol.[32]

To accelerate the start of production and reduce the supervisory burden on Bristol, the participating firms recommended that they should each be assigned a limited number of parts of the engine; two firms only would assemble and test complete units. Freeman and Newall, then AMSO, argued fiercely against this system because of its vulnerability to bomb attack, since damage to the only factory making a component could hold up completion of all the finished engines. The companies argued, however, that if they were asked to make too many different components they might not be able to produce the 4,000 engines the Air Ministry needed by March 1939; Freeman and Newall were over-ruled.[33]

On most other occasions, however, Freeman was able to make a more positive contribution to production. By guaranteeing an order, he helped to persuade Rolls-Royce and Bristol jointly to establish a new company, Rotol, suggested by Roy Fedden, for the development of variable-pitch mechanisms† for propellers,[34] and he was deeply involved in the establishment of other shadow factories for propellers, machine-guns, canons and carburettors. The propeller plant managed by de Havilland at Lostock ultimately produced more than half of all the propellers made in Britain during the Second World War.

The 1936 aircraft orders had been placed in the expectation that deliveries of new models would begin in the summer of 1937, but by the autumn, progress,

---

* Suitable buildings were erected, complete with services and machine tools, so that when extra production was necessary, staff could put them into operation without delay.
† The Curtiss Electric version was preferred for single-engined aircraft because of hydraulic leaks.

in terms of completed aircraft, was most unsatisfactory, and it was obvious that the production programme was in deep trouble. All the firms had difficulties, and Air Ministry confidence in their technical and managerial ability ebbed as more delivery dates were deferred. Swinton and Weir resolutely opposed pressure from some members of the Air Council for direct state intervention* to resolve the problems, because they knew all too well how state control stifled initiative and diminished responsibility.[35]

For their part, the firms responded indignantly to charges of inefficiency, and accused the Air Ministry of being excessively bureaucratic and of demanding too many modifications, and Freeman tried to respond constructively to their complaints, for there was some justification in the allegations. Air Ministry staff spent far too much time attending committees†, and he told them that their results would be more valuable 'if those attending ... had time to study the subjects on the agenda before the meetings, and then to carry out the resulting recommendations'.[36]

Besides curbing bureaucracy, Freeman did what he could to control the spate of modifications. Mass production was not possible without the use of specially designed jigs and tools, based on a standard design, but the pressure for expansion was so great that new designs were rarely fully standardised by the time production orders were placed: modifications often had to be incorporated, sometimes retrospectively, causing serious delays.

Hoping to reduce the number of modifications to aircraft from the first production runs, the Air Council eventually agreed to leave such decisions to Freeman, and laid down that, once the final design conference between the manufacturer and the RAF had taken place, no further alterations to new types of aircraft would be made without his express authority. He undertook to visit firms the day after their final design conference with Air Ministry officials, so that he could review the proposed alterations, and make a personal decision as to which alterations – if any – were essential.[37] His decisions would be final.

Despite these initiatives, trust and respect between the Air Ministry and the aircraft firms which formed the Society of British Aircraft Constructors (SBAC) continued to deteriorate. In an attempt to improve matters, a joint Air Ministry/SBAC committee was set up, including AMRD and AMSO, to examine design, development and production problems. After a meeting with the Prime Minister, the SBAC eventually agreed to appoint a new full-time chairman, choosing the Bank of England's industrial advisor, Sir Charles Bruce-Gardner, who soon became one of Freeman's most trusted and helpful colleagues.

After less than two years as AMRD, Freeman could see the essentials of his

* It was just such a 'national' sector of industry, controlled by the Air Minister and the civil servants of the Air Ministry, which had been responsible for building the R.101 airship. The stringent test conditions of its building contract had been waived by Air Ministry officials, to allow it to set off on its last flight despite known and obvious faults. The final authorisation however, was given by the AMSR, Air Marshal Sir Hugh Dowding.

† One official was a member of thirteen committees and over four months 'had attended no less than 37 conferences'.

job with extraordinary clarity. The development of most of the new airframes and engines was obviously going to take several years and whilst he thought it essential to order airframe prototypes from at least two firms for each specification, the same engines could be used for various aircraft, so the number under development could be limited. Once a factory had been equipped to make a new airframe however, much output would be lost before it could be re-tooled to make a different airframe and most, if not all, advances in performance seemed likely to come from extracting greater power from the engines. He realised the vital importance of high rates of climb, and of the ability to maintain power at altitude, and from 1938 onwards he was always pressing the engine firms for improvements. He wanted better cooling, greater reliability and time between overhauls; he asked for better superchargers, if possible, with two- and three-speed gears, and two stages, to give the highest possible power at all altitudes, and above all, he invariably insisted on quality, if necessary at the expense of quantity.

Nowhere was that more important than in air warfare – but it took a man of Freeman's calibre to go on insisting on it – and get his way – in times when popular and political pressure was all for bigger and better numbers.[38]

By December 1937 Freeman had decided that a fundamental revision of procurement policy was now essential, and that the Air Ministry must extend its control of production planning, so as to ensure that the RAF got the maximum long-term use out of the aircraft it was buying. In a long memorandum entitled 'Design and Production' submitted to the Air Council, he recommended that the Air Ministry should take limited powers to intervene in the management of aircraft factories. On his advice, the Air Council accepted (in principle, but not as yet in practice), that new specifications should be issued each year, that specifications should give designers more latitude, that all firms should get a planned flow of design and production work, that the Air Ministry should pay the full cost of prototypes, that there should be a reduction in the number of types in service, that the service life of aircraft should be extended by engine development, and finally, that firms would have to subcontract as much production as possible, so that aircraft factories were primarily used for assembly work.[39] Some of these matters were strictly outside his jurisdiction as AMRD, since they impinged on production issues, but Freeman had already perceived the need to merge the Air Ministry's Development and Production Departments.[40]

Besides this general revision of policy, other more specific steps were taken to increase output, and a limited number of production officers were appointed to the Director of Aeronautical Production's department. Although Swinton, Weir and Freeman agreed that their appointment should not lead to aircraft firms being pressurised into adopting new production techniques which were still at the experimental stage, it was nevertheless Freeman's belief that, in addition to offering 'suggestion, persuasion and guidance', these officers should also be charged with 'obtaining information with regard to the production methods of the various firms'.[41] The rearmament crisis was too acute for secrecy, and he renewed this quest for information in 1938, when the pace of rearmament accelerated.[42]

In private, Freeman was very uneasy about the international situation and the state of British politics, distrusting Baldwin, Chamberlain and Churchill. He told Anne that he preferred what he knew of the *ideals* of Communism to Fascism, but disliked both. Deeply as he distrusted the motives of the pacifist 'Left', he was appalled by the staggering rate of the weapons build up; rearmament on such a scale could only result in war.[43]

Developments in the German aircraft industry were better understood in Britain by 1937, because, in the hope of discouraging competition, the German Air Ministry decided that the time had come to display to the RAF the rapid progress of their preparations for war. Freeman, who loathed pompous, ceremonial occasions, refused, but some very senior officers, including Courtney, the Deputy CAS, Douglas and Evill, accepted invitations to visit Germany,[44] and they were shown some of the latest aircraft plants, including the huge Junkers works near Leipzig. What they saw confirmed the worst fears of the British Chiefs of Staff: the scale of German rearmament was colossal.

Very senior British engineers and industrialists were also invited, including Major G.P. Bulman from the Air Ministry, A.G. Elliot, Harry Swift and Jimmy Ellor of Rolls-Royce, and Roy Fedden of Bristol.[44] Bulman was stunned by the sight of the huge modern aero-engine factories, about a mile long, fully equipped with machine tools and test equipment: it was evident that the same comprehensive planning had been applied to airframes and armament.[45] Bulman's report on his visit, which Freeman passed to the Secretary of State, was received incredulously, but it was soon confirmed and enhanced by the Rolls-Royce team, and Fedden's reports were even more disconcerting.[46] Germany's preparations were on a enormous scale: the factories were spotless, lavish, and working fast and effortlessly on a single shift.[47] Britain was falling behind.

Air Chief Marshal Sir Edward Ellington was succeeded by Newall as Chief of the Air Staff in September 1937. The information coming out of Germany by then was so ominous that the Air Council presented the Cabinet with a new expansion plan, Scheme J, which implicitly recognized that German production capacity was going to be much greater than Britain's in the near future. It required a 40 per cent increase in the number of bombers and a 25 per cent increase in fighters: an overall average of 35 per cent. Sir Thomas Inskip, the new Minister for the Coordination of Defence,* thought the cost excessive, however, and the Air Council eventually put forward Scheme K, a cut-price version of Scheme J, with most of the increase focused on extra fighter squadrons for the Metropolitan (home defence) Air Force.[48]

The deadlock over the pace and scope of rearmament, which continued throughout the winter of 1937–8, was partially broken when Germany in-

* A letter to Anne reported: 'the S of S ... on sick leave so I deal with Inskip - a genial and clever man – quick on the uptake and with sound judgement'

vaded Austria in March 1938. War seemed increasingly likely, an accelerated air rearmament programme was essential, and Scheme L, yet another expansion programme, was adopted, whereby the Government agreed to purchase as many aircraft as the industry could produce by April 1940. The necessary industrial resources were to be provided at last, regardless of the interference that this would cause to the normal course of trade, but even then the Chamberlain Government continued to hesitate in the hope that war could be avoided, and again refused to agree the Air Council's plan to create a large force of heavy bombers.[49]

Responsibility for the implementation of Scheme L was given to an Air Council sub-committee which became known as the Air Council Sub-committee on Supply (or 'Supply Committee'). The members, besides Swinton and Weir, were Freeman, Air Marshal Welsh (the new AMSO) Air Vice-Marshal Peirse (then DCAS), Henry Self (Second Deputy Under-Secretary), Bruce-Gardner, and Edward Bridges of the Treasury. Bridges was given the power to authorise expenditure for any proposal which needed prompt action, without reference to the Treasury, and until war was declared he was able to give instant sanction to a whole series of expensive expansion plans.[50] Additional contracts were now placed with all the aircraft firms, and the Government agreed to pay for all the capital extensions required to fulfil them.[51]

Right at the top of the Supply Committee's agenda was the expansion of Rolls-Royce engine production. No arrangements had been made to 'shadow' Rolls-Royce production during 1936 and 1937 because none of their new engines had passed their 100-hour tests. Their designs had not been ready for large-scale production, demand for Rolls-Royce engines was insufficient to justify the erection of new factories,* and the management actually opposed the entire principle of shadow pro-duction on the grounds that it would involve the disclosure of technical information to potential competitors.

In September 1937, however, the company's new General Works Manager, Ernest Hives, persuaded the Rolls-Royce Board to reverse this stance, and in October the Air Ministry was informed that Rolls were willing to allow their products to be produced in a new shadow factory. Once Scheme L was authorised, an extra 1,900 Merlins and 50 additional Vultures were ordered for delivery by March 1940,[52] and by moving their motor car division, Rolls-Royce doubled the output of Merlins at Derby to 60 per week. They had to ask for a government contribution of £600,000 towards the extra capital cost of equipping the aero-engine line at Derby, having spent £750,000 of their own capital since the beginning of rearmament.[53]

Worried that the increasingly vital Rolls-Royce aero-engines were all being made at Derby, Freeman now insisted that they set up a shadow factory,[54] which they could run themselves, and Rolls-Royce asked for a provisional allotment of £1,500,000 to build and equip it.[55] Despite the rising demand for Merlins, the decision to create a Rolls-Royce shadow factory was never-

* As late as May 1938, the Rolls-Royce factory at Derby could not produce more than 30 Merlins a week.

Ernest Hives (later Lord Hives CH MBE) with King George VI and Queen Elizabeth at the Derby works in the summer of 1940. Hives joined Rolls Royce as an experimental tester in 1908 and became General Works Manager in September 1937.

theless deferred for another six months whilst a suitable site was found and the Cabinet considered the scope and expense of the next rearmament scheme. A 'greenfield site' near Crewe was eventually chosen and the first Merlin left the Crewe factory in 1939, 361 days after building work started.

Although there was a dramatic acceleration of rearmament planning after the Anschluss, it was clear to Parliament that parity with the German air force had not been maintained, and there was strong criticism of the Air Ministry from Conservative back-benchers like Churchill and from the Labour Opposition. Freeman understood their unease, having chafed at the industrial restrictions insisted on by Chamberlain. 'I have by chance ... got into a position in which I am likely to be affected by the political wind', he told Anne. 'I might find myself without a job at any moment now. I don't think the fault lies with me ... I have worked hard and ... been told that I have done well ... The trouble is that I am on the side of the critics and can do nothing.'[56]

Much of the shortfall could be directly attributed to Chamberlain's secret insistence that rearmament should not interfere with the normal course of trade, but Swinton had to accept the blame for the consequences of this 'undisclosed constraint,* and on 16 May 1938, he and Weir both resigned[57]. Swinton's replacement was Sir Kingsley Wood, a 'funny, pleasant little cockney'[58] lawyer (soon nicknamed 'Little Sir Echo' by the Air Staff), who frankly admitted that he 'did not know one end of an aircraft from another'.

Freeman was deeply distressed by the ignorant bias of the Air Ministry's critics,[59] and seriously worried by the resignations. 'The whole of my world seems to have been topsy-turvey', he wrote to Weir, 'but I must now write and thank you for your unvarying kindness and help over a period of more than two years, and to say how much I shall miss your advice and insistence on essentials and avoidance of trivialities.'[60] To Swinton he wrote:

> I felt too depressed on Monday to express adequately, or even intelligently, my sorrow at your going and my disgust at the way it was brought about ... No one could have worked harder or better ... No one can achieve the impossible, but you came near to doing that – but even the impossible wouldn't have been sufficient to confound critics who wanted someone's blood ... I have never served a better or more considerate master than yourself ... If we win through in the end, it will only be because of the foundations you have laid.[61]

Close association with these rich and influential men, at the highest level, had been clearly vital to Freeman's career. He had a clear, quick mind, ruthless honesty, and a tireless capacity for work; he took great pride in the new service he had helped to create, and he demonstrated, over and over again, the essential qualities of leadership. He had not forgotten the ghastly experience of sending aircrews out to fight in obsolete aircraft in the First World War, and knew that unless he could give them the finest possible equipment, it would all be repeated.

Until 1936 however, he had no experience of industry, had never worked with aircraft manufacturers, and had never been involved in extracting decisions out of the stately procedures of the Civil Service. Swinton had soon realised that Freeman had technical perception, and executive and administrative ability of the highest order,[62] and taught him how to work with politicians and the Air Ministry's Civil Servants in a frank and efficient manner. Weir's advice was industrial, and from him Freeman learned that he must trust the independent aircraft and engine companies to develop and manage new factories, and design and produce new aircraft; government intervention must, if possible, be restricted to guidance and supervision.

Shortly before his resignation Weir had recommended that responsibility for technical development and supply should be combined at Air Council level: the production directorates should be transferred from the AMSO to the AMRD so that co-ordination between the Air Ministry's design and supply functions was improved.[63] He furthermore proposed, obviously with Swinton's

---

* According to F.M. Hyde, in *British Air Policy between the wars*, Swinton later regretted that he had not challenged these restraints.

support, that the heavy responsibility of this new position on the Air Council should be given to Freeman.[64] Kingsley Wood accepted their advice, and acted on it, telling Parliament in June 1938 that Freeman would in future control production as well as research and development, his new appointment being redesignated 'Air Member for Development and Production'.

Freeman was thus entrusted with one of the most urgent and awesome industrial responsibilities ever given to a serving officer;* 'the first man to be responsible for the whole process, from research to the production of the finished article'.[65] The nature of the coming attack was clear, the RAF would have to meet it, and would have to be fully re-equipped to do so. 'No burden except that of the Prime Minister could have been greater.'[66]

FAMILY LIFE

Freeman's personal life had been much happier since his divorce and remarriage in April 1935. Emulating his brother Alan, he entertained frequently, both at Andover and in the London house he leased at 10 Canning Place, delighted to find that Elizabeth enjoyed being the focus of attention at meetings and dinners, and could keep her end up amongst Freeman's older colleagues and business friends from the Staff College, industry and the Air Council. He much preferred entertaining at home, where he could chose his company, control the surroundings and match both food and wine to the occasion, and was a wonderfully stimulating host. But he despised the London night life and the fashionable 'Tatler' scene, and criticised the way so many of the rich young men he knew wasted their time and talents socialising when they could have applied their wealth and intelligence to responsible jobs in the manufacturing and service industries, and made a real contribution to management.[67] He was careful about visitors while he was working at home on research projects, and absolutely scrupulous about his impartiality over decisions on aircraft orders: the gold cigarette cases sent by aircraft companies were always returned.

Anne, his eldest child, an impressionable teenager, remembered him at his very best in the 1930s. He wrote her light, confiding letters, arranged for her and a friend, aged 15, to be flown down from school to Andover in a Puss Moth and on a visit, charmed her headmistress into the unheard of privilege of allowing Anne to join him for breakfast at his hotel. His remarriage to Elizabeth made no difference: she was only nine years older than Anne, and shared her interests. Anne sometimes travelled with Freeman to Murtle, burdened with the 'heavy responsibility' of map reading on the familiar roads he had travelled so often; she was thrilled to have him on her own and

* The roles of Themistocles, who arranged for the construction of the Athenian fleet of triremes in the year before Salamis, and of Admiral 'Jackie' Fisher, who forced through an equally vital programme of naval rearmament and modernisation in the decade before the First World War, were roughly similar, but they acted from positions of greater executive power. Acknowledging congratulations from Hives, Freeman added 'I think it ought to have included some lines of sympathy'.

to stay at hotels as they went north. He taught her to share his love of books, reading aloud a miscellany which included 'good tripe' like the best of the Dornford Yates 'Berry' books which had them both in helpless laughter, poems like 'The Scholar Gypsy', 'The Song of Honour', and his favourite, 'They told me Heraclitus'.[68]*

After his divorce Freeman's access to his children by his first marriage was restricted at first by G, and a court order was needed before Anne and Elizabeth were allowed to meet. Nevertheless, the charming, flattering and frequent letters to Anne continued, and all sorts of 'jollies' and expeditions were planned as restrictions eased; they were clearly devoted to each other. Keith, who was three years younger and naturally more influenced by his mother's resentment of Elizabeth, found it much more difficult to adjust, and Freeman sensed that he was hostile to his new wife, a reaction which he seldom wholly forgave. Keith was naturally plump, and nicknamed 'podge' by his father, who told Anne after a visit to him at prep-school, 'he was looking well and not so stout as I expected'. Anne did her best to ease their relationship, but the petty discourtesies of youth, such as failing to answer letters, were noticed; Keith was irked by Freeman's easy rapport with Anne: the fact that he lived with his mother did not help.

Anne Freeman, aged 16.

Freeman's second daughter, Joan, was born in August 1936, when he was 48. Elizabeth found pregnancy difficult, often feeling unwell, and was disappointed not to have had a son, but Freeman was intensely proud of his new family, and his flippant references to Elizabeth's 'bun in the oven' were soon coded to 'Bunting' or 'Bunt', and eventually to 'Mrs B', a nickname which Joan carried for many years. Their social life was restricted by her pregnancy, but by 1938 Freeman was desperately busy attending endless meetings with ministers, service chiefs and captains of industry, and urgently building the infrastructure to support an air force which would be much larger and infinitely more technically advanced than ever before.

---

* The last was written by William Cory Johnson, the author's great, great-uncle.

CHAPTER 5

Development and production
1938–39

O NCE FREEMAN'S NEW APPOINTMENT as AMDP became effective, he asked for full-time assistance to cope with the enormous increase in the range and scope of his responsibilities; someone with production and organisational experience to replace Weir on the Air Council. Ernest Lemon, from the LMS railway, joined his department to become Director General of Production (DGP),[1] and he in turn appointed Lewis Ord, a Canadian industrial consultant and production engineer, and T.S. Smith, a senior consultant from the Bedaux group, to control the planning of production and help him mediate between firms and the Air Ministry on technical matters.[2] With Freeman's support, Lemon enlarged the Air Ministry's production department by creating eight new directorates with jurisdiction over airframes, aero-engines, subcontracting, equipment, materials, factory construction, statistics and planning, and war production planning.

Lemon is usually credited with the introduction of the policy of subcontracting component manufacture which the Air Ministry started in the final months of 1938, but Freeman had actually proposed the creation of 'a new satellite sub-contracting organisation' to help fulfill the next expansion plan as early as December 1937.[3] His recommendations had been accepted in principle, but had not been implemented immediately.

Installed as DGP, Lemon undertook a thorough survey of British aircraft production at Freeman's request, and told the Air Council in September 1938 that deliveries were not matching forecasts because the aircraft firms were unable to absorb and train enough skilled labour. To complete the current programme on time the labour force would have to rise from just over 60,000 in September 1938 to a peak of well over 180,000 in January 1939, four months later. Since the industry had hitherto been unable to assimilate new labour at a rate of more than 10 per cent per month, a change of system was essential.[4] Subcontracting was the only solution.

Lemon recommended that access to additional resources of skilled labour would be best achieved if parent firms subcontracted at least 35 per cent of their outstanding orders to the type of general engineering firms which would not have normally undertaken aircraft work: his proposals were immediately accepted and rapidly implemented. By July 1939 more than 1,200 firms were engaged in airframe subcontracts, accounting for fifteen per cent of total airframe labour.[5]

Apart from establishing Lemon as DGP, Freeman also insisted on recalling Air Vice-Marshal Arthur Tedder, then AOC Far East, based in Singapore, to handle the research and development functions of his department, explaining that he didn't feel like taking on the job unless Tedder joined him. Privately nicknamed 'Tirpitz' by Freeman in 1917, when found in a corner of their RFC Mess, quietly correcting the proofs of his book on naval history, Tedder relieved Freeman of much detailed work on R & D so that he could concentrate on production problems. Tedder wrote of Freeman:

> He had a very quick and sometimes impish sense of humour, and whether playing chess or gossiping about books, music, or politics, he was wonderfully refreshing ... He could be a little intolerant at times, but his judgement of individuals was shrewd, and as AMDP in those critical days, there was no time to be wasted on fools. He was able to imbue the Ministry with a due sense of urgency, without panic.[6]

The Secretary of State's progress meetings were suspended during August 1938, and Freeman took leave at the end of the month, joining Elizabeth, Ralph, and other members of the family at Murtle Den. The 'family' house had come back on to the market shortly after the sale of the Murtle estate, and Wilfrid had persuaded Ralph to buy it with him and share the costs of running it. He was delighted to have recovered a base on Deeside, a retreat from the pressures of his awesome responsibilities, and a country home for his second family. Ralph, who could now afford both the time and expense of flying home from Kenya every year, happily renewed his links with Murtle and the familiar surroundings of Aberdeen and Deeside for his holidays in Britain, and the brothers enjoyed each other's company as much as ever.

Freeman also changed his London home, and leased 24 Ilchester Place; it was large enough for Keith and Anne to have their own rooms so that they could come to London more often. Anne had spent the previous six months in Germany, before going up to Somerville College, Oxford, to read languages, and had fallen foul of the Customs on her return journey. Freeman was anxious about her, and postponed his leave until the end of August, so that she could join him at Murtle. She made friends easily, and her father found some of them uncongenial; she was escaping the 'tidy compartment' in which he had known her until then.

The reorganisation of the Air Ministry's development and production departments had barely been completed when the Czechoslovak Sudetenland crisis erupted. Freeman was recalled from leave, and as they travelled into London, together, Kingsley Wood asked him what could be done to accelerate aircraft production. Freeman explained the measures that could be taken if war broke out that autumn, but warned that each had objectionable features.[7]

His most urgent government recommendation was for action to restrict German access to high octane grades of petrol and crude-oil stocks, and to increase Britain's own capacity to produce high octane fuel and essential additives.[8] Turning to airframe production, he proposed that the Speke shadow factory should be taken out of Rootes' management and handed to Bristol or Avro. 'It would entail heavy compensation to Rootes', he wrote, 'since it would cast an obvious, and in my opinion highly justifiable, slur on the management. By doing so and appointing efficient management, aircraft would probably be produced before the end of the year instead of next spring, and production would reach 15 or 20 a week instead of 10.'[9] He also recommended increasing production of Blenheims and Battles if war was imminent, but warned that this would delay the introduction of more modern designs: 'in 1941 the RAF would be accepting obsolescent aircraft'. Airframe production might also be accelerated by changes of procedure: for example, by stopping the anodic treatment of metal, or by relaxing inspection regulations.[10]

Arrangements to make 20mm Hispano cannon[11] and variable-pitch propellers had been completed by the end of 1937,[12] and power-operated turrets were being developed, pending availability of suitable aircraft to carry them.

On the last day of September 1938, as the Czechoslovakian crisis reached its peak, Tedder, Buchanan, the Director of Aircraft Development, and Bulman were told to wait in Freeman's office in case war was declared. Bulman's memoirs recall it vividly:

> Freeman had gone off to Whitehall in uniform, leaving word that [we] were to wait his return, however late. I joined Tedder and we spent some time getting to know each other better, the first real opportunity to do so. ... About 5.30pm Freeman sent word to assemble in his office. The three of us had just sat down at his conference table when the door opened at the far end of the long room in Alexandra House, Kingsway, and Wilfrid entered. He paused a moment on the threshold, took off his brass hat and to our amazement threw it whirling down the room to land bang on his hat stand. 'It's all over chaps, no war. Neville Chamberlain has just got back from Germany with his umbrella and a bit of paper signed by Hitler agreeing there will be no war in our time. I left him at No. 10 in cheerful triumph and relief, waving the bit of paper and saying Peace in our time.' We sat dumb at this dramatic news as he crossed the room. He sat down at the head of the table. 'Peace in our time ...; that means we have a few more months to get ready. How can we increase our programme:' – and we sat on for two hours, doing just that, with no authority from anyone save Freeman. He needed no instructions as he was responsible. There was so very little time. We began to implement the decisions made that evening, immediately.[13]

Freeman now asked the Cabinet for a decision on timing: should the RAF plan for war in 1939, or continue Scheme L, which was due for completion in March 1940.[14] In response, the decision was taken to raise the first-line targets established under Scheme L, and to sanction industrial capacity for a so-called 'War Potential' programme. This envisaged the production of 17,000 aircraft in the first twelve months of a war beginning in October 1939, and for a wartime capacity of 2,000 aircraft per month by the end of 1941. Not unreasonably, the Government refused to sanction wartime levels of production in peacetime, and right up to the outbreak of war, a substantial gap remained between the peacetime programme (renamed Scheme M) and the War Potential programme. Freeman's work was hideously complicated by the prevailing uncertainty as to when to merge the two programmes, and as late as the summer of 1939, he was still asking the Government to clarify its long-term objectives.[15]

AIRFRAMES

Short-term production planning witnessed a decisive shift from bombers to fighters in 1938. By the time that Kingsley Wood took over as Secretary of State Lord Nuffield* had been persuaded to start building and equipping an airframe shadow factory at Castle Bromwich to produce Spitfires rather than

Battles.[16] It became clear, after Munich, that Britain would only have two-thirds as many long-range bombers as Germany by April 1940, and less than half their number of fighters, and the Air Council decided that defence had to be given even greater priority. A maximum effort would be applied to increasing the fighter force through the creation of the largest possible productive capacity and fully adequate reserves of aircraft and personnel would be provided: twelve additional fighter squadrons were to be established.

The Air Staff was aware that counter-offensive action by Bomber Command would not, alone, be sufficient to protect Britain from German air attack, but continued to emphasise that the long-term policy had not been changed to a defensive strategy at the expense of a counter-offensive; there must be a bomber force at least comparable in power to that of Germany. Numerical parity with the German bomber force was neither possible in the short term, nor necessary: a striking force (consisting of the latest two- and four-engined heavy bombers), capable of delivering an equal tonnage of bombs, was the alternative.[17] Freeman therefore asked

Viscount Nuffield. Patriotism made the millionaire motor-car magnate eager to help Britain rearm. But Kingsley Wood should not have chosen him to run the aircraft Civilian Repair Organisation; his experience and the management resources of the Nuffield group were not suitable for the nationwide job of salvaging and repairing aircraft.

for authority to order many more of these types: 'It was essential to resist a wholly defensive posture in war', he wrote later: 'It was simply not enough to avoid losing, it had to be won'.

* Due to a petulant quarrel with Swinton, Nuffield had refused to allow Morris to participate when the other motor firms co-operated for the first shadow factories, in 1936.

Freeman argued that Britain would save money by adopting the heavy bomber instead of older, smaller types, and Tedder* prepared a memorandum which outlined the minimum requirements in speed, range, bomb load and defensive armament, and the comparative costs of producing enough twin-engined medium bombers and four-engined heavy bombers, together with the necessary aircrews, to deliver 4,000 tons of bombs on Germany.[18]

	Heavy Bomber	Medium Bomber
Average bomb load; lb.	10,000	2,500
Number of aircraft required	896	3,584
Cost (£ million)	47	79
Labour units needed	1,926	3,584
Number of engines needed	3,584	7,168
Flying personnel (aircrew)	6,720	22,400
Flying schools ratio	1	4
Maintenance personnel	14,000	42,000

The evidence seemed incontrovertible, but the Treasury still hesitated. In February 1937 the RAF share of total expenditure for the five years 1937–41 had been forecast as £567 million, 32 per cent of the rearmament budget. The extra cost of a large heavy bomber programme would add £350 million (55 per cent) to the RAF's existing budget, and raise their share of the total rearmament cost to nearly 40 per cent.[19] Clinging to his belief that war could be avoided, Chamberlain once more deferred the decision to develop and construct the heavy bomber force, 'for further consideration'. A programme for 3,700 additional fighters was authorised by the Cabinet, and firm orders were given for at least half that total, but heavy bomber production plans were not to be increased.[20]

The obvious quality of the Wellington led to a firm decision to expand production, and a Wellington production group comprising Gloster, Austin and Armstrong Whitworth was planned. By May 1938, however, Vickers was still unable to release completed production drawings to the other firms, and Freeman realised that long delays could be expected before production could start on a large-scale. Having accepted that substantial numbers of Wellingtons could not be expected from makers other than Vickers, the Air Ministry revised the Wellington group idea: Gloster was directed to join Hawker in producing Hurricanes, and Armstrong Whitworth and Austin had to go on making the Whitley and Battle bombers until one or more of the new heavy bombers could be brought into production.[21] Wellington production was thereafter to be restricted to Vickers-Armstrongs, the parent company of the two Vickers aircraft firms.

Freeman then approached Sir Charles Craven, the managing director of Vickers-Armstrongs, and proposed that 'the wide organisation and experience of the Vickers-Armstrongs group might profitably be applied to the setting up

* Freeman was recovering from an appendix operation.

of a comprehensive scheme designed to accelerate production'.[22] Craven agreed to co-operate fully, and merged the two Vickers aircraft subsidiaries under Vickers-Armstrongs for management purposes.[23] During 1939 an extensive network of subcontractors was established in the North-West to supply Wellington parts to an assembly factory in Chester, and this was later augmented by a similar network centred on Blackpool, and by increased production at Vickers-Armstrongs' Weybridge factory. The Chester and Blackpool factories were originally intended to produce a total of 100 aircraft per month, and the target was raised to 150 during the first year of the war.[24]

In December 1938 Freeman proposed the creation of several other 'group schemes' for the manufacture of both heavy bombers and fighters, and despite the Treasury's misgivings his plan was accepted as an interim measure which would enable production to start as soon as financial restraints were lifted.[25] Aircraft factories would be organised into groups; committees, chaired by Lemon, would be appointed to co-ordinate the work of each group, and Freeman estimated the capital cost of these production facilities as:

Manchester group:	£7.75 million
Stirling group:	£11.75 million
Halifax group:	£0.75 million
Westland and fighter group:	£0.75 million
Hawker and Gloster group:	£3.50 million

Avro and Armstrong Whitworth would build Manchesters; Austin would make the Stirling, and Handley Page the Halifax. Rootes, who were originally expected to produce Manchesters, were to make Halifaxes instead. An offer from George Nelson, of English Electric, to resume making aircraft at his company's Preston works was gratefully accepted, and the firm was given a small educational order for Hampdens and told to put the Halifax into production there as soon as possible.[26] English Electric eventually became the largest producer of Halifaxes.

The group schemes were intended by Freeman to focus production on the most modern aircraft types, and all three types of heavy bombers were selected for group production to insure the RAF against the very real danger of technical failure: if one of the new bombers proved unsuccessful, industrial resources could be diverted to another. He also attempted to develop geographical specialisation within the aircraft industry to make the best possible use of parent firms and their subcontractors when Scheme L was completed in March 1940. Manchesters would be made in the Manchester area by a group headed by Avro and including Fairey and Metropolitan Vickers, helped by subcontractors from manufacturing areas of the North-West. The Halifax group, comprising Handley Page and English Electric, would employ subcontractors in north Lancashire and London, and similar groups were proposed for the Stirling.[27] As more experience was gained about the quality of the new designs, however, the group's constituents were revised, and the planned geographical concentration was sometimes affected.

The Lockheed Hudson which Freeman ordered in 1938 for maritime reconnaissance duties with Coastal Command. The first American aircraft to be delivered by air, it was the only really modern aircraft in Coastal Command in 1939. It had a maximum speed of 253 mph and a range of 2,160 miles.

The creation of the group schemes for bombers and fighters naturally absorbed much of Freeman's time while he was AMDP, but the production of other classes of aircraft, such as trainers and Fleet Air Arm designs was not neglected. For trainers he looked to de Havilland,[28] Airspeed and Phillips and Powis (Miles) in Britain, and North American in the USA, from whom he ordered the AT-6, or 'Harvard'[29]. Fleet Air Arm aircraft were to be built by branches of Fairey, and Blackburn. Freeman also ordered Lockheed's 'Hudson' for maritime reconnaissance duties with Coastal Command.[30]

The Cabinet finally lost its remaining illusions about Hitler when Germany seized the rump of Czechoslovakia in March 1939, and Freeman saw that war was imminent.* The vital importance of the aircraft programme was at last recognized, and Freeman was given the unprecedented privilege of dealing directly with the Treasury; all requests for finance had previously been channelled through the Air Council.[31] Normal procedures were abandoned. 'It is of the utmost importance', Freeman's department was warned:

> that the action taken as a result of the Supply Committee's decision should be as rapid as possible. Action first and paper afterwards. On no account should criticisms or discussions of the details be permitted to delay action. Any official aware of any hold-up or having in mind a legitimate criticism which might result in a hold-up, should bring the matter immediately to the notice of his Director or Head of Division who will have immediate access to AMDP or Second DUS with a view to clearance of the difficulty.[32]

* According to family records he warned his sister Sibyl, whose teenage sons wanted to join the RAF, before the end of March.

Briefing Kingsley Wood, via Henry Self for new discussions with the Chancellor, Freeman asked for stop-gap orders for another 1,000 aircraft (at a cost of £12.5 million), to keep the factories in production.[33] Production arrangements for the new heavy bombers could at last be finalised.

ENGINES

Plans to produce four-engined bombers, when added to the existing orders for other aircraft, had significantly increased the demand for aero-engines. By February 1939, Freeman realised that there would be a serious engine shortage unless further industrial capacity was created, and asked for immediate authority to buy all the machine tools needed to complete the principal engine shadow factories.[34] He recommended that subcontracting for both Rolls-Royce and Bristol should be intensively developed and that funds be allocated for the third section of the Rolls-Royce factory at Crewe.[35] The following month, Kingsley Wood was warned that another £300,000 was needed for plant to increase Mercury and Pegasus engine capacity, as an insurance in case there was no solution to the apparently insoluble manufacturing problems affecting Bristol's new range of sleeve-valve engines.[36]

Beyond the immediate demands of the current aircraft programme, Freeman had also to consider the even higher levels of output which would be needed in the event of war. If war broke out in 1940, 24,000 airframes might be needed in the first year of hostilities, involving a huge increase in the production of engines, as well as carburettors, airscrews, armament, turrets, and raw materials. Early in March 1939 Freeman therefore proposed to the Treasury measures costing £14 million, to raise the output of Merlin engines to 1,000 per month and of Bristol engines to 800 per month (of which 600 would be the new two-row sleeve-valve Taurus and Hercules), explaining that this would meet the requirements of the new twin-engined fighters and four-engined bombers, when production began in 1940.[37] After the seizure of Czechoslovakia, Freeman raised this to a total of £30 million to cover both engines and ancillary equipment.[38]

Knowing that Chamberlain still hoped that war, and thus the full expenditure, could be avoided, Freeman presented his requests as if they were instalments, proposing the creation of industrial capacity for war on the basis that the £30 million he required would be spread forward '... in three approximately equal parts' and asked for at least £9.45 million immediately.

> The main problem is to find the additional capacity for engines, light alloys, turrets, guns ... and some money for accessories. The ... difficulty is that whatever is spent in the first quarter must be a complete unit in itself, otherwise we get no value for [this] expenditure if [the Chancellor's] axe should come down.

– as it would do if the threat of war receded.[39] Three days later Self reported back: 'As regards the proposal for [spending] £30 million ... the Chancellor thought it difficult to justify giving sanction at this stage.'[40]

Undaunted, Freeman asked Barlow, the Permanent Secretary of the Treasury, for immediate authority to spend £4.5 million on a new Rolls-Royce factory: the balance of £2 million – also required for this factory – could be left until the autumn:

'As regards Bristol, we have asked for an immediate authority for £5 millions [but can probably manage with] … £3 millions, leaving the second half of two new factories until the autumn … In effect … we are asking for one-third instalment of the £30 million'. The total amount involved was £12 million 'leaving the balances … to be pursued in two further instalments, one towards the end of the year and the other early in 1940'.[41]

Barlow replied that the Chancellor 'can finance these in 1939, but he could give no guarantee of his ability to do so in later years.' It was nevertheless agreed that sanction for the proposed new Rolls-Royce and Bristol factories could be given and stop-gap orders placed for 2,000 aircraft of current types at a cost of £25 million.[42]

Freeman had got what he needed for the next stage.

Rolls-Royce's second new factory was built at Hillington, near Glasgow. Designed to produce 500 Merlins a month, plus spares, on a double-shift basis, it was entirely self-contained, and had to be equipped with a high proportion of the most modern automatic machine tools to compensate for the fact that most of the workforce was unskilled: it was therefore much more expensive than the Crewe factory, costing roughly £6.3 million.[43]

Planning for Bristol engines was much more complex. Since the beginning of the shadow aero-engine scheme, it had been assumed that the Bristol shadow factories would switch production from the old poppet-valve Mercury and Pegasus engines to the newer and more powerful sleeve-valve Hercules by the end of 1939. By Easter 1939, however, the prospects for mass-producing the Hercules were so indefinite that the risks of such a switch had become unacceptable. Stirlings were to use the Hercules, but if there were delays getting the big aircraft into service, production of Wellingtons, Hampdens and Blenheims would have to continue, and there would be a serious crisis if production of the Mercury and Pegasus engines they needed had been stopped, and the factories converted to make the Hercules.[44] Freeman had no option but to keep the Mercury and the Pegasus in production, and so *four* more shadow factories were set up to make the Hercules when it was eventually ready; production was planned to start in the spring of 1940.[45] As before, the four new factories were to be run by the motor firms, Standard, Daimler, Rover and Rootes, but this time they were organised into pairs, so that each pair could produce complete engines.[46] A fifth new factory at Accrington, if built, was to be managed by Bristol.

Freeman disliked gambling on the Hercules in this way, and was acutely conscious of the horrendous consequences should mass production of the engine prove impossible. Hercules production was so gravely behind schedule that he had briefly considered using Vultures instead, which would have thoroughly disrupted the Rolls Royce production programme at Derby.[47] He hedged his position by asking Rolls-Royce to develop their 36-litre V-12 Griffon engine as an alternative, in the hope that it could be developed with far less risk than the Vulture: finance was provided for Griffon jigs and tools.[48]

The future prospects of the Vulture were closely linked to the success of the Manchester and the Tornado however, and by August 1939, it was clear that the Manchester airframe and the Vulture were both overweight,[49]* and that the aircraft was seriously underpowered. Rolls-Royce asked to be allowed to stop development of the Vulture, but Freeman again refused.[50]

Although the new expansion plans would greatly increase production within two years, Freeman and the Supply Committee still anticipated a shortage of aero-engines in 1940, and his vague plans to make aero-engines in the Austin car factories were jolted by the news that Austin wished to accept War Office contracts for cars. It was clear by then that only about 30–40 per cent of the motor industry's plant would be suitable for aero-engine manufacture, but the motor firms would be a valuable source of additional skilled labour which Freeman was reluctant to lose, and he immediately tried to formalise plans for converting the Austin and Humber works to the production of complete Rolls-Royce engines as soon as war started.[51] His initiative failed[52] but it was agreed that Austins would work as subcontractors for Rolls-Royce in wartime, that Armstrong Siddeley engines would be made at Standard and Jaguar, and the Rover and Rootes car factories would be turned over to the repair of Rolls-Royce aero-engines. He also encouraged Rolls-Royce to use Alvis for sub-contract work and engine repairs.

ANCILLARY EQUIPMENT AND MATERIALS

The expansion of airframe and aero-engine capacity absorbed most of Freeman's time in the months following the Munich crisis, but steps were also taken to increase output of ancillary equipment such as airscrews, magnetos, carburettors, aircraft instruments, armament and turrets, and to expand productive capacity for high explosives and incendiary bombs. Production of aircraft for the Fleet Air Arm, and of barrage balloon equipment were increased, as was bomb storage capacity and the output of plastics, machine tools and extrusion presses. The Director of War Production Planning drew up a series of war programmes: airframe production was placed at the centre of the programme, and requirements for ancillary items were then analysed in detail. Among the major projects launched as a result were two carburettor shadow factories, increased capacity for Rotol airscrews, and an enlarged organisation for gun turret production involving Lucas, Daimler, Brockhouse Engineering, Parnall and Boulton Paul.[53]

It would be tedious to describe in detail all of the measures taken by Freeman in 1938 and 1939, but the depth and scope of his expansion plans for one particular sector, aluminium, may be taken as representative of his

* Estimated tare weight: air-frame, 18,623, actual 29,360 lb. The Vulture estimated weight was 2,100 lb, actual weight was 2,450 lb.

work for the aircraft industry as a whole. As late as the summer of 1938, Freeman had been reassured by the light alloy industry that there was plenty of capacity for the aircraft programme. Larger aircraft, however, required much greater quantities of light alloys than those produced in the early stages of rearmament, and once the heavy bombers were ordered, and the government clarified its long-term requirements, it became obvious that the existing UK capacity for producing and fabricating light alloys was totally inadequate.

After the Munich crisis and the acceleration of Scheme L, immediate shortages were overcome by importing supplies from abroad, and factory extensions were sanctioned to raise production of aluminium-alloy sheet and strip from about 20,000 to 30,000 tons per year, yet even this still fell far short of estimated wartime requirements. Freeman therefore proposed the erection of three new alloy works with a total annual capacity of 30,500 tons per annum (tpa), an extension of the Northern Aluminium (Noral) works at Banbury, and new works in Canada, each to add a further 5,000 tpa, at an overall cost of £4.6 million. He tactfully told the Treasury that only 'between one-third and one-half [of this] will need to be incurred now, to produce one-third of the war potential capacity, and the balance ... at the end of 1940 or at the outbreak of war, whichever is the earlier'. Once again he persuaded a worried Treasury to fill another vital gap in the industrial infrastructure.[54]

A matter of increasing concern was the supply of light alloy extrusions, the use of which had become widespread in aircraft design since 1935*, and Freeman made arrangements to double Britain's extrusion capacity in 1939. New orders were placed for German extrusion presses, and steps were taken to accelerate press manufacture in Britain by recruiting a suitably experienced engineer to act as adviser to British firms.[55] The Air Ministry scoured the world's markets for presses and diverted a number to Britain which would otherwise have been exported elsewhere. Extrusion press deliveries from Germany were closely monitored; the last German press built for Britain was snatched from the Hamburg dockside just before war was declared.

A further response to the threat of light alloy shortages came at the administrative level. In January 1939 a new committee of industrialists and Air Ministry officials was established to supervise light alloy distribution,[56] chaired by Samuel Beale, a director of GKN. He was a skilled negotiator, well able to persuade rather than compel firms to co-operate,† and the committee became the model for the voluntary control organisation established by the light alloy industry on the outbreak of war.

Freeman believed that British alloy manufacturers would be able to meet most of the requirements of the aircraft programme when these plans were complete, but British production of raw aluminium fell far short of requirements. The Air Ministry calculated, for example, that in 1939 the aircraft

---

* An extrusion press squeezes large billets of metal through specially shaped, narrow nozzles at great pressure, forming long, thin sections or spars which have structural strength.

† Beale was very able, and could 'cut the cackle and make everybody laugh'. A.R.Gray to author.

programme would absorb 90,000 tons of raw aluminium per annum, whereas total British output was only 30,000 tons. British production could be increased to 41,000 tons, but the rest would have to be imported.

Freeman initially expected that most of this material would come from the United States,[57] but during 1939 he became increasingly interested in the potential of the Canadian aluminium industry, which had a capacity of 100,000 tpa, and extra construction was authorised on 6 April 1939. When war finally broke out in September 1939 the Air Ministry was prepared, and had arranged to import 60 per cent of Canadian aluminium output.

QUANTITY VS. QUALITY

Although a large proportion of his time was devoted to production matters, by 1939, Freeman's primary role as AMDP was to co-ordinate research and development, and he never lost sight of the importance of maintaining technical quality of service aircraft at the highest possible level. As production pressures increased, he realised that shortages of staff were severely impeding the progress of long-term design: draughtsmen were frequently being diverted to deal with production drawings and the flow of modifications. 'Progress ... has been disappointing', he wrote. 'None of our new bombers or fighters has passed its preliminary trials and only one [of our heavy bombers] has as yet been in the air.'[58]

The industry's design resources were clearly overstretched, and Freeman decided that he had to ration new projects to ease the burden of development work. In September 1938 he had even gone so far as to warn the SBAC that, for a time, drawing offices should not waste their time on further new designs as 'he would refuse to look at them',[59] although, in fact, he continued to encourage the most promising new ventures. He became increasingly interested in the Whittle engine at this time, and insisted that its development should continue. 'This engine is based on jet propulsion', he explained at one of the Progress Meetings, 'and the results of tests already carried out had exceeded expectations'. He was particularly attracted to the engine because, if successful, 'it would be cheap to produce, as it contained comparatively few mechanical parts. It ... required no airscrew.'[60]

Despite the long term contribution to aircraft performance expected from research and development, Freeman was well aware that the use of 100 octane fuel would give a huge and immediate benefit. The RAF had been using 87 octane for some years, but a change to the higher grade would permit safe use of higher supercharger pressures (boost), and extract the maximum value from the new engines and variable pitch propellers. The production capacity of German refineries was estimated to be roughly 970,000 tpa of 100 octane by 1938,[61] and it was clear that to remain competitive, the RAF would have to start using 100 octane fuel for operational aircraft as soon as possible.[62]

Free world production of 100 octane fuel at this time was roughly 1,000,000 tpa,[63] of which Britain contributed only 125,000, and Freeman urged the Government to establish capacity to meet potential deficiencies as a matter of the utmost importance, recommending the erection of three huge new hydrogenation plants, one in Britain for 200,000 and two in Trinidad, one for 200,000 and one for 300,000 tpa, at a total cost of £9 million.[64] His proposals were amended after extensive deliberations by the Treasury and the Committee of Imperial Defence. The 157th and 158th Progress Meetings on 7 March 1939 recorded that Treasury authority had been received to construct two new refineries with a capacity of 720,000 tpa, and that ICI would build a small plant at Billingham to produce iso-octane, an essential additive. Another 100 octane refinery, in Trinidad, was sanctioned immediately after the outbreak of war.

REPAIRS

Historians have often overlooked or understated the vital importance of Britain's aircraft repairs and maintenance organisation during the Second World War. Between 1940 and 1945, no fewer than 79,000 repaired aircraft were delivered by the repairs organisation to the Metropolitan Air Force[†], representing 48 per cent of total MAF deliveries; 35 per cent of all the Spitfires and Hurricanes reaching the RAF during August 1940, and more than 40 per cent in September and October, were repaired aircraft.[65] It was far more economical to use industrial resources for repairs than new production: the material used to repair 3,816 Lancaster bombers between 1942 and 1945 would have made only 622 new aircraft.

Most of the aircraft of the biplane era had been repaired on RAF stations, but Freeman recognized that the stations would be quite unable to cope with the new generation of metal monoplanes, and as soon as he joined the Air Council in 1936, he recommended the establishment of five aircraft repair depots.[66] Ellington, the CAS, and a majority of the Air Council, blocked the proposal on the grounds that a modern air war would be so short and destructive that wrecked aircraft would have to be replaced by new machines. Freeman had to wait until Ellington retired* before he could resume his pressure for a proper repair organisation.

However Newall, the AMSO, agreed with Freeman and having set Air Vice-Marshal Portal to work on plans to form a new Maintenance Command,[67] he accepted the recommendations as soon as he became CAS.[†] Progress was slow, because the difficulty of getting the Treasury to provide funds for a

---

* RAFM, Trenchard papers; 23.2.48. Freeman's letter to Trenchard '... you made Ellington CAS, the worst we ever had.' 24.2.48. Trenchard agreed. 'He never understood a big job, or any job except detail, and that not too well'. 'He was too shy to be an effective head of a rapidly growing service, and, until overruled by Swinton, he actually opposed the training of Fighter Command in the use of Radar, because it might end the dominance of the bomber.' [H.M.Hyde *British Air Policy between the Wars*.]

† Portal recommended that repairs and salvage be entrusted to a service department run wholly by the Royal Air Force, employing civilian labour and civilian contractors, but not involving private industry. There were to be six large general repair depots, three to be wholly staffed by Royal Air Force personnel and three Civilian Repair Depots (CRDs), staffed by civilians, but under Royal Air Force control.

major new department (in anticipation of a yet unquantified need) was under-estimated by Air Marshal Welsh, who succeeded Newall as AMSO, and it was July 1938 before the new Maintenance Command HQ was set up at Andover: it remained very understaffed. Freeman found the sluggish development of the Command and its repair depots a source of mounting frustration and, in an attempt to accelerate the organisation's development, he began to involve himself more closely in its affairs.

By the time he became AMDP, progress on the acquisition of sites for the repair of airframes under the new Maintenance Command had been negligible, and realising that the administrative division between repairs and production within the Air Ministry was part of the problem, he proposed that the repair responsibilities should become part of his department.[68]* Repairs were discussed at the Progress Meetings of 4 October and 29 November 1938, after the first depot had finally been authorised, but progress remained dilatory, and it was March 1939 before the advisory panel of industrialists, set up to assist the Secretary of State, supported a suggestion of Freeman's that the McAlpine company be consulted on construction of depots, and that experts from the aircraft industry should advise on layout, complements and staff. Even then, a site for the third depot (at Stoke-on-Trent) was not decided until June 1939, by when AMSO was responsible for statements about the future development of repair depots.[69]

Fretting at the delays and indecision, Freeman asked Major Barlow, of Fairey Aviation, to report on the projected repair factory at Warrington, and Barlow responded that Air Commodore Quentin Brand, the Director of Repairs and Maintenance (DRM), had underestimated the difficulties of administration. Barlow thought that 'service control of civilian factories by RAF officers [was] impractical [and that the need to act] through Groups, Commands, etc, [would not give] the efficiency and output [required]'.[70] Tedder disagreed, and supported Brand, on the grounds that good RAF engineer officers would know more about the wide variety of airframes and aero-engines then in use than any civilian manager, and that this was more important than experience of managing factories.[71] Freeman respected Barlow's advice, and thought that there would be little difference between repair and production. He wanted the depots to be run by a big civilian organisation which would call on its own experienced pesonnel if war came and referred the matter to Lemon.[72]

Freeman's views about Civilian Repair Depots (CRDs) had been clarified by these exchanges, and the matter was reviewed at the 178th Progress Meeting late in July 1939.[73] Welsh wanted the depots to be commanded by RAF officers but managed by civilians, 'men with engineering and good organising and

---

* Freeman knew and respected Percy Cooper, the former Inspector of Accidents for the Air Ministry, who had just retired, and realised the importance of his reports. Cooper's careful studies of accidents had revealed much technical information about engines and airframes and the causes of failure, and brought about a significant improvement in the reliability and strength of aircraft, and the safety of aircrews: both were quite as important as the benefits of rapid repair.

administration experience', but Freeman envisaged agency arrangements with large engineering firms, arguing that:

> the *civilian* depots would have little to do in peacetime, as most of the repair work would [be done by] . . . *Service* depots . . . In war . . . the civilian depots would be very busy . . . needing large staffs, run by experienced industrial organisations' and men with experience in labour management.

At meetings in August,[74] which involved all the relevant departments, Freeman and Welsh decided to try both methods, and compare the results, and to arrange for one of the sites to be managed by an industrial firm, on an agency basis, and for another to be run for the RAF by a suitably qualified civilian manager. It was agreed that Kingsley Wood should ask Lord Nuffield either to lend some of his staff as a nucleus for one of the CRDs, or to take over its management and run it on 'shadow' lines,[75] but war was declared on 3 September 1939 before any action had been taken.

Arrangements for repairing aero-engines developed much more satisfactorily during the rearmament years. Major repairs had been carried out by their makers in the twenties and early thirties, and this arrangement continued, Bristol setting up separate workshops large enough to repair 15 to 20 engines a week, so that such work would not interfere with production.[76] Rolls-Royce, however, only had a cramped workshop which was mainly occupied with derating Kestrel engines into Kestrel XXXs for the Miles Master advanced trainer.[77]

Freeman understood from the first that the repair process made a vital contribution to identifying and correcting defects in engines, and he firmly believed that responsibility for engine repairs should remain under AMRD's control. Realising that the Rolls-Royce repair facilities were inadequate, he deftly suggested that service or civilian depots should perform the semi-skilled work of stripping, cleaning and reassembling Rolls-Royce engines under the company's supervision.[78] Stung by this suggestion, the Board of Rolls-Royce accepted that adequate repair facilities were of national importance, stopped production of cars,[79] and planned to treble their repair capacity to 50 Merlins per week by 31 December.[80] Alvis took over the job of converting and repairing Kestrel engines and, subsequently, Merlins; by March 1940 the Clement-Talbot car factory was also nearly ready for Merlin repairs. Bristol set up a similar, dispersed, system for repairing their engines, centred on the parent factory, and airscrew repairs were planned on the same basis.

PROGRESS BY 1939

By 3 September 1939, Freeman had achieved many of his targets. Scheme F had not been fulfilled by its original target date of 1 April 1939, and less than 50 per cent of the first Spitfire contract, and only 52 per cent of the first Hurricane contract had been completed by August. Nevertheless, deliveries had begun to exceed the programme by the beginning of the year, and by the end of June 1939 the industry had produced 598 more aeroplanes than the

1938 forecast. Total output in 1939 was 180 per cent higher than in 1938, and monthly output exceeded that of Germany by the outbreak of war, a dramatic acceleration which made up some of the deficiencies which had accumulated since 1936. The production record was steadily improving.

Where planning was concerned, the picture was even more impressive. During 1938 the Air Ministry's procurement apparatus had been completely reorganised, and planning and programming methods immeasurably enhanced; by September 1939 official production programmes had been developed which stretched forward to 1941.

Between the Anschluss and Germany's invasion of Poland, Freeman had fought for and obtained approval for an enormous increase in expenditure on new industrial capacity for aircraft and associated products: group production schemes had been organised, the aircraft industry and its 'shadows' were expanded, and many more general engineering firms became involved in aircraft manufacturing. Sub-contracting was adopted as official policy, and elaborate plans were initiated to increase the supply of aircraft equipment, aluminium and 100 octane fuel.

The availability of skilled manpower was carefully considered before new projects were approved. New factories had to be located so as to make the best possible use of available labour and most of the new shadow factories were built in close proximity to parent companies and run as part of their organisation to ease the task of management, The threat of German bombing was also taken into account, and efforts were made to provide more than one source of supply for all items, as an insurance in case one was bombed. Freeman asked the Treasury to sanction the duplication of jigs, tools and drawings, once designs had been fully standardised.[81]

By September 1939 Freeman had laid the foundations of Britain's wartime aircraft economy. Approximately 8 million square feet of productive floor space were in operation in the airframe industry alone, and plans were in progress to increase this figure to 19 million square feet by 1941 – to be used initially to augment the output of fighters and medium bombers like the Wellington, but capable of conversion to make the new heavy bombers.

The planned expansion was far from complete, however. Major new capital projects, such as the Castle Bromwich Spitfire factory, were well behind schedule, and although Rolls-Royce delivered a complete Merlin from their Crewe factory less than a year after starting it on a 'greenfield site', it was at least two years after authorisation of new capacity before most of the other firms were in production. During the first months of hostilities, Freeman and his staff had to face the formidable challenge of bridging the gap between the solid achievements of 1938 and 1939 and preparations for war which could not become fully effective until 1941.

CHAPTER 6

War: the production
alternatives clarified

T
HE POLISH CRISIS deepened in August 1939, and with his new family
settled at Murtle Den, Freeman was called back to London, moving to
live at 14 Gilston Road with his sister Josephine. He jotted down notes
at this critical time in almost daily letters to Elizabeth: his hope that Hitler
would climb down, his relief that the humiliation of Munich would not be
repeated, his concern at the prospect of losing Tedder if he got a command, and
his fear that he himself might be posted to an overseas command like India, or
some other backwater, away from the work he knew so well. Despite these
anxieties, he put on a mask of optimism, both at work and at home: Josephine
made him very welcome.*

In scribbled letters, he told Elizabeth his fleeting thoughts: his depression
at the grey, unenterprising, sombre figures collected around Chamberlain as
a War Cabinet, except for one, unspecified, member, (presumably Churchill).
He described what he knew of the hostilities between Germany and Poland
as a 'half-hearted business . . . I expect Chamberlain will threaten them with
another speech if they don't stop fighting'. As for himself, he noted that his
executive powers had been increased: 'I seem to be accumulating quite considerable powers which makes things easy, as I don't have to explain'.[1]

He was particularly anxious that his brother Ralph should stay in Britain
for the war, and on the eve of hostilities begged him not return to Kenya[2], an
interesting and unusual concern for a happily married man in charge of a
vital sector of the nation's armaments. For the previous twenty years Ralph
had made his home in Kenya, most of his friends were there, and he had
built up a flourishing coffee farm from nothing. Behind Wilfrid's request lay
his recognition that he would probably remain one of the most influential
officers in the RAF, deeply immersed in the day-to-day conduct of the war,
and he would need a confidant. The military responsibilities that he would
have to carry would be such that they could not be discussed with anyone
whose discretion was not complete. He knew that his young wife, with whom
he was still deeply in love, lacked the maturity, experience, and perhaps the
discretion, to have to think about state secrets; the task of sharing his load
and relieving him of the lonely burden of leadership would have worried her
desperately. Ralph, however, had served in MI6 in the First World War,[3] and
besides being as congenial as ever, he was the only member of the family to
be trusted with military secrets. He would have preferred to return to Kenya,

---

* He was touched to discover that the fresh flowers in his room were bought for him by her two
maids, Violet and Dorothy

Ralph Freeman, Wilfrid's brother and his invaluable confidant throughout the war.

but he realised that he was badly needed by his brother, and accepted the extraordinary role he had been offered.

Ralph by then was an exceptionally serene, charming and intelligent man, delightful company, poised and well read, in whose company everyone seemed able, effortlessly, to give of their best. He had an inexhaustible well of ideas, books, family and friends to talk about, perfect tact, and an unexpected, often delightful, kind, irreverent wit. Behind his slightly austere features, there was an enchanting personality, with a gentle perception that always buoyed his companions, an absence of ambition which took that distraction out of the equation, and absolute discretion which was put at his brother's service. Over the next five years, the support of his mature wisdom was very precious to Wilfrid who wrote to him about his work and fled to Murtle Den and Ralph's company whenever he could.*

MOBILISATION

As soon as Germany invaded Poland on 1 September 1939, Freeman made a desperate appeal to Kingsley Wood to release finance for the American machine tools needed to complete the new aero-engine factories planned earlier in the year, and for new capacity for equally essential raw materials. Without these, engine and material production would be insufficient for the requirements of the aircraft programme during 1940 and 1941 (assuming Britain declared war in 1939). He warned that a new inter-departmental committee, set up under Treasury aegis to control dollar commitments, was already holding up schemes which had previously been approved, and that further government controls were likely to obstruct expenditure plans even further.

There was a grim determination behind his demands, and Kingsley Wood was left in no doubt about the dire consequences of refusal. 'Frankly I cannot face the appalling delay which must follow', Freeman wrote. 'We are virtually at war and I must advise you with all the emphasis at my command that we must take action at once if we are to have any hope of keeping engine production and raw material supplies in line with [airframe] output.' Knowing that he must 'genuflect' towards the Treasury to achieve what he wanted, he agreed that 'the American machine tools involved will only be released with the approval of the new Treasury Committee', while insisting, at the same time, that authorisation of purchase could not be postponed. 'We shall have to rise above departmental procedure if action is to be taken in time'.[4]

After the first few days of war, Freeman assessed his own prospects.[5] 'I am preparing for a three and a half years war at a minimum', he wrote, 'it seems the only safe thing to do'. Having held nothing but staff positions since returning from Palestine, he thought that he would be 'useless at commanding any operations', but he also expressed doubts as to whether he was going to hold his present job. He was particularly grateful for the support and trust he was receiving from Bruce-Gardner, who knew better than anyone the burden he was carrying, and asked Elizabeth to write 'spontaneously' to tell Bruce-Gardner how much he appreciated his kindness and cheerfulness, and his unvarying support and help.[6]

Assuming that the war would last three years, the Air Council planned to increase monthly production from 2,000 aircraft to 3,000 as soon as possible.[7]

* In 1942, when he was under severe stress, Freeman wrote; 'If I could spend two days every month at Murtle, I know I would do better work'.

New factories would have to be set up and provision made for machine tools and other plant, 80 per cent of which had to be imported.[8] More raw materials would be needed, and extra facilities for aluminium fabrication, and the capital cost of these totalled £168 million. The labour requirement would be about 1.6 million workers, and the annual cost of aircraft, £900 million – a daunting responsibility.[9]

Such a programme needed the support of the SBAC and of the Ministries of Supply and Labour, and Freeman got neither agreement nor alternative proposals from any of them. The only solution was intensive discussions with each of the individual companies, and although these disclosed looming deficiencies, particularly supplies of alloy sheet, extrusions and Embodiment Loan equipment (EL)* a smaller programme was eventually agreed, named the 'Harrogate Programme', because Freeman's department had been evacuated there before the end of September. The monthly target for the third year of the war, to include 250 heavy bombers, was set to reach 2,550 by July 1942, assuming that Canada and Australia would by then be producing 250 aircraft a month.[10] In the first six months of the war, few of the targets set by the Harrogate programme were achieved, but in the longer term the programme was reasonably accurate, indeed, until 1943 it was the only estimate of future production that bore some relation to reality. Bruce-Gardner subsequently confirmed to Freeman that his meetings with the SBAC members had done a great deal of good: he had the support of every member of the Council and they all wished to help as much as they could.[11]

The evacuation of AMDP's department to Harrogate had been planned long before the war started because of the fear of bombing attacks on London; Freeman himself left for Harrogate on 14 September. He found his work severely hampered by the move, which he was soon trying to reverse, but he immediately got down to the task of producing the extra engines, EL equipment and materials required for the new programme.[12] He told Bruce-Gardner that he was especially concerned over the supply of light alloys:

> Aircraft production is not now [limited by] ... floor space, labour, man hours and so forth, it's limited by the amount of aluminium available and the amount of capacity for rolling, extruding or forging the light alloy. We cannot produce more than a certain *weight* of aircraft at present; that is a fundamental fact.[13]

Some short-term measures could nevertheless be taken to ameliorate shortages of materials and to increase aero-engine production. At the outbreak of war, for example, Ernest Hives of Rolls-Royce, recommended that material rejected because of minor flaws should be used for non-stressed aero-engine parts, and Freeman willingly agreed.[14] Greater output could also be achieved by standardisation, and Freeman allowed Rolls-Royce to halt work on the Boreas

---

* EL equipment comprised ancillary items like gunsights, radios, turrets, wheels, propellers and instruments, which were ordered separately by the Air Ministry, and supplied to the airframe maker free of charge.

engine.[15] Hives was actually hoping to be allowed to stop work on the Vulture as well, but was told it must continue, as also development of the 37-litre Griffon, which offered the prospect of replacing the Merlin in airframes like the Spitfire. Freeman recognized that the Griffon*, based on the Schneider Trophy 'R' engine, might be easier to develop than the Vulture.[16]

Recycling scrap and standardising production might achieve an immediate increase in the output of Rolls-Royce engines, but in the longer term, it was clear that much more capacity was needed. Humber's facilities would be required for engine repairs, and when Austins proved more enthusiastic about producing aero-engine parts than complete engines,[17] Freeman approached Lord Perry, the chairman of Ford, Great Britain.[18] He had visited Ford's Dagenham factory in 1935, when Commandant of the Staff College, and had been impressed by the character and ability of Rowland Smith, their Managing Director. After meeting Perry and his staff in London on 31 October 1939, Ford agreed to set up a new Merlin factory at Manchester, and began talks with the Rolls-Royce management immediately.

In designing the Manchester factory, Ford faced the same fundamental problem which had confronted Rolls-Royce at Hillington, near Glasgow: the only labour available at Manchester had no experience of precision engineering. Ford, however, could draw on the experience gained by Rolls-Royce's planning engineers at Hillington, and on their help to train key supervisory workers from Ford, such as tool setters, so the factory was set up and went into production with the minimum of delays and mistakes. As at Hillington, it was equipped with the latest special-purpose machine tools which could produce accurate components when operated by semi-skilled workers. But by then Rolls-Royce had seconded senior production managers and foremen to the Crewe and Hillington Factories, and could no longer spare the same degree of help to Ford. The Ford managers, who were used to mass-production systems, soon realised that Rolls-Royce's existing Merlin drawings, were not accurate enough to be used by the unskilled Ford labour force, without such supervision, and decided that the engine had to be completely 'redrawn' before production could begin.† The first 'Ford' Merlin XX was delivered in June 1941.

The Ford Merlin factory represented only part of a much larger capital expenditure programme launched after the outbreak of the war, and between September and December 1939[19] Freeman managed to obtain much of what was needed: capital commitments for military aircraft production doubled. But he was deeply depressed by the Chamberlain Government's approach to the war and, especially by the activities of his own Secretary of State, Kingsley Wood, and he now began to chafe at the inaction of the 'phoney war'. As early as October, when a paper for the Cabinet was being discussed by the Air

---

* Hives offered Freeman the Griffon in January 1939, and proposed a development programme for it in February.

† For the same reasons all the drawings were reworked by Packard, and adapted to allow for different American engineering practices.

Council, he let fly at Kingsley Wood, telling Elizabeth later some of what he had said:

> Do I gather that the Cabinet have not yet made up their minds as to how they will win this war? Have they no plans?' When Kingsley Wood admitted that they had not; '... After all, the war has only been going about seven weeks', Freeman turned on him: 'Then all I can say is that you are taking the high road to losing it'.

Naturally enough, the Secretary of State did not appreciate his criticism, but Freeman was unrepentant. 'I am feeling a bit unhappy about the Government', he told Elizabeth. 'We must find a statesman and a strong one.'[20]

PRODUCTION

The increase in aircraft production after the outbreak of war was very disappointing. Although factories were expected to operate a two-shift system, subcontracting was extended, and it was assumed that labour intake and working hours would both increase; such hopes were unrealised.[21] Shortages of fabricated alloys and EL items were the main cause, and although extensive plans to raise the output of these sectors had been sanctioned by the early months of 1940, much of the new capacity had only been authorised in 1939, and would not come into production until late 1940, or 1941. It became increasingly difficult to balance the supply system. Freeman tried to ensure that materials and equipment were evenly distributed, by a circular to all makers. '[With] 9,000 different articles ... [making up] the aeroplanes of an Air Force', he ruled, 'no firm should have in store a greater number of embodiment loan items than is required to marry up their production ... [otherwise] some other firm will go short',[22] but shortages developed, and production suffered.

Public and political criticism of the Air Ministry steadily increased over the following months, and Freeman became more and more uneasy. Critics focused on two aspects, on the fact that despite the imposition of government controls over the economy, production had failed to expand as rapidly as had been expected after the formal declaration of hostilities, and on the managerial problems that continued to bedevil the airframe repair organisation. By the spring of 1940, there was serious political pressure on the Air Council. No one worked harder than Freeman to solve the twin problems of production and repairs, but as the political unrest increased, his relations with Kingsley Wood deteriorated,[23] and he began to be anxious about his own position as AMDP.

Shortages of equipment and materials imposed such severe restrictions on production between January and March 1940 that labour intake nearly stopped:[24] there were reports of idle time in the factories, and some workers were even laid off[25]. But these were not the only reasons why aircraft deliveries failed to match the programme. The completion of factory projects, like Castle Bromwich, were delayed,* and reservists were called up, disrupting

---

* Nuffield rejected suggestions that the factory should be brought into operation 'a bay at a time', insisting that production did not start until the whole factory was ready.

output:[26] Vickers lost 8 per cent of their personnel to the armed services.[27] Several factories were changing over to new types of aircraft, which inevitably involved some temporary loss of production,[28] and there were fewer working days in December because of the Christmas break. The vile weather conditions in the new year hampered commuters, and restricted the pre-delivery test-flying schedules; influenza caused high absenteeism throughout the industry.[29]

The problems were compounded by a shortage of spare parts, so sudden and serious that the aircraft industry had in some cases to sacrifice the output of complete aircraft to increase spares production.[30] Output was significantly greater than in the first half of 1939, but the Air Ministry was failing to meet its initial wartime targets, the undertow of political criticism got stronger,[31] and Freeman found himself increasingly at odds with his Secretary of State. He 'is now nervous of his tenure of office', he told Elizabeth, 'and wishes me to [promise] greater output of aircraft in the future than I believe will be achieved.'[32] He steadfastly refused to do this, but he worried lest he himself would 'soon be replaced by someone ... more amenable.[33]

He realised that despite his achievements, there were members of the Government who thought 'the right industrialist' would be able to run a production department better than a Royal Air Force officer, and he began to experience the type of political problems he was to face all too often over the next four years. Harrogate was out of contact with the mainstream of events in London, and he felt uneasy and very suspicious about the rising political pressures in the capital. At the end of November he confided in Elizabeth that 'Things have not been going too well, a lot of work, changes in programme, much keeping of the peace and a feeling that ... a good many people in London are working against us.'[34]

The balance between quantity and quality, one of the most essential aspects of Freeman's work as AMDP, had been maintained by new specifications and a constant vigil on development projects, but by November 1939 the doctrine of quality was coming under attack from two quarters, of which the Cabinet was the most influential. The Government was facing growing criticism from both the Opposition and some of their own backbenchers over its conduct of the war, and although Parliament did not have hard figures at its disposal, the general unease over munitions supply would not have been allayed by Freeman's arguments about the importance of maintaining quality. Such critics could only be pacified by numbers.

The SBAC was also restive. Aircraft contractors were predictably reluctant to take responsibility for the production shortfalls in the first months of the war, and argued that higher output could have been achieved by greater 'standardisation'. In practice, this would have meant delaying the introduction of new models, producing more Blenheims, Whitleys and Wellingtons and, in the longer term, focusing heavy bomber production on one type, rather than three. Modifications were unpopular because they delayed completions, and all firms asked for bigger stocks of raw materials and ancillary equipment at their factories.

The Defiant. Despite an initial success when operated against German day fighters, the Defiant was too slow and heavy to compete against the day fighters and was in August 1940 switched to operating as a night fighter.

Freeman understood the Cabinet's position, and sympathised with the industry, but his primary consideration was always the operational efficiency of the RAF. The Service required the maximum number of the best available aircraft, incorporating all the latest modifications, and they also wanted newer types and better engines to be introduced as soon as possible, even if some loss of output was involved, and Freeman was determined that these demands should be satisfied. Service aircraft must be designed for war, and if additions such as self-sealing tanks and armour became essential, such modifications would have to be introduced.

The main bone of contention was Freeman's insistence on maintaining the quality of service aircraft. It had always been tempting to sacrifice this for quantity in response to urgent demands from the Services and political pressure for results, and at times such sacrifices had to be made. Many of the aircraft specifications issued by the Air Ministry in the early 1930s, like the Wellington, Whitley and Spitfire, had been good, but the operational requirements for others, such as the Battle and the Defiant, proved faulty.* There were obvious reasons why it was often impossible to switch production quickly to other aircraft, such as the Beaufighter, the Halifax and the Manchester, but delays in finalising new designs were often exacerbated by a shortage of

* The top speed of the Battle exceeded its specification by more than 50mph, but the new fighters were even faster: the Defiant was intended to mount 'standing patrols', so as to attack unescorted bombers. By the time the Luftwaffe began raiding Britain from bases on the channel coast, they were escorted by Me109s.

draughtsmen and jig and tool designers in the aircraft industry. Tool-makers were scarce by 1939, Merlin engines were in short supply, and the Hercules was still not ready for mass-production.

In these circumstances the Air Ministry had no option but to place so-called 'stop-gap' orders for obsolete aircraft. The continued production of such types was a better alternative than the closure of the factories concerned and the dispersal of their tools and workforces. Production of the Fairey Battle therefore continued up to December 1940, while the Rootes shadow factory went on building Blenheims until 1943: the 'quality' option was all too often simply 'not available'. As soon as they were ready however, Freeman always insisted that new airframes, and more advanced engines were brought into production, even if output fell somewhat as a result. The clearest expression of his views on the correct balance between quantity and quality can be found in the memorandum he circulated to the Air Council in April 1940.

> My department has been asked on many occasions whether they can increase output. There is no doubt that it might be increased if we are prepared to sacrifice quality and reasonable caution. Caution is the motive behind the decision to order three types of heavy bomber, and quality the factor that causes us to modify and improve [aircraft].

Production could, of course, be increased if the number of different aircraft types was reduced, if designs were simplified, and if there was a complete embargo on modifications. Equally, the production of extrusions, a vital bottleneck at that time, could be accelerated by halving the number of different types and sections. This could only be achieved, however, by jeopardising the

Fairey Battle light bombers over northern France in the winter of 1939/40. Outclassed in performance and armament they were slaughtered by Me 109s and the excellent German light 'flak'.

operational capability of service aircraft. As long as output did not fall below 75 per cent of programme, Freeman insisted that quality should remain of overriding importance.

> The only argument of any force in favour of quantity is that 'God is on the side of the big battalions' – the story of David and Goliath being forgotten'. An aeroplane that is brought down by the enemy only once in ten flights, is of more value than two which normally only survive four or five flights. (the saving in pilots and crew ... must [also] be taken into account) ... I suggest that we should openly adhere to the policy of quality as opposed to quantity and we should continue to modify and improve our aircraft as much as possible.[35]

Freeman kept faith with this philosophy throughout the war, and as the pressure for numbers built up, he was always planning new developments to insure the RAF against impending obsolescence. In 1939 he was worried that the performance of the Hurricane and Spitfire would become inadequate by 1941, but he planned to go on making them until the cannon fighters, the Whirlwind and Beaufighter and the new Tornado/Typhoon day fighters, were in full production, and could replace them.[36] He also authorised the new B.1/39 heavy bomber specification,* hoping that it could go into production to replace aircraft like the Halifax or the Stirling, by 1943.

Apart from supporting the development of the 37-litre V12 Griffon, he sent Roy Fedden, head of the Bristol Engine Department, to Canada in May 1940, hoping that the Canadians could establish a factory to produce the 54-litre Centaurus.[37] He also included Frank Whittle's jet engine in a limited class of 'war winning devices', and devised arrangements for its development and production. Whittle was determined not to allow his enterprise to be swamped by one of the established aero-engine companies, and had himself proposed collaboration between his firm, Power Jets, and Rover. The extreme difficulty of agreeing formal terms of co-operation between the two companies, and their intransigence, obliged Freeman and Tedder to insist that they worked together, but the independence of Whittle's company was not thereby jeopardised.[38]

As for bomber production, Freeman wanted the Halifax, Manchester and Stirling to be introduced as soon as possible.[39] He knew that the Air Staff would prefer to receive fewer of these aircraft rather than many more medium bombers, because a heavy bomber could carry the load of twelve Blenheims, and needed only a single crew. The aggregate saving in pilots and crews, staff, schools, flying instructors and maintenance personnel, would be vital to the expansion of the operational forces.

Freeman fought hard to maintain the doctrine of quality, but he realised that the Air Ministry's critics were very influential, and in January 1940, he asked for the support of an experienced industrialist to counter the political influence of Harold Balfour, the Under-Secretary of State, and the burning

---

* The B.1/39 would have had .5in. guns in its turrets, and been larger and faster with a higher ceiling.

The cannon fighters. (*above*) The size of the Westland Whirlwind was restricted to the absolute minimum required to carry four 20-mm cannon in the nose of the fuselage. It then became possible to mount such cannon in the wings of single-engined fighters, production of its Peregrine engines ceased and the Whirlwind airframe was too small for other engines and too specialised for other roles. (*below*) The Bristol Beaufighter was much larger than the Whirlwind. It proved to be a successful long-range day fighter against bombers, an adequate night fighter, and a superb anti-shipping torpedo and strike aircraft, capable of carrying eight 60-lb rockets as well as a torpedo and four 20-mm cannons.

ambitions and unpredictable policies of Nuffield. Kingsley Wood agreed to appoint Lord Riverdale, formerly Arthur Balfour, Chairman of the eponymous specialist Sheffield steel company, to the Air Council to present unbiased industrialist opinion.* Freeman was delighted: 'He is a grand old man, and more than a match for Lemon and Nuffield ... he will be a great help to me, if he doesn't get rid of me.'[40]

SALVAGE AND REPAIRS

With direct responsibility for every aspect of aircraft procurement, Freeman had to react to criticism of his department from Parliament and elsewhere. He was not responsible for the organisation which salvaged aircraft and controlled the repair of damaged airframes, the other target of the Air Ministry's critics, but for the first eight months of the war he did all he could to resolve the problems created by Kingsley Wood's decision to involve Lord Nuffield in the aircraft repair problem.

The delays and muddled arrangements had worried Freeman since 1936. Although construction work on the six general repair depots eventually started in 1938, the only one ready by September 1939, at Sealand, was promptly commandeered for training and other purposes: the depots at Stoke and Abbottsinch were incomplete and those at St Athan and Henlow lacked much equipment. Skilled workers, recruited for the depots, were moved to other jobs, and most repair work on lighter aircraft had to be allocated to private contractors[41]. Progress on the repair depots had been so unsatisfactory by September 1939 that Freeman thought Welsh would not be able to put it right, and tried to have airframe repairs transferred to his department.[†]

Nuffield meanwhile had agreed to manage the Burtonwood depot without profit, and before Freeman could arrange for the transfer of responsibility for the depots from AMSO, Oliver Boden, Nuffield's 'right hand man', had proposed a more widespread and radical alternative using capacity from a number of branches of industry in general. Freeman respected Boden, but still wanted ultimate control to be transferred from AMSO to Lemon, his DGP.[*42]

The 186th SSPM held on 10 October reported the conclusions of a separate meeting four days earlier,[43] at which Kingsley Wood decided to keep control of repair under AMSO, and to transfer the whole salvage and repair responsibility to a Civilian Repair Organisation, CRO, to be run by Boden on attachment to the Air Ministry. Freeman and Lemon had been strongly against this solution. Freeman's preference for management by 'large engineering firms whose own work was likely to diminish in time of war'[44] was not satisfied by the choice of Nuffield's group which did not have adequate experience to be able to handle such an intricate task. The work would be detrimental to the efficiency of Nuffield's completion of the Castle Bromwich Spitfire shadow

---

* The choice of Riverdale was probably made by Weir who had served with Riverdale and Sir James Lithgow, on an important supply committee between 1933 and 1935.
† 'I have decided to take over all repairs from Sinbad'. Freeman preferred this sobriquet for Welsh to 'Sailor', the RAF alternative.

Ernest Lemon brought production experience and the invaluable services of industrial consultants to the expansion programme when he joined Freeman's production department as Director-General.

factory. There would be a duplication of effort and wastage if the repair of airframes was not placed under Lemon, the DGP, whilst the need to guide and train an inexperienced organisation like the CRO while they gained experience in repairs, would be a serious distraction for the aircraft manufacturers.[45] Lured by the prospect of profit-free help from the great industrialist, Kingsley Wood disregarded Freeman's opposition, and accepted Nuffield's proposals.

Freeman's original concept that the CRO would use servicing and industrial resources which became idle in wartime was not, in itself, illogical, but very few of the staff of Nuffield's new units had any knowledge of aircraft technology. The management of a diverse and highly technical salvage and repair organisation was far too large and complex for the managers seconded from Morris Motors, and Nuffield, Boden and their staff soon found themselves out of their depth. Aircraft were salvaged, but the backlog of work on repairs steadily increased, and Welsh became unduly reliant on Nuffield's support. Hearing rumours that Welsh was unlikely to remain in his present job, Freeman told Elizabeth:

> Sinbad is getting more and more difficult, and is of course making the most of his association with Nuffield. I am quite sure that Nuffield will have my job before 1940 is out, even though he has megalomania, as did Napoleon and Northcliffe. Hitler should change his name to one starting with 'N'.[46]

Air Chief Marshal Sir Cyril Newall (*left*) and Air Marshal Sir Christopher Courtney leaving 10 Downing Street with the Secretary of State for Air, Sir Kingsley Wood.

Of course the fundamental problems, caused by the separation of responsibility for aircraft repairs from aircraft production, were not solved by Nuffield's intervention. His new CRO, formed within Morris Motors, was based at Cowley, and operated under contract to the Air Ministry, subcontracting work to numerous independent firms. Nuffield, the new Director General of Maintenance (DGM), was supposed to direct it from the AMSO's department at the Air Ministry, with assistance from both Freeman's Directorate of Production and AMSO's Maintenance Command, but Freeman recognized at once that this arrangement divided control: the repair contractors were working between two authorities.

Freeman was determined that his own department should not be held responsible for the incompetence of Welsh and Nuffield, and knowing that there would be chaos unless the repair functions of the two Air Ministry departments were clearly defined, he tried to clarify the position with a series of meetings and minutes. Under the new system, apart from the separate problem of the repair of engines, he suggested that AMSO should be wholly responsible for administering the repair and maintenance of aircraft in service, but he wanted AMDP to be allowed to set up a new Directorate of

Maintenance Design (DMD) to ensure that equipment was designed with due regard for ease of maintenance and repair, and to define the methods and standards of repair work.[47]

The aero-engine situation was happily different, as engine repairs were already controlled by the AMDP, and this scheme proved very successful. Predictably, Welsh pressed for engine repairs to be transferred to his department, and it was only steadfast opposition from Freeman which prevented this. His argument was simple enough. Unless those responsible for development were also responsible for repair, there was little chance of improving the performance and reliability of aero-engines. Freeman's expert staff alone had the technical knowledge to be able to insist that the latest improvements were built in to engines sent for overhaul or repair. Dismissing suggestions that 'it was a prestige matter for the CRO', Freeman explained,

> Lord Nuffield has taken on a gigantic task, [and] until we see repaired aircraft, guns, turrets, instruments and other equipment coming out ... it would be a mistake to saddle the civilian repair organisation with yet another problem.[48]

Five months earlier, in July 1939, the Air Council had accepted that the link between aero-engine production and repair should not be broken, but despite the Council's ruling, Freeman had again to defend his position before the Secretary of State in December, and it was not until March 1940 that the retention of engine repairs within his department was finally confirmed.[49]

Air Marshal Sir Christopher Courtney, Deputy Chief of the Air Staff in 1935/36, took over from Welsh as AMSO on 1 February 1940. Courtney was very able and he might have taken over Fighter Command from Dowding in 1939, had Dowding's retirement not been postponed. But he seems to have been unable to achieve very much on aircraft repairs in his first three months as AMSO. The CRO was run by Nuffield who only reported to AMSO, and Courtney may not have realised the seriousness of the situation at the repair depots. The sudden death of Oliver Boden, who could influence Nuffield, must have further disorganised the CRO, and large stocks of new or salvaged EL equipment, urgently required for new aircraft, accumulated at maintenance units and repair depots. The SBAC claimed that any repairs worth doing were being done by the aircraft industry, and that aircraft which could have been repaired were condemned for break up by the CRO. The Assistant Director of Aircraft Inspection, who worked for Freeman, concluded that the CRO simply did not understand when damage could be repaired and when it could not.[50]

Matters came to a head a month later, when reports reached Freeman, via Quentin Brand (now DMD), which revealed just how little practical repair and salvage work was being done.[51] More than 500 damaged aircraft were waiting to be dismantled for repair or write-off, and storage space at depots was so short that salvage teams were being asked not to send any more. The shortage of EL equipment was seriously hampering production of new aircraft and because of the desperate need to recover anything that could be repaired for reissue to the aircraft firms, Freeman went straight to the CAS and the Air Minister, and got permission to launch an inter-departmental raid by AHDP staff on the AMSO depot at Kidbrooke.

Reporting back to Newall on 5 May 1940, Freeman disclosed that every item of equipment which featured in the current shortages had been discovered, either serviceable or easily repairable. About 90,000 items of equipment awaiting repair had accumulated over many months, and it was thought that a further 30,000 had been retained by operational units. Only 2,000 items had actually been repaired by then, although forms for the repair of 65,000 had been issued. The incompetence of those responsible stunned Freeman. 'I cannot understand', he wrote, 'how Maintenance Command can have been unaware of a situation which is entirely within their control.'[52] Freeman knew that if adequate extra space was added to the producers' factories,[53] it would be far more economical in time, labour and materials to repair aircraft than to manufacture them 'de novo', and promptly diverted all repairable equipment to the component factories to get it serviceable as soon as possible.

NEW APPOINTMENTS AT THE AIR MINISTRY

In April 1940 the disappointing production figures, the chaos within the repairs organisation and the criticism from the Press and Parliament finally convinced the Cabinet that changes were needed at the Air Ministry, and Sir Samuel Hoare, previously Lord Privy Seal, exchanged jobs with Kingsley Wood. Hoare had been Air Minister in the 1920s, and was therefore much more experienced than his predecessor. Guided by members of the SBAC, who knew the work-load that Freeman was carrying, he promptly appointed Craven to the Air Council as the first full-time Civil Member for Development and Production. This position replaced that formerly held by Lemon, the DGP, but whereas Lemon had been Freeman's subordinate on the Air Council, Craven was made his equal. He immediately assumed many of Freeman's industrial responsibilities.

Freeman had worked with Craven on aircraft matters for the past four years, and if he had any reservations about this appointment, they would have concerned Craven's health,* not his experience or his ability. Hoare may in fact have meant Craven to replace Freeman – the 'top industrialist' alternative, for he offered Freeman the new post of Vice-Chief of Air Staff, which Freeman refused because he realised that the position would involve responsibility with very little power. The RAF was not at that stage equipped to make any significant offensive contribution to strategy, and the Government had very little idea how the Allies were going to defeat Germany: Freeman felt he could do more for the RAF where he was.

* Sir Charles Craven was a naval submariner who joined Vickers in 1918 becoming Chairman of Vickers Armstrongs in 1936. He was 'tough, able and coercively charming', but by 1940, still buoyant and energetic, he had overstrained his heart, and was frequently too ill to work. He died in 1944.

Marshal of the Royal Air Force Sir John Salmond. Freeman recommended that the former CAS should take over responsibility for the armament research, design and production departments.

Bill Payne, one of his ADCs, must actually have written to him suggesting that he take over as CAS, and Freeman passed on his letter to Elizabeth, commenting:

> It is a good summing up of the position. Of course, it is quite useless for me to take Cyril's* place, since I disagree so heartily with our position of wait and see. So far as I can see we have no strategy, no plan, no courage and no foresight. With these sort of views it is no good my making things more difficult and starting dissension.[54]

The change of ministers, and Craven's appointment, added to Freeman's workload at first. Hoare demanded information on new aircraft,[55] a matter about which Craven knew little, so it was Freeman who submitted a four-page response to the new Secretary of State on 22 April.[56] He also prepared other briefing notes for Craven setting out his priorities, and gave him the small notebook in which he kept data on aircraft performance. There was a pressing need for more capacity for Bristol's Hercules and Centaurus engines, for

* Air Chief Marshal Sir Cyril Newall, the Chief of Air Staff.

magnesium, and for machine-guns, but raw material supplies were the worst problem. Capacity for extrusions, forgings and stampings had to be rapidly increased, and the shortage of special alloy steels for engines was serious.[57] He advised Craven to amalgamate the armament research, design and production departments under the former CAS, Sir John Salmond. Conversely, he felt that Bulman, who was supervising both development and production of engines, had too big a load, and suggested dividing the two functions between separate departments. Craven took over as Chairman of the Supply Committee – which had met every day for the previous two years – and Freeman sent him a list of capital expenditure schemes which had been passed by the Treasury, costing in total more than £115 million. He added; 'Although I should not perhaps say so, this is a mere formality as I have never known the Council to disagree with any of the Committee's recommendations.'[58] Freeman also warned that there was only one factory making ceramic components for radio valves. This had originally been constructed by a German company, and as the Germans were fully aware of its location, and of its vital importance to the RAF, it was extremely vulnerable.[59]

While the fighting in Norway continued, a reassessment of German aircraft production for the CAS, calculated (erroneously in fact), that Germany was producing twice as many aircraft as Britain. When Hoare asked what could be done to increase the aircraft programme beyond 2,550 a month, Freeman called a meeting to consider the effect on output of concentrating on twin-engined medium bombers instead of two- or four-engined heavy bombers.

Their conclusion was that if production of medium bombers continued, and the introduction of heavy bombers was postponed, an extra 600-700 aircraft per month could be produced. To achieve this, however, more aluminium and steel would have to be imported, five existing airframe factories would have to be enlarged, and others converted, and more machine tools would have to be purchased. An extra 1,200 aero-engines would also be needed which would mean doubling the capacity of the Bristol shadow group and extending the Glasgow and Ford Merlin plants, neither of which could be in production for some time. It was obvious that a general switch to twin-engined designs would not produce significantly greater numbers of aircraft for at least eighteen months.[60]

CHAPTER 7

Aircraft design and development:
September 1939 to May 1940

THE WIDE RANGE of aircraft and engines with which Freeman was involved as AMDP and later, confronted him with constant design and development problems and difficult production decisions throughout the rearmament and wartime years, but the eight month period of the 'phoney war' was a good opportunity to review progress and plan future development. The doubts of the Government's hesitant rearmament policy had been resolved by the outbreak of war, and the phoney war period allowed major omissions, such as self-sealing petrol tanks, and supply bottlenecks, to be corrected before the 'dam broke'. Existing projects, many dating back to 1936, were reviewed, and new specifications, for more advanced military aircraft, or to meet unforseen operational requirements, were prepared.

By September 1939, the more successful aircraft ordered at the beginning of rearmament were coming into production, and early prototypes which had obvious defects, and engines that were defective, or faced insuperable weight or development problems, were cancelled. But aircraft designed to meet more recent specifications – fighters such as the Tornado/Typhoon and Whirlwind, and bombers such as the Stirling and Manchester – also ran into difficulties, and Freeman's wartime design programme has been criticised on that account. Although the de Havilland Mosquito was a shining exception to this generalisation, the hypercritical Correlli Barnett considered:

> 'the British wartime record in the design and development of new types of aircraft, and in the speed at which they were put into production, [to be] . . . markedly inferior to the American or even the German [record].'[1]

In fact, all the major countries had serious difficulties with most of their designs, and faced the same airframe and engine development problems and technical difficulties as Freeman. The production programme was too complicated and interdependent for rapid changes, and Freeman's policy, and his real task, was to maintain quality: to pick the winners, make the best possible use of the second-rate, and terminate production of the unsatisfactory, as soon as the factories concerned could be put to better use. He was willing 'to accept responsibility – to back his own judgement – and to run risks . . . qualities with which [he] was supremely endowed. Some of his most important and fruitful decisions such as . . . the Mosquito and . . . Whittle's jet were taken against formidable technical advice . . .'[2] The fact that the Americans were able to build huge factories that were immune from the risk of enemy bombing simply compounded the benefits derived from the sheer size and depth of an electronic and engineering industry serving 140 million people, and contributed greatly to the success of their aircraft production programme from 1941 onwards. Even so, apart from their naval aircraft, which were ordered by 'carrier' Admirals, and infinitely superior to most British naval aircraft, the ultimate success of their Army Air Force procurement policy was to owe much to Freeman's activities and advice.*

The technological revolution of the mid-1930s had confronted both the Air Ministry technicians and the designers of the aircraft industry with serious and fundamental problems. Mastering the new technology of the metal monoplane, with its need for hydraulic, electric or pneumatic control of undercarriage, flaps, turrets and airscrews was always certain to be a long and complex process, but the scale of the task was invariably underestimated. Competition for orders between aircraft firms often overburdened the capacity of their design teams, a factor which the Air Ministry initially overlooked when apportioning work, and technical staff, who were scarce, were dispersed among too many different projects. Hawker and Blackburn, for example, neither of whom maintained particularly large technical teams, received design contracts for no fewer than seven different types in 1936[3],†

Chamberlain's refusal to allow the Air Ministry to insist on priority for their work, meant that despite the Air Ministry's order for 600 Hurricanes in 1936, Hawkers continued to develop and produce (profitable) versions of their obsolete biplane aircraft for export, well into 1938. The diversion of effort to the design of other prototype aircraft like the P.4/34 bomber and the Hotspur turret fighter, may also have had side effects, but modifications such as substituting metal-cladding instead of Hawker's traditional fabric-covered wings would have come sooner, but for the lack of priority for RAF work.[4]

Freeman rationed new projects as soon as the shortage of design capacity became apparent, and thereafter the pace of aeronautical development in Britain was restricted by the availability of design capacity. Design teams were swamped by the service demands for modifications and refinements to existing models which emerged as soon as their aircraft were tested in war, and technical staff were diverted from longer-term development. Men were sometimes seconded between other companies, but de Havilland, which had concentrated their pre-war design efforts on the civil market, was one of the few firms with the capacity to start designing a new military aircraft in 1939.

THE MOSQUITO

Despite attempts to reduce the delays between design and production of a new aircraft, it remained a long and complex business. Orders could not be placed until a new specification had been agreed between Freeman's department, the Air Staff, – or the Admiralty if naval types were involved – and the

---

* A more technical summary of the problems and developments of the more important engines and aircraft is given in Appendices IX and X.

† Two of the types ordered from Blackburn were, however, 80 per cent interchangeable. The Air Ministry had detailed information about drawing office employment in the industry.

The graceful four-engined Albatross proved that de Havilland was capable of building wooden aircraft which met high performance specifications.

RAF Command for which the aircraft was being purchased, a process which could also be influenced by input from the aircraft industry and from government research establishments.

Disputes were frequent. The Director of Technical Development had complained in 1935, that '... Air Staff [requirements were] ... dotted about all over the specification',[5] and, nearly three years later, Freeman criticised Air Staff specifications for being 'far too detailed'. He went on to suggest that 'specifications should be simplified to the extent of concentrating on the fundamental requirements, leaving more latitude to designers than at present.'[6] Sometimes the reverse was true: orders for the de Havilland 'Don' trainer were ruthlessly cut when the weight of the extra RAF equipment, added *after* it had been designed, overloaded the airframe.[7]

In September 1939, Freeman resumed work on the concept of an unarmed high-speed bomber, which ultimately emerged as the de Havilland Mosquito, one of the finest British aircraft of the Second World War. The idea had been discussed with Geoffrey de Havilland more than once since February 1938. Merlin-powered adaptations of both the Albatross and the Flamingo had been considered, despite the Air Ministry's reservations about de Havilland's design record.* But the timing of de Havilland's first offer of a new, smaller, bomber, in which armament was sacrificed for speed, had been wrong. Nevertheless the technical and production successes of their 1934 racing monoplane, the Comet, and the sleek and uniquely beautiful four-engined wooden airliner,

---

* Apart from the Don, accidents to Puss Moths in the 1930s had been due to a structural defect.

the Albatross*, had proved that de Havilland was capable of building wooden aircraft which met – indeed exceeded – performance expectations, and achieving a demanding development schedule.

Freeman by then could marshal a formidable range of compelling arguments in favour of an unarmed, high speed aircraft. The difficulties of developing and producing adequate gun turrets had been such that, in 1937, many bombers had been delivered before their defensive armament could be fitted:[8] redesign of their armament installations delayed deliveries of the Handley Page Hampden and the Avro Manchester for months.[9] The effect of such turrets on aircraft handling was unpredictable, and sometimes interfered disastrously with their flying characteristics, whilst aerodynamics showed that the performance of faster aircraft could be significantly enhanced by eliminating external protrusions.

Before the Mosquito could be ordered, however, Freeman's department had to get agreement from the Air Staff and Bomber Command, and there was strong opposition from each of them. The technical 'minefield' through which this specification had to pass illustrates all too clearly the prejudices and lack of operational foresight that so nearly rejected its development.

On 20 September 1939 de Havilland proposed the design of a wooden bomber powered by two Merlins, with a crew of two, and a range of 1,500 miles, carrying a 1,500lb bomb load at an exceptionally high speed – a concept which closely matched the requirements for an unarmed bomber which Freeman had formulated in February 1938. Tedder's response confirmed that Freeman had been hard at work on the project, well before war started, and he suggested that de Havilland should plan for a 2,000lb bomb load[†] and a 2,000 mile range, insisting nevertheless that the complete absence of defensive armament 'was not generally accepted: its acceptance would depend very much on the additional speed it would permit, as demonstrated in tests on the prototype.'[10]

Tedder instinctively disliked the idea of an unarmed bomber, and whilst de Havilland forecast a maximum speed of 405mph, and a cruising speed of 320mph (which was faster than most contemporary fighters), Liptrot's estimates of 350 and 325mph respectively, were based on the assumption that the aircraft would be heavier than forecast, and would use more fuel.[11] Other Air Ministry doubters considered de Havilland's figures scanty, and were even more pessimistic.[12] Fresh estimates were then made, showing the effect of adding a gun turret.

When de Havilland design staff and the Air Ministry's technical experts met in Harrogate on 14 October 1939, de Havilland were pressed to consider the inclusion of rearward-facing guns in unpowered positions like those of the Hampden, and the subsequent series of meetings all confirmed the size of

---

* The Albatross was ordered in January, 1936 and the aircraft and its new engines were ready for the first flight in May 1937: the first production aircraft had been delivered in October 1938, and averaged 219mph delivering mail to Cairo, that Christmas.

† This was double the 1,000lb capacity of the Blenheim, then just coming into service.

the credibility gap.* Most of the technicians and Air Force officers simply did not believe de Havilland's performance forecasts, and were determined to encumber the aircraft with a defensive turret. Various alternatives were considered and rejected. Sholto Douglas, by then ACAS, called for 'a Griffin- (*sic*) engined bomber with a 4-gun turret',[13] but de Havilland warned that even if the Griffon came into production before 1942, it would take two years to design and produce such an aircraft.

Despite the Air Ministry's doubts, there was agreement that a new design should be ordered from the company on production grounds alone. The de Havilland design team was not engaged in any other military work; their experience of wooden construction was well established, and there was already strong official interest in the development of a wooden or composite aircraft which would not impose further demands on Britain's scarce aluminium resources. An order for two prototypes was considered, one unarmed with a crew of two, and another with a rear turret and an extra gunner, but when Douglas minuted Freeman on 20 November 1939, confirming that the Air Staff's requirements were for an aircraft with 'a bomb load of 1,000 lb, and a range of 1,500 miles at a speed high enough to make interception by the contemporary fighter difficult if not impossible ... not be less than 350 mph', his failure to recognize the potential of the concept is shown by his added comment:

> As it is almost certain that the highest speed which we can get would still not enable the bomber altogether to avoid being intercepted by fighters, we must have some defensive armaments.[14]

Confident that de Havilland could design an unarmed aircraft which really was fast, Freeman's reply 'nailed' the fallacy of insisting on a gun turret, for he wrote on 22 November:

> You want a bomber so fast that it will have the legs of an enemy fighter ... [but] you decide that it will not be fast enough ... and will therefore make it slower by adding defensive armament, and it is probable that you will achieve a compromise which will not fit the bill in either of these two characteristics. It seems to me that we must rely on engine development to give us what we want, and I am inclined to think that we should aim at getting a new bomber into the air each year, sacrificing everything for speed. If we bank on the compromise, we will have to turn out in 1941 a bomber with a speed of 350 mph with two Griffon engines and a four-gun turret. This machine can not be either quickly designed or quickly manufactured, since the turret and hydraulics complicate matters to an extraordinary extent. Moreover, in this case I very much doubt whether the Griffon engines would be available.[15]

He then attended a pre-arranged meeting at Harrogate between his department and the de Havilland designers, and went much further than Tedder in

---

* De Havilland thought this would delay production of the prototype, and reduce speed by 25–30 mph .

meeting the firm's request for a production order. Freeman envisaged a series of aircraft, based on the same concept, starting with a twin-Merlin aircraft of 350mph, then a twin-Griffon model of 370–380mph, and finally a twin-Sabre model with a speed of over 400mph, to enter service in 1942.* His far-reaching proposals must have rather stunned the de Havilland staff, for he agreed that if the firm would guarantee to produce an unarmed Merlin aircraft within nine months, and then start building the Griffon-engined successor, and subsequently a Sabre-engined version, 'he would be prepared to recommend it to the Air Council, ... as a gamble.'[16]

From the start, Freeman's wish to order a new aircraft from de Havilland had been opposed by Ludlow-Hewitt, the AOC-in-C, Bomber Command, who was anxious to obtain a new high-speed bomber as soon as possible. He rightly feared that building an aircraft from scratch would impose further delays, but wanted to adapt the 300mph Beaufighter as a bomber, a solution which missed the whole point of Freeman's concept.[17]

Luckily, by November 1939, Freeman had recognized that there was a need for a new specification: a very fast and very high flying photo-reconnaissance (PR) aircraft,[18] first requested by Bomber Command in March 1939. 'War experience has shown', he wrote, 'the need for a very fast unarmed aircraft for reconnaissance and photographic duties at high altitude.'[19] Moreover the two high-speed specifications, for a PR aircraft and an unarmed bomber, overlapped,† and a minute by Farren on 23 November summarised the RAF's requirements from de Havilland as a two-seat long-range reconnaissance aircraft with no defensive armament, which could be developed into a high-speed bomber; he specified a weight of 18,500lb and a top speed of 370mph.[20] An outline of the provisional specification, as discussed with de Havilland by Farren, is dated 23 November 1939.

Anxious to thrash out an agreed requirement as soon as possible, Freeman summoned all the interested parties to meetings on 7 December 1939, but at the last moment, Douglas must have asked for them to be postponed, and held in London, starting at 10.30 on 12 December.[21] Freeman therefore arranged for his team to have an earlier meeting with the de Havilland team, at which he told them that detailed requirements for the aircraft would be finalised later that day.[22] Despite the Air Ministry's emphasis on defensive armament at previous discussions, Freeman now decided to commit himself to de Havilland's original concept of an unarmed design, and told them that 'the firm were to look on him as the ultimate authority on requirements, and were not to take instructions from anyone else', stressing that 'speed of production was of first importance'. He wanted an unarmed, two-seat, twin-Merlin model, with the highest possible speed.[23]

---

* Subsequent references to the projected 'Griffon Mosquito' show that Freeman realised the extra weight of the larger engines meant that the original airframe could not be used unmodified.
† The structure of the PR version was very similar to that of the bomber alternative. Conversion from one to the other was much easier than altering the day and night fighter fuselages, with their cannon armament.

By the time they joined Douglas, Ludlow-Hewitt and other representatives from the Air Staff, Freeman had made up his mind, and brought Tedder, Lemon, Farren and the rest of his staff firmly into line. Douglas chaired the meeting and repeated his ill-founded argument that an unarmed bomber aircraft would be a poor compromise. Freeman's response was that speed versus armament was the crux of the question and that, from the production point of view, the provision of armament would delay and disrupt the present programme. Tedder supported Freeman's argument and the two men worked together and persuaded the meeting that, on production and technical grounds, the aircraft should be unarmed. The alternatives proposed by Bomber Command would have insufficient speed and ineffective armament.

Freeman suggested that it would be necessary to build two distinct types, the unarmed bomber and the photo-reconnaissance aircraft: the former would have to be re-engined each year to maintain its ascendancy over contemporary fighters. Buchanan, Deputy Director General of Production, then confirmed that a wooden aircraft could be designed and produced quickly; de Havilland's design staff were under-employed and could start work on the project immediately. A wooden aircraft could be developed much more rapidly than a metal one, scarce aluminium would not be required, and there were plenty of skilled craftsmen from the woodworking industry.[24]

Wilfrid Freeman with the Hon. Richard Casey, the Australian member of the War cabinet, A.S. Butler, the Chairman of the de Havilland Company, and Major Hereward de Havilland (Geoffrey de Havilland's brother), at a demonstration of the Mosquito's amazing versatility at Hatfield.

Despite his personal commitment, and the cogent arguments in favour of an unarmed bomber, Freeman still lacked authority to place an order for the bomber version without a Bomber Command requisition, and Ludlow-Hewitt stubbornly maintained that he had no operational use for an unarmed aircraft, except for photo-reconnaissance work. The first order for 50 aircraft was therefore agreed on the understanding that they would be used for photographic reconnaissance, though this would not preclude the development of bomber and fighter variants.[25] A revised draft of the Air Staff requirements, of which paragraph 4 confirmed that 'the total elimination of defensive armament is proposed', was sent to de Havilland by Farren on 12 December, immediately after the meeting with Douglas.[26] Three weeks later, when the order had finally been placed, Freeman summoned Buchanan and J.V. Connolly, from the Department of Aircraft Production, to a meeting with Geoffrey de Havilland on 1 January 1940: de Havilland put outline drawings on the table, and there and then, Buchanan and Connolly drew up specification B.1/40, for the aircraft which became the Mosquito.[27]

With official interference kept to a minimum, the Mosquito's design was uncompromising, and because of its unconventional wooden construction, it was assembled very quickly. Apart from insisting that the aircraft should not be armed, Freeman made other provisions that were essential for its rapid development. The airframe was to be as simple as possible, incorporating the minimum of equipment; parts which could be made without drawings would be developed in de Havilland's experimental department to the requirements of the drawing office, and the normal interchangeability regulations would be waived for the first batch of aircraft.[28]

The result was so unlike any other warplane that for the first two years of its existence it was known as 'Freeman's Folly'. He was its champion and its main defender, and without his support, Douglas and Ludlow-Hewitt would have killed it in 1939 – or Portal in December 1940. It was July 1940, before the Air Ministry finally accepted de Havilland's proposals for making a fighter version, and July 1941 before the company was at last allowed to proceed with the unarmed bomber alternative. 'Failure is an orphan; success has many parents', but Freeman was unquestionably the Mosquito's single parent. Although its development, and operational success as a bomber was retarded by a prolonged failure to make best use of its remarkable qualities,[29] it ultimately proved to be one of the finest and most versatile military aircraft of the Second World War.

The Mosquito was almost unique in that variants with single-stage Merlins like those of the prototype, continued in production until the end of the war. Freeman had expected to instal more powerful engines in larger versions of the basic aircraft in the future, but the Mosquito's exceptionally 'clean' aerodynamic form enabled it to outpace enemy fighters when operating at its

OPPOSITE: **Freeman's Folly** – three variants of the Mosquito which show its amazing versatility: (*top*) W4051, the prototype reconnaissance version; (*centre*) W4052, the prototype fighter; (*bottom*) B. Mk IV, the first bomber version to go into service.

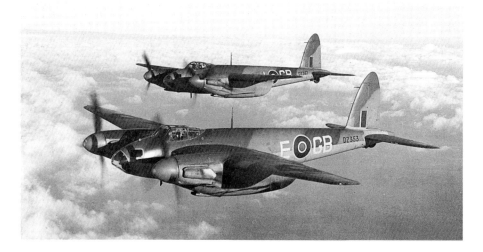

proper altitude*.[30] Greater performance would be achieved by installing two-stage Merlins, and by a simple enlargement of the bomb-bay which doubled the weight of bombs that could be carried.

But the almost 'effortless' success of the Mosquito airframe was exceptional:[†] many of the prototypes which Freeman ordered needed extensive modification, and some failed altogether.

DEVELOPMENT FAILURES

Three of the Blackburn designs, the Skua, the Roc and the Botha proved unsatisfactory. Some of their defects were due to the compromises required by the range of duties required of them by the Admiralty, but all three aircraft were overweight, and underpowered by their Perseus engines.[31‡] The Skua and the Roc were top-heavy, and the Skua's fuselage had to be lengthened by 2ft 5in because it was far too unstable, longitudinally.[32] The Botha, as a torpedo-bomber, was also a failure, unable to maintain level flight on one engine, and production was finally stopped in September 1940.[33] Blackburn also made a flying boat on which both hull and wing floats were retractable. It was powered by two Vulture engines and proved to be very fast, but the operational requirement for a heavy flying boat with a speed of 340mph was questionable, and when the prototype broke up during a high-speed run, killing the pilot, the project was cancelled.[34]

Freeman's lack of confidence in the competence of the Blackburn design team extended also to Saunders Roe, as both their new flying boats proved to be disastrous failures. Their four-engined parasol-winged prototype combined structural weaknesses with an inability to take off in adverse sea conditions, and its whole wing structure collapsed before it was airborne.[35] Their Lerwick flying boat was almost as bad. It was intended to replace the Sunderland, but had a tendency to swing viciously during take-off – and could not take off with a full service load. Its single-engine performance was unacceptably bad, and operation of the gun turrets in flight caused loss of control.[36] The RAF's attempts to improve the aircraft's flying characteristics were unavailing; only 21 were made, and the production line of the Short Sunderland had to be reinstated when the Lerwick was cancelled.

Inevitably, the new fighters were not without development troubles, but the worst problems with Hurricanes and Spitfires were over by 1940. Production was rising steadily, and the first set of modifications, such as three-bladed, variable-pitch propellers and 100 octane fuel for both aircraft, and two-speed superchargers for the Hurricanes, came through in time for

---

* Tests confirmed that when operating above 20,000ft, the Mosquito could outpace most enemy fighters, by gaining speed in a gentle dive. The German radar usually failed to predict the course of intruders in time for conventional fighters, climbing at speeds of about 220mph, to be able to intercept, and attack Mosquitoes cruising at 320mph, and capable of 380–400mph.

† Apart from buffeting of the tailplane at high speeds, cured by enlarging it and lengthening the engine nacelles, even the prototype was virtually faultless; it achieved 392mph in May, 1941.

‡ Freeman had flatly refused to allow Bristol to instal Perseus engines in the Beaufort, and insisted on the Taurus; this was more powerful, – but even more unreliable than the Perseus!

The second Typhoon. Note the thick wing – which affected its handling at speed – and the position of the engine; roughly half the engine was behind the leading edge of the wing because fuel was carried in the wings not the fuselage.

the Battle of Britain, and gave significant increases in performance. By then, Freeman had reconciled himself to the certainty that alternative fighters with a superior performance would not be available for a year or more: he would have to rely on improved versions of these two.

Hawker's new fighters, the Vulture-powered Tornado and the Sabre-powered Typhoon, had many engine and airframe problems. The Tornado's first flight was in October 1939, the Typhoon's in February 1940, and neither could be expected to enter service for another 18 months. The decision to stop Vulture production caused the Tornado production line to be dismantled: Hawker then concentrated on the Typhoon, but the thick wing affected its handling at speed, and Freeman asked for a new, 'thin-winged' version, the Typhoon II in 1940. Their Sabre engines were desperately unreliable, and performed badly at height although other defects, such as a cockpit hood with no rear vision, were easily remedied. The help of the RAE was needed to identify a design defect in the elevator mass balance as the reason why the tail sometimes broke off in flight.[37]

Fortunately the steady development of the Rolls-Royce Merlin, and the remarkable development potential of, and appropriate improvements to, Mitchell's superb Spitfire airframe, were to ensure that the RAF had a 'combat fighter' which was technically superior for most of the war years – a potential that was difficult to forecast before 1941.

The cannon fighter was another technical 'cul-de-sac'. The Air Ministry had recognised the need for 20mm cannons to replace .303 machine-guns as early as 1937, but assumed that the cannons would be too heavy to be fitted in the wings of the new single-engined monoplanes. Their new specification therefore called for twin-engined aircraft, mounting the cannons in the nose, and the Westland Whirlwind, and Bristol Beaufighter were chosen*. Teddy Petter, Westland's chief designer, decided to use 21-litre Rolls-Royce Peregrine engines instead of heavier Merlins, to keep the size of the airframe to the minimum required to carry four 20mm cannons in its fuselage. The airframe of the prototype Whirlwind had design faults and aerodynamic problems, and by the time these had been overcome, 20mm cannons had been successfully installed in the wings of conventional fighters, and development of the Peregrine had stopped. The Whirlwind airframe was too small to take Merlins instead, so production was halted: the limited number delivered by Westland were used as low-level fighter-bombers.

There was nothing fundamentally wrong with the concept of a twin-engined fighter, but they were invariably heavier than 'singles', and thus less manoeuvrable, a disadvantage that was compounded by the extra fuel capacity to give them a longer range. The Beaufighter was slower than the Whirlwind, but its Merlin or Hercules engines remained in production, and it was larger and could carry a navigator, bombs and torpedoes, so output continued, and it performed well in various roles.

A detailed account of the full development history of the aircraft ordered by Freeman would be lengthy, and although he was faced by the same procurement problems as the other services – and those of the other combatant nations – the remarkable success of his track record will emerge in later chapters.

ENGINE DEVELOPMENT

The massive advances in performance from the last 1930s biplane fighters, with top speeds of 220–250mph, to the 330–360mph of the early monoplane fighters, and from 150–180mph to 250–280mph for the bombers, owed much to better streamlining and aerodynamics, but most to the increased power of larger engines, better superchargers, 100 octane fuel, and variable-pitch propellers.

All the main powers expected that future, and roughly comparable gains in aircraft performance would emerge from the design and installation of even larger engines, and planned their production for new fighters and bombers. Freeman expected similar progress, and made plans to use Vultures and Sabres widely: development of the Griffon and the Centaurus were authorised by 1939. But he was quick to realise that developing the larger engines to give great power reliably was a slow process: significant gains in performance were likely to demand a disproportionate investment in research and development.

Enormous technical problems were encountered with all the biggest engines; there were long delays before their introduction, and some were eventually cancelled. Britain stopped production of the Vulture, and experienced acute difficulties with the Sabre; the Griffon had to be redesigned to accept a two-stage supercharger, and cooling problems with the Centaurus delayed its

* Mitchell at Supermarine designed a Merlin-powered alternative, but the firm was too busy on Spitfires and their B.12/36 prototype.

use. Germany devoted a massive technical effort to the huge Junkers Jumo 213 and the Daimler Benz 603 engines, but their design difficulties were endless, 'with the result that factory space was tied up unproductively for considerable periods of time'.[38] In the USA, although development of the 18-cylinder Wright R-3350 engine started in 1936, its reliability was still disastrously bad in 1943, and the company was under such pressure that engines which were known to be defective were actually issued.[39]

Apart from the challenges of different technologies, the Air Ministry and aircraft industry faced serious problems accommodating military requirements in new aircraft. The failure of the de Havilland Don was relatively unimportant, but when the performance of the Stirling fell short of expectations, the effects were much more serious. Designed to meet the B12/36 specification *for a bomber/transport* to carry 24 troops, the Stirling was 17ft longer than the other two heavy bombers, the Halifax and the Manchester/Lancaster,* and apart from its longer fuselage the Stirling had been strengthened so as to be capable of being launched with catapult assistance.[40] The prototype was destroyed when the undercarriage collapsed, but although its handling characteristics were excellent, and its wing loading was less than the Lancaster's, the extra weight and the shortcomings of its Hercules engines meant that at cruise power the available hp/lb was 30 per cent less than the Lancaster at 15,000ft.

Most of the aircraft ordered for the RAF during the first rearmament schemes were, in fact, extremely successful, despite the complexity of service requirements, and Freeman went out of his way to simplify Air Ministry specifications: the Mosquito clearly benefited.

By contrast, most of the aircraft designed to Admiralty specifications proved unsatisfactory; problems which the Senior Service never recognized as 'home baked'. Because the 18in torpedo was very fragile,† the Admiralty selected the 160mph biplane Albacore as a replacement for the 130mph Swordfish, in 1937, instead of a monoplane, and throughout the rearmament years it failed to identify the potential value of the RAF's modern single-seater land fighters for fleet carriers. Admiralty fighter specifications still insisted on two-seater aircraft as late as 1939, and the crucial importance of high performance in fleet fighters was only acknowledged after the commencement of hostilities. Small wonder, then, that such confused specifications as 'torpedo-spotter-reconnaissance' or 'fighter-dive-bomber' rarely produced aeroplanes of very great operational utility. Indeed, they provide the best illustrations of how a multiplicity of service requirements 'Jack of all trades' specifications, prepared by the Navy on the basis of what seemed operationally desirable, rather than technically feasible, inexorably reduced the ultimate quality of aircraft design.[41]

---

* A Stirling fuselage was 87ft long; the empty aircraft weighed 43,200lb. Comparable figures for the Lancaster were 69.5ft and 36,900lb, for the Halifax 70ft and 38,240lb. The wing loadings, empty, were: Stirling: 33.8 lb/sq.ft, Lancaster; 35.14 lb/sq.ft, Halifax: 33.3 lb/sq.ft.
† It had to be dropped at a slow speed, by an aircraft flying very near the water.

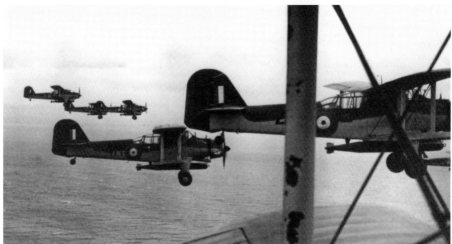

TOP: **The primitive Swordfish** could operate off small carriers and when not opposed by modern fighters was successful. This Swordfish I is flying over *Ark Royal*. It could carry a torpedo, depth charges, bombs or mines and had a maximum speed of 138 mph.
BOTTOM: **The Albacore** was the 'saloon version' of the Swordfish, hampered by its Taurus engines. With a maximum speed of 161 mph it could carry a torpedo or up to 2,000 lb of bombs.

The shortcomings of Admiralty specifications help to explain the high incidence of design failure at Blackburn, who specialised in naval work.

Freeman recognized that aircraft technology was going through a period of rapid transition and was resigned to the likelyhood that some of the types he selected would be technically unsatisfactory. Unlike the policy of concentration pursued by the German Air Ministry which (disastrously) gambled on single designs for most operational functions, he ordered more than one design for each military role, as insurance against failure.

By 1941, the British programme would be producing outstanding new aircraft like the Lancaster and the Mosquito to spearhead the strategic bombing offensive for the remainder of the war, while the German design programme was on the brink of near total collapse. Aircraft like the Heinkel He177, the Junkers Ju288, and the Messerschmitt Me210 and 410 were

The He 177. Selected as the only GAF heavy bomber for quantity production, it was a disastrous choice. Daimler-Benz never perfected the huge 72-litre double DB606 engines, and it proved impossible to stress it for dive-bombing as Hitler insisted.

plagued by technical problems and consistently failed to match performance targets.[42] The American P-38 was structurally unsafe above an indicated air speed of 375mph, the mid-engined Airacobra P-39 was armed with guns of three different calibres, and too short-ranged and slow for air fighting: the two–stage Allison needed for its successor, the P-63, was developed too late for production. The early B-17s, without turbo-chargers, and front and rear power-operated turrets, would have been slaughtered by the German fighters, and the RAF had to supply the 8th Air Force with Spitfires in 1942, because the P-39s, P-40s and early P-38s could not compete against the Luftwaffe FW190s and Me109Gs in Western Europe.[43] Spitfires were the only fighters to operate with the 8th AAF from 26 July 1942 to 5 April 1943.

There were technical failures in Britain too, but had Freeman remained in charge between May, 1940 and October, 1942, they would have been identified promptly, and if correction was not feasible, production runs would have been promptly curtailed. Until he returned as Chief Executive of the Ministry of Aircraft Production however, such decisiveness was unusual, and problems were rarely rectified. But his achievements after he returned to MAP would show that his control of military aircraft procurement was far more effective than that of his German rivals.

Two of the papers that Freeman prepared for Samuel Hoare when he became Secretary of State for Air, are summarised at Appendix II. Hoare concluded that the first priority was for 'long range bombers in much greater numbers', and he questioned the decision to put three different heavy bombers into production. When Churchill replaced Chamberlain as Prime Minister, on 10 May 1940, Hoare was sent off to Spain as Ambassador, and the compliant Liberal leader, Sir Archibald Sinclair, installed as Secretary of State for Air. A civilian Ministry of Aircraft Production was formed from Freeman's department, and as an RAF officer, without executive powers, Freeman found himself working for the new minister, the Canadian press baron, Lord Beaverbrook.

CHAPTER 8

'Magic is nine-tenths illusion' – the Beaverbrook myth

W HILE THE GOVERNMENT'S CONDUCT of the Norwegian campaign was being debated, and heavily criticised, in the House of Commons on 9 May 1940, Freeman gloomily forecast an imminent German offensive against France and the Low Countries.[1] 'Every ounce of her strength will be behind the effort', he wrote. Chamberlain resigned as the German attack started on 10th May, and when Churchill formed a coalition government, he replaced Hoare as Air Minister and set up a new Ministry of Aircraft Production (MAP) by transferring the Air Ministry's Development and Production organisation to it, including its joint heads, Freeman and Craven – a decision which seriously hampered production and development of aircraft over the next two or three years.

Churchill believed that the governments of the 1930s had not paid adequate attention to his warnings about the danger which the new German Air Force posed to Britain, and had persuaded himself that the Royal Air Force could by then have been equipped with many more modern aircraft if the Air Ministry had been more competently managed. His experience as Minister of Munitions in the First World War had convinced him that output could be increased by placing production under a civilian ministry, by 'cutting red tape', and by active political propaganda. Knowing nothing about aircraft production, he failed to recognize that rebuilding the RAF and the British aircraft industry would take *time*. Time and expert planning and massive financial help had been required to set up the infrastructure to supply the raw materials, construct the factories for mass production and equip them with jigs and modern machine tools, without which mere 'enthusiasm' would be ineffective. Aircraft had to be designed and developed to the new technology of the all-metal monoplane, and large, well tested aero-engines selected and put into production: workers had to be trained to make them. Even the pilots and aircrews could not be produced by magic, requiring aerodromes, training aircraft and instructors.

Control of the new ministry was given to one of Churchill's oldest friends, the newspaper magnate, Lord Beaverbrook, whose optimism and reputed power to inspire and drive seemed to Churchill qualities that were necessary to invigorate aircraft production at this crisis of the war, – and by doing so, Churchill also secured the support of the Beaverbrook newspapers.* Even

---

* Churchill had been ruthlessly excluded from office before the war by the Baldwin and Chamberlain governments, and was far from confident that he would be loyally supported by all the Conservative Members of Parliament.

before Beaverbrook had taken up office, the Germans were streaming across the Meuse at Sedan, and more than half the RAF aircraft in France were out of action after four days of fighting. There seemed little prospect of halting the German advance, and the Air Council realised that Britain might soon be attacked by aircraft based in Holland and Belgium – possibly even in northern France. The maximum number of aircraft would be needed as soon as possible.

As soon as Beaverbrook was appointed, two experienced Civil Servants were brought in to run his private office, and a third, Archibald Rowlands, was transferred from the Treasury to become the Permanent Under-Secretary of the new ministry. Beaverbrook summoned a few of his old friends to help him, many of them useless, but he also added some able industrialists. Patrick Hennessey, general manager of Ford in the UK, was soon given control of raw material production, while Mittman, of Northern Aluminium and Devereux of High Duty Alloys were placed in charge of light alloys; between them they supervised a further expansion of material capacity. Trevor Westbrook, the former general manager of Vickers Aviation, was put in charge of repairs, and made responsible for reorganising the Castle Bromwich aircraft factory. Craven agreed to work on as CMDP, Tedder remained DGRD, and Freeman remained AMDP and the senior Air Force officer in the Ministry.*

Beaverbrook ran the MAP from Stornoway House, his London home, until he could take over suitable offices and, after failing to commandeer the Shell-Mex building on the Strand from the Petroleum Board,† he took over ICI's building at Millbank.

Transfer to a civilian ministry left Freeman's position ill defined and his responsibilities divided. He was nominally chief executive of the MAP, and most of his working hours were spent advising his new minister, but despite his rank and experience, the fact that he was not a Civil Servant meant that he had no executive powers in the new civilian ministry. As AMDP and a member of the Air Council, however, he continued to be jointly responsible for administering the RAF, sitting on promotion boards, and advising Sinclair on RAF policy matters other than aircraft production. When, on 27th May, he was promoted to Air Chief Marshal at Beaverbrook's request, the ultimate decision had to be taken by Sinclair.

The invidiousness of Freeman's position soon became clear as the MAP found itself locked in series of jurisdictional disputes with the Air Ministry, which had not taken kindly to losing control of aircraft development and production. The close links between the RAF, which used the aircraft, and the aircraft industry, which supplied them, were thereby to be seriously impaired, for control of selection and supply had been given to politicians and civil servants, with different aims and priorities to those of the Royal Air Force.

* According to Kingston McCloughry, Courtney was also considered for this post.
† Beaverbrook did not accept his defeat by Sir Andrew Agnew, head of the Petroleum Board, which was based at Shell-Mex House, with dignity and the disgraceful story of his attempted revenge is given in Appendix IV.

Beaverbrook frankly asserted his 'definite and declared policy ... to pay no attention to the Service's requirements as stated by the Air Ministry. The MAP should be the judge as to what the Service should get'.[2]

The most immediate and serious of these disputes concerned the anomalous status of the Civilian Repair Organization. But for Kingsley Wood's decision to put Nuffield in charge of aircraft repairs and create the CRO, the transfer of that responsibility from the AMSO's department to the AMDP's might have gone through in September 1939, when it was first suggested by Freeman. Newall had confirmed that the best interests of the RAF were much more important than the sanctity of departmental divisions within the Air Ministry, when he allowed Freeman's staff to investigate the state of the repair depots in April and May 1940, and had MAP not been created, jurisdiction over salvage and repair might well have been transferred to Freeman, within the Air Ministry, in May or June.

Once AMDP's department had become a separate ministry however, Sinclair, Newall and Courtney became deeply concerned by the prospect of further reductions of the Air Ministry's functions and stubbornly defended Nuffield against Beaverbrook's demand for control over the CRO.[3]

Freeman had no option but to take Beaverbrook's side on the matter. Well before MAP's creation, the evidence of mounting chaos in the repair depots* had convinced him that Nuffield's executive control over repairs must be ended, and a firm departmental link between the aircraft production and repair branches re-established. The onset of active hostilities after the end of the 'phoney war' had created a veritable flood of salvage and repair work which overwhelmed the totally inadequate repairs organisation, and Freeman realised that the interests of the country and the RAF must have priority over the niceties of departmental self-esteem. In the desperate military circumstances of May-June 1940, any changes which helped to supply the Royal Air Force squadrons should not be opposed.

He was also quick to realise that Beaverbrook's attention was focused almost exclusively on one single aspect of his job, the production of new aircraft; everything else would be subordinated to that end. Spares production, vital to aircraft repair and maintenance, was bound to suffer, the problems of the repair organisation would remain unsolved, and serviceability levels would fall. If, however, repairs were transferred to the MAP, Beaverbrook would get credit for the growing number of repaired aircraft reaching the Aircraft Storage Units (ASUs), and might be less reluctant to divert resources away from new production into spares.

Immediate action was urgently needed, and once Freeman had explained the situation, Beaverbrook began the administrative changes needed to transfer the salvage and repair system from Nuffield's incompetent grasp.

But for a man with Beaverbrook's newspaper background, a more dramatic change seemed necessary, in the light of the disastrous news of the German

* Clearing the backlog left by the Air Ministry, Tedder's men found about 1500 airscrews at the Ruislip repair depot; Kidbrooke yielded 331 wireless sets.

breakthrough in France. The conclusions of the AMDP's meeting about making more twin-engined bombers and fewer four-engined ones[4] had been reported to Hoare on 12th May, just before MAP was set up, and Beaverbrook saw them and decided that until the end of September 1940, everything in the way of production should be sacrificed to increase the output of five types: the Wellington, Whitley and Blenheim bombers discussed in Freeman's memorandum, and the Hurricane and Spitfire fighters.

Beaverbrook issued the ministerial instruction giving priority to the 'big five' and to all 'materials, equipment, engines etc., which can possibly be used to accelerate deliveries' on 18 May 1940.[5] He disregarded Freeman's warnings about the immediate shortage of engines and the long-term effect of his decision on the quality of aircraft in service, but demanded that other measures advocated by Freeman should 'be taken at once' and having committed himself to this strategy he refused at first to alter it. It's propaganda value appealed to him and he cared too little about the long-term future of aircraft production to recognize that the potential benefits were strictly limited.

In fact, the effect on the planned production of other types of engines and aircraft would have been disastrous if an absolute priority had been enforced and maintained for a long period. The 'big five' policy involved the cancellation of orders for thousands of heavy bombers, the reduction of orders for other types, and the withdrawal of aircraft, pilots and personnel from experimental stations and drawing offices where the next generation of aircraft and engines were being tested and developed. Production at the new Hercules engine factories was delayed by the transfer of machine tools to the plants producing the older Mercury and Pegasus engines for Blenheims and Wellingtons. Fedden was summoned home from New York on 19 May[6] and the offer by General Motors to build the Bristol Centaurus engine in America was rejected because Beaverbrook had forbidden all long-term development projects.

Frustrated by months of inaction from Nuffield, Welsh and Courtney, Freeman admired the ruthless way Beaverbrook forced through the administrative changes which transferred the entire salvage and repair organisation to the MAP and the speed at which it was integrated it into the MAP.[7] Nobody else, he felt, could have made such radical changes in such a short time, and fought so relentlessly to get the maximum priorities over plant, materials and labour.

> I wouldn't have believed it was possible for anyone to go on as [Beaverbrook] does, day after day, with only six hours off. His house is always packed, mostly with politicians, [but with] a sprinkling of industrialists. The odds against us at times seem overwhelming; that's one advantage in the Beaver, he does lessen the odds and over-ride difficulties as no other politician would do, or even dare to attempt.[8]

Beaverbrook's solution to one particular bottleneck, the shortage of presses for extruded alloy sections, was a typical example of the unorthodox approach which so impressed Freeman. The acknowledged expert in their design was

Ludwig Loewy, a German Jew who had fled to England with his staff in 1938, and although Loewy had been allowed to continue his work after the outbreak of war, many of his assistants were interned. Having learned of this, Beaverbrook simply sent a couple of German-speaking Jews round all the internment camps on his ministerial authority, and Loewy's colleagues and other experienced aircraft engineers were rescued and put to work for the MAP, regardless of security regulations. Their employment raised a storm of protest which Beaverbrook ignored.[9]

In the very short-term, two or three hundred more aircraft may have been obtained by concentrating on the 'big five', but Freeman was very sceptical about the policy. The emergency was such that he accepted that there were grounds for suspending long-term research projects, but important plans to develop the so-called 'ideal bomber', the B. 1/39, and produce 0.5 in- machine-gun turrets, the *immediate repercussions* of which would have little effect, were actually cancelled.* He firmly resisted, however, the complete cessation of research and development work and continually reminded Beaverbrook that the 'big five' strategy 'could not go on without complete disorganisation'. Beaverbrook eventually agreed that the policy would be halted on 1st July, 'but in the meanwhile he was determined to be a driving force to try and obtain maximum output by any method, no matter how irregular'.[10]†

Forced to accept the short-term priorities imposed by the emergency, Freeman went on trying to get Beaverbrook to relax his ruling about the five priority types, because, 'as long as it is in force it must upset other operational types and in the end mean less aeroplanes'. He fought continuously to keep the general policy looking at least twelve months ahead, because there would be serious long-term effects on aircraft production, the supply of aircrew, and the quality of aircraft, if Beaverbrook's more drastic measures were carried out to the letter.[11]

Less than a fortnight after Beaverbrook's appointment, Freeman decided to mount a high-level damage-limitation operation to prevent his wilder ideas from seriously impairing both current and future production. He was particularly concerned that the immediate drive for maximum output of the 'big five' would obscure the vital importance of long-term planning for a wider variety of aircraft, but realised that it would be futile to confront the minister head-on; the only authority likely to alter Beaverbrook's priorities was the War Cabinet, and the War Cabinet would, in turn, be advised by the Chiefs of Staff. Agreement on a common policy with the Air Staff was now essential.

With this objective in mind, an informal meeting between MAP and Air Ministry officials took place on 29 May. The meeting acknowledged that

* The B.1/39 specification was for an even larger four-engined bomber with 0.5in. machine-gun turrets. Had it not been cancelled, it might have been available to replace Halifaxes and Lancasters by 1944.

† When Tizard consulted Freeman about his trip to the USA with the latest British inventions, and asked why Beaverbrook refused to see him, Freeman explained that Tizard had failed to come immediately when summoned by Beaverbrook. Tizard was shocked; 'The man must be mad'. 'Of course he's mad' said Freeman, 'didn't you know that?'

although 'the notion of a three year war [may have] gone by the board ... it would be disastrous to allow a three months notion to take its place'. The Air Ministry representatives agreed that an Air Staff paper should be sent to the Chiefs of Staff Committee supporting Freeman's position on production planning.[12] He explained to Tedder. 'We should plan for maximum production by June 1941: nothing that cannot be in production by that date has any interest.'[13] The programme could then be reviewed: the production of several types would be reduced or deferred, but it would still be possible to develop a plan encompassing many more aircraft than Beaverbrook's 'big five'.

The Air Staff's views were duly passed by the Chiefs of Staff Committee to the War Cabinet, and by 5 June 1940 the log-jam on priorities created by the 'big five' directive had been broken. A variety of general reconnaissance aircraft and trainers were reinstated alongside the fighters and bombers on the lists. Beaverbrook ordered 1,000 Spitfires, 300 Defiants, 1,000 Blenheims, 300 Whitleys, 500 Wellingtons and 100 Oxfords; Beaufighter, Albemarle and Typhoon/Tornado programmes were reduced, and orders for heavy bombers were limited to 150 Stirlings, 200 Manchesters and 200 Halifaxes.[14] The best news for the RAF was probably the renewed emphasis on training aircraft without which, as Tedder told Freeman, 'we will have Service aircraft without the trained personnel to fly them'.[15] Development and production of the three heavy bombers was, however, severely retarded.

Lord Beaverbrook with his son Wing Commander Max Aitken, December 1942.

The Vickers Wellington was one of the most successful aircraft in the Second World War. It first entered service in 1938 and was one of the five types on which Beaverbrook instructed production facilities were to be concentrated.

Apart from persuading Beaverbrook, and the stray friends and 'experts' he had added to his staff, to ease or alter instructions that were obviously mistaken, Freeman simply ignored those that were clearly wrong. The first production order for the Mosquito was maintained, although Beaverbrook tried to cancel it, but work on the prototype ceased to have priority status for a while.[16] Via Tedder, Freeman asked Joubert, the Assistant Chief of Air Staff with special responsibility for radio, to dissuade Beaverbrook from halting the development of Airborne Interception radar (because his son, Max, a day fighter pilot, said that it was useless),[17] and he went so far as to conceal the existence of the Whittle project from Beaverbrook for nearly a week with the result that it was not cancelled, and merely lost its priority status from 20 May to 11 June 1940.[18]

The obsession with numbers was the defining characteristic of Beaverbrook's term of office at the MAP. He attached to the aircraft production statistics the same importance that he attached to the circulation figures of his newspapers.[19] To him they were the most important measures of his success; they could be crowed about to Churchill, the Government, and the public; they were his defence against criticism, indeed the myth of his 'achievement' is still very much 'alive and quoted'

At first, his methods appeared to have been very successful: the number of aircraft reaching RAF squadrons increased significantly in the months following his appointment. Churchill, delighted with the rising figures, told Sinclair that Beaverbrook had made a surprising improvement in the supply and repair of aeroplanes.[20] The idea that Beaverbrook personally engineered a 'production miracle' was actively propagated by Churchill to justify his decision to create the MAP, and by Beaverbrook himself, whilst Dowding, who had become thoroughly ill-disposed towards Sinclair, actually asserted that the effect of Beaverbrook's appointment was 'magical'.[21] But when Churchill told Ernest Bevin (who detested Beaverbrook), that he was a magician to have achieved such results, Bevin replied, 'You are right PM, I was always told that magic is 9/10ths illusion'.[22]

In fact, production had been rising strongly since March: average monthly output of Wellingtons for the second quarter of 1940 was 170 per cent higher than for the first quarter; for the Whitley the figure was 100 per cent, for the Hurricane 120 per cent, and for the Spitfire 95 per cent,[23] increases which were almost entirely due to measures taken before the creation of the MAP. It is true that there was another huge rise in Spitfire deliveries from Supermarine in the third quarter, from 231 to 363, but even this was mainly due to the expansion plans made by the Air Ministry in November 1939:[24] Castle Bromwich produced 10 in June, 119 in the third quarter, and 225 in the fourth.[25] Production of the rest of the 'big five' rose again slightly in the third quarter of 1940, but fell back thereafter. Comparisons between the average monthly output in the second quarter of 1940 and that in the six months ending 31 March 1941 show an increase for Wellingtons of 36 per cent, for Blenheims 21 per cent, and for Hurricanes 8 per cent, while the output of Whitleys fell 21 per cent. This was hardly a 'production miracle'. A more significant 84 per cent rise in Spitfire production for this period was largely due to rising deliveries from Castle Bromwich.

Beaverbrook's achievement was therefore ephemeral. Modern aircraft do not appear miraculously, overnight, and all new aircraft completed in 1940 were made by plant laid down a year or two before. The government-sponsored shadow factories planned by Swinton, Freeman and the Supply Committee, and erected by 1939, entered production early in 1940, and made possible the steep rise in the output figures between February and July 1940, thereby sustaining Fighter Command during the Battle of Britain. The repair organisation which Freeman had fought so hard to improve since September 1939 also began to fulfil its true potential. Apart from these factors, the rate at which production could expand was determined by the capacity of the available jigs and tools, and by the lengths of shifts. The multiple shifts envisaged by Freeman before the war were seldom possible, and although some factories worked single shifts of twelve hours per day, seven days per

* Work on the Castle Bromwich factory was started in June 1938, and the first Spitfire produced would have emerged later than June 1940, but for Beaverbrook's transfer of its management from Nuffield to Vickers in May.

week, because of the crisis, the stamina of the work force began to flag after two or three months, and working hours were subsequently reduced.

Commenting later, Freeman argued that, apart from getting rid of Nuffield, and putting Sir William Rootes in charge of aero-engine production, instead of Lord Austin, such increases of new aircraft as were achieved by Beaverbrook's methods were the result of four short-term factors:

(1) The fall of France and the Battle of Britain had created a crisis atmosphere in the aircraft factories,

(2) Spare parts, some taken from operational units, had been used to bolster the output of new aircraft,

(3) Aircraft awaiting scarce ancillaries had been completed using EL equipment found in the repair depots, and

(4) Some aircraft had been delivered incomplete.[26]

Beaverbrook was warned that withdrawing spares from squadrons was bound to hinder and delay repairs 'on unit', but he refused to change his instructions, since 'aircraft repaired on unit' would not feature in his output statistics. He put so much pressure on Bristol's engine division that they began to deliver Mercury engines without carburettors.[27]

The measures that Beaverbrook took while he was still prepared to be guided by Freeman seemed so successful that he became over-confident. He did not entirely cease to accept informed advice, but he grew increasingly devious, unreliable, and quarrelsome about the failure of the more impractical measures on which he had insisted, blaming others for their lack of success. On one occasion he went so far as to demand that his staff should sign certificates guaranteeing the achievement of their output targets. Freeman himself refused to promise that the output of aircraft equipment would meet the requirements of the aircraft programme. 'I am not ... responsible for calculating the quantities required to equip new aircraft and to satisfy wastage in RAF units', he told Beaverbrook. 'Any certificate given by me would therefore contain so many provisos as to be quite useless.'[28]

Despite his difficulties with Beaverbrook, Freeman never lost sight of his main task, that of ensuring that the RAF always had the maximum number of the best available aircraft, and his relentless quest for even better aircraft was never relaxed. Changes in engine policy, which stopped development of the R-R Peregrine and Vulture, had caused the cancellation of the Whirlwind, Tornado and Manchester,[29] but work on the Sabre versions of the new Hawker fighter continued, and he asked Hawkers to work on an alternative 'Tempest wing' for it before the end of 1940.[30] He pressed Rolls-Royce and Bristol to develop their larger, more powerful engines and more highly supercharged versions of existing engines like the Merlin and the Hercules, and nagged at them to increase production.[31]

Three of Freeman's decisions during the spring and summer of 1940 were among the most important of his career. Brave, decisive and far-sighted, they were to have a significant effect on the outcome of the war. First, he ordered

320 new fighters from a small US firm, North American, who were 'not bogged down with high priority stuff' like Curtiss, and were already supplying the RAF with their AT-6 'Harvard' advanced trainer. Curtiss was the only US aircraft firm with the capacity to make modern fighter aircraft in large numbers, but they were so fully committed to making P-40s for the US Army Air Corps that they were unable to proceed with their even newer XP-46 design. Colonel Oliver Echols, head of the Air Corps' Experimental section, helpfully suggested that the British should approach North American, and allowed the technical data on the Curtiss XP-46 to be sold to North American – for $56,000. Helped by this research, and using hydraulics, brakes, wheels and electrics from their AT-6, the prototype of the NA-73X, later named the Mustang, had its first flight on 26 October 1940 – 178 days after the order had been placed. Britain's first production order was increased by 300 in September.[32]

A second, and equally vital, decision was the award of a contract to Packard to set up a factory to make Merlin engines in the USA. When Hives first suggested that Rolls-Royce engines should be produced in America,[33] Freeman had been unable to follow his advice,[34] presumably because of the shortage of dollars and the uncertainties of the US neutrality laws. By April 1940, however, arms from the USA were available on a 'cash and carry' basis, and the need for Rolls-Royce engines was so great that demand seemed certain to outstrip the combined production of the Derby, Crewe, Glasgow and Manchester factories. On 26 June 1940, the MAP entered into an agreement with the American motor company, Packard, for the production of Merlin engines.[35] Freeman's initiatives in getting both the Mustang airframe and the Packard Merlin engine into production by 1941 were to prove perfectly timed technical decisions of almost incalculable value in the later stages of hostilities.

The third problem on which Freeman took decisive action in August 1940 was that of the Vulture-powered Manchester, the sole remaining heavy bomber still being made to the twin-engined P.13/36 specification. By 1940 many of the Vulture's early design faults had been eliminated, but production versions of the engine were still seriously overweight, and without a radical redesign, the potential for weight reduction or power increases was limited. The problem

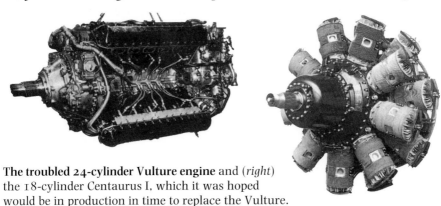

The troubled 24-cylinder Vulture engine and (*right*) the 18-cylinder Centaurus I, which it was hoped would be in production in time to replace the Vulture.

The **Avro Manchester** *(top)*, a heavy bomber designed to take two of the new Rolls-Royce Vulture engines. The airframe was overweight and the Vulture underpowered and unreliable. Avro disliked the Vulture and were relieved to be allowed to redesign the airframe for four Merlin engines and name it the **Lancaster** *(bottom)*. The similarity of the two airframes is striking, as are the different engine nacelles, those for the Merlins of Rolls-Royce design. Roy Chadwick, Avro's chief designer wrote to Freeman: 'I am confident that the Lancaster will prove to be the outstanding aircraft of the war, and it is largely due to you that it has come into existence'.

was compounded by the fact that the Manchester airframe was very much heavier than had originally been estimated.[36]

Both Hives at Rolls-Royce and Chadwick at Avro had serious doubts about the Vulture, and realising that he faced a major production crisis if production of the engine stopped, Freeman asked Bristol whether their Centaurus would be in production in time to replace the Vulture.* Cancellation of the whole Manchester airframe would involve re-tooling and rejigging the relevant factories to make a different aircraft, a process which would take nine to twelve months and a huge consequential loss of output. Supplies of Centaurus were obviously going to be inadequate, but Chadwick managed to convince Freeman that Avro could redesign and extend the Manchester wing

* The Bristol Directors Committee on 8 February 1940 forecast that production would not reach 75 a month until 1942, and agreed that this would not be enough for the Air Ministry.

to accept four of the now very reliable Merlin engines. Other parts of the airframe would have to be strengthened to cope with the extra weight, but most of the basic Manchester airframe could remain in production, and the changes could be made relatively quickly. Freeman persuaded Beaverbrook to place orders for the 'Four-Merlin' Manchester, and, renamed the Lancaster, and it proved to be Britain's best heavy bomber of the war. [37]

Freeman's emphasis on the importance of long-term planning contrasted sharply with Beaverbrook's short-termism, but in the atmosphere of crisis which prevailed during the summer of 1940, Freeman was sometimes prepared to abandon established procedures in favour of less orthodox methods, not always dissimilar to those employed by his minister. When a shortage of Merlin engines seemed imminent, he attempted to recover 100 Merlin IIIs from France before the Franco-German armistice on 18 June.* Ater trying to divert French orders for Swiss machine tools to Britain, [38] he intervened to rescue key parts and technical drawings for Halifax undercarriages from Messier's factory in Paris.

On this occasion Freeman personally arranged for the Navy to land Louis Armandias, Messier's UK representative, in southern France. From there he made his way to Paris, commandeered a truck, loaded it with the parts and design data, and drove it back to Nice. His triumphant return to Britain was, however, frustrated by the Dover customs officials, who refused entry of the 'contraband' goods until a telephone call from Freeman released them. They were then rushed to Handley Page. [39]

Freeman's admiration for Beaverbrook's 'piratical ways' was shortlived. As soon as the transfer of the salvage and repair organisation from the Air Ministry to MAP was completed, Beaverbrook began an underhand and devious campaign to obtain jurisdiction over other spheres of Air Ministry work which could be linked in any way to aircraft production. He demanded control of the Atlantic Ferry Pools because they carried equipment and supplies for the MAP, [40] and he actually asked Sinclair for the Air Ministry's equipment department. [41] Inevitably, Sinclair and Newall opposed these further amputations, with the result that the two ministries were locked in continuous dispute throughout the summer of 1940. No one could have worked harder or more patiently to resolve their differences than Freeman, but the disputes and jurisdictional arguments severely strained relations between the two departments.

The difficulty of working with Beaverbrook was exacerbated by another extraordinary example of his subversive methods. To strengthen his case and undermine 'establishment' confidence in the Air Ministry, he arranged for a series of anonymous papers about alleged failings of the RAF and its senior officers to be written and circulated in Whitehall. One of them, describing the Air Ministry as 'a most cumbersome and ill-working administrative machine', was seen by Churchill in June. [42]

The papers were written by Edgar James Kingston-McCloughry, then a

---

* They were to have been installed on Amiot 356 bombers.

Wing Commander in the Air Ministry's Department of War Organisation (DWO). McCloughry had been outraged when he was passed over for promotion in June 1940, and his vitriolic attacks on the RAF high command appear to have started at about this time. Besides his friendship with Beaverbrook, McCloughry had wide acquaintance in political circles, and was well known in Parliament. His papers indicate that he often dined with Beaverbrook in the spring of 1940, before the MAP was created, and he claimed that he had personally suggested either Freeman or Courtney for the senior Air Force post in the ministry.[43]

It was no coincidence that McCloughry's anonymous papers began to appear as soon as the Air Ministry made clear its opposition to Beaverbrook's plans. There is strong evidence that an attack on Newall entitled 'A Weak Link in the Nation's Defences' was prepared and circulated with Beaverbrook's connivance, if not his guidance and encouragement,[44] and it is not unreasonable to assume that he sponsored all of McCloughry's memoranda. He took a mischievous delight in stimulating people to criticise their seniors, and having found McCloughry intelligent and outspoken, he probably encouraged him to offer his opinions about people in the RAF, and to disclose inside information about the service.[45]

Freeman discovered the identity of the anonymous author early in July 1940. 'I am worried', he told Elizabeth, 'because there is an officer in the Air Ministry who has been corresponding with ... [Beaverbrook] for some months and running down his seniors to him and giving him certain evidence against Cyril [Newall]'.[46] Beaverbrook tried to have McCloughry transferred to MAP,[47] but the Air Council refused, and decided to post McCloughry to South Africa, out of harm's way, a posting delayed by McCloughry's illness.

As an Air Chief Marshal and a member of the Air Council, the fact that Freeman's minister was so obviously plotting against the RAF high command, made his position almost intolerable, and he decided that if McCloughry was transferred to MAP, he would leave the ministry. 'I don't think I have ever worked under such unpleasant conditions as at present', Freeman wrote, 'Indeed I never imagined that I would be called upon to do so.'[48] He told Newall about McCloughry's activities at once, but the CAS himself was having such difficulty with Beaverbrook and the Government, that he could neither advise nor offer help: Freeman could only bide his time. Beaverbrook went on 'moving heaven and earth to get McCloughry on his staff',[49] and the matter was not finally resolved until yet another of McCloughry's memoranda came to Freeman's notice in September. This new document concerned the officers responsible for aircrew training and was typically scathing about their abilities. It had been prepared on Beaverbrook's instructions, and Freeman found it whilst running the MAP in his minister's absence, and took it to Newall. McCloughry was posted off to South Africa the following day.[50]

The accuracy of McCloughry's assertions can perhaps be judged by a draft of a memorandum which attacked Freeman himself: '... It is largely due to his lack of drive, coupled with his scanty technical knowledge, that our output has not approached that of Germany'.[51] In fact, British aircraft production overtook that of Germany during 1939, and in 1940 Britain produced more aircraft than any other country in the world.

Apart from the appalling McCloughry saga, and Beaverbrook's part in it, Freeman had become deeply concerned about a number of other issues in the three months after the creation of MAP. The ministry was constantly being reorganised, and in August proposals for a further management shake-up so alarmed him that he wrote to Beaverbrook pointing out the obvious defects of his plans. In the first of four ruthlessly trenchant letters or memoranda,[52] he argued that ultimate responsibility for supervising the output of any one type of product, instrument, or engine could not be shared among a number of people. Stressing that most of his production duties had been taken over by Beaverbrook, and that Tedder was already controlling research and development very competently, he suggested that he should be allowed to leave the MAP and go back to the Air Ministry if a suitable RAF job could be found for him. A second letter, on 5 September 1940, exposed even more clearly the administrative muddle of the new organisation.[53]

No sooner had it been sent, however, than Freeman learned of yet another unwelcome proposal from his minister: the formation of an Army Air Force. This force would be entirely separate from the RAF and would be controlled by the War Office. Freeman saw this, correctly, as a vindictive and provocative attempt to reduce still further the powers of the Air Ministry, and he therefore wrote to Beaverbrook yet again, asking to be allowed to leave the MAP writing: 'My position as the senior Air Force Officer in your Ministry is unbearable'. . . I disagree with you on so many other points of policy . . .

> [that] it would be better if someone who is more in line with your views should hold this position . . . I do not understand your policy of non cooperation with the Air Ministry . . . [which] may seriously prejudice the proper conduct of the war.[54]

Finally, on 7 September, Freeman explained at length the inanity of Beaverbrook's inclination to re-establish an Army Air Force, pointing out that if the output of any part of the aircraft industry in the pre-war rearmament period had been diverted to this end, the RAF would not have had enough aeroplanes to win the Battle of Britain; the war would have already been lost.[55]

It took Beaverbrook a few days to recover from this barrage, but he eventually replied, evasively, that relations between the MAP and the Air Ministry were in fact 'very good' and that Freeman had actually supported him on a number of occasions when he had opposed the Air Ministry's plans:

> . . . The major issues at which I have been at variance [with the Air Ministry] are training and the transfer to training units to Canada. In both of these issues I had your support. . . . I must say that I think you have made as many difficulties for me at the Air Ministry as I have made for myself.[56]

But he refused to allow Freeman to leave the MAP.

CHAPTER 9

An unwelcome role:
Vice-Chief of the Air Staff

B Y SEPTEMBER 1940 Freeman's position in the MAP had become almost intolerable. He had reached the conclusion that he should leave the ministry even if there was no suitable post for him at the Air Ministry, but Beaverbrook would not let him go, an impasse with only two solutions. The first was that Beaverbrook might leave the MAP – and by September, Churchill was, in fact, hoping to move him to the Ministry of Supply.[1] If this happened, systematic planning could soon have restarted at MAP, and if Freeman had been able to recover his lost executive authority, he would happily have remained AMDP. As a serving officer, however, the Secretary of State for Air and the Chief of the Air Staff could insist on his return to the Air Ministry at any time.

There were no vacancies on the Air Council for an officer of the rank of Air Chief Marshal, but apart from the entirely unofficial idea that he should become CAS in place of Newall,[2] Freeman was also well qualified for the post of Air Member for Supply and Organisation, due to his long experience in aircraft development and production. Courtney had only been appointed in February, however, and as he was obviously able, it would have been wrong to move him so soon, merely to find a job for Freeman.

Although Freeman would have preferred to stay at the MAP, *without* Beaverbrook, there were other changes in the RAF high command at the beginning of October which left him no option but to return to the Air Ministry as Vice-Chief of the Air Staff.

Until August 1940 Newall had retained the support of his minister and his service, but his standing as Chief of the Air Staff with the Government had undoubtedly been undermined by the unscrupulous political intrigue orchestrated by Beaverbrook throughout the summer of 1940. But by September 1940, two of the most senior Air Force officers began to be critical of his operational decisions, and for reasons which were influenced by other overriding considerations, they lent their weight to Beaverbrook's campaign against him, intervention which proved decisive; Newall was replaced by Sir Charles Portal in October, and Portal, almost immediately insisted that Freeman returned to the Air Ministry as his VCAS.

The prolonged dispute between the Air Ministry and the Prime Minister over Dowding's position as AOC-in C, Fighter Command, was a major factor in the considerations which culminated in Newall's replacement. By July 1940 both the Air Staff and the Secretary of State for Air had decided to replace Dowding – whose appointment had already been extended beyond the normal retirement age. Churchill was so strongly opposed to any sugge-stion of Dowding's removal that he asked Sinclair to prolong his appoint-ment indefinitely, adding '... this would not of course preclude his being moved to a higher position ...'[3]

This unquivocal prime-ministerial backing stopped any attempts to replace Dowding until early September, when the first concentrated night bombing raids by the Luftwaffe provoked a heated controversy between the Air Staff and Fighter Command over air defence tactics. But it also raised the spectre that Churchill might seek to impose Dowding on the Royal Air Force as CAS.

The details of the dispute about night fighting lie beyond the scope of this book, but matters came to a head on 11 September when Marshal of the Royal Air Force Sir John Salmond (then Director of Armament Production in the MAP) submitted a paper to Beaverbrook, his minister, which effectively asked for an enquiry into night air defence: Newall supported the proposal. After several meetings, which he attended, Salmond concluded that Dowding was in the wrong and should be replaced, an opinion which was heartily

Air Chief Marshal Dowding and some of his famous Fighter Command 'chicks', (*from left to right*) W/Cdr Max Aitken DSO DFC, W/Cdr A.G. 'Sailor' Malan DSO DFC, S/Ldr A.C. Deere DFC (RNZAF), Dowding, Flight Officer E.C. Henderson MM (WAAF), F/Lt R.H. Hillary, W/Cdr J.A. Kent DFC AFC and W/Cdr C.B. Kingcombe DFC.

Marshal of the Royal Air Force Lord Trenchard, the 'Father of the Royal Air Force'. Seen here with Air Marshal Harry Broadhurst, Wing Commander Robin Johnston, RNZAF, and some of their fighter pilots in Normandy in 1944. Trenchard was deeply involved when the decision was taken to replace Newall as CAS, consulting Salmond and Freeman in the process.

seconded by Salmond's closest service confidant, Marshal of the Royal Air Force Lord Trenchard.[4] When he reported this to Beaverbrook, however, Salmond discovered that both he and Churchill thought highly of Dowding and were unwilling to remove him. Salmond's attempt to have the matter discussed at the Air Council was then blocked by Newall.

A CAS would normally expect to exert a decisive influence over the term of appointment of operational commanders, but the weakness of his political position, and the corresponding strength of Dowding's, meant that Newall was unable to do so. Quite apart from the knowledge that the Prime Minister admired Dowding, Newall must have realised that he himself might be held equally responsible for the RAF's unreadiness to combat night bombing. Salmond obviously failed to recognize the difficulties of Newall's situation, for he thought Newall's opposition 'incomprehensible'.[5]

Once they began to doubt whether adequate pressure for Dowding's removal could be brought to bear while Newall remained CAS, the two Marshals of the RAF decided that the one sure way of ensuring that Dowding did not succeed Newall, was for Newall to be replaced as CAS whilst Dowding was still at Fighter Command. Salmond proposed this to Trenchard on 25 September.[6]

Trenchard's faith in Newall had been dwindling throughout the summer for very different reasons. Newall held completely orthodox air force views on the question of bombing policy, championing the concept of strategic bombing and strenuously opposing the use of bombers in direct support of ground forces. But on the outbreak of war he was compelled to recognize that Bomber Command was too weak to launch an offensive against Germany, and having eventually bowed to political pressure to use the command in other ways,[7] he thereby lost the support of Trenchard, the 'Father of the Royal Air Force', who was impatiently awaiting the commencement of the strategic bombing assault.[8]

On 25 September, the very day that Salmond denounced Newall, Trenchard wrote directly to Churchill deploring the employment of Bomber Command in operations against the German invasion fleet. In a transparent attempt to overturn the bombing policy agreed between Newall and the Cabinet, he questioned 'whether the C-in-Chief of the Bombing Force should not be given all the freedom to bomb the oil and power stations, the Ruhr and some of the great manufacturing plants in Germany, and to use the maximum of his force for this purpose'.[9]

The exact sequence of meetings between 25 September and 2 October cannot be documented with certainty, because virtually all the relevant papers, minutes and letters have disappeared, but the decision to appoint Portal CAS had been taken by 2 October. Beaverbrook and the former Chiefs of Air Staff, Trenchard and Salmond, were obviously involved, and Trenchard had been consulting Freeman confidentially, as the senior Service member of the Air Council, after the CAS.[10]

Correspondence in the Salmond papers show him and Trenchard to be the secret 'kingmakers' of the RAF,[11] with Salmond lobbying senior members of the Service, and Trenchard using his influence in both Parliament and the Royal Air Force. Beaverbrook probably helped to persuade Churchill that Newall should go, but it is most unlikely that he took any part in the choice of Portal to succeed him.[12]

Portal's appointment as CAS began on 25 October, his promotion to Air Chief Marshal having been back-dated to 26 May, the day before Freeman's, to give him one day's artificial seniority. Less than a week later, Portal insisted that Freeman be released by MAP to join him as his VCAS, an appointment which Freeman had already refused twice. Pierse, from whom Freeman took over as VCAS, and Portal, under whom he would then serve, were less experienced, four or five years younger and junior in rank: both had been his pupils when he was instructing at the Staff College in 1922. The strange story of the discussions which led to these appointments and of the people concerned is unlikely ever to emerge in full, but some of the factors can be pieced together.

By September 1940, among the senior officers who had been members of the Air Council and were still young enough to be appointed CAS, Freeman was the most experienced. His outstanding success as AMRD and AMDP, and his part in creating a modern aircraft industry and re-equipping the RAF with superior aircraft in time to win the Battle of Britain, was recognized; he had been party to all the pre-war discussions and appointments by the Air Council, and he had an intimate knowledge of Air Ministry staff and methods.

Besides being thoroughly familiar with the technical capabilities of modern aircaft (having chosen and had most of them made), he knew more about the characters and abilities of the senior RAF officers than his contemporaries, because of his spells at the Staff College and his years on the Air Council. Most of their experience had been obtained in operational commands in the Empire, or in other, less senior, staff positions. Freeman was decisive and very hard working; he had exceptional charm and great and proven powers of leadership and persuasion, and over the four and a half years to September 1940 he had demonstrated an ability to work effectively and harmoniously with ministers, Civil Servants, industry – even with Beaverbrook! – against a background of almost continuous emergency.

In fact, he had received a perfect training for the post of CAS.

Why, then, were Freeman's many proven qualities rejected in favour of Portal, his younger, less experienced, former pupil? Freeman cited his own lack of recent operational experience as an adequate reason for twice refusing the job of Vice-Chief of Air Staff,[13] but this is wholly unconvincing. He was always modest in self-assessment, and frequently expressed doubts about his own future prospects which were completely unwarranted.* That neither Sinclair, Portal nor Churchill shared Freeman's reservations concerning the 'operational side of the Air Force', is proved by the fact that they offered him at least two key operational commands later in the war,† and had he accepted either post, he would surely have mastered them as quickly as his many other demanding roles.

His exchanges with Portal about bombing policy a year later were to show that Freeman understood the problems of training and building up an effective night-bomber force far better than did Portal, despite the latter's operational experience.[14]

Operational experience was not essential, although it could be helpful in assessing the performance of Commanders in Chief: leadership, general experience, strength of character and moral courage were far more important. It is hard to believe that the six months Portal spent at Bomber Command, directing the operations of about 240 aircraft (of which only about 160 would be serviceable at any one time),[15] uniquely qualified him to be CAS above all the other senior RAF officers. If operational experience was the most important criterion, Dowding was an infinitely stronger candidate.

Freeman had, of course, been seconded from the Air Ministry to the MAP since May 1940, but the fact that he had loyally worked with Beaverbrook

---

* For example, his letter to Elizabeth of 25 November 1939, wondering whether he would be replaced as AMDP.
† Freeman could have elected to take over from Tedder as AOC-in-C Middle East in October, 1941. He refused to allow his name to go forward for an even more important post, probably as head of air operations for 'Overlord', in July 1943.

in conditions which he himself described as 'intolerable', should not have disqualified him from the top Air Force post; the transfer of his department to the MAP hardly affected his position, for he kept both his RAF rank and his seat on the Air Council as AMDP.

Portal was only forty-six when he was offered the post of CAS. A student at the RAF Staff College in 1922/3, when Freeman was on the directing staff, he later went to the Senior Officers' course at Greenwich in 1926, which Freeman had attended eight years before. After serving as AOC Aden, from January 1933 to December 1935, he returned to instruct at the Imperial Defence College, and then worked under Welsh in the AMSO's department from 1937 until his appointment as Air Member for Personnel in 1939. As AMP, he implemented major changes in the RAF's recruitment and training systems, started the Women's Auxiliary Air Force (WAAF), and made a vital contribution to the Empire Flying Training Schools, but he took over Bomber Command from Ludlow-Hewitt in April 1940, after only fourteen months on the Air Council.

Portal's record at Bomber Command was not particularly distinguished. He was unaware of the limitations of his bomber forces, and seems genuinely to have believed in Trenchard's view that the poorly trained and ill-equipped squadrons of Bomber Command could achieve decisive results in 1940 by bombing industrial areas of Germany by night. He had ceased to fly himself, and obviously did not understand the difficulties of night navigation: at the famous meeting of the War Cabinet on 21 June 1940, at which the existence of the German 'blind bombing beam' was disclosed, Portal did not disagree when the Cabinet was assured that the RAF's bombers did not need electronic aids, and could rely on astro-navigation.[16]

The responsiblity for the decision to replace Newall in October 1940 was very largely that of Trenchard and Salmond, and they were so self confident about their influence that even after the decision to appoint Portal as CAS had been made, they were corresponding about the possibility of attaching conditions to his appointment, presumably during discussions with Churchill.[17] Although Trenchard had an exceptionally high regard for Portal,[18] the few surviving documents show that the only serving officer consulted by Trenchard and Salmond over the replacement of the CAS was Freeman: they obviously thought him their best advisor as to the abilities of the serving senior officers.

Trenchard told Salmond and Freeman on 24 September that he was going to see Beaverbrook, and they both asked to 'brief' him before he did so. Salmond was asked to do so on the 25th, as Trenchard was trying to fix a time to see Beaverbrook on the 27th or 28th September, and Trenchard's letter to Freeman added '. . . I had better know what is in your letter [to me] so that I do not give you away.' . . . He also asked Freeman to lunch with him at Brooke's on Monday, 30 September.[19]

Exactly when Portal was summoned to London, and persuaded to accept the appointment of CAS, is unknown, but it was Freeman who told him that he was to be offered the position and who persuaded him to accept. Portal himself was surprised and bewildered by the thought of the huge respon-sibilities involved: 'My first thoughts', he wrote, 'were serious doubts whether I could tackle the job'.[20]

Virtually no written evidence has survived about the high-level discussions that must have taken place before Portal's appointment, and absence of corre-spondence which seems distinctly odd in the circumstances: most top service appointments – Gort as CIGS in December 1937, his successors, Ironside, Dill and Brooke – are well documented. But the very fact that there are no documents to explain the choice of Portal to replace Newall may well be sig-nificant: it seems possible that an attempt has been made to conceal the true circumstances of Portal's selection. Churchill's assertion that Portal was 'the accepted star of the Air Force'[21] is appropriately vague, for he hardly knew Portal, and was obviously quoting others.*

Fortunately, the all-important meeting between Freeman and Portal was witnessed by Freeman's chauffeur, Davies, who drove for him throughout the war, and moved with him to Courtaulds in 1945, when he left the MAP. Sometime after Freeman's death, Davies described the crucial meeting to his new boss, and the gist of the story was as follows.†

Davies brought the car round to the office door, and Wilfrid Freeman and Portal, the C-in-C of Bomber Command got in the back; Davies was told to drive round and round Hyde Park while they talked. There was no partition, so he heard the conversation over a period of two hours. Wilfrid said that the Chief of Air Staff, Newall, was about to be retired, that Portal had been chosen to succeed him, and that he must accept, as he could do the job. Portal was horrified at the thought, and claimed that he did not have enough experience on the Air Council, and did not know enough about the top people in the RAF to be able to choose the right men for the top appoint-ments. He countered by telling Wilfrid that he would be a much better CAS, and they talked round the matter until Wilfrid eventually explained: 'The King will not accept me; I've had a divorce'.

After further persuasion, Portal suggested that he might be able to do the job if Wilfrid would join him as Vice-Chief of the Air Staff, and despite Wilfrid's belief that he could best serve the RAF by remaining at the MAP, instead of moving to the Air Ministry, Portal clung to the idea almost as a condition of even thinking of accepting. Wilfrid went on trying to convince Portal that he could hold down the job, and that he was the only Air Marshal

---

* An example of Churchill's willingness to gloss over awkward facts is revealed by the back-ground to his account of the Dieppe raid as disclosed by B.L.Villa's book *Unauthorised Action*.

† Freeman died in 1953, and Davies, his chauffeur, who had worked for him since 1940, or earlier, and transferred with him to Courtaulds in 1945, became chauffeur to Ronald Kerr-Muir, another Courtaulds Director. The author met Kerr-Muir at Nannerch, North Wales in the early 1960s and asked what had happened to Davies, and then, whether he had ever talked about Freeman.[6] Kerr-Muir repeated what Davies had told him about the Freeman family and Murtle, and finally his account of the Freeman/Portal conversation during their drive around Hyde Park. (The story was not prompted in any way: the thought of writing a biography of my uncle had never entered my head. AWF)

with the application and intelligence to take on the role – and eventually he talked him into accepting.

It thus seems to have been Freeman's divorce, five years earlier, which barred him from the top RAF job, and which resulted in the appointment of the reluctant and inexperienced Portal. Not surprisingly, the truth was never officially acknowledged, and the disappearance of all the relevant records has protected those involved, from Sinclair and Churchill upwards, from adverse comment.*

From a modern perspective it seems remarkable that such a consideration could have counted against Freeman at that time of national crisis, but the appointment of Chiefs of Staff was subject to the approval of King George VI and the Prime Minister. The abdication crisis of 1936, which forced the shy and reluctant Duke of York to succeed his brother, enhanced the total Royal disapproval of both parties to a divorce. Moreover, Churchill, a senior Privy Councillor, had been deeply involved in the crisis and had no illusions whatever about the strength of Royal feeling on the divorce issue.[22]

Divorce was also a 'black mark' on a service career. Montgomery-Massingberd, the CIGS from 1933 to 1936, was known to have pressed for the compulsory retirement of divorced army officers, and Percy Hobart, one of the few brilliant Generals of the period, was nearly barred from an appointment because of his invovement in a divorce,[23] a negative view which was shared by the Royal Air Force. The RAF was the junior service; most of its officers lacked the social status of many in the Army and Navy, and Trenchard and Salmond, the only Chiefs of Air Staff between 1919 and 1933, undoubtedly tried to emulate this outlook and values, and avoid criticism of the Air Force by the other services. After his divorce in 1935, Freeman was planning on the assumption that he would have to retire at the age of 47, a fate from which he was saved by Swinton's intervention.

Immediately after Portal became CAS-Designate, Freeman was offered the post of Vice-Chief of Air Staff – for the second time. After discussing the subject with Beaverbrook and Portal, he opted to remain at the MAP, writing to Sinclair on 7 October 'I can best serve the interests of the RAF if I . . . refuse the offer . . . My principal reason is that I have been so long away from the operational side of the Air Force that I do not believe that I would be of that assistance to Portal that either you or he expect.'[24]

The implausibility of this argument has already been noted. That this was not the real explanation for his refusal is clear from the letter which he addressed to Portal on the same day. 'I cannot of course put all my reasons

* All Sinclair's private files were stored in an isolated cottage on the Thurso estate. The author recently established that those relating to Freeman were shown by Robin Sinclair to Freeman's son Keith, and his wife, when they visited Robin shortly after the end of the war, whilst Sir Archibald was still alive. The files were destroyed in a fire which caused the death of an estate worker, but, apart from the possible impropriety of reading them before the death of his father, the 2nd Lord Thurso obviously felt that much of their content was so controversial that neither the fact that he had seen them nor the matters which concerned Freeman could be disclosed to the author, when they exchanged letters in July 1985.

[for declining the offer] to the S of S', Freeman wrote, 'but can assure you I have considered only the interests of the RAF'.[25]

In fact, despite the difficulties and responsibilities of the previous four and a half years, Freeman had revelled in his work as AMDP. He loathed working under Beaverbrook of course, and frankly told him that he wished to return to the Air Ministry 'without any conditions', but he knew exactly what would happen if aircraft orders were no longer influenced by the Air Ministry. Without an experienced leader at the MAP, one with the strength of character to insist on the production of the aircraft and engines required by the RAF, the political pressure for 'numbers' would be irresistible. The aircraft industry would concentrate production on aircraft that were easy to produce in quantity, leaving the Air Force no option but to fly them, regardless of their quality, and Freeman cared too passionately about the service, its aircrews, and its operational effectiveness to allow this.

He had also begun to 'hope that by October the Beaver will have gone to some other job; he won't be satisfied with this one much longer'.[26] If he could last out Beaverbrook, there was a more than full-sized job to be done at the MAP. Freeman was far more aware of its desperate importance than most of his RAF colleagues, and knew that he could manage aircraft development and production better than anyone else.

For a few weeks it seemed as if he might be allowed to stay with the MAP. The American government had realised that the Battle of Britain had effectively been won, that Britain would fight on, and would need all the help that America could give them, and that one of the top British airmen would be their best 'mentor' as to American aircraft production policy. Sinclair specifically asked Beaverbrook to release Freeman, to lead the liaison mission to the USA to discuss the American aircraft production programme and aircraft supplies for Britain that they had so urgently requested.[27] Beaverbrook obdurately refused to release him, but the matter was still under consideration when Portal intervened to insist that Freeman be appointed VCAS, and Beaverbrook could not refuse to allow this.

Less than a week after taking over from Newall, Portal had realised the full scale of his responsibilities at the head of a rapidly expanding and highly active service, and recognized his inexperience, the validity of his doubts about accepting the post, and his need for help from the senior and much more experienced Freeman. They both knew that for Freeman it would be a step down, but there was no real alternative. Apart from the former Chiefs of Staff, Trenchard and Salmond, there was no one else in the RAF with such a balanced, independent mind, or with such vision; no one with his intimate knowledge of the Air Council's work, and knowledge of the strengths and weaknesses of all the service's senior officers.

Freeman had all the qualities needed by a CAS; to appoint him VCAS would put a thoroughbred into the shafts of a hansom cab. Nevertheless, Portal had to be given the support he said that he needed, so despite Freeman's reluctance, and the likely effect of his transfer on aircraft development and production, Sinclair, as Air Minister, realised that he had to ask for his help. Thanking Beaverbrook for releasing Freeman, the Secretary of State for Air wrote:

> I have asked you to release him because I am convinced that his quali-
> fications for the post [of VCAS] are unique among those of available officers
> and, above all, because the new Chief of the Air Staff feels strongly that he
> needs him, – and in assuming the heavy responsibilities of his new post,
> Portal needs all the help that we can give him.[28]

Freeman had no option in the matter, and no illusions about the need to efface himself so as not to overshadow his former pupil. Diana Richmond reported that he was 'gloomy at his change and at the fact that he is allowed no apparent influence on policy',* well aware that the work would be that of an assistant, administering the RAF, deputising for Portal, but with little executive power; he could influence policy only indirectly through the CAS. His attitude to his new role was explained in a letter from Elizabeth to her brother John Richmond, dated 1.1.41;

> ... he was pushed, against his will and, as he declares, his better judge-
> ment, into accepting the post of VCAS. Portal, the CAS was very insistent
> that W. should take it, for he himself, being junior to W. and several years
> younger, felt that he wanted the advice and moral support of an older man,
> and one such as W who shared his views. Wilfrid on the other hand believed
> – and still believes – that aircraft production is more important still, and
> that he, with unrivalled knowledge in that sphere, could be of better service
> to the RAF [there] than in the field of operations – one that he has entirely
> neglected for the last five years. I think he is right in that; but I also believe
> that he had no option but to join Portal, since the latter, who is after all his
> chief, maintained that Wilfrid was absolutely essential to him.[29]

His reservations were confirmed by the experience of serving, month after month in a role where he so little right to take decisions, and later, after a period of intense mental strain, he let off steam in a letter to Elizabeth, probably written in April or May, 1942, when he had just heard from Portal that Churchill had refused to let him return to MAP.

> I was so happy in production until the Beaver arrived ... No one knows
> better than you how much I loathe this intangible job, always with a
> feeling of failure and frustration.

---

* An important addition to the household at Murtle Den in the late summer was Elizabeth's sister-in-law, Diana, John Richmond's wife, and her infant twin daughters. John Richmond was in Cairo when Italy joined the war – and France left it – and could not get back to Britain. They were without a house of their own, and it suited both Diana and the Freemans for her and the twins to share the house-keeping and spend the war at Murtle Den. Diana Richmond's weekly letters, hereafter DR, were kept by her husband, later Sir John Richmond, and generously made available for this biography, giving brief vignettes about Wilfrid Freeman's visits.

He went on to describe how he despised

> the misery of a job ... [in which] you have little or no interest ... its the same use as a nurse is to a grown up family – no use, but ... she will try to stop them letting themselves down' ... and even 'tick off' the parents ...[30]

His farewell letter to Beaverbrook on leaving the MAP, frankly acknowledged that he thought he could make a bigger contribution to the Royal Air Force by continuing to work in aircraft development and production, but conceded:

> It is not for me to judge where I am most needed. My first duty must be to Portal. Since he so strongly urges that I can best serve the interests of the Service [as] VCAS, I feel I have no alternative but to do as he wishes. That by so doing I am taking a step down rather than up the ladder, is a consideration which cannot count at such a time.[31]

He had no illusions about Beaverbrook, and he knew the dangers of arousing his animosity, so, despite his inumerable difficulties since May, he tried to ensure that they parted company on friendly terms. His letter gave proper recognition of Beaverbrook's achievement in forcing through the transfer of responsibility for aircraft repairs, to the MAP, in time for the Battle of Britain, and he wrote with genuine respect that

> ...without the ever increasing flow of aircraft from the ASUs, for which you were entirely responsible our pilots could never have won such a resounding victory.

and finished - with a 'double entendre' and then some outrageous flattery which he must have enjoyed composing –

> It has indeed been a great privilege and an abiding lesson to serve under you, and if at any future date I can serve you again in any capacity, I shall indeed be grateful for the opportunity. Yours sincerely.*

To this day, Beaverbrook is often given personal credit for engineering the so-called 'production miracle' of the summer of 1940. Nothing could refute this popular misconception more completely than his own response to Freeman's farewell letter.

'This Ministry', Beaverbrook wrote, 'is being weakened by the departure of one who more than any other man gave the Royal Air Force the machines, whose superior quality won the vital battles of this summer. ... To your vision more than any other factor, do we owe the victories that saved our country ...'.[32]

---

* Beaverbrook was delighted and wrote on a copy 'COPY OF W-F-'S LETTER. I MAY WANT IT AT ANY TIME'

Freeman's dislike of publicity is obvious in this posed portrait of the two Air Chief Marshals, Portal the CAS and his VCAS 'examining' a German incendiary bomb.

CHAPTER 10

The supremely competent VCAS

FREEMAN BEGAN working as Portal's VCAS in mid-November 1940, and served him for nearly two years. He found the post utterly uncongenial, but his knowledge of the senior officers of the RAF, his insight into the needs of the air war, and the potential of the aeroplane industry were thereby made available to its leaders, and the range of his activities over this period was extraordinary, and invaluable to Portal, the Royal Air Force and the British and American governments. This chapter deals mainly with the general responsibilities he assumed in that post, and the extent to which he shared in Portal's work. It covers Freeman's relationships with Churchill and Portal, his work within the Air Staff and the RAF High Command, his supervision of the RAF's expansion and administration of its separate commands, and his continued involvement in Britain's aircraft development and production programme. His wider activities during this period, tasks, many of them vital, for which his character, experience and ability made him uniquely suitable, need to be explained in greater detail, and are covered in later chapters.

Freeman had moved to a flat in Berkeley Square when his sister Josephine's house in London was damaged by bombs during the Blitz, and he shared it at first with Jo and their cousin Paul Patrick. This was a mistake for both were talkative, and Freeman was too busy to be congenial when he came in late, and dog-tired. He did not eat properly; there was no canteen at the Air Ministry and London restaurants closed at 9pm, long before the end of his day's work. He had caught 'flu at the end of October, so he took some leave at Murtle Den before starting work as VCAS.

The atmosphere at Murtle was relaxed; Diana found Wilfrid 'as kindly and provocative and jovial as ever... [but] gloomy at his change [to be VCAS].'[1]

Freeman's new appointment brought him into close contact with the Prime Minister and, realising Freeman's importance, and wanting to know him better, Churchill invited him to Chequers for the night on 26 December 1940. 'P.M. a bit caustic until after dinner,' Freeman wrote to Elizabeth, 'but mellowed as drink and food of the best were consumed.' Following dinner with the Churchill family, Freeman found himself alone with the Prime Minister. 'He talked and I listened', Freeman recorded:

> Once, after a harangue lasting about three-quarters of an hour ..., he suddenly said 'Criticise that'. I proceeded to do so and was interrupted; I tried again and was interrupted, so I said at last 'You don't give me a chance to criticise'. He laughed and said 'Go ahead, I'll give you ten minutes.' ... I doubt I did have it but we had some good arguments on a variety of subjects ... I don't think it was unuseful and he asked me to come down again soon.[2]

Of greater importance was the new working relationship which Freeman had to establish with Portal, who was not a congenial man. Schooled at Winchester, which has a reputation for good manners, Portal was definitely atypical. He was unsociable, aloof by nature, intellectually arrogant and intolerant, happiest in the company of his six brothers, and in the leisured comfort of his family's estate, and unsoftened by the influence of sisters. Although a brilliant games player at Winchester, he made few friends, preferring solitary, perfectionist sports like fishing, sailing and falconry. He went through life like a lone wolf.

Portal had a patrician reluctance to explain things that were obvious to him, and was sometimes ruthless and quite unreasonable to those who failed to interpret his unspoken wishes. Even Freeman found him 'so bad at explaining what he would like done'.[3] Nevertheless he recognized Portal's ability and his unsparing hard work, and applied himself steadily to the task of making a close friend of that exceptionally austere man – yet another of Freeman's major contributions to the Royal Air Force and to the conduct of the war. He dined with Portal, joked with him, talked in his outrageous, uninhibited way about the war leaders and their colleagues in all three services, and broke the hard grind of their routines with relaxed and happy moments.

No wonder Portal called him 'The embodiment of wisdom, candour and loyalty'[4] and wrote that Freeman's utter loyalty and conscientiousness, his shining intellectual honesty, and, almost above all, his happy wit and delightfully mischievous sense of humour combined to make him not only one of the greatest officers of his time but also the most lovable and dependable of friends.[5]

Even so, there were moments when the strain of work tested Freeman's tolerance: 'Peter (his family and close friends called him Peter) has arrived back from his leave in rather bad temper', he wrote to Elizabeth on one occasion, 'and when he is like that he is damnably difficult'[6]

Portal's admiration for Freeman was unqualified, and for two years they ran the RAF together in mutual trust. Freeman only attended the Chiefs of Staff Committee when Portal was away or otherwise committed, but the Vice-Chiefs Committee, to which much staff business was delegated, was a regular commitment, and Freeman seems to have been Portal's 'alter ego' across the entire spectrum of RAF business. For obvious reasons, Freeman handled much of the liaison work with the MAP, and although, officially, he had no formal involvement in operational policy, his office was next to Portal's, he saw all the CAS's papers, shared much of the work, and the scope of his activities was always very much wider than would normally be allocated to a Vice-Chief of Staff. Slessor, who had the good fortune to serve them as ACAS(P), wrote:

> [Freeman's] ... wise, unrattled, humorous efficiency in the day-to-day running of the Service, the build-up of the expansion, and in dealing with Commanders-in-Chief and other Members of Council left Portal far more free than would otherwise have been possible, for his wider responsibilities in the Chiefs of Staff Committee.[7]

and later quoted Portal, about Freeman's work as VCAS:

> ... in this work, as in all he did, [he] was a tower of strength ... brilliantly successful in foreseeing the needs of the Service... He showed real genius for distinguishing what was right from what was merely clever – for finding the truth and exposing the superficial and specious. And he displayed steadfast courage in making and defending many crucial and difficult decisions.[8]

He loathed being VCAS, because he was by nature perceptive and decisive. There was more important work for him at MAP, but he had been forced by circumstances to accept as a No.2, a post of great responsibility, which had effectively no direct involvement in strategic and operational matters. Nevertheless, even as VCAS, he was a major influence in the politics of both the RAF and the MAP, and he remained deeply, if indirectly, involved in aircraft and engine development and production planning – distractions which complicated a workload that was already crushing.

All the C-in-Cs turned to Freeman for help, advice, equipment and personnel. He coped with complaints from, and difficulties with, the other services, and constantly played the role of mediator in disputes between the RAF Commands. He remained in close contact with scientists like Tizard, and Watson Watt of Radar Research, who found him a pillar of support, and with industrialists such as Ernest Hives of Rolls-Royce. Fedden at Bristol was almost alone in distrusting him.*

Portal and he worked long hours, often well past 10pm; leave was only two weeks a year, and when, in January, Freeman became ill again with 'flu and overwork, he once more retreated to Murtle Den where he could briefly relax. Diana found him 'far from well; ... he looks extremely tired'; and yet he remained 'merry and delightful as ever. ... Pheasant for dinner, good claret and vintage port and then Brahms and early to bed', Diana recorded; there was good conversation, too, a 'clamorous argument on Freemasonry and later Pain and Euthanasia ...'.[9]

Freeman gossiped discreetly about Churchill and other Cabinet ministers such as Woolton and Bevin.[10] Thanking Beaverbrook who sent him a 'golden' basket of fruit from Cherkley – grapes, oranges and grapefruit –, Freeman added: 'I hope your asthma is keeping clear; if it doesn't, I shall have to come back ... to make you angry, which you told me was your cure.'[11] After his return to London, his sister Sibyl sent him a weekly parcel of eggs and butter from her farm in Gloucestershire, and his health improved.

A report from R.V. Jones, awaited his return; an account of the German beam system for guiding aircraft at night, and a witty exposure of the

* Fedden was in charge of engine development at the Bristol Company until October 1942. Statements by Fedden about Freeman, reported in the original edition of Bill Gunston's book, *By Jupiter* included the suggestion that 'he ought to have been impeached for impeding the war effort' and that he 'rejected' the Centaurus. In his subsequent book *Fedden* Gunston distanced himself from these allegations. The minutes of the Bristol Directors Committee between 1936 and 1942 raise questions as to the reliability of Fedden's recollections.

lamentable failure by 80 Wing, the Royal Air Force's countermeasures organisation, to investigate, digest and act on the information available about the new 'X' beams used by the Luftwaffe's KG.100 pathfinder force.[12] Air Commodore Lywood, who commanded 80 Wing, and was ultimately responsible for such intelligence, had persuaded Portal to have most copies of the report 'recalled' whilst Freeman was on sick leave, but when he had read the report, it was reissued, unaltered, with a more limited circulation, and arrangements were promptly made to prevent the head of any other unit from restricting the flow of information to the Air Staff. The effect of Freeman's intervention was immediately obvious, for a new post, Assistant Chief of Air Staff (Intelligence) was created for Air Vice-Marshal Medhurst, who outranked Lywood, and Jones was promoted to be Assistant Director of Intelligence (Science) on the Air Staff executive, reporting direct to Medhurst.[13]

The young R.V. Jones – a 1937 portrait. He became Assistant Director of Intelligence (Science) on the Air Staff executive in 1941, and showed exceptional intuitive and technical ability, invaluable to the Air Staff.

Meanwhile, Freeman had written a personal letter, telling Jones that he had read his admirable report with the greatest interest; 'A good deal of it is beyond me, but I hope to find time to go into it more thoroughly and so learn a bit more' – encouragement in its proper sense, and typical of Freeman's courtesy.[14] He knew that Jones was young and relatively junior, but he had had the courage and self confidence to worry away at the slivers of information he could find about the 'beams' used for navigation by KGr.100, and to force the implications of his findings on his unwilling superiors: Jones was immensely heartened to know that he had got through to one of the top people.

Lywood remained in charge of 80 Wing and when KGr.100 made the modulation changes which Jones had forecast in his report, the alteration was overlooked, with the result that the guidance beams for the Baedeker raids, which caused grievous damage to some ancient cities in April and May 1942, were not jammed.*[15]

As VCAS, Freeman automatically assumed control of the Air Staff in

* Lywood deserved well of his country for he not only developed the Typex coding machine which served the RAF with total security throughout the war, but was responsible for introducing VHF for aircraft radios. His lapses concerning the German 'beams' probably stemmed from over-confidence, on technical matters with which he was unfamiliar. The radio beam was inaudible to the human ear and had to be modulated to be audible. The German's choice of a different musical note was not discovered soon enough.

Portal's absence. His longest, and most arduous term as Acting-CAS occurred at the end of 1941, when Japan and America entered the war, and Churchill took Portal to Washington for five weeks. Freeman's reservations about Churchill were such that he doubted whether their visit was necessary, believing that there was more important work to be done in Britain, and on Portal's return there occurred one of the few serious arguments ever recorded between them. 'I nearly told Portal that he had better get a new VCAS, but held myself back because he was so worried and tired and with good reason.'[16]

In Portal's absence, Freeman had to cope with the near insuperable problem of reinforcing India, Burma and Malaya to help stem Japan's relentless advance. Even this extra burden represented a relatively minor part of his enormous workload in the first half of 1942, during which he was involved in revising the Target Force 'E' expansion programme, making staff changes to improve the effectiveness of the bombing campaign, negotiating future deliveries of American aircraft, and planning to base the first American squadrons in Britain. His relentless quest for improvements in the quality of aircraft continued, and despite Churchill's refusal to allow him to return to the MAP, Freeman mounted a sustained campaign through Sinclair and the two ministries for better aircraft and engines, greater factory capacity for the aircraft industry, and increased production of heavy bombers.

THE AIR STAFF AND THE RAF HIGH COMMAND

As one of the two most senior serving officers in the RAF, Freeman was naturally obliged to delegate the detailed implementation of high policy to his subordinates in the Air Staff and in the top ranks of the Service. If the administrative machine over which he presided was to function smoothly, it was essential for key appointments to be held by high-calibre officers; he therefore took a keen interest in higher appointments and promotion matters, and kept a close eye on the performance of officers selected for important positions.

The activities of the Air Staff were supervised at regular morning meetings attended by directors of the Air Ministry's departments, and although Freeman usually attended, and sometimes ran them himself, they were normally chaired by the DCAS or by the ACAS(O). The meetings were always of considerable importance, and if for any reason Freeman was absent, he was invariably required to pass retrospective judgement on questions which lay beyond the jurisdiction of the DCAS.[17]

Freeman was determined that the meetings should be run with his own brisk efficiency, and when they became too prolonged, as they did in March 1942, he took his subordinates to task, writing:

> Too many of those who attend the morning Staff conference appear to be using it as a place for clarifying their own minds ... [and] read lengthy statements which they have failed to study in advance. It may be necessary for a Director to plough through masses of unimportant or irrelevant detail, but he should not do so in public: the only result is to transfer his confusion of mind to his listeners.[18]

The officer immediately beneath him in the Air Staff hierarchy was the DCAS, a post held first by Harris and then Bottomley. Despite his frequent criticism of Harris, Freeman recognized that his decisiveness and capacity for work was far greater than that of his successor, indeed, when Bottomley took over from Harris, Freeman's workload increased perceptibly. 'It has been a bloody day after a series of late nights and bad days', Freeman wrote to Elizabeth at this time.

> Both Portal and Bottomley are away . . . and that gives me a heavy addit-ional load . . . P[ortal] will only go away if I am here, and yet B[ottomley] must get away as he is not strong. I miss Harris tremendously . . . He was a much better man than B[ottomley][19].

Despite his own prodigious experience, Freeman, as VCAS, did not hesitate to draw on the expertise and measured judgement of retired senior Air Force officers, such as Salmond and Ludlow-Hewitt, and they both carried out their tasks with tact and efficiency. Equally, he did not waste time on those who simply refused to co-operate, such as Dowding, whose visit to America after he left Fighter Command, had been a disaster.* Despite pressure from Chur-chill, the Air Ministry refused to appoint Dowding either to Army Co-operation Command in June 1941, or as C-in-C, Middle East in September, and when Sinclair eventually had to ask him to review RAF manpower on Freeman's behalf, the two Air Chief Marshals were soon at loggerheads.

Dowding made the mistake of complaining to Churchill, before telling Sinclair, the Air Minister, that Freeman's disagreement represented 'gratuitous impertinence from an officer junior to myself' and his superiors finally abandoned any residual hope of accommodating him, and accepted his resig-nation with relief.

Freeman recognized that the efficiency of the entire Air Force depended on the qualities of its most senior officers. He closely monitored promotions above the rank of Air Commodore, and profoundly influenced senior air force appointments policy throughout the Second World War. Many of the confi-dential minutes which he wrote on this subject have been preserved among Portal's papers, and they represent frank, personal comments to a trusted colleague about men known to both of them. If, at times, they show a clearer perception of the failings rather than the strengths of the officers concerned, they must be considered in their proper context. Freeman was a clever, critical observer with very high standards of his own. He was decisive, clear headed, and intensely hard working, had a passionate commitment to the service he had done so much to create, and which Portal and he effectively ruled for the time being, and he was as determined to promote the capable as he was to retire those who had reached the limits of their abilities.

Typical of the advice Freeman gave to Portal was a note on Leigh-Mallory

* Sent to the USA early in 1941, as the hero of the Battle of Britain, to promote the interests of the RAF, he actually advised the Americans to stop making lots of bombers and make tanks instead! He was soon recalled.

Leigh-Mallory was ambitious and competent, and many of his operational ideas were correct, but he was dogmatic, obstinate and hot-tempered. When under stress he was apt to take counsel of his fears, and he was never wholly trusted by the Americans.

written in February 1942, concerning the possibility of his appointment to the Air Council as Air Member for Training: 'I think you or the S of S should speak [to him so that he avoids] the usual mistakes which are the pitfalls of an obstinate and self-opinionated man', Freeman wrote. '[He may] be too forthright and difficult with the C-in-Cs who are ... much senior to himself ... he can get a lot of value by *listening* (he is a bad listener) to other people who have both knowledge, experience and ideas.'[20]

Freeman was particularly concerned at the extent to which the highest Air Force ranks were dominated by older officers, many of whom had been brought out of retirement on the outbreak of war in 1939. He focused his attention on two groups, the Air Chief Marshals, of which he was one, and the much larger group of older officers who were ripe for retirement because of poor health, bad leadership qualities or inexperience with modern aviation technology. He was willing to use their services if they could 'perform useful work in the training sphere', but equally prepared to acknowledge that many senior officers in responsible positions had 'outlived their usefulness'.[21]

In recommending more rapid promotion for younger officers, Freeman accepted that such a policy, impartially applied, might affect his own position, and early in 1942, at the age of 53, he repeated his offer to drop a rank and serve as an Air Marshal 'if the Air Council wish to retain my services'. He pointed out that the average age of the seven Air Chief Marshals in 1942, excluding the Chief of Air Staff, was nearly 56. 'At the end of the last war, Trenchard was 46, Geoffrey Salmond 39, John Salmond 37, Sykes 42, Ellington 41, Sefton Brancker 40, Longcroft 35. The present Air Marshals and acting Air Marshals are all around 50 ... mature enough for any responsibility'.[22] His offer was not accepted.

Some of his observations on appointments and promotions, instinctively recognized the 'Peter Principle' – and thus the importance of *not* promoting people above the level of their competence. A typical case was provided by a Group Captain, an old friend, who had been promoted because he had done well as a Station Commander. After promotion he was too senior to remain a Station Commander, and then found that none of those in charge of larger

RAF Groups wanted him in the role of an Air Commodore. Ultimately, however, the quality of the high command of the RAF, many of whom he did not respect, would only be preserved by maintaining a continuous influx of high-calibre recruits into the lower ranks, and this too was a worry. 'We have wonderful pilots but they will never make administrators because, once they are off flying, they want to spend their time with girls and movies, games and drinking; they don't want to get down to the drudgery of real hard work.'[23]

Apart from his work at the top of the RAF hierarchy, Freeman had also to maintain close contacts with senior officers from the other armed services. Their principal point of contact was the Vice-Chiefs of Staff Committee. Freeman got on particularly well with Tom Phillips, the VCNS, and they soon found they could be frank with each other. One product of their collaboration, after German Focke-Wulf 200s began attacking shipping in 1940 and shadowing convoys to report them to U-boats, was the so-called 'catapult merchantman'. Freeman suggested putting an expendable fighter on one of the ships of a convoy, which could be catapulted off to attack the raider:[24] the scheme proved a deterrent until supplanted by 'merchant aircraft carriers'.*

In October 1941 Phillips was given command of reinforcements for the Far Eastern Fleet. He had always strongly supported the theory that warships could defend themselves from aerial attack,[25†] and his farewell letter to Freeman, just before he sailed for Singapore in HMS *Prince of Wales* is poignant:

> My Dear Wilfrid ... A line ... to say how much I have enjoyed our VCOS contacts ... I shall think of you all slaving away burning the midnight oil while I am living my life of ease in the future ...‡

RAF EXPANSION AND ADMINISTRATION

In the two years to 1 October 1942, the period which covers most nearly Freeman's time as VCAS, the number of RAF personnel increased from 437,473 to 1,042,015,[26] and his task, undertaken with the help of the Assistant Chief of Air Staff (G), was to supervise this expansion programme.

The operational needs of the RAF had changed when advanced bases in Europe were lost, since only the heavier bombers could now carry out offensive attacks against Germany. Portal's first expansion plan, for 75 heavy and 25 medium bomber squadrons, was soon overtaken when Freeman put the full weight of the Air Council behind a demand for a vastly increased force of 4,500 heavy bombers. The (rather simplistic) calculation that ostensibly lay behind this proposal was that in June 1941 the Luftwaffe bomber strength would be 2,250: British aircraft had twice as far to fly to their

---

* Freeman also wanted to bomb the Focke-Wulf factory.
† Harris jeered at the way Phillips asserted that modern battleships were able to defend themselves against air attack. [When at war with Japan] '... out of cloud will come a squadron of Japanese bombers and as your great ship capsizes, you will ... say " That was a whopping great mine we hit"'.
‡ Seven weeks later, HMS *Prince of Wales* and HMS *Repulse* were sunk by Japanese aircraft: Phillips went down with his ship.

targets and Britain therefore required twice as many aircraft.[27] The Air Staff may not have been entirely serious in requesting such a force, but in competition with the Army and the Navy, their principal concern may simply have been to ensure that the RAF obtained as many heavy bombers as available resources would allow. The main factors about the heavy bomber programme are summarised in Appendix VIII.

Freeman called a meeting to consider the 'interim' expansion programme in November 1940, and insisted that the task of attacking Germany in the immediate future would fall largely on the RAF. The heavy bomber force was then 26 squadrons, most of them equipped with Whitleys and Wellingtons and would have to appropriately re-equipped.[28] Since the 100 squadrons of 'Target Force C' could not possibly be sustained by current manning and production plans, the plans to increase fighter strength, and to expand Army Co-operation Command would need drastic reductions. More medium bombers were required,[29] and there was an urgent need for more training aircraft to ensure that expansion was not delayed by a shortage of trained aircrew.[30] There was a limit to the total number of aircraft that could be built in Britain, so all the extra planes would have to come from America, and Freeman hoped that Army's tactical requirements could be met by American aircraft like the Douglas DB-7 'Boston'. Freeman was able to defer the build-up of the RAF's Army Co-operation Command in the UK, and transfer some of the command's pilots to meet pressing Air Force needs elsewhere. He nevertheless reassured the Army that 'every effort would be made to withdraw only pilots with less than six months experience in squadrons';[31] other RAF commands were not getting preferential treatment.

Although the expansion of the RAF absorbed much of Freeman's time while he was VCAS, he was also responsible for many aspects of the Service's organisation and administration. His vital contribution to the work of Bomber Command and Middle East Command is discussed in subsequent chapters, but his intervention was needed in almost every sphere of RAF activity, including Coastal Command, Air Sea Rescue and photographic reconnaissance.

Coastal Command was the branch of the RAF that operated over the sea from coastal or inland bases. During the early stages of the war, its serviceability record had been poor, partly because its C-in-C, Air Marshal Bowhill, allowed its aircraft to perform the endless – and ineffective – long distance 'offensive' patrols prescribed by naval doctrine. Soon after Portal and Freeman took over the Air Staff, Coastal Command became the focus of yet another struggle with Beaverbrook. The Air Ministry had refused Bowhill's request for a larger establishment, and Beaverbrook promptly proposed that jurisdiction over Coastal Command should be transferred to the Admiralty,[32] a proposal which Freeman defeated by threatening resignation.[33] He was appalled by the discovery that aircrews were spending more than 1,000 hours in the air per U-boat sighting, trundling up and down the Navy's fixed patrol lines, and Joubert soon replaced Bowhill.

At the heart of the Coastal Command dispute was the all-important

The later Bristol Beaufighters were capable of carrying a torpedo and two 250-lb bombs or eight 90-lb rocket projectiles in addition to their 20-mm cannons. This Beaufighter has just fired a salvo of eight rockets.

question of aircraft supply, and if in this instance the Air Ministry rejected the command's request for more equipment, Freeman always did his best to ensure that available aircraft were equitably distributed between the different RAF commands. In 1942, for example, he personally sponsored Coastal Command's re-equipment with Beaufighters.[34]*

Freeman had been deeply concerned by Coastal Command's losses of light bomber aircraft in anti-shipping operations since September 1941, when he first suggested the use of cannon-firing aircraft for anti-shipping strikes.[35] By February 1942, before airborne rockets had come into use, he decided that the torpedo was by far the most effective weapon against shipping:

> We should therefore rely primarily on the expansion and development of the torpedo bomber force for the destruction of enemy vessels. I am now considering the proposal for accelerating the formation of squadrons. One of the factors is the production of torpedoes.[36]

Coastal Command was still using the Taurus-powered, Beaufort torpedo bomber, the performance of which had never really been adequate, and although Bomber Command eventually released some of the Hampdens they used for minelaying,[37] Joubert asked for the Beauforts to be replaced by Beaufighters adapted to carry torpedoes as well as their formidable fixed armament of four 20-mm cannons. He was delighted by the first tests of these aircraft, and begged Freeman 'as a matter of great urgency to fill up Coastal Command Fighter Squadrons with Beaufighters equipped to carry torpedoes; in the dual role they would be of the utmost value'.[38] Freeman referred this to Sorley, the ACAS(T), who agreed that cannon-firing aircraft could also support the anti-shipping strike squadrons by harassing the escorting ships with heavy gunfire during the torpedo attack and be able to look after themselves against fighters at low altitude.[39]

Freeman knew that the Mosquito would eventually supersede the Beaufighter as the standard nightfighter, that the fighter version of the Beaufighter was basically the same as the torpedo alternative, and that there would be a surplus of about 60 night fighters and 60 'coastal' Beaufighters at the end of the year.[40] He acted at once, telling the DWO, DNC, and ACAS (T) on 1 June 1942: 'I would like Coastal Command to have a Beaufighter-type torpedo aircraft at the earliest possible date'. Ten days later he was able to tell Joubert that 'CRD has already [started] the conversion of fifteen Beaufighters'.[41]

Fighter Command Beaufighters lacked W/T – which was long wave and needed an operator – but navigational difficulties at short ranges could be overcome. Freeman therefore asked the MAP to increase the output of Beaufighters to twenty-five a month by September, and planned to introduce them as the main torpedo carrier in two stages. The first 100 aircraft would be delivered without Anti-Surface Vessel (ASV) radar or sensitive altimeter and without a number of smaller modifications; subsequently, an adapted torpedo version would be built, embodying all necessary modifications.

Anticipating a negative reaction from the Admiralty to the stop-gap version of the Beaufighter, he could not resist adding: 'Do what you can to dissuade the Admiralty from rushing into print on the need to be fitted with ASV and other things. We will get you the fully modified article by the earliest possible date and no amount of petulant letters from their Lordships can possibly produce it earlier.'[42]

Freeman also reorganised the Air Sea Rescue Service [ASR] and the Photographic Reconnaissance Units [PRUs]. During 1941, concern over the performance of ASR had been mounting and by July, Peirse, the C-in-C Bomber Command, declared that its organisation was inadequate and its results disquieting. Of 60 aircraft which had gone 'missing' in June, only 20 had signalled that they were coming down in the sea. The Germans often claimed to have shot down fewer aircraft than were missing, so more may have come down there.

Reluctant to blame Group Captain Croke, the ASR Director, for the inadequacy of his service, without more information, Freeman decided to establish a new Directorate of Aircraft Safety to take over both ASR and regional control, and asked Sir John Salmond to run it.[43] Salmond soon realised that the ASR organisation was inadequately equipped, and asked for, and promptly received, two squadrons of Hudsons for deep search purposes; Croke retained operational command.[44]

Freeman was equally distressed by the way that losses of PR aircraft were rising during 1941 for he kept a special place in his heart for the PR pilots on their long, dangerous and lonely missions. He had asked Rolls-Royce to see what they could do to raise the ceiling of the PRU Spitfires on 2 December

1940,[45] knowing that, all too few of the fast, long-range Mosquitoes were available for PR work, because production orders had been so delayed by the Air Ministry's deep distrust of the unarmed aircraft. He directed that from January 1942 the first two 'bomber type Mosquitoes each month were to be fitted up for PR work.[46] Freeman's concern to maintain the quality of the aircraft used by PR units, and to conserve such aircraft as they had, made him study their casualties with great care, and he soon realised that each Command and Service was scheduling its own targets and sorties: several sorties were often being made, in quick succession, to the same target.* PR aircraft were too scarce to be misused in this way, so Freeman unified the PR service, creating one impartial organisation to serve all the different Air Force commands.[47]

As an administrator, Freeman had to maintain a lower profile than those who directed military operations; yet his work was no less controversial than theirs. He was continuously called on to overrule operational commanders – strong personalities, unused to compromise – but did so with a unique combination of authority, tact and evenhandedness. On one occasion in 1942, when Peirse, by then AOC-in-C India, sent home a bad-tempered and sarcastic letter of protest after his plan to separate the operational and administrative branches of his command was rejected,[48] Freeman's reply was a model of courteous reproof and immediate help:

> None of us are omniscient and the experience of all, some with even more experience than yourself, is that the divorce of administrative and operational control is unsound. I deprecate most strongly the tone of your signal, which apart from its impropriety in an official communication to the Air Ministry, must exasperate officers who are working their hardest and doing their best to help you in your task.

He then promised that Ludlow-Hewitt, the Inspector General, who was in the area, would discuss with Peirse his entire organisation. '[He] has full authority to decide, on the spot, what is best.'[49]

AIRCRAFT DEVELOPMENT

Despite his absence from the MAP, Freeman found it impossible to disengage himself completely from the work of his former department. The success or failure of the Air Ministry and the MAP were so closely interlinked, and his name and record so inextricably bonded to procurement policy, that he continued to exert a major influence on aircraft production and development. Indeed, as evidence of incompetence, indecision and mismanagement at the Ministry accumulated, Freeman's determination to improve the situation inexorably reinvolved him in its affairs, and procurement became another onerous, if unofficial, duty; by the summer of 1942 it was accounting for a significant proportion of his time.

* Warned by a successful raid or by the first sortie that some port or town was of interest, the Luftwaffe could guess that there would be subsequent visits, and patrol fighters at height to intercept.

Tizard had stayed on the Air Council in 1940, hoping to co-ordinate Air Ministry and MAP policy as Freeman had done, but Beaverbrook disregarded his advice,[50]* and Portal told him to take his problems on development policy to Freeman.[51] When Portal dismissed the Mosquito as 'useless' early in December 1940,[52] Freeman instantly intervened:[53] another 150 were to be ordered by 30 December 1940,[54] and by 23 January 1941, the Air Ministry asked for the 'new order for 150 to be day and night fighters.[55] By August, the MAP was being asked for 160 Mosquitoes *a month*, 100 fighters, 50 bombers and 10 PR.[56]

In April 1941, Freeman can be found influencing fighter development policy, when a dispute broke out between Tizard, at MAP, and the Controller of Research and Development (CRD), Air Vice-Marshal Linnell. Tizard believed that the new Hawker Typhoon would soon replace the Hurricane and Spitfire, while Linnell knew that it was inadequate until improved. He told Tizard that the Spitfire V and IV approached RAF requirements much more nearly and were the only non-pressurised fighters

Sir Henry Tizard had been a pilot in the RFC. As Chairman of the Committee for the Scientific Study of Air Defence and Scientific Advisor to the RAF, he made a magnificent contribution to its operational efficiency between 1934 and 1940. Excluded from radar development by Lindemann thereafter, he was still being consulted by Freeman and Portal two years later.

which did so. Linnell also insisted that Tizard's hopes for the unproven Whittle jet engine for the longer term were premature; efforts to develop other fighters should not be relaxed.[57] Freeman wholeheartedly supported him. 'You set out my views far better than I could do myself', Freeman told him:

> Tizard is fundamentally unsound in gambling on a dayfighter force ... equipped entirely with Typhoons ... and the problematical Whittle ... You cannot sacrifice performance ... and performance means specialisation. You cannot afford to gamble on the equipment of your fighter force. Tizard ... believes in ... delivery and performance [promises] which have no basis for justification and I will not agree to sacrifice a really good certainty for the doubtful Whittle and the Typhoon ... which we know will not be able to operate at great heights. I take it that this file will not go to ... Tizard.[58]

As scientific adviser to the RAF, Tizard had earned Freeman's respect, but his appointment to fill Freeman's former role at the MAP had been a mistake

* Beaverbrook used to throw his memos into the wastepaper basket unread.

and by the spring of 1941 he had lost the confidence of the Air Staff, in that role. Freeman therefore proposed that Tizard's responsibilities for research and development should all be transferred to Linnell, who should also choose the types and numbers of aircraft produced for the RAF.[59]

It was an important change, but Freeman lacked the formal responsibility for improving the higher direction of the MAP, and he monitored developments from the Air Ministry, with mounting concern. Leading industrialists, such as Hives, shared his anxiety, and instinctively looked to him to find a solution. Writing to Freeman in June 1941, Hives described how, as in the First World War, ['technically literate'] Civil Servants and 'experts' at the MAP were making over-optimistic guesses about the performance of new aircraft and engines, based on the unproven forecasts of their designers, and backing them at the expense of proven alternatives. Too much of the Ministry's time, effort and equipment was being spent on undeveloped engines, meetings were chaotic, crowded and indecisive, and the controlling influence of the Air Staff was badly missed. Warning Freeman of the creeping inertia of indecision, he wrote:

> I've never yet attended a meeting at MAP that I have not left with a stomach ache and a feeling that it has been a waste of time ... Since we now have to go through the Civil Service routine, it is impossible to get any decisions ... The only safe thing to bank on in quantity for next year is something which exists today ... Hurricane Is and Spitfire Is, if converted to take Merlin 45s, or Merlin 66s ... can be as good as any of the front-line aircraft.[60]

Freeman, Linnell and Hives were soon vindicated. The Spitfire V, and its Merlin-45 engine with an improved single-stage supercharger and 100 octane fuel, became standard equipment in Fighter Command in 1941, and began to be supplemented by the Mark IX, with a two-stage Merlin, in 1942; the Spitfire was never replaced by the Typhoon.*

In the following months, any success achieved by the MAP in the field of aircraft design resulted not from its own policies but from the outcome of decisions taken by Freeman when he was AMDP. Production of the Halifax, Lancaster and Mosquito were steadily increasing, as were deliveries of Beaufighters, once the teething troubles of the airframe and its Hercules engines were solved. Together with new Spitfire and Hurricane variants, these models significantly enhanced the operational capability of the RAF, and the MAP received much of the credit for their development. Freeman recognized, however, that new design projects, such as the Whittle and Sabre engines, were stagnating, and that production of the all-important two-stage Merlins and Griffons was rising very slowly: if these programmes were not driven forward more energetically, the Air Force might eventually lose the qualitative advantage which it had hitherto enjoyed over the Luftwaffe.

His concern deepened during the early months of 1942 following the appearance of an outstanding new German fighter, the Focke-Wulf 190. 'In

---

* The Spitfire III, designed for the two-speed Merlin XX never went into production, but the airframe became the basis of the Mark Vc and later varients.

the Royal Air Force', he told Elizabeth, 'we started the war with superior equipment but the superiority has been eroded from us slowly, not because we can't have it but because the Minister is only concerned with numbers . . . It is pitiful if not tragic. I am about to have a tussle on this.'[61]

He was indeed. In May 1942 Freeman drafted an adverse report to the ministry about its 1943 programme, making scathing comments about production plans for combat fighters, the type of aircraft about which he was exceptionally sensitive.

> The mountain has again produced a mouse and substantially the same old mouse at that. Engine design has not been forced ahead to provide sufficiently high power for new fighters, and production capacity has never included allowance for the introduction of new types without interfering with those in production. . . . If we persist in . . . production of types inferior to those of the enemy, our defeat in the air is certain.[62]

Freeman's paper caused such a major flutter at the MAP that in subsequent communications with the ministry he had to moderate his tone somewhat.[63] He was unrepentant however, having bluntly warned MAP that no new types of aircraft or engines could be brought into service quickly: 'all we can hope for', he wrote, 'is the development of existing types.'[64] The position seemed bleak: there were never enough fighters despite all the MAP's promises, US production was largely devoted to unwanted types,* and Freeman was certain that American fighter squadrons operating in Britain would have to be equipped with Spitfires.[65] He rejected the Typhoon as a combat fighter because there was no role for such a low altitude aircraft in current operations over France,[66] and concluded, (erroneously for once) 'the absence of a new design of engine with better power:weight ratio absolutely precludes any radical improvement in fighter efficiency.'[67]

Neither of the large Bristol engines appeared to offer a solution, although roughly half the engines for operational aircraft still had to come from Bristol, regardless of their shortcomings. The high-altitude performance of the Hercules compared unfavourably with that of the smaller Merlin[68], and progress on the Centaurus was hampered by cooling problems, production difficulties and the lack of suitable airframes. Merlin-powered Lancasters had high ceilings, even with full loads, but the bomb loads of Merlin-engined Halifax IIs and Vs, and of Stirlings, Halifax IIIs and IVs (and the 300 Lancaster IIs) with Hercules VIs or XVIs had to be restricted because of their low ceilings; their targets were often selected to reduce the high casualty rates caused by their need to operate at a lower altitude.[69] Other marks of Hercules engines, and the other Bristol radials, were used on aircraft for which good performance at height was less essential.*

For the most important first-line aircraft, Freeman knew that the RAF was

---

* In 1941, despite long term plans to adopt the new P-47, US production of fighter aircraft was concentrated on the P-39 and P-40, both with the single stage Allison engine: the P-38, with two such Allisons, had yet to be given turbo-chargers. None of the latter would have been able to compete with German Me109s and FW190s.

highly dependent on Rolls-Royce to develop more powerful versions of the Merlin, and higher capacity engines like the Griffon. He therefore made sure that the engine manufacturers were fully appraised of their respective roles in the future aircraft programme. (see Appendix X)

Freeman's criticism of the MAP did in fact result in a dramatic acceleration of engine development, for Rolls-Royce was able to rise to the challenge immediately, but many fundamental technical problems remained unsolved when he finally returned to MAP as its Chief Executive in October 1942. His worries about the quality of Allied fighters would have proved entirely justified had it not been for the development potential of the Spitfire, and for the extraordinary performance of the Merlin Mustang. As soon as the Mustang's potential qualities became clear, in May 1942, Freeman became its strongest and most influential proponent.

Freeman also tried to keep four alternative options open for light bomber development: a Griffon-Mosquito, the Centaurus-powered Buckingham, a Sabre-engined bomber from Hawker, and a bomber version of the Beaufighter, to replace the Beaufort. But once the performance of the Mosquito with the Merlin 61 was established, Freeman cancelled the Griffon Mosquito, the Beau-bomber and the Hawker bomber, and slowed work on the Buckingham, decisions explained further in Appendices IX and X.

Despite his preoccupations and the mass of detailed work he undertook for the Air Staff as VCAS, in Portal's shadow, Freeman obviously continued to exercise a dominating influence on aircraft development. The factors he considered at this time, the selections he made from the mass of technical alternatives available, his relentless drive for engines with superchargers which performed well at high altitudes, and above all his willingness to adapt policy to new opportunities as they emerged, show that he still had absolute mastery of the process of aircraft selection for quality, and that he remained the '*deus ex machina*' of the production organisation he had set up and been forced to leave in 1940.

Churchill finally recognized Freeman's unrivalled ability to direct both aircraft development and production, and in October 1942, after serving Portal as VCAS for nearly two years, he returned to MAP with full executive control of development and production, the position from which he had been removed by the creation of MAP in May 1940.[†] The background to that decision is covered in greater detail in subsequent chapters.

---

* The casualty rates for aircraft which did not return early from the Nuremberg raid in 1944, were 17.5% for Halifaxes, 11.75% for Lancasters. 'Height spells safety' was a sign in the crew room at Binbrook. (*The Nuremberg Raid* by M. Middlebrook)
† Churchill at the time had referred to 'the muddle and scandal' of aircraft production.

Developing a Tactical Air Force: the Middle East, 1940–42

ROM JUNE 1940 to November 1942, apart from the campaign in Italian East Africa, the Eastern Mediterranean was the only theatre in which the British Army was opposed by either German or Italian land forces. Linking the western and eastern extremities of her empire, the Middle East was of vital strategic importance to Britain, and she was resolutely committed to its defence. Beside the RAF squadrons based in Iraq, Palestine, Trans-Jordan, Egypt, Cyprus and Malta, there were units at Aden and East Africa, all of them under the control of the AOC-in-C, Middle East Command, based in Cairo. Their principal peacetime function had been imperial policing.

In 1940 the Command was far from ready to conduct hostilities against Italy and Germany, major powers equipped with large numbers of modern aircraft. The forces at its disposal were widely dispersed, many of its aircraft were obsolete, and it possessed neither the logistical nor the training infrastructures necessary to support a modern air force in protracted operations. Yet it was soon faced with a variety of strategic and tactical commitments which had somehow to be fulfilled with very limited resources, and the formidable administrative task of expansion.

Predictably, therefore, the problems of the Middle East absorbed much of Freeman's time whilst he was VCAS. Together with Portal, he determined the most important command appointments; in collaboration with Courtney, he controlled aircraft allocations to the Middle East; he worked with the AOC-in-C to improve the Command's repair and maintenance organisation; he ensured that the Middle East was supplied with experienced pilots from Britain, kept up a limited transport service with wholly inadequate resources, and did his utmost to develop the Command's own operational training facilities. Finally, he studied the systems of army-air co-operation which were developing as a result of the active operations of the desert war, and drew on their experience to shape the air support systems created in Britain at the end of 1942, for the liberation of Europe.

MIDDLE EAST COMMAND

The innumerable strategic and logistical problems facing the Royal Air Force in the Middle East could only be solved by an outstandingly capable officer who enjoyed the unequivocal support of Churchill and the Air Staff. Air Marshal Sir Arthur Tedder was eventually accepted as the right leader, but for much of 1941 the status of the C-in-C Middle East Command was uncertain, to say the least. Sent to the Middle East to act as deputy to Air Chief Marshal Sir

Arthur Longmore, Tedder replaced Longmore in June 1941, and in October was nearly replaced himself. Freeman's role in ensuring that he retained his position as C-in-C was of crucial importance.

Longmore had been appointed AOC-in-C Middle East Command in May 1940, less than one month before Italy entered the war on Germany's side. With only 29 squadrons of obsolete or, at best, obsolescent aircraft, logistical support appropriate only for peacetime operations, and with a sphere of command stretching from the Balkans to Kenya, and from Aden and the Persian Gulf to Malta, Longmore was confronted with the unwelcome prospect of fighting against forces which were, numerically, vastly superior to his own. His problems were compounded by the closure of the Mediterranean supply route, by Italian air attacks on Malta and, in October, by the invasion of Greece.

Soon after Portal and Freeman assumed control of the Air Staff, they decided that the work-load on Longmore should be eased by the appointment of a Deputy C-in-C in the Middle East, and considered a number of possible alternatives. Freeman favoured the former CAS, Sir John Salmond, still only 59, still exceptionally able, but he warned Portal that 'the RAF . . . would not like it – another old man we've got rid of and brought back'. Barratt had, in his view, both strengths and weaknesses, the latter tending to outweigh the former. 'He's pig-headed', Freeman wrote, 'and may antagonise the PM.'

This left Peirse, then at Bomber Command, as 'the best solution' and Tedder. 'We won't go far wrong with Tedder,' Freeman wrote, 'he understands the problems at this end.'[1] Freeman had originally hoped that Tedder would remain at the MAP to maintain the vital liaison between the ministry and the Air Force, but he was selected, only to find that Churchill promptly cancelled his appointment, probably on Beaverbrook's advice. Air Marshal Boyd was chosen instead, but his aircraft landed in Sicily by mistake on its way to Egypt, Boyd was captured and Tedder's appointment was promptly reinstated: he left for Egypt on 30 November 1940.[2] Whilst at MAP, Tedder had learned a great deal about the salvage and repair of aircraft, experience which would prove exceptionally valuable, for the Middle East Command's maintenance arrangements were far from perfect, and badly stretched by the wide geographical spread of operations.

A succession of disagreements over strategy and aircraft supply to the Middle East in the first few months of 1941 caused both Churchill and Portal to question Longmore's competence. His consistent and entirely understandable complaint was that he was being asked to undertake an excessive range of responsibilities with totally inadequate manpower and material, and being pressed by the Chiefs of Staff to accept ever more extensive commitments. Extra Blenheim and Hurricane squadrons were sent to Greece, as Germany advanced into the Balkans, and Turkey was offered RAF help. There was even talk of preparing enough airfields to operate a total force of ten fighter squadrons in Turkey and Greece by April,[3] proposals which completely disregarded the chronic supply difficulties of Middle East Command.

Longmore naturally faced stiff competition for aircraft from the home commands, but even when his forces were allocated more aircraft there were protracted delays before they could be deployed in the main theatre of operations. The Mediterranean was virtually closed to British shipping after Italy joined the war in June 1940, although aircraft with a range of 1,200 miles or more could be flown out to Egypt via Gibraltar and Malta, and Hurricanes with long-range tanks could reach Malta from Egypt when the Cyrenaican airfields were in British hands.* All other supplies to the Middle East had either to be sent on the long journey round the Cape, which made huge demands on scarce shipping, or landed at the Gold Coast port of Takoradi and then flown across Africa to Khartoum and up the Nile to Cairo, a journey of more than 3,000 miles,[4] – after which they needed an overhaul before they could be put into service.

Longmore's supply problems might have been viewed more sympathetically in London had his maintenance and repair organisation been able to sustain higher levels of serviceability, but the onset of hostilities overwhelmed the existing support services, and opened a yawning gulf between the number of aircraft 'on charge' in the Middle East and the number immediately available for operations. It was a gulf which Churchill could not, or would not, but certainly never did, understand. Believing that large numbers of aircraft were standing idle in the Middle East, he became increasingly frustrated by Longmore's reluctance to assume further operational commitments and by his incessant requests for more supplies. The C-in-C's stock fell even further after the German offensives drove British forces out of Greece and Cyrenaica in April 1941.

Freeman sympathised with Longmore's troubles. He realised the military absurdity of committing more forces to the Balkans, but reminded Tedder that 'the Greek frontier is important. [If we do not intervene] Turkey will think that we will leave her in the lurch ... and she will not in fact go into action.'[5] Conscious of the difficulties of trying to meet the many demands from London which began 'You must ... ', he told Tedder, dryly: 'I sometimes feel we might end the next telegram by saying 'you must win the war'.[6]

But he also recognized the extent to which supply problems dominated the activities of Middle East Command. The speed of German transfers over interior lines of communication worried him, and he asked to be notified of the departure of all aircraft from Takoradi. When, in February and March 1941, these were 40 per cent below target,[7] he urged Courtney to increase deliveries, and he was particularly anxious to deploy American aircraft more rapidly: 'we want all the bombers, particularly heavy bombers, that we can get and any long range fighters that are available', he wrote. But he monitored the suitability of reinforcements carefully, and when Churchill offered to send additional Wellingtons to Middle East Command, Freeman went so far as to tell Sinclair to refuse: the transfer of aircraft overseas without the necessary supporting organisation simply didn't make sense. 'Any attempt to add more

* There were experiments which came to nothing for fitting a slip-wing on a Hurricane. The extra wing, which could be jettisoned when airborne, would allow the aircraft to take-off with a heavy fuel load.

to the area would go beyond the saturation point', he wrote. The standard of maintenance will fall, the percentage of unserviceability will rise, and there will be more wastage. The sponge is full, it can hold no more water'.[8]

Although the difficulty of maintaining aircraft in the dusty conditions of the Middle East was compounded by the desperate shortage of spares and by the lack of base maintenance facilities, Freeman, like Churchill, was far from satisfied that aircraft which were available were being efficiently employed. Whilst not unsympathetic to Longmore's predicament, and to the way his forces were being stretched, the persistently negative tone of his communications became increasingly irritating to Churchill and the Air Staff. Their patience finally ran out when another signal, dated 30 April, passed on complaints from the other C-in-Cs, that the Middle East was not getting its fair share of modern aircraft, and asked about the availability of new designs like the Typhoon, Beaufighter, Whirlwind, Manchester and Stirling.[9] The questions betrayed a fundamental failure to understand the vital contribution that salvage and repair could make to keeping the squadrons supplied: for Longmore to pass them on, asking for unproven new aircraft with all the problems of maintenance and spares at the end of such a tenuous supply line, was inane. Longmore was summoned home and told on 19 May that his return to the Middle East was to be postponed.

Tedder was left in charge, his formal appointment as C-in-C coming in June. Knowing Tedder's failings,* Freeman harboured some reservations, fearing that, despite his ability, Tedder lacked leadership qualities, and the self-confidence and 'presence' to hold down a high command.[10] But he respected Tedder's intelligence and loyalty, and was impressed by the energy and determination with which he tackled his job as Longmore's deputy: his respect for Tedder steadily increased after he became AOC-in-C.

By October 1941, however, Churchill was beginning to doubt Tedder's 'offensive spirit'. Shortly before the commencement of the 'Crusader' offensive, Tedder cabled London cautiously forecasting that the RAF would start the campaign without *numerical* superiority. Churchill had seen 'Ultra' versions of Luftwaffe reports from Libya which contradicted Tedder's figures, and having promised the Australian and New Zealand governments that the RAF would have adequate air superiority before the next offensive, he was deeply incensed, and sent Freeman out to Cairo to investigate.

Freeman was given full authority to discuss policy with senior officers and government representatives in Cairo, in the light of the current plans and Ultra information, but Churchill specifically invited Freeman to consult him personally: 'You should report normally to the CAS for Sinclair but you are also free if you consider it necessary to communicate directly with me as Minister of Defence.'[11] Freeman guessed – correctly – that Churchill was planning to replace Tedder, and before he left UK, he took the precaution of

---

* He had a very direct and 'pawky' sense of humour which was easily misunderstood. Warning his staff, in the presence of George Nelson, to 'lock up the silver' because of his visitor, caused lasting offence. (2nd Lord Nelson to the author)

agreeing with Portal that they would both resign if Churchill tried to insist that he took Tedder's place.[12]

Freeman travelled to the Middle East with Group Captain Basil Embry in an Australian-manned Sunderland, leaving at about 5 o'clock in the fading light on 18 October, and entering cloud almost at once.[13] After it arrived at Gibraltar, the aircraft had to fly around for 1½ hours until the sea was calm enough to land. The dangers of the Mediterranean route at that time are evident from Embry's account of the flight:

> We left Gibraltar shortly before mid-day on 19th reaching Malta about 10 o'clock that night. The last few hundred miles into Malta had to be flown in darkness to avoid enemy fighters. About 50 miles from Malta we were told that a night fighter was coming in from the rear, but it proved a false alarm. We landed safely at Malta, and remained only long enough to refuel as we had to be east of a certain latitude before first light. Seven hours later we landed on the Nile and motored into Cairo on 20th.[14]

Safely in Cairo, Freeman held talks with Tedder, Field Marshal Auchinleck, the GOC-in-C, and Oliver Lyttelton, the Minister of State in the Middle East. He explained the reason for his mission, and delivered personally to Auchinleck a sealed letter from Churchill which disclosed that the Prime Minister had indeed lost confidence in Tedder: 'You will find Freeman an officer of

A Short Sunderland of the Royal Australian Air Force. The Sunderland had a cruising speed of 133 mph and a range of 2,690 miles.

altogether larger calibre', Churchill wrote, 'and if you feel he would be a greater help to you and that you would have more confidence in the Air Command if he assumed it, you should not hesitate to tell me so.'[15] Almost immediately Freeman received a cable from Portal warning him about Churchill's proposal, and asking for his views.

Freeman replied: 'Has your visit led you to think that a change in command would improve Crusader's chance of success? ... 'no'. Would you accept command if offered? 'certainly not, repeat not. Minister and Auchinleck, if questioned, will agree; delighted to think we may both go.' And he continued:

> It is obvious that evidence of friend [Freeman] sent to help is being used to incriminate. You and S of S will understand that the role of Judas is one I cannot fill. Am convinced it would be fatal mistake to change now. Obvious he [Tedder] knows highest has no confidence in him which would certainly sap self-confidence if he felt he had lost yours. Your confidence is all he needs and wants. I gave him assurances.[16]

Tedder's appraisal of the relative strengths of the opposing air forces was 'massaged' on Freeman's advice to present a less pessimistic overall view. New figures were drawn up by recalling aircraft on detachment, by allowing for enemy maintenance problems (no doubt using data from Ultra decrypts), and by stressing the superior serviceability of the British aircraft. Churchill was then able to reassure the Dominion governments, and he calmed down. Nevertheless, his confidence in the RAF, already shaken by evidence of the inaccuracy of bombing raids on Germany, declined further, and his relations with Portal and Freeman became strained.

THE MIDDLE EAST REPAIR ORGANISATION

The disputes which broke out between London and Middle East Command over aircraft supplies were exacerbated by the low serviceability rates of aircraft deployed in that theatre. This stemmed, in turn, from the Command's inadequate salvage, repair and maintenance facilities, and in recommending Tedder's appointment as Longmore's deputy, Freeman's principal expectation had been that he (Tedder) would draw on his experience in the MAP to reorganise and improve repair and maintenance in the Middle East.

At the time of Tedder's appointment, repairs represented but one of the innumerable responsibilities of the Air Officer Administration (AOA), Air Vice-Marshal A.C. Maund, and was not accorded the separate status which it had acquired in Britain, and which its importance undoubtedly deserved. Moreover, another organisational change which had transformed the Home repairs organisation had not been implemented in the Middle East: Maund's activities were still directly supervised by AMSO, the Air Ministry's department of Supply and Organisation.

The aircraft repair and maintenance problem was discussed in London at the very highest levels. The War Cabinet eventually agreed to a proposal made by Lord Beaverbrook that Air Vice-Marshal Dawson, Director of Repair and

Maintenance in the MAP, should be sent to examine the true situation in the Middle East, and to explain how repairs had been reorganised in Britain. Dawson arrived in Cairo in June, and soon proposed radical changes on the lines advocated by Freeman between 1938 and 1940. All maintenance, repairs, salvage units and air stores parks should be placed in a separate Command, to be run by a Chief Maintenance and Supply Officer (CMSO) – Dawson himself – directly under the C-in-C: repairs would no longer be subordinated to the AOA. The new Command would thus undertake the functions performed in Britain by Maintenance Command and the MAP's Salvage and Repair units.

The Air Staff supported the proposed reorganisation in almost every respect, and although Courtney strongly resisted the recommendation that the AOA should cease to be involved, Tedder and Dawson proceeded with the scheme. During the following months Dawson opened the huge Masara Caves complex, on the outskirts of Cairo to deal with storage, repair and the overhaul of engines, formed another large unit at Heliopolis, and made other repair and servicing units mobile and self-supporting. Recovery schemes were devised and many spares, especially for engines, were saved from the scrap heap and reconditioned.[17] The result was a steady improvement in aircraft serviceability levels in Middle East Command.[18]

The transformation of repair and maintenance was part of a much more extensive reorganization of Middle East Command undertaken by Tedder in

A squadron of RAF Bostons taking off in line abreast from a desert airfield. Without proper filters, dust badly damaged aero-engines.

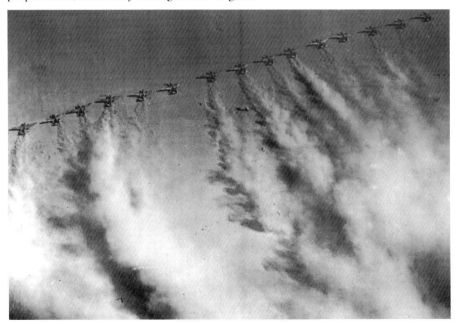

the summer of 1941. His proposals, however, had to be sanctioned by a so-called Establishments Committee sent out from London, and under Courtney's influence, and in spite of Dawson's remarkable achievements, the committee insisted that maintenance should remain under the jurisdiction of the AOA. Tedder, in turn, was determined that Dawson should keep his independent status, and when protracted discussions failed to produce a solution, he appealed to Freeman:[19] shortly afterwards, the Establishments Committee was withdrawn to London; Dawson retained the position of Chief Maintenance and Supply Officer.

Freeman probably hoped that this would end Tedder's problems, but when Portal accompanied Churchill to the Arcadia conference in the United States, in December 1941, Courtney tried to take advantage of his absence by enforcing the recommendations of the Establishments Committee: Dawson was to be demoted, his independence ended, and his responsibilities in the Middle East subordinated to the AOA, and thereby to the AMSO in London. Many of Tedder's aircraft had just been diverted to the Far East, and Tedder knew that he could rely on Freeman to quash the move, telling him: 'Dawson ... is handling it exceptionally well ... It would be an appalling mistake to remove him and ... ludicrous to demote him. The vital importance of our maintenance and repair organisation has been further increased'.[20] '[Dawson's] vision and drive are essential if the organisation, which is in its infancy, is to meet our pressing needs.'[21]

Freeman had to confront Courtney again; he was 'very difficult about it,' but Freeman was insistent. 'The CAS feels that Tedder's organisation has worked, and he is unwilling to upset it', Freeman wrote.

> There can be no doubt that [Dawson] has done remarkably well, and I think we should accept the fact that we have a CMSO of the rank of Air Vice Marshal and an Assistant CMSO of the rank of Air Commodore. I should, however, like to get this settled up, because I know it is worrying Tedder a good deal at the present time.[22]

This settled the question once and for all; there were no further attempts to wrest the Middle East repairs organisation from Dawson's control.

PILOTS AND AIRCREW

The improvement of aircraft supply and serviceability solved many of Middle East Command's difficulties, but aircraft alone were of little use to Tedder without adequate numbers of trained pilots and aircrew to operate them. As new aircraft became available for allocation to overseas theatres, Freeman controlled the type of aircraft supplied, and Courtney the number. Aircrew however, were different, and in 1940 Middle East Command largely depended on British OTUs for operationally qualified pilots, OTUs which were controlled by the Cs-in-C of the home commands.

By the time Freeman became VCAS, the shortcomings of this approach were already becoming clear. Home Cs-in-C, like Sholto Douglas and Peirse, were themselves short of well-trained aircrews, and reluctant to release their better pilots: Middle East Command tended to be allocated those who could be more easily spared.[23] The Middle East Command had no OTUs of its own in 1940 and clearly needed some as soon as possible.

Freeman recognized this, and, besides doing his utmost to improve the supply of qualified aircrew to the theatre in the first half of 1941, he planned to make Middle East Command entirely self-sufficient in OTUs for all major classes of aircraft. He had helped to set up the first flying school in the area in 1916; the first Middle East OTU came into existence in November 1940, and two more were established in nucleus form in March 1941.[24] He also recommended the creation of new training establishments in Britain to prepare aircrew for the specific requirements of overseas service, so that most of them could go directly abroad, by-passing the home commands. No. 14 OTU at Harwell was allotted exclusively to the task of training Wellington crews for Middle East service in April 1941,[25] and by November 1941 there were five OTUs in the Middle East.[26]

While these plans developed, Freeman closely monitored the quality of pilots selected for Middle East Command. The critical importance of posting operationally qualified fighter pilots to that theatre was obvious, and yet he found himself engaged in an almost continuous struggle to persuade Sholto Douglas to release more experienced personnel. When Lloyd, the AOC Malta, complained that Fighter Command had sent him three pilots with virtually no operational experience, Freeman minuted on the message [obviously to Portal] 'Can [Douglas] laugh this one off? I suggest you ... ask him [for] the operational experience of the officers he recommended – without mentioning this signal. W.'[27]

The new OTUs were slow to develop, because of the acute shortage of instructors, ground staff and aircraft, and when Freeman visited Cairo in October, he found that the shortage of pilots was so drastic that squadrons were, on average, one-third ineffective. 'The best help the Air Staff could give the Middle East', he told Portal, 'is to hasten the despatch of the batch of 100 fighter pilots ... 75 of these should arrive by 1 November 1941, and these should have not less than 70 to 75 hours in an operational unit. They should also include at least fifteen Flight Commanders.'[28] An extra OTU for Army Co-operation was set up after his visit.[29]

A general improvement in operational training for Tedder's forces might reasonably have been expected by the beginning of 1942, but the outbreak of war with Japan in December diverted large numbers of aircraft and pilots to the Far East and the Middle East OTUs were the first to suffer. Their output was, in fact, lower in March 1942 than in the previous October, and operationally trained aircrew had still to be sent out from Britain in large numbers.

As a result, the operational commands continued to compete with one another for aircrew and Freeman was constantly confronted with the difficult task of adjudicating between their rival claims. As the desert campaign wore on, however it became clear that fighter leaders and other experts in the

Desert Air Force were gaining much more experience in ground support operations than their counterparts in Fighter Command. The coming invasion of Europe made this an aspect of great significance, and Freeman wanted the best of them returned to Britain to pass on their skills to the new Tactical Air Forces. He knew, however, that Tedder was not getting equally experienced replacements from Douglas,[30] and would be increasingly reluctant to help unless this changed. He explained to Portal;

> The personnel, even of Squadron Leader rank we have sent out to him have been inferior; you and I know quite well that Douglas will not nominate his best and will never do so[31] ... This is not fair on Tedder and it is not fair on the officers in this country who should be given wider experience.*

Freeman suggested that in future Wing Commanders and Group Captains for overseas theatres should be selected by the Air Ministry, not by home commanders. He was equally determined to supervise more closely the posting of more junior officers, and asked for a nominal role to be drawn up of Station and Squadron Commanders with at least six months' experience in their current posts.

The conflicts which broke out between home and overseas commands over the allocation of experienced personnel could never be entirely resolved, however, and were still in evidence when Freeman left the Air Ministry.

MIDDLE EAST COMMAND IN 1942

Hitler declared war on the USA on 11 December and, to the great relief of the British leaders, Roosevelt agreed a 'Germany First' policy, and began to apply the full might of American industry to the war in Europe. Churchill set off on HMS *Duke of York* to Washington the following day, taking Portal and Admiral Sir Dudley Pound, the First Sea Lord, with him and leaving Freeman to act as CAS, and take the innumerable decisions forced by the Japanese advance in the Far East. Malaya and Burma were desperately short of aircraft, and such aircraft as were available were mainly obsolete. There was no immediate prospect of increased aircraft supplies from America,[†] so reinforcements for the Far East would have to be British: the Middle East was the nearest available reservoir.

Although Middle East Command was still engaged in the all-important operation 'Crusader', there was no alternative to sending the Far East every aircraft that could possibly be spared, and Freeman stripped Tedder's forces quite ruthlessly, telling him: 'Our aim in the Far East is to raise the strength of bomber and fighter squadrons at Singapore from five to eight respectively. Fifty-two Hudsons are being flown out from England [to Singapore] ... equiv-

---

* Freeman knew Douglas well, and accepted him as a forceful personality, successful in some responsible postings such as DCAS and C-in-C Fighter Command. Douglas liked and admired Freeman, and wrote his entry in the *Dictionary of National Biography*: Freeman thought Douglas 'devoid of self discipline' and lacking 'the instinct for preferring the gentleman to the cad'.
† The US Government imposed a temporary 'panic' embargo on exports of warplanes after Pearl Harbor.

alent to one squadron with reserves for the existing squadrons there. Our deficiency in bombers at Singapore is therefore two squadrons'. He went on to explain that 99 Hurricanes were on their way to Singapore by sea, with the pilots of two, and ground personnel of four squadrons; Burma needed personnel for four bomber squadrons and aircraft for five: Tedder was to arrange to fly two batches there, each of 18 Hurricane IIs and three Blenheim squadrons each of 24 aircraft, two to Burma and one to Singapore.[32]

Tedder was stunned by the scale of the reinforcements and cabled, 'Please confirm this is an executive order to despatch reinforcements', but he added: 'Will begin immediately first squadrons ready. The 36 Hurricane IIs will also be sent.'[33] In all, Tedder had to send nearly 450 of his aircraft to the Far East.[34]

With three operational theatres to support, British aircraft supplies were now more thinly spread than ever, and aircraft shortages threatened not only the operational capability of front-line forces but also, as we have seen, the development of operational training facilities. The Government had been subjected to intense political pressure to send fighters to the Soviet Union, however, and it was eventually decided that some 200 Hurricanes per month should be dispatched there. Although the first hundred aircraft could be supplied from Britain, the second hundred had to be withdrawn from Middle East Command.

Freeman was adamant that this would seriously weaken the Desert Air Force, and argued that other models would satisfy Soviet requirements equally well. 'The [Allison-powered] Airacobra and Mustang were precisely the type of Army Support fighters the Russians required* and it would suit us far better to supply [these] than Hurricanes or Spitfires'.[35] Russia should be asked to accept the American types in whatever quantity Britain had to send them.[36]

He eventually asked the War Cabinet's Defence Committee for a temporary cut in the rate at which fighters were going to Russia, explaining:

> The withdrawal of about 17 squadrons of fighters, all ... from Fighter Command or its reserve [comes when] the Empire [is] in a relatively more grave situation than that facing Russia over the next three months ... If the monthly supply to Russia was cut by 50% it was not likely to affect the issue of the war in Russia decisively. Britain on the other hand would almost certainly need 100 more fighters a month during the coming months.[37]

But the political pressure to assist the USSR was too strong and Freeman's request was refused.

By the end of December, it was clear that wastage in Middle East Command would not be made up for nearly two months because of the diversion of Hurricanes to the Far East. Freeman had to accept this situation; Tedder's Hurricanes were the nearest, speed was essential, and half measures in reinforcement useless. Tedder, too, fully appreciated the importance of reinforcing Burma and Malaya.

---

* The Russians used large numbers of fighers for low-level army support operations, for which the limitations of the Allison supercharger were unimportant.

Spitfires on HMS *Eagle*. Although HMS *Eagle* and HMS *Ark Royal* both displaced 22,000 tons, *Eagle* had space, early in 1942, for only 16 Spitfires. She had been converted from a Chilean battleship between 1918 and 1924.

In the circumstances, Freeman could only sweeten Tedder's troubles with praise and occasional 'goodies' like Spitfires and Mosquitoes. 'The ASV Wellingtons are reaching you and I have told them to ship Spitfires, even though they have not been tropicalised', Freeman wrote.† [Joubert is parting with] two PRU Mosquitoes at the earliest date.'[38] Tomahawks and Kittihawks were also sent to Egypt to compensate for the lost Hurricanes and an extra 157 Hurricanes were shipped out via Takoradi.

While hostilities were beginning in the Far East and 'Crusader' operations continued in North Africa, Luftwaffe bombers based in Sicily mounted a sustained assault on the island of Malta. Aircraft and submarines based there had been decimating Axis convoys between Italy and Libya, adding significantly to Rommel's logistical problems in Cyrenaica, but by January 1942, convoys to Malta from Gibraltar and Alexandria were being subjected to such relentless air attacks that the island's supplies began to reach dangerously low levels.

Once Portal was back from America, Freeman turned his attention to Malta's problems. Embry had stayed there for four weeks on his way back to Britain, and had realised at once that the island's elderly Hurricanes must be replaced by Spitfires if German aircraft from Sicily were to be intercepted before reaching their targets, and that better radar equipment was needed to

† The essential 'mod' for desert operations was a dust filter.

control them from the ground. Lloyd, the AOC Malta, asked for an experienced controller as a top priority,[39] and Freeman sent out experts from Britain to chose a site for the radar before Embry left. The re-equipment of Malta's fighter squadrons posed greater problems. Short-range aircraft bound for the island had to be brought within range by aircraft carriers and flown the rest of the way. Freeman told Portal on 20 February:

> I have arranged with MAP for . . . parties to work day and night to prepare 16 Spitfires for another 'spotter' operation . . . Ready to leave . . . with long range tanks in approximately one week. Understand the journey from this country to Gib takes ten days. Allowing for hitches, we ought to be able to get the Spits to Gibraltar in just under three weeks . . . We should order shipping space at once, i.e. today.[40]

Fifteen Spitfires landed in Malta on 7 March 1942, ferried by HMS *Eagle*, and another 16 followed later that month. More were soon urgently needed, however, and since HMS *Eagle* could only carry 16 fighters at that time, the US Navy generously agreed that USS *Wasp* should load 47 Spitfires in the UK and fly them into Malta.[41] The operation was soon repeated, and these supplies just enabled the island to fend off the German onslaught until May, when the Axis leaders decided that Malta should be captured outright and called off the bombing offensive. In the event, the island was never invaded.

It is well known that Malta received the collective award of the George Cross for its stoic endurance of the German bombing; the island is still correctly known as 'Malta GC'. Far less well known is the fact that Wilfrid Freeman initiated the award. Aware of the intensity of the German assault, Freeman had the insight to recognize how the Maltese would value world recognition of their heroic resistance, and he told Portal on 27 March: 'Malta is having a tough time . . . Encouragement from [the King] . . . would do much to hearten them.[42] The island's GC was awarded on 15 April 1942.

By May 1942 the worst of Malta's trauma was over, and the desert war was once more commanding Freeman's attention. In the subsequent land fighting which led to the fall of Tobruk and the retreat to El Alamein, the consequences of poor generalship and inferior army equipment were glaringly obvious to the Air Staff. Freeman was appalled by what he heard of the quality of some of the desert generals, and the superiority of German guns and tanks.* 'The advantage of superior equipment and superior generalship have never been so obvious in war', he told Elizabeth in June 1942.

> The news from Libya gets worse and worse, and I must admit that the first thought in my mind is admiration for Rommel and his forces. What he has done is quite beyond the capacity of our Generals . . . I could never have believed that the Army and its equipment could be so bad . . . and that's almost treason these days.

* Charles Moran, Churchill's doctor, quoted an eminent scientist's remark in 1942: 'if we had been as inefficient in providing aircraft as we have been in turning out tanks, the war would have been lost already.

He recognized that the desert war would ultimately be won and lost in the air. 'The Royal Air Force is having prodigious casualties trying to stem the tide', he wrote. 'That expression is not fair because it suggests the impossible and it *is* possible [but] at terrific cost. We will pay that cost'.[43] Supply difficulties persisted, however. Between 24 May and 7 July 1942, as the 8th Army retreated from Gazala to El Alamein, 202 Desert Air Force (DAF) fighters were lost on operations alone; the wastage rate for Kittyhawks was more than 100 per cent, and two squadrons found themselves without any aircraft at all. Shortages also developed in RAF squadrons using American aircraft because of the American decision to supply complete units of American forces – aircraft and pilots, untrained for desert conditions in the Middle East – instead of aircraft to equip British squadrons. The new American squadrons remained inactive while their pilots acquired experience: the fastest Mark II Kittyhawks, with Packard Merlin engines, were issued to American squadrons 'which had yet to train to Desert standards'.[44]

Excluding Malta, Tedder's units were once more seriously short of aircraft by July. American supplies would ultimately provide the solution, but the US authorities initially estimated 'wastage' at only 20 per cent per month. Freeman sent a tactful letter via the RAF delegation in Washington, complimenting them on their reinforcement provisions, but stressing his experience that 'replacements had to be planned on the basis of 50 per cent per month for fighters, and $33^1/_3$ per cent per month for bombers': he asked for an immediate flow of aircraft and crews to meet wastage, over and above the aircraft already sent on RAF account.[45] This was one of the last occasions on which the aircraft supply question returned to trouble Freeman: during the next few months Allied air forces in the Middle East established an overwhelming numerical superiority over their Axis counterparts.

Quality differentials had also intruded in July 1942, when Tedder told him that the Desert Air Force was losing 'first class, experienced pilots', especially those flying Kittihawks and Hurricanes, because of their inferiority to German Me 109Fs. He promptly allocated Tedder six of the latest Spitfire IXs, the first of which had only reached Fighter Command during the previous month, telling him 'I suggest we pack up half a dozen Spit 9's at once and send them to Takoradi [on the basis that] the aircraft are tropicalised when they reach the Middle East. We are straining our resources to the utmost to send you 150 Spitfire [Vs] in August and September and thereafter about 100 a month including Malta. No use asking for more, they don't exist.'[46]* Six fast, low level Typhoons were to follow. Medhurst and Evill were much slower to react to the same problem when the Me 109Gs and FW 190s established a similar degree of local air superiority in Tunisia, early in 1943.

---

* Far too many Spitfire Vs were being squandered by Portal and Douglas over northern France and Belgium.

Experience gained in the desert war had profound implications for the organisation of the British armed forces at home. Following the collapse of France in 1940, the RAF had faced the accusation that it had provided insufficient support for British ground forces and had neglected completely many of the tactical problems associated with army co-operation. On the basis of this argument, critics of the Air Force in the press and in Parliament began to campaign for the creation of an army air corps which would be controlled by the army itself. Freeman and Portal accepted that much more attention would have to be devoted to army co-operation in future, especially if an attempt was eventually to be made to liberate northern Europe, and agreed to the establishment of Army Co-operation Command in December 1940. But they were strongly opposed to the concept of a separate army air corps and successfully blocked every attempt to re-create one during 1941.

The Army's most forthright attempt to acquire its own air force had been during the early months of 1941. Under Brooke's direction, and with Beaverbrook's mischievous encouragement, demands were formulated for an enormous air force – an air component of possibly 80 squadrons of specially designed aircraft, under direct Army control – to give close support to an army of 15 armoured divisions and 42 infantry divisions.[47] Not to be outdone, the Admiralty also planned to set up their own Naval Air Force of 2,000 first line aircraft, with reconnaissance aircraft, bombers and fighters all working under Naval operational control.[48]

In all, the combined demands of the Army and Navy totalled 6,000 aircraft for limited and specialised roles. Freeman remarked scathingly that even if the Fleet Air Arm was excluded, 'the combined demands exceed by a considerable margin the total strength of the Luftwaffe'. To meet such demands would automatically extinguish any hope of developing the bomber offensive that had been postulated by the Chiefs of Staff for winning, as opposed to not losing, the war.[49]

When Sinclair received confirmation of the Army's requirements for a force of nearly 4,000 aircraft, on 20 May 1941, Freeman and Portal killed the proposal immediately by simply asking to see the General Staff's (non-existent) plans for the use of the divisions in question.[50] Apart from the fact that the Germans would be able to concentrate vastly superior forces against the largest British force that could be landed on the Continent at that time, it was obvious that an opposed landing could not take place until air superiority had been gained, that this could only be achieved by expansion of the heavy bomber force, a development which would be impossible if the RAF's programme was distorted by the need to produce different aircraft for the Army. Army pressure for a separate air component subsequently eased.

Once the matter had been decided in favour of the Air Staff, Army Co-operation developed along a number of different paths. Closer links were forged between the Army and Bomber Command, and important theoretical work on battlefield co-operation was undertaken by Army Co-operation Command.

Serious efforts to improve air support techniques were also being made in the Middle East, which was rapidly emerging as a testing ground for an entirely new approach to the problems of army co-operation: between August and October 1941 an inter-service committee, assisted by Ludlow-Hewitt, the Inspector General, was established to investigate and rationalise the whole system of army-air co-operation.

Two fundamental conclusions emerged. First, the provision of air support should not be confined to specialised forces of the type demanded by the Army after the fall of France; on the contrary, if necessary, the entire available air power should be employed in gaining air superiority and supporting ground operations. Second, existing systems of air support control were inadequate: it was essential to develop better communications between ground and air forces by reorganising command and control structures, procuring better communications equipment and providing more specialised training to operational units.[51]

Ludlow-Hewitt confirmed that hostilities in the previous six months had proved conclusively the decisive power of well directed air forces, working in close co-operation with the Army. The most effective form of attack against small thin-skinned targets would be fighters rather than bombers. 'We should', Ludlow-Hewitt wrote, 'be directing all the Royal Air Force energies towards the utmost development of the fullest possible co-operation with the Army'. He urged an even closer liaison, to create a better understanding of the possibilities for air support among Army staff and troops in the rearward areas, and suggested that the functions and organisation of the specialist Tactical Reconnaissance Squadrons of the RAF should be clarified, and improvements made in air transport.

Portal and Freeman agreed with this, and by the end of 1941 the measures were bearing fruit. After an uncertain beginning, the new air support system developed there proved itself during 'Crusader' at the end of 1941, and Freeman looked on in admiration from London. 'I must start off by congratulating you and everybody ... on the wonderful work done in the Libyan campaign', he wrote to Tedder at the end of December.[52]

Not everyone was so appreciative, and in February 1942, following fresh reverses in the Far East, the General Staff renewed its campaign for an army air corps. Once more, their proposals were successfully blocked by Freeman and Portal. The Air Staff stressed once again, that the Army's primary need was for general air superiority, and that an army co-operation force would be backed by the full weight of the Metropolitan Air Force in Continental operations.

Searching for a compromise, however, they proposed that a number of fighter squadrons be provided with specialised training for air support.[53] Although this satisfied Brooke, now CIGS, elements within the Army's high command remained critical of the Air Ministry's provisions for army co-operation. When a memorandum by Nye, the VCIGS, inferred that the Army's reverses 'from Narvik to Singapore were linked, if not due, to the Air Ministry's refusal to recognize and fulfil the Army's need for air support', Freeman rejected his allegations by drawing directly on the lessons of the Middle East. That Army/RAF relations in the Middle East had greatly improved was, he argued, because the question of air support had been tackled from the top.

> Good co-operation was achieved because the C-in-C had set his heart upon it; it did not arise spontaneously from air superiority. You appear to think that co-operation follows from satisfactory air support, but in fact the reverse is true.[54]

As the flow of aircraft improved in the autumn of 1942, after the huge diversions to the Far East and Russia, the Mediterranean Air Force turned the tide of battle decisively against the Axis powers, and Freeman quickly recognized that a similar system could be developed, on a much larger scale, for operations in north-western Europe.[55] He suggested that an officer from the UK-based Army Co-operation Command should be sent out to the Middle East to learn about the new systems,[56] and refused once again to accept the Army's constant pressure to separate low-level reconnaissance ('Tac-R') squadrons for highly specialised training by the Army. 'The pilots must not be trained for a complicated system', he wrote, 'but worked as normal intelligent individuals ... able to assimilate clear tactical instructions'.[57]

In June the GHQ Home Forces proposed a compromise solution to the army-air co-operation controversy which had periodically soured relations between the two services since 1940, involving the creation of a Royal Air Force Army Air Support Group of twelve squadrons within Army Co-operation Command. Drawing on experience from the Middle East, it was proposed that these squadrons should be equipped with fighters and that they should be available for general air activity until the beginning of land operations.[58] Portal's initial response was to reject the Army's plan outright, and it was Freeman who recognized the similarity between the GHQ proposals and the air support organisation already established in the desert, and saw the scope for employing the same approach in Europe. 'I am not so sure', he told Portal, 'that we should turn these proposals down in quite so flat a manner. Home Forces have put up a compromise in the hope that we will ... meet them ... In the Middle East we have virtually been doing what [was] recommended.'[59]

The Air Staff therefore tabled their own compromise plan on 21 July 1942. Instead of confining their response to the isolated question of the Air Support Group, their proposals encompassed many broader questions concerning the organisation of air support during an invasion of Continental Europe. They sought, first and foremost, to establish in Britain precisely the same command structures as those developed in the Middle East – in other words, that all Air Force Commands involved in invasion operations, including Army Co-operation Command, would be subordinated to a single AOC-in-C. In so far as this officer would himself be answerable to a Supreme Commander of all ground, sea and air forces, the Army was assured that almost the entire Metropolitan Air Force would be available for army support in the widest

Churchill greeting Air Marshal Tedder first, before the diplomats and other senior officers in the welcoming party, at Cairo in August 1942.

sense of the term. All Air Force units would, however, remain under the operational control of the RAF. The Air Staff also agreed that the new Air Support Force of twelve fighter squadrons should be created, but recommended that they should form in 11 Group (Fighter Command) instead of within Army Co-operation Command, as GHQ originally proposed.[60]

Brooke refused to accept this alternative. All the Air Staff's proposals seemed to him to be tied to one particular operation, the liberation of Europe, whereas he wanted immediate changes in the air support organisation, beginning with the formation of the 12-squadron Air Support Force in Army Co-operation Command.[61] Portal at first felt he should comply, but again Freeman urged caution. He knew that the superb performance of the Desert Air Force in the defensive fighting near Alamein in July and August 1942 had finally changed Churchill's opinion of Tedder. Visiting Cairo with Brooke, in August 1942, Churchill emerged from his Liberator dressed as an Air Commodore,* and singling out Tedder, to the exclusion of the rest of the high ranking welcoming party, he apologised for having accepted Beaverbrook's views. '... I

* Churchill was the Honorary Air Commodore of No.615 Auxiliary Squadron.

was told you were just a nuts and bolts man. ... I was not told the truth. I am sorry.'[62] Beaverbrook had been out of the Government for some months, conducting an irresponsible campaign for a 'Second front now', so his baleful influence had waned, and Tedder's achievements were being properly evaluated.*

The entire question of Army air support was therefore referred to the Prime Minister, and in October Freeman and Portal obtained virtually all the decisions they wanted on air support matters. Although Churchill actually allocated the new Air Support Force to Army Co-operation Command, his principal ruling was that, in the forthcoming invasion of Europe, all RAF commands, including Army Co-operation Command, were to be controlled by a single AOC-in-C. The Air Support Force would be operated as part of the 'Tactical Air Force' system which had been developed in the Middle East under Tedder, in actual fighting against a well equipped and resolute enemy.[63]

On the basis of Ludlow-Hewitt's reports and of his own close study of Tedder's systems Freeman had shaped, between June and October 1942, the new Tactical Air Force which was formally established in Britain in the following year.

Freeman's work in the Middle East between November 1940 and October 1942 was an exercise in the art of the possible: he knew that performance would be limited by the resources available and did his utmost to maximise these. Even with American help there simply weren't enough aircraft at his disposal to meet the combined requirements of the home and overseas commands, and of allies like the Soviet Union, and he had therefore continuously to ration the available resources between these different forces. Each, on occasion, inevitably lost out.

The imbalance between resources and commitments was inevitable, given Britain's wide range of strategic commitments, and if the Middle East Command often found itself short of aircraft, and unable to develop its operational training facilities at adequate speed, its requirements were never neglected by the Air Staff. More and better fighters could in fact have been sent out after the German attack on Russia. But Freeman could not challenge the decision to retain them in Fighter Command, and use them over France and Belgium, on highly unprofitable 'sweeps', and as escorts for bombing raids by light bombers, however much he disagreed.[†][64]

Notwithstanding these constraints, Freeman did everything within his power to ensure that the command was competently led, and adequately supplied and maintained. He was instrumental in Tedder's initial appointment to the Middle East and quick to recognize his ability as AOC-in-C: when Churchill attempted to replace Tedder in October 1941, Freeman's part in his defence was decisive. He was equally impressed by Dawson's reorgan-

---

* Air Chief Marshal Cross was present, and understood exactly the intention of Churchill's gesture. (Cross to author, 1996)

† Freeman warned Portal that the scale of the bombing, and the restricted range of escort fighters would be unlikely to lure the German fighters to attack, unless on terms that were much in their favour. He was right.

'Air superiority would bring all else in its train': the meaning of the phrase is well displayed in this photograph of a Luftwaffe 'graveyard' in the Desert. Airborne, these machines were formidable enemies; air superiority had reduced them to so much junk.

isation of aircraft repair and maintenance, and twice prevented Courtney from demoting him. He also personally monitored the supply of aircraft and pilots to the Middle East, and if, on occasion, he was forced to divert materiel to other theatres, he repeatedly used his authority to allocate to Tedder his fair share of available resources.

Many factors contributed to the Allies' attainment of air superiority in the Middle East by the later months of 1942, but Freeman's crucial role in the success of the desert campaign merits greater recognition than it has so far received. Moreover, it was Freeman, as much as Portal, who took the lessons of the desert war to heart during the debates in London over army co-operation in 1942, and who thereby determined that the principles of air support which had been developed in the Middle East, were applied to the successful new command structures for the invasion of Continental Europe.

CHAPTER 12

Freeman and RAF bombing policy

FREEMAN HAD BEEN a prominent member of the team that devised the two new heavy bomber specifications in 1936, and he bore the main responsibility for the selection and construction of the bombers themselves and of their engines. He patiently nursed them into existence during 1939 and 1940, replaced orders for them after Beaverbrook's cancellations, and saved the Manchester airframe, or most of it, as the Lancaster, when the problems of the Vulture seemed likely to leave the airframe in the dustbin of history.

By 1941 the four-engined variants of the P.13/36, the Halifax and the Lancaster, showed promise, and when the bomber offensive faltered in 1942 and the performance of the Stirling and the early Halifaxes proved disappointing, it was Freeman, reinstated as CEO of his former department, now the Ministry of Aircraft Production, who took the decisions which ended production of Stirling bombers, increased Lancaster output, and re-engined the Halifax, eventually giving it a performance nearer to Lancaster standards, once the Hercules 100 engines became available. But his influence as VCAS on issues vital to the future success of Bomber Command was equally important, and his support for the creation of a Path Finder Force within the Command, in June 1942, was decisive. His contribution to the Allied bombing offensive merits a special chapter.

Bomber Command entered the Second World War equipped with only rudimentary systems of navigation. Consecutive pre-war C-in-Cs knew of the direction-finding and navigational aids available to civil aviation, but had little evidence to show that these would be of use to the RAF. They had ceased to fly themselves, and assumed that astro-navigation alone would enable bomber crews to find their targets on clear nights, without checking whether such confidence was justified. The concept of 'blind bombing' was not really considered.

Ludlow-Hewitt, the C-in-C from September 1937 to April 1940, ruthlessly criticised the alternative bombing policies which emerged from an Air Staff review, but he was more at ease demolishing the plans and theories of others than implementing his own proposals. He knew that his crews would have to fly both by day and by night, and realised, after his appointment, that Bomber Command was 'entirely unprepared for war, [and] unable to operate except in fine weather'.[1] He was well-informed, and very sound on paper, and he frequently recommended the provision of navigational aids and improvements in aircrew training, but he failed to ensure that his proposals were put into effect. Having alerted the Air Staff to the shortcomings of his Command, he made little effort to rouse them into action, because, when it came to the point of making decisions, he was incorrigibly indecisive '. . . as a Commander, a hopeless bungler and fuddler, unable to make up his mind.'[2]

After nearly two years as C-in-C, Ludlow-Hewitt shamelessly admitted that *less than 60 per cent of his aircrews could find a target in a friendly city in daylight.*[3]

The outbreak of war did not lead to any immediate improvements in target-finding. As soon as the RAF started unescorted day raids on the German fleet, their casualties proved that without self-sealing tanks, Wellingtons which lacked dorsal turrets, and Hampdens with inadequate traverse for their guns, were almost defenceless against beam attacks by German fighters;[4] Bomber Command would have to operate by night. Unfortunately, Portal, who took over from Ludlow-Hewitt, showed no more interest than his predecessors in scientific methods of night navigation. Neither he, nor his group commanders, flew with their crews, and none of them made any attempt to check the accuracy of their aircrews' navigation and target-finding. They therefore failed to realise that the crews were inadequately trained and that most of them were incapable of locating their objectives with any certainty.

Except as a member of the Air Council, it was not Freeman's task to influence bombing policy during his years as AMRD and AMDP. Through his regular contacts with Sir Henry Tizard, the RAF's scientific adviser, he knew that the application of scientific research to air warfare was far more advanced in Fighter Command than in Bomber Command. But by 1939, with the huge burden of production added to his remit, he already had more to do than any other member of the Air Council; he was thus hardly likely to interfere in matters which were not, directly, his responsibility.

Operational matters were within the formal jurisdiction of the CAS however, and after Freeman's appointment as VCAS, he was at last able, indirectly, to influence intervention in decisions about night navigation. During 1940 he had learned from Tizard about the German KGr.100 target-finding force and the extraordinary accuracy of some of the German night raids, and from R.V. Jones, about the 'beams' used by the Luftwaffe to guide aircraft to their objectives. He quickly recognized that Bomber Command would have to employ similar methods to achieve comparable levels of accuracy at night.

The surviving Air Staff documents on the formulation of bombing policy show clearly that Freeman soon developed his own, distinctive ideas about the subject. In June 1941, for example, his emphasis on attacking industrial targets contrasted markedly with Trenchard's proposals for an assault on German morale, or Portal's insistence on launching small raids on Berlin.[5] He was also sceptical when Portal inaugurated the so-called 'Circuses' during 1941.[6] These daylight attacks on northern France and the Low Countries, mainly by formations of Blenheims with fighter escorts, proved costly and largely ineffective, and starved the other operational sectors like the Middle East and Malta of the Spitfires they so badly needed.[7]

It was, however, the Butt Report of September 1941 which led Freeman to make his clearest statement on bombing policy, a statement induced by one

F.A. Lindemann *(third from left)* with some of the staff of the Royal Aircraft Factory, Farnborough. Having learnt to fly in 1916, by July 1917 he had worked out the aerodynamic reasons why aircraft 'spun'and proved them by solo experiments. He was scientific advisor to Churchill from 1934 to 1945, becoming Lord Cherwell in 1941. Mr Butt of the 'Butt Report' was a member of his staff.

of his very few serious disagreements with Portal, and one which establishes that Freeman had a far clearer understanding of the problems facing Bomber Command than the CAS.

The Report, commissioned by Lord Cherwell, Churchill's aide on scientific matters, was based on the evidence of more than 600 photographs taken by night-bomber aircraft during June and July 1941, and on operational summaries and other records. It concluded that only one-third of the aircraft recorded as attacking their targets got within five miles of them, and in moonless conditions the proportion was only one in fifteen.

The Butt Report not only exposed the inadequacy of Bomber Command training, and the desperate need for navigational aids for night operations, but inferred that the key task of being the main offensive force of the British armed forces, that had been assigned to it, was a role that the command was at present incapable of performing. This in turn raised doubts about the justification for its claim for a substantial proportion of the nation's industrial resources. If the planned force of 4,000 heavy bombers[8] was to be created, Cabinet confidence in the effectiveness of their operations had to be restored.

The subsequent Air Staff review of bombing policy revealed fundamental differences of opinion between Freeman and Portal. Assuming that 75 per cent of Bomber Command's bomb lift would not fall on the assigned target, Portal proposed a so-called 'nuisance plan', suggesting that on nights when aircraft could not identify targets visually they should attack twenty or thirty widely scattered towns all over Germany, rather than trying to concentrate their bombs on the estimated positions of a few.[9]

In a long memorandum, quoted in full in Appendix VI, Freeman dissented. The evidence of German attacks on Britain had shown him that concentration should be the key objective of strategic bombing operations, and he doubted whether any significant morale or material damage could be inflicted by sending out older, medium bombers to wander around German airspace, dropping bombs more or less at random. He knew that standards of aircrew training had fallen because of the rapid expansion of the RAF. Accidents were frequent, and he sensibly recommended that on nights when the weather over Germany was cloudy, it would be far better to train pilots and navigators over Britain,* so as to accumulate experienced aircrews to man the new heavy bombers when they became available. He understood the patience needed to create a highly trained force under the stress of war, and the need to resist the political pressure to use it too soon.

Portal's response ignored most of the serious thinking behind Freeman's advice, especially the need for improved aircrew training. He agreed with Freeman's views about concentration, but if weather conditions did not permit concentration, what, Portal asked, should the RAF do?

> 'Are we to stay at home or go out: are we to try for material damage – which requires concentration – or morale damage which I maintain, though you do not agree, can be obtained by dispersal?'[10]

The differences of both attitude and maturity could not have been more pronounced. Freeman was the supreme professional, with a deep understanding of the increasing complexity of the highly technical force he was trying to assemble. Quite apart from his sensitivity to the private anguish caused by aircrew losses,† he chafed at the waste of sending out half-trained crews on dangerous missions in obsolescent aircraft. Portal, by contrast, was a much less sensitive man who had accepted without question Bomber Command's blind confidence in astro-navigation, and failed to test whether its claims were justified. When confronted with the Butt Report, he was unwilling to face the stark conclusion that his existing bomber crews were

---

* There was a serious shortage of staff and equipment for new bomber OTUs, where qualified but inexperienced pilots could be given *operational* training before joining their Squadrons.

† Freeman kept a close watch on aircrew casualties, and pined at the casualties suffered by the PRU pilots on their lonely journeys. He wrote to J.A.D. Freeman, a distant cousin, when his younger brother, Patrick, was killed flying a bomber over Germany in 1942.

effectively being put at risk for propaganda purposes. His failure to conserve them was to delay the expansion of Bomber Command, and would ultimately impair its ability to make the decisive contribution to the defeat of Germany in 1944.

Freeman's memorandum on bombing policy illustrates both his grave concern over the associated problems of night navigation and target finding, and his methodical, scientific approach to solving those problems. Convincing as his arguments were, however, Portal decided to continue with dispersed raids. Bomber Command's aircraft therefore went on wandering around Germany, dropping less than 25 per cent of their bombs within five miles of their targets, and 488 of the aircraft sent out on operations, and several thousand aircrew, were lost in the six months to 31 May 1942.

Sadly, operations which were, to a great extent, politically motivated, required political intervention before they could be restricted. During raids in bad weather on several different targets on the night of 7/8 November 1941, exceptionally high casualties were sustained by Bomber Command. Peirse, Portal's successor as C-in-C, Bomber Command, blamed the losses on the weather conditions over northern Europe and on the insufficient training and experience of some aircrews. Freeman was furious; he thought his response 'objectionable', and the reference to the crews 'a damning admission'; if they were insufficiently trained, he argued, it was the commander's duty to train them.[11] When Churchill was informed of the casualty figures, he sent an abrupt minute to Sinclair and Portal which stated, unequivocally, 'We cannot afford losses on that scale',[12] and Portal had to accept the arguments which Freeman had addressed to him so cogently in September. 'The most effective and immediate method of reducing our losses', he replied to the Prime Minister, 'is to limit our operational effort, and instructions to this effect have been issued.'[13]

Portal was thus compelled to follow the policy of conservation of Bomber Command that Freeman had advised. But this did not mean inaction, and the Air Staff now stepped up their efforts to improve flying safety, night navigation and target finding. A highly qualified and innovative bomber pilot with operational experience, Group Captain S.O.Bufton* was brought in as Deputy Director of Bomber Operations [DDBO] at the Air Ministry and, despite Treasury opposition,[14] he promptly persuaded the Air Staff to arrange for Carnaby, Woodbridge and Manston to be specially enlarged as emergency airfields on which crippled aircraft could be landed safely.†

In the later months of 1941, hopes were pinned on a radio-based navigation system known as 'Gee', which would be specially valuable to 'home' aircraft

* Bufton had commanded No.10 Squadron from July 1940 to April 1941, so had operational experience, as well as six months in command of the bomber station at Pocklington.
† The runways were 75 yards wide and 3,000 yards long with huge grass extensions at either end. They cost about £250,000 each, but more than 1,500 Allied aircraft, mainly heavy bombers, made forced landings on these three airfields. Since each such aircraft was worth at least £75,000 in terms of cost of aircraft and of training the crews, the subsequent savings were immense, including thousands of lives.

back to base after sorties. Henry Tizard was actively involved in its development.* But after flying in an aircraft fitted with *Gee* the following year, accompanied by a very experienced navigator, Tizard warned Freeman, that at long range, the system was far too inaccurate to be an aid to blind bombing an area such as the Ruhr, some 350 miles from Britain. In Tizard's opinion, *Gee*, and the newer and still experimental H2S, would be unsuccessful unless used by a well-trained, specialist, skilled and efficient force.[15]

Tizard was by no means the first to reach this conclusion for Cherwell had recommended the creation of a specially equipped target-finding force after passing the Butt Report to Churchill.[16] Most operational aircrew in Bomber Command believed, as early as February 1941, that such a force should be established, and Bufton had quickly reached the conclusion that a British target-finding force, similar to the German KGr.100, would significantly raise the operational efficiency of Bomber Command.[17]

The documents do not disclose when Freeman first heard of the proposal to create a target-finding force,

Group Captain S.O. Bufton with his fiancée, Susan Browne. Bufton had had considerable operational experience before he became Deputy Director of Bomber Operations at the Air Ministry.

but by April 1942, he had declared himself strongly in favour of the scheme.[18] He had been ruefully conscious of the achievements of KGr.100 in 1940, and he recognized that the RAF must create a similar force when navigational aids became available; indeed, as he learned about the limitations of *Gee* from Tizard, he realised that its creation was not only desirable, but essential.

Astonishingly, opposition to the formation of the new force came only from Bomber Command's most senior officers. In February 1942, Peirse had been replaced as AOC-in-C, Bomber Command, by Air Marshal Sir Arthur Harris. Freeman and Portal had been impressed by Harris when he was DCAS: they had found him decisive, hard working and capable, if inclined to flamboyant language. His subsequent posting to the United States had been

---

* Lindemann, by then Lord Cherwell, had spitefully excluded Tizard from membership of all committees involved in Radar, but *Gee* was 'radio-based'.

less successful, however: his supercilious manner and forthright opinions had antagonised the Americans, and his cabled messages to the CAS, had been so destructively critical of Britain's main supplier and future ally that Freeman and Portal had been obliged to restrict circulation of parts of his signals to London.[19]

Harris shared the unshakable conviction of virtually all senior air force officers that the bomber offensive, if vigorously enough pursued, would inflict a decisive defeat on Hitler's Germany. He doubted, however, that a target-finding force would greatly improve the effectiveness of bombing operations, and stated that this opinion was shared by most, if not all, his group commanders. As none of them took part in operations, and all of them were well aware that Harris 'did not welcome independent opinions',* its not uncharitable to suggest that the views they expressed lacked an element of integrity. Although he formed, trained, equipped and continuously supported 617 Squadron, by far the most expert and 'Elite' unit in the wartime RAF,† Harris claimed a deep-rooted and irrational antipathy towards anything resembling a *corps d'élite* – if suggested by others! – and believed that the transfer of the best aircrew into a single specialist force would gravely weaken the morale of the remainder. He thought it would be sufficient for Bomber Command's existing groups merely to send the most experienced crews into the attack first 'to illuminate the target for the rabbits'.[20]

Harris took over his new Command shortly before the launch of a highly successful raid against the French Renault factory at Billancourt. This had been planned with advice from Bufton, well before Harris arrived at Bomber Command. The raid, led by an experimental target-finding force, achieved an unprecedented degree of bombing concentration, and severely damaged the Renault plant.[21] This encouraging result inevitably strengthened the arguments for establishing a permanent target-finding force, and encouraged its advocates, most notably Bufton at the Air Ministry, to press the case more firmly with Bomber Command.

Harris was distinctly impressed by the results of the Billancourt raid, and invited Bufton to write to him with his ideas, and the first of his letters was dated 17 March 1942. Anxious to have the personal reactions and comments of the Squadron Commanders and Commanding Officers at the Bomber Stations to the concept of a Target Finding Force, the Directorate sent each of them questionnaires, and every reply on the files at the PRO, without exception, accepted the proposal.[22] Bufton sent Harris the results of his survey on 11 April, confident that the unanimous opinion of the senior operational aircrews was bound to convince Harris and his Group Commanders, none of whom had flown on operations in the current war.‡

---

* 'I don't ask opinions, I give orders.' Bufton, quoting Harris to author, 14 November 1991.
† A posting to 617 Squadron was the ultimate compliment to the skill of an airman.
‡ Among those who replied thus were Don Bennett, 'Tirpitz' Tait and 'Connie' Constantine. Singleton confirmed that all the operational officers he had interviewed were utterly convinced of the need for a Path Finder Force.

Air Marshal Sir Arthur Harris who was appointed Air Officer Commander-in-Chief of Bomber Command in February 1942.

 The evidence went down like a lead balloon, and although Harris made a series of alternative suggestions which edged gradually towards the selection of better crews as raid leaders, it is obvious that he remained implacably opposed to most of Bufton's proposals. Another meeting was called, and the five Group Commanders, and the five specially selected Squadron Commanders they brought to the meeting announced their unanimous conclusion that there was no case for forming a special Target Finding Force. The degree of independent opinion allowed, and its likely effect on the career prospects of dissenters, can be judged by the fact that Harris was present, and prefaced their conclusions by saying that he 'was totally against the idea'.*

 The deadlock between Bomber Command and the Air Staff was only broken by Freeman's decisive intervention in June.

 In the first few months after Harris's appointment to Bomber Command, Freeman tactfully refrained from insisting on immediate consideration of the target-finding force. He told Bottomley, the DCAS, that 'Harris is still going through what he calls 'the whole gamut of experimentation of bomber tactics' with the new *Gee* equipment before he will make any decision'.[23] Freeman wanted a quick decision on whether 'a specially trained and constituted target finding force is necessary to achieve the concentration which is essential to the success of our operations' because he knew that the Germans would soon start jamming *Gee*,[24] and he must have expected that Harris would conclude that such a force was indeed necessary, once he had weighed the evidence, and would take whatever steps were required to create it.

* Slessor at that time Commander of No 5 Group, subsequently apologised to Bufton, confessing that he had been wrong to support Harris.

If this was Freeman's expectation, he can only have been disappointed, because for the next few months Harris not only continued to block the target-finding force scheme, but resisted by counter-proposals, virtually every other Air Ministry suggestion for improving the operational effectiveness of Bomber Command. His disregard of well informed advice was so contemptuous that it caused needless offence to those whose only purpose was to improve the performance of the huge organisation of which he was the head, and casts serious doubt, both on his judgement and on his integrity. By June 1942 Freeman realised that Harris would only co-operate if compelled to do so.

The attack on the Renault Works on the night of 3 March 1942 was the first accurate night raid. It was carried out by 233 aircraft, which dropped 470 tons of bombs from heights of 1,200 to 4,000 ft. The target was identified by reliable crews and thereafter continuously illuminated by flares. as planned by Bufton.

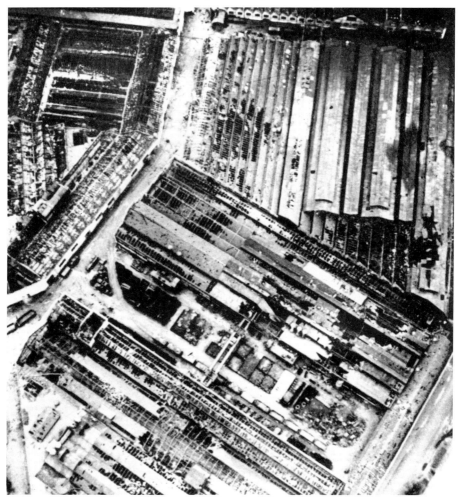

A typical exchange between the two men occurred in April 1942. A vitally important question facing Bomber Command at this time was whether, 'our best means of destruction of built-up areas is primarily by incendiarism, or by high explosive.'[25] Freeman monitored the numbers of each type of bomb employed in raids on German cities, and following an attack on Rostock on 27 April, he wrote to Harris suggesting that more incendiaries should be used. The ratio of incendiary to high explosive bombs had been far lower at Rostock than at Lubeck, and much less damage was inflicted. Freeman concluded that only large-scale incendiary attacks, concentrated in time and space, would achieve a decisive degree of destruction.

> If 50,000 × 4lb incendiaries is effective against Lubeck it follows a larger number will be required for bigger cities. On Cologne for example we might hope to produce a catastrophic effect by getting 100,000 incendiaries inside an hour.[26]

Harris responded that Lubeck was an exceptional target, 'built more like a firelighter than a human habitation', and could not be compared with other towns. 'I am always being pressed to concentrate entirely on incendiaries', he wrote, 'but I do not agree. The moral effect of high explosive bombs is vast'. He also maintained that high explosive did, in any case, help to spread incendiarism.[27]

Disagreements like this between the Air Staff and the operational commanders were by no means unusual, but the tone of Harris's response was striking. Freeman's suggestions had been made in good faith and in a co-operative spirit, his single objective being to increase the destructive impact of bombing raids, not to question Harris's authority by interfering in the administration of his command. Harris, however, seems to have resented Freeman's intervention just as strongly as he rejected other advice. His reply refused to acknowledge any basis for collaboration between the Air Staff and Bomber Command, making it clear, that on the contrary, advice from the Air Ministry was most unwelcome. Moreover, by deliberately misrepresenting Freeman's arguments – Freeman at no time recommended concentrating 'entirely on incendiaries' – Harris made a perfectly sound case appear irrational.

Equally striking is the contrast in their reasoning between Freeman's concern with material destruction and Harris's emphasis on morale. Material damage is tangible and can be scientifically measured; claims about 'the moral effect of high explosive' cannot – which was, no doubt, precisely why Harris chose this line of argument. Freeman, however, had been confronted by similar claims throughout 1941; he had not accepted them then, and he was no more disposed to do so now. Harris's assertion that Lubeck was an exceptional town merely proved Freeman's point. 'Much of the damage', Freeman wrote , 'was done by one house setting fire to its next door neighbour, or even one some distance away. In the case of Rostock you do not get this advantage and we therefore need to drop a far larger number of incendiaries.'[28]

If Freeman's faith in Harris was shaken by this dispute, he must have been even more disconcerted by their next altercation. In April 1942 a Bomber Command memorandum, issued by Harris himself, recommended a resumption of daylight attacks on suitable targets in Germany by small formations of heavy bombers, and high-level daylight attacks on the Pas de Calais area by heavy bombers with fighter cover. Freeman obviously approved of the memorandum, and arranged for some Lancasters to be armoured, so that they could be used in experimental daylight raids.

'I should like to use the Lancasters in the first instance over *occupied* territory,' he wrote to Harris on 26 May 1942.

> Although these operations should not be limited to raids with direct fighter cover, it will clearly be necessary to consult Douglas so that he can provide cover for the Lancasters on their way to and from the targets and give indirect protection by means of diversionary sweeps.

The official history, *The Strategic Air Offensive against Germany*, presents a misleading account of this affair by ignoring Freeman's emphasis on the importance of fighter cover and implying that he personally proposed the resumption of daylight operations and had in mind 'the use of *unescorted* heavy bombers in daylight'.[29] In fact, Bomber Command itself had recommended a return to daylight raids, and neither Freeman nor Harris made any mention of 'unescorted' bombers at this time.[30]

The armoured Lancaster proposal was not unreasonable. Lightly loaded Lancasters were regularly tested to 29,000 feet,[31] well above the altitude at which they would escape most 'flak', and fighter escorts would have welcomed the chance to tackle the Luftwaffe fighters. As Freeman himself pointed out, 'It was recognized that a reduction in the maximum bomb load would be necessary, but why not, if the weight of bombs reaching the target is greater than it otherwise would have been?*[32]

Harris promptly concluded that daylight bombing operations should not be resumed, and vehemently opposed the scheme. 'The object of putting the special aircraft on to day bombing', he wrote to Freeman, 'is apparently to attempt assessment of their vulnerability as compared with the ordinary Lancaster, by exposing them to the attacks of enemy fighters and recording the result.

> If, however, the formation was intercepted by an overwhelming number of fighters there is no doubt that very few . . . would survive and their fate would depend on chance, not armour'.[33]

This was ostensibly a rational argument, yet Harris was again completely misrepresenting Freeman's position. In a characteristically forthright response Freeman reminded Harris that a return to daylight raiding was being considered at the time when the armoured Lancaster proposal was made. Far from jeopardising lives, the scheme was intended to reduce casualties to the

---

* The Blenheim carried 1,000 lb of bombs; the Lancaster could carry 14,000 lb, but would have been much less heavily loaded when armoured.

minimum. 'I thought that over a period of one and a half years I had got accustomed to your truculent style, loose expression and flamboyant hyperbole', Freeman replied, 'but I am not used to being told ... that I am deliberately proposing to risk human lives in order to test out an idea of my own, which in your opinion is wrong'.*

Harris was now abruptly directed to execute the orders given to him on the 26th of May,[34] although there is no record that such raids took place. Freeman could have drawn but one conclusion: only the most peremptory methods would bring the C-in-C Bomber Command into line.

Harris's obstructive behaviour cannot have encouraged Freeman to expect that the all-important target-finding force would soon be established within Bomber Command. Bufton, at the Air Ministry's Directorate of Bombing Operations, had been corresponding with Harris on the subject since March, but had achieved very little progress. The matter had, in the meantime, increased in significance due to the appearance of the official Report on the Bombing of Germany, by Mr Justice Singleton. Presented to Churchill on 20 May 1942, the report quoted two operational officers 'of great experience' who were 'firmly convinced of the desirability of a specially trained Target Finding Force'.[35]

Harris obstinately refused to accept the concept. Although he declared himself ready to appoint regular 'raid leaders' within the ordinary squadrons, he attempted to refute the advice of the Singleton Report by citing the opinions of five, specially selected, squadron commanders. Knowing the likely consequences of disagreement, they too were just as unanimous in their support of the C-in-C's position as the Group Commanders.[36] By 12 June, when Bufton's last letter to Harris of 8 May was still unanswered, he was gloomily pondering the impasse when his door opened and Freeman looked in to ask if he had any problems. Portal was away on one of his few periods of leave at the time, and Freeman was checking to ensure that nothing was being held up by the CAS's absence.

Bufton replied that there was nothing really, except for the delay in establishing the target-finding force. Freeman borrowed the relevant file, read it, and telephoned Bufton about an hour later:

'This last letter,† have you had a reply to that?'
'No Sir.'
'Do you know why?'
'No Sir.'
'Because there isn't an answer to it. You have beaten Bert at his own game.'[37]

Bufton's letter was courteous and good mannered, but ruthlessly logical and well informed, and Harris simply stopped writing to him. As soon as he read Bufton's file, Freeman realised that Harris was no longer trying to refute the unanswerable case for a target-finding force but simply prevaricating about it, and he promptly intervened, decisively.

* 'The only way with Bert is to treat him rough.' (Freeman to Bufton: Bufton papers)
† Bufton's letter is quoted in full in Appendix VII.

First, he arranged a meeting between Bufton and Tizard for the following day. 'We discussed [the target-finding force]', Bufton later recalled, 'and Sir Henry obviously told Sir Wilfrid that he was entirely in support of everything I had said.'[38] Second, together with Tizard, he briefed Portal about the situation when the CAS returned from leave on 15 June.[39] Both Freeman and Tizard had been convinced for some months that a special target-finding force must be formed; they now persuaded Portal to overrule Harris's objections once and for all.

Freeman may well have drafted the letter Portal subsequently sent to Harris, for it was dated 14 June 1942, the day before Portal's return to the Air Ministry. The letter referred to the inadequate and inaccurate results which Bomber Command was achieving by its present 'rule of thumb' tactical methods using unsegregated crews, and baldly stated that 'the problem confronting us is clearly so great that nothing less than the best will do.' The difficulties were appreciated, but none of them were insuperable. The succession of evasive compromises proposed by Harris were then summarily rejected; they all, of course, implied his admission of the need for a specialist target-finding force.

> Over a period of three months your attitude seems to have progressed from the complete rejection of the target finding force proposal, through a target finding squadron phase, to this present 'raid leader' suggestion. I cannot feel it is logical that you should now reject the final and essential step of welding selected crews into one closely knit organisation ... In the opinion of the Air Staff, the formation of the special force would open up a new field for improvement, raising the standard of accuracy of bombing, and thus morale, throughout Bomber Command.[40]

It was wholly in character that Portal then added to the draft that is now in the PRO:

> I am reluctant to impose the Air Staff proposal upon you while you object so strongly to it. I would therefore like to discuss the subject with you tomorrow – and I hope we shall be able to formulate an agreeable scheme.

The version of this letter in the Portal papers omits this addition, and the fact that Harris agreed so promptly, probably implies that he received the version without that extra paragraph.*

At a meeting between Portal and Harris the following day, at which Freeman may well have been present, Harris is said to have started by stating – 'A target-finding force would only be established over my dead body'. They must have talked it through, for Harris was told to 'go away and think about it' and let Portal know his conclusions the following day. Harris realised that he must accept the implied ultimatum and agreed to establish what he decided to name a 'Path Finder Force'. Bufton had no doubt, however, that it was the 'fortuitous intervention of Freeman' that pushed the formation of the new force through

---

* Bufton told Freeman that 'he wished to disassociate himself entirely from the possibility of compromise'. (Bufton papers)

against the shifting and evasive procrastinations of Harris, and that it was only the united determination of Portal and Freeman that made Harris give way.[41]

Freeman was well aware that the only language Harris understood must be as blunt and outspoken as his own. By being careful to ensure that his arguments for the target-finding force were supported by Tizard, Portal had made sure that he had the backing of both his own Vice-Chief and the Air Ministry's scientific adviser, before he decided to confront Harris; Freeman was probably present.* The speed at which the decision to form the new force was taken once Freeman had made up his mind to intervene, provides a tantalising glimpse of how firmly and decisively he could act on one of the rare occasions when he was allowed to involve himself in operational matters.

Development of the Path Finder Force was slow at first. Harris deeply resented the fact that he had been compelled to form it,[†] and the force never received any priority in the allocation of the latest aircraft, the best equipment or the most experienced aircrews. As late as February, 1943, when 5 Group had been completely re-equipped with Lancasters, there were Pathfinder squadrons using Wellingtons, Stirlings and Halifaxes, all of them aircraft which had been bitterly criticised by Harris for inadequate performance.[‡] The Pathfinders had many practical problems which were only to be resolved by continuous, painstaking experimentation, nevertheless, their record steadily improved. Between 19 August and 31 December 1942 the force led 26 attacks on Germany. On six occasions, when the weather was poor, it failed to find the target; but in good or moderate weather conditions, targets were located and marked three times out of every four.[42] The contrast with the navigational record described in the Butt Report in September 1941 could hardly have been more pronounced.

Summarising Freeman's contribution to bombing policy between 1940 and 1942, it is clear that he strongly advised both constant training and concentration of bombing effort. He realised that it was vital to inflict tangible, material damage on the enemy, and his concern with material damage stemmed, in turn, from his quest to find empirical methods of gauging Bomber Command's effectiveness. Above all he attached supreme importance to training and the application of systematic, methodical and scientific measures to improve the accuracy of bombing raids. An immediate change for the better could only be achieved if aircrew training was improved and the new navigation aids were concentrated in the target-finding force. When he could intervene he provided a firm directing hand. He had the determination and strength of character to implement new policy initiatives, and was able – and willing, when necessary – to override the protests of Harris.

* Bufton was not present, but, asked whether Freeman was, he replied 'Very likely. I think Freeman was in at every stage of the whole operation'.

† Harris irrationally 'hated the PFF idea'. (Bufton tapes)

‡ The extent to which Harris favoured 5 Group is emphasised by his subsequent decision to allow them to 'mark' their own targets. The fact that four squadrons were transferred from PFF to 5 Group to assist the process rather vitiates the claim that their success proved that the formation of the PFF was unnecessary.

Air Vice-Marshal D.C.T. Bennett. A former airline pilot, he was appointed Commander of the Path Finder Force. Harris described him as 'the most efficient airman ever and brave as a lion'.

Bomber crews and ground staff in front of a Lancaster, before setting out on one of the Path Finder Force's first great successes, a 250-bomber raid on Dusseldorf on 10–11 September 1942.

He thus provided a counter-balance to those within the Air Staff and Bomber Command who had very different opinions about bombing policy. Alive to the political pressure for endless news of air attacks, they believed in the nuisance value of dispersed operations, content to gratify those concerned with the assault on that most intangible of targets, German morale.* They did not share Freeman's understanding of the enormous technical problems involved in moulding Bomber Command into an effective offensive force.

The difficulty of persuading Harris to create the Path Finder Force should have shown Portal that the arrogance and self-importance which had marred his otherwise excellent performance in earlier staff jobs had not been checked, but once Freeman had gone back to the MAP, Portal's control of Harris became increasingly ineffective. It was obvious, from this episode, that Harris was quite impervious to the polite and reasoned arguments that Portal employed with his other subordinates, but he shrank from using the forceful language that Harris understood, and became increasingly reluctant to impose his will. By 1944 Harris was effectively out of control,[43] resisting or ignoring Portal's courteous attempts to persuade him to comply with Air Staff policy, and replying to his letters with insolence which still makes painful reading.

Max Hastings makes the point forcefully in his book *Bomber Command*; he summarises the position:

> That winter, when Harris made clear his continuing commitment to the area offensive despite the major reservations of the Chief of Air Staff, he should have been sacked. The obliteration of Germany's cities in the spring of 1945, when all possible strategic justification had vanished, is a lasting blot on the Allied conduct of the war and on the judgement of senior Allied airmen.... By his indecision and weakness in handling Harris and the bombing offensive in the last eight months of the war, Sir Charles Portal disqualified himself from consideration as a great, or even as an effective, commander of air forces, whatever his merits as a joint-service committee-man.

Freeman would have had no such inhibitions.

---

* Disgusted by the clichés in Bomber Command's communiqués, Freeman minuted, through Peck; 'The attached note records two clichés which were "attacked" yesterday and which I hope can now be categorized as "probably destroyed".... The juxtaposition of the two adjectives "heavy" and "successful" has the affect of an emetic upon me.'

CHAPTER 13

Freeman's influence on US aircraft procurement policy

WHILST HE WAS Vice-Chief of Air Staff, Freeman also played a vital part in selecting the types and number of American aircraft to be supplied to the United Kingdom, and influencing the production priorities of the USA. Although supplies, including aircraft, were covered by the terms of the Lend-Lease Act after March 1941, Britain had ordered and paid for large numbers of American aircraft between April 1938 and February 1941, including the Hudson reconnaissance/bomber, the Harvard trainer, the Catalina flying boat and the P-40 Tomahawk fighter. By the later months of 1940, however, it was clear that what the Air Staff needed from the United States more than any other type were heavy bombers.

The paramount importance of these reflected Britain's strategic position after the fall of France and the successful conclusion of the Battle of Britain. Churchill and the Chiefs of Staff recognized that Bomber Command provided the only means by which Britain could wage offensive war against her principal enemy. As soon as Portal and Freeman assumed control of the Air Staff therefore, ambitious expansion plans were initiated, culminating in 'Target Force E', which envisaged a colossal operating force of 4,000 heavy bombers by the spring of 1943.

The British aircraft industry would never have been able to produce enough aircraft to meet such a target, even if their own expansion plans had been achieved, and to reach it vast numbers of aircraft would have to come from America. Beaverbrook had cancelled 90 per cent of the orders for British heavy bombers in May 1940, and the delay in reinstating those orders meant that output of bombers, such as the Halifax, Manchester, Lancaster and Stirling, increased much more slowly than had been expected, a shortfall which simply raised the number of aircraft that would be needed from the United States.

The American government took the basic decision to support Britain in October 1940, and even before the Lend-Lease Act was passed, a few months later, Freeman was working hard to persuade them to make a *vast* increase in their capacity to produce heavy bombers, and to obtain as many of them as possible for the RAF: until Russia entered the war they were the only British manned weapons capable of inflicting a decisive defeat upon Germany. His efforts soon brought him into direct confrontation with Lord Beaverbrook, who claimed jurisdiction over American orders for the MAP, and, like the Air Staff, looked to the American aircraft industry to make up for production shortfalls in Britain. Beaverbrook, however, was much more interested in the number of aircraft likely to be supplied, than the operational quality of aircraft ordered from the United States.

His discussions with Freeman in April 1941 convinced General 'Hap' Arnold, head of the US Army Air Corps, that there must be an enormous increase in America's heavy bomber production. Freeman therefore accompanied Churchill to his first wartime conference with Roosevelt in August 1941, to discuss air strategy with the US Chiefs of Staff and explain British requirements.

But for his appointment as VCAS, Freeman might well have had an invaluable opportunity to influence US production policy and the supply of American aircraft to Britain, as early as October 1940. Soon after Portal became CAS-designate, the United States government realised that the German attempt to defeat the RAF by daylight air attacks had failed, and that the Luftwaffe had lost the Battle of Britain. Reports reaching the President from Joseph Kennedy, the American ambassador and from the US War Plans Division had been, and were still, very pessimistic about Britain's chances of survival. But the triumph of the RAF led to a reassessment of the situation and Henry Morgenthau, Roosevelt's Treasury Secretary, reopened the whole matter of US aircraft supplies to Britain with Arthur Purvis, head of the British Purchasing Commission in Washington. Purvis was asked if the new CAS could visit the United States and explain Britain's air strategy and operational needs to the US administration, so as to bring about a concerted effort to meet their requirements.[1]

Purvis duly relayed this request to the Air Ministry, suggesting that if Portal could not come, someone with 'position, experience, personality and ability to present the general picture convincingly' should be sent instead. Lord Lothian, the British Ambassador, went further, asking for Portal to choose 'a high air officer, with ... war experience, knowledge of strategy, and enthusiasm [who could] kindle the interest of the US Administration and airmen on this side ... He could in a week or two exercise a great influence on the US decisions, not only about production and types so important to ourselves, but also on the US own programmes'.[2]

Sinclair suggested Freeman, then still at the MAP, describing him to Beaverbrook as 'the ideal man to give the Americans the right brief on Britain's behalf'.[3] Beaverbrook, however, was so reluctant to delegate his own authority over American aircraft supplies, that he flatly refused to allow Freeman – or any other member of the MAP hierarchy – to travel to the United States.[4] Eventually, Sinclair appealed to Churchill, telling him that Freeman 'could put our case to the US Administration with more authority and grasp than any other officer we have,'[5] and by thus asking for a definitive ruling from Churchill, Freeman might well have been allowed to go to the USA, had Portal not intervened.

Portal had accepted his new post without insisting on a named Vice-Chief of Air Staff, and after less than a week as CAS, he must have told Sinclair that he could not cope with his new role unless Freeman joined him. Having consented to the appointment of the younger man, Sinclair could only agree,

Freeman with General Arnold, head of the US Army Air Corps, on board HMS *Prince of Wales*, August 1942. Unposed, it epitomises the trusting friendship formed in April 1941 when Arnold visited Britain. Freeman convinced him of the need for America to produce more heavy bombers.

and Slessor, the Director of Plans at the Air Ministry, was therefore sent to the USA without the help of Freeman or any other senior representative of MAP. Slessor's first, tentative, agreement with Arnold, was that Britain would receive most of the aircraft produced from new American factories, and whilst this might have been ratified by the USA if their isolationist mood continued, its supersession after Roosevelt's re-election was inevitable.

For several months after Slessor's arrival, British representatives in the United States spoke with two voices. Slessor presented the views of the British

Air Staff, emphasising, in particular, Britain's need for American heavy bombers. The British Air Commission spoke for Lord Beaverbrook, and Beaverbrook's concern was simply to obtain as many American aircraft as possible, irrespective of their operational utility. Since America's capacity to produce short-range, light and medium bombers and fighters was then far greater than its capacity to produce heavy bombers, there was a very real danger that the US authorities would be more amenable to the MAP's demands than to those of the Air Staff. The RAF might then find itself lumbered with large numbers of completely useless aeroplanes.

Once Roosevelt had been re-elected President in November 1940, and his Lend-Lease proposals had been announced, Harry Hopkins, his great friend and confidant, was told that he would be given the job of administering the new scheme. By the time the Lend-Lease Bill was submitted to Congress, Hopkins had arrived in Britain, and Churchill instructed Beaverbrook to give him the latest information about British aircraft production. Other US appointments soon followed: a new American Ambassador, John Winant, took over from the pessimistic, anglophobe Kennedy,* and Averell Harriman arrived to become Hopkins' London representative on Lend-Lease matters. The change in attitude soon became obvious to Freeman and the rest of the Air Staff. Hopkins, Winant, and Harriman were dedicated opponents of Hitler's Germany, and staunch friends to Britain, and Freeman – and Britain's allies – had good cause to be grateful for their advice and support over the next four years.

The commencement of Lend-Lease quickly revealed the deep divisions between the Air Staff and the MAP over American aircraft orders. Given access to MAP's figures by a very reluctant Beaverbrook,[6] the US Air Attaché, Scanlon, told Hopkins; 'The Air Ministry wants bombers [while] Beaverbrook thinks they need fighters. I think the Air Ministry is right'[7] Without telling the Air Ministry, Beaverbrook also tried to persuade the Army to place large orders in the USA for dive bombers,[8] – which they refused to do.[9]

By the end of March 1941, Sir Henry Self, head of the British Air Commission [BAC] in Washington, had drawn up a programme, probably on MAP advice, for the delivery to Britain of 3,000 medium bombers, 4,000 light bombers, 1,400 dive bombers, 6,500 single-engined fighters and 1,000 twin-engined fighters. A high proportion of these aircraft would, in fact, have been completely useless for RAF operations, because of their short range, and poor performance, whilst only 600 four-engined bombers were scheduled for delivery to Britain between January 1941 and June 1942. As soon as Freeman saw the programme, he slated it as 'deplorable' and 'grossly immoral'.

> We will be unable to use many of the aircraft which will be delivered . . . They are paid for by a foreign nation, and their performance rules them out of the sky.[10]

* Roosevelt asked Hopkins to investigate the rumour that when he was US Ambassador, Kennedy had used secret diplomatic information to make a fortune by speculating in Czech bonds. He was replaced by Winant almost immediately.

To prove his point, he ordered the Air Ministry's Director of Bombing Operations to produce a map to show how the short range of the American light bombers would restrict their operational utility if they were flown from typical UK East-Anglian bases.[11] Courtney was advised to tell Self not to place these additional orders, and to instruct the Americans that the factories concerned should be instructed to turn over forthwith to heavy bombers. 'If they refuse, the raw materials [to make these useless aircraft] should instead be fabricated to our needs and embodied in British heavy bomber types such as the Halifax and Lancaster.'[12]

But it was the job of Beaverbrook at MAP, to condemn the programme, and on 7 April, in a prompt volte-face, MAP cabled BAC in Washington to press for a review:

> The programme is quite unacceptable in its present form; too few heavy bombers; too many fighters. Additional heavy bomber production must be obtained by diverting existing capacity from other types and creating new capacity.[13]

By March 1941, Freeman had convinced Hopkins and Scanlon that heavy bombers were of far greater importance than other types, offering huge advantages in terms of operating costs, but he was still desperately worried by the mounting evidence of Beaverbrook's quest for 'numbers', regardless of whether the aircraft were of any use to the RAF, and he realised that Beaverbrook's influence over aircraft production must be terminated as soon as possible.

The opportunity to strike an effective blow against him emerged on 23 April 1941, when Beaverbrook was scheduled to speak about aircraft production in the House of Lords. Beaverbrook did his best to dissuade Trenchard from intervening, but Trenchard insisted on doing so,[14] and arranged for the House of Lords to go into secret session, so that he could speak frankly and at length. He carefully avoided the pitfalls that always followed criticism of Beaverbrook, by an adroit ruse. He posed a series of very well informed questions about American aircraft supply and other important procurement issues, phrasing them in such a way that Beaverbrook's activities would have been exposed if he answered them.*[15] Rather than do so, Beaverbrook resigned from the MAP within a week.†

Beaverbrook's departure from MAP ended the confusion in Washington over the true British aircraft requirements. Their far-reaching implications for American aircraft production had been further clarified when General Arnold, the head of the US Army Air Corps, at the suggestion of Hopkins,

---

* An almost indecipherable copy of Trenchard's speech is uncharacteristically methodical. The key issues were well chosen, probably by Freeman, who knew that Beaverbrook was a dangerous enemy. Trenchard therefore avoided direct accusations and asked a series of awkward questions.

† Beaverbrook's involvement in production matters continued however, because Churchill reappointed him Minister of State.

visited Britain in April 1941. His visit gave Freeman a welcome opportunity for direct influence on American aircraft procurement policy.

Hopkins had recognised that existing American plans could not meet the demands of both the American and British Air Forces, and was already urging the government in Washington to make a major increase in aircraft production in general, and in the production of heavy bombers in particular. As soon as he realised that Arnold was demanding that aircraft supplies to his own force should be given priority over the needs of the RAF,[16] Hopkins persuaded Roosevelt to send him to Britain to learn more about Britain's needs and about the operational requirements of the European air war*.

Before his arrival, Freeman agreed with the Air Staff that the inadequacy of the American heavy bomber programme should be brought home to Arnold during his visit. He should be left in no doubt that to operate aircraft with a bomb load of less than 2,000lb and a range of less than 1,500 miles, was uneconomic in crews, aircraft and aerodromes. Freeman hoped that Arnold could be persuaded to press the US government for a huge increase in the industrial capacity allocated to heavy bombers.[17]

On his first night in London, Arnold dined with Portal at the Dorchester. The evening was not a great success, for Arnold was irked by Portal's formality and the urgency of his repeated requests for all sorts of aircraft, and thought that he had failed to grasp the enormity of the problems facing the Americans.[18] His subsequent talks with Freeman went much better. Apart from being exceptionally well informed about the potential of the most modern aircraft, Freeman was able to convey his knowledge in a friendly and amusing fashion. They got on so well that Freeman was asked to help draft a cable from Arnold to the USA.

Freeman's draft[19] stressed that the Air Ministry was planning to create a heavy bomber force of 4,000 first-line aircraft, all of them with the long range, large bomb load and good defence essential for operations against Germany. Roughly 1,000 heavy bombers a month would be needed to complete the programme during 1942, of which Britain might produce 500, so the balance would have to come from the USA.

America's production plans, which at that time envisaged an output rising to a maximum of only 226 heavy bombers per month by April 1943, were obviously inadequate and far too heavily orientated in the direction of lighter aircraft:

> ... production of light bombers was of secondary importance and abundant deliveries of these would in no way make up for failure to produce heavy types.[20]

Basing his cable to Washington on Freeman's draft, Arnold described the RAF's plans for a first-line bomber force of 4,000 aircraft, and stressed the

---

* Hopkins saw letters from Arnold demanding an end to the diversion of US-made aircraft to Britain, and thought that talks with RAF leaders would give Arnold a greater understanding of the problems of an air war against Germany.

inadequacy of existing production plans for heavy bombers, and the advantages of these aircraft over other types, not least the 'great saving in the number of crews required'. Using Freeman's own phrases he concluded:

> Light bombers are of secondary importance and do not in any way make up for our failure to deliver heavy bombers.[21]

Arnold was totally converted by Freeman, and returned to the USA with enough information at his disposal to initiate vitally important changes in the American aircraft production and development programmes. On 4 May 1941, Roosevelt formally directed Stimson, his Secretary of War to arrange for the appropriate priorities for plant to increase production of heavy bombers to 500 per month.[22] An immediate consequence was the creation of the so-called Joint Airplane Production Programs which provided for the mass production by six companies of the B-17 and B-24 heavy bombers.

They were programs which produced the overwhelming majority of American heavy bombers during the next five years.

In the same month, Arnold took the decision to order 250 'very long range' bombers which eventually became the B-29, ordered purely on the evidence of half-completed prototypes and a 'mock-up'. The creation of full production facilities for the B-29 was not sanctioned until after Pearl Harbor, and the project encountered such acute technical and design difficulties that production versions were not available until late in 1943: B-29 operations only began in 1944. Upon entering service, the B-29 proved itself by far the best heavy bomber in the world, but had it not been ordered 'off the drawing board' in 1941, it would have been unlikely to see wartime service.

Freeman's influence on the United States aircraft production programme during the spring of 1941 was profound. He convinced Arnold of the operational advantages of heavy bombers and the inadequacy of existing British and American plans for their production, and gave him the evidence to convince Roosevelt's administration of the need for a vastly more ambitious heavy bomber production and development plans. Although, at this time, Freeman had the RAF's interests at heart, there can be no doubt that the US Army Air Corps benefited immeasurably from his actions after America's entry into the war. Roosevelt himself recognized in May 1941, 'Additional bombers ... could, of course, be used by our Army as well as the British.'[23]

Arnold indeed was so impressed by Freeman that he supported the suggestion that the US Army Air Corps should allow members of their staff in Britain to liaise with the RAF 'to learn about tactical and technical information on ... aids to navigation and radio ... maintenance and repair ... airplanes and ... accessories'.[24]

The RAF's requirements for American heavy bombers, as conveyed by Freeman to Arnold, were based on the latest estimates of the British production programme, which had been reinstated after the Beaverbrook cancellations of 1940. During the first half of 1941, however, British production expanded much more slowly than anticipated: heavy bomber deliveries for the first three-quarters of 1941 totalled only 75, 102 and 150 respectively. The chances of achieving a front line of 4,000 heavy bombers in the spring of 1943 receded rapidly, and the only solution seemed to be to persuade the Americans to make a further substantial increase in their production capacity.

When Hopkins returned to Britain for further discussions in July, Freeman acted as the sole representative of both the Air Ministry and the MAP, and once again stressed the need for accelerated heavy bomber production in the USA.[25] They became good friends, and it was soon agreed that Freeman should represent the British Air Staff at the 'Riviera' conference, the first wartime meeting between Churchill and Roosevelt, in August, to explain the British position and its implications to the American Chiefs of Staff.

Freeman took leave during the last week of July at Murtle Den, bringing with him a bottle of Haut-Brion 1903, which he had been given by Sir Frederick Handley Page.* His health had greatly improved, and he gossiped happily about Harry Hopkins and his meetings with the Americans. On a day out with Liz and Diana, they drove through Aberdeenshire in the summer sunshine, passing through the Coreen Hills, and Huntly where Wilfrid's parents were married, and lunched at the edge of a pine wood looking down 300ft into a steep little valley with a mill and a ford. 'He has been cheery and argumentative, with a rather nice touch of humility that discounts all his own achievements.'[26]

The August 1941 meeting between Roosevelt and Churchill, held at Placentia Bay, Newfoundland, played an extremely significant part in the development of Anglo-American co-operation in the months before the United States entered the war, and in their subsequent plans. The first of a number of meetings between Churchill, Roosevelt and their staffs, it gave rise to the Atlantic Charter declaration of the 'Four Freedoms', American participation in convoy work in the North Atlantic, and the supply of more American aircraft to Britain.

By August 1941, the prospect of receiving the lion's share of output from the new US factories, generous and potentially realistic whilst the US was still opposed to involvement in the European war, was fading, and bound to be amended. Hitler had invaded Russia in June, and the influence of the isolationists in America rapidly waned as the dangers posed by Nazi Germany to the entire civilised world became increasingly clear. Huge expansion and re-equipment programmes were begun for America's armed forces, but America wanted to aid Russia, China and the Dutch colonies as well as Britain, and the US Chiefs of Staff came to Placentia Bay determined to stress just how little they could afford to supply to Britain in the immediate future.

Freeman's job at the conference was to rescue what he could from the ruins of the Arnold-Slessor agreement, by securing for Britain a significant allocation of American heavy bombers, and to reinforce the messages he had given to Hopkins and Arnold in previous months concerning a huge increase

---

* Sir Frederick was not known as a lavish maker of gifts, and Freeman rarely accepted anything from people in the aircraft industry, so this was a notable event.

The 'Riviera' conference (*above from left to right*) Air Chief Marshal Sir Wilfrid Freeman,
General 'Hap' Arnold, Admiral H.R. Stark, Admiral of the Fleet Sir Dudley Pound,
Fleet Admiral Ernest J. King, General George Marshall, Field Marshal Sir John Dill
and Rear Admiral Kelly Turner, on the *Prince of Wales*, at Placentia Bay, Newfoundland.
(*below*) '**A damned cold business.**' Harry Hopkins, Churchill, Dill, Freeman and Pound.
'We were posing for Movietone News . . . if you want to see how five people can waste
their time during the greatest war in history . . . ' (Freeman's diary).

in the aircraft production capacity of the USA. The policy agreed by all three British Chiefs of Staff was that only the heavy bomber could produce the conditions under which any other offensive could be employed, and that 'to achieve our object within a reasonable time, the bombing offensive must be of the heaviest possible scale.'

Freeman set off for Placentia Bay on 3 August, travelling to Thurso in Churchill's special train, with Dill, Dudley Pound, Cadogan and Hopkins. Arriving at Thurso the following morning they were taken by a destroyer to HMS *Prince of Wales* at Scapa Flow and, after lunching with Admiral Tovey, the voyage to Newfoundland began at around 4pm. Almost immediately the *Prince of Wales* ran into heavy seas, which forced her to abandon her destroyer escort; she had also to alter course after a U-boat was reported in her path. But the battleship duly arrived, unscathed, at Placentia Bay on the morning of the 9th.

The voyage gave Freeman further opportunity to observe Churchill at close quarters. In his diary there are repeated notes of the Prime Minister's 'brilliant' and 'sparkling' conversation: given the critical importance of their mission, it was doubtless reassuring to find him in 'superb form'.[27]*

They did not always see eye-to-eye, however, and Freeman recorded how, on 7 August, Churchill had lectured the Chiefs of Staff 'on what he wanted to do with and get from the President'. . . . 'I couldn't possibly agree to some of the proposals, and D[udley] P[ound] and Dill eventually agreed with me.'[28] Also during the voyage there were regular discussions, both formal and informal, with the other Chiefs of Staff, and with other key participants in the forthcoming meeting with the President, including Hopkins.

Warnings came from Harris, by then head of the RAF delegation in Washington, of 'Attempts . . . to persuade President to alter ratio or even rescind release of aircraft under Slessor Agreement,'[29] and from Portal of 'large allocation of heavy bombers . . . to US Army contracts at the expense of Lend-Lease. Difficulties are bound to intensify. . . .'[30]

Freeman attended a number of meetings with the American Chiefs of Staff between the 9th and 12th of August, and much of their time was spent discussing production questions. It soon became clear that General Marshall and Admiral Stark intended to ask the President to curtail the heavy bomber programme he had initiated in May, and would oppose the release of substantial numbers of heavy bombers to Britain. Even Arnold, who favoured increased heavy bomber production, was now unhappy with the Slessor agreement and its allocation of such aircraft to the RAF.

Freeman listened gloomily whilst Marshall and Stark tried to bias Dill and Pound against the heavy bomber programme, telling Dill that it would retard

---

* He also recorded; 'The amount he drinks is amazing and it is quite obvious that he now could not do without it. At lunch two whiskies, one port, and 2 or 3 brandies and generous brandies at that. In the evening 4 glasses of champagne and at least 3 brandies and 1 port; after dinner a couple of whiskies, whisky instead of tea. That is a formidable ration of alcohol for 24 hours.'

tank production, and Pound that it would interfere with shipbuilding and Catalina production. 'All this in spite of the fact that no one has put forward any alternative method of winning the war.'[31] Arnold was more helpful, however, claiming that the aircraft programme would not interfere with shipbuilding and that the only real bottleneck as regards heavy bombers was the time taken to get aircraft factories into production.[32]

Realising that the Americans would offer less than he wanted, Freeman demanded more than they could possibly give, and a somewhat startled Arnold noted, hyperbole which Freeman would have much appreciated:

> They asked for 100% of our production. They would have taken all the Army, Navy, British, Chinese, and Dutch planes and engines ... They asked [us to set up] ... depots [from] Iceland to Singapore to repair and maintain all their American planes ... to train their combat crews ... [to ferry] two- and four-engined planes across the Atlantic [and] ... all

Pound, Dill, Churchill and Freeman at a staff meeting on the *Prince of Wales*. Frequent discussions ensured unanimity when they met Roosevelt and his staff.

bombers possible across with our pilots ... [and] to send Bomber and Pursuit Squadrons complete with all their equipment to become acquainted with the British communication and command systems. I must admit that Freeman accepted our refusals gracefully ...[33]

Arnold responded by showing Freeman production figures for heavy bombers far lower than those given to the British Purchasing Commission, which made it obvious that the Americans did not have nearly enough aircraft for their own needs in 1941. Maximum deliveries to Britain would be 34 heavy bombers per month from August to December, and none at all from January to July 1942. Supplies would restart in August 1942, rising to ninety B-24s per month by February 1943. Assuming Britain received 50 per cent of total American production, about 2,300 heavy bombers might be delivered by June 1943, but there was no commitment. Freeman had to pass these figures on to Portal, with the unwelcome, but not unexpected, news that the Americans did 'not intend to agree to further releases of heavy bombers'.[34]

Harriman and Arnold agreed however, to investigate the possibility of turning some of the existing aircraft factories over to B-17 or B-24 heavy bombers, especially the Vega and Omaha plants planned for the production of medium bombers, which had not yet been jigged or tooled for any aircraft. Nevertheless, the sum total of US and UK heavy bomber production from August 1941 to the end of December 1942 still left Bomber Command short of 1,500 aircraft.

Freeman suggested that the US might consider sending ground units of their Army Air Corps to the UK immediately, so as to gain experience of the RAF's administrative and operational machinery, but Arnold was non-committal, explaining that only 50 B-17s were in service in the Army Air Corps at the time, and that he was having the greatest difficulty assembling a total of 400 aircraft of all types for large-scale manoeuvres in September 1941.[35] Arrangements to train RAF bomber crews in the US would, however, begin at once.

Hopkins reassured Freeman that it was the President who would allocate aircraft, not Marshall or Stark, but Freeman had no opportunity to raise the matter with Roosevelt personally during the conference.[36]* Overall, he could only conclude that progress had been slow. 'We are not getting as much out of this visit as I had hoped', he recorded. 'There is immense good will but that is all and we want more.'[37]

Apart from facing competition from the American military leaders, one of the difficulties confronting Freeman in the negotiations was the absence of any centralised American authority with responsibility for aircraft production or allocation. 'The sole rep for the Air for Britain is Freeman', Arnold wrote.

With the US, Admiral Stark, General Marshall, Admiral Turner, General Burns, Commander Sherman, General Arnold and ... Colonel Bundy ...

* Hopkins warned Freeman not to raise the matter with Roosevelt 'unless a favourable opportunity arose'.

give ideas and opinions re aircraft and their use. No wonder that Freeman said: 'When Portal comes over, I am going to insist that he sees just two people, the President and you.'[38]

In these circumstances it is hardly surprising that Freeman continued to work through Hopkins, the American official he now knew as a personal friend. Hopkins recognised the overriding importance of quality, and the need for vast fleets of heavy bombers, and could be relied upon to press their case with the President. Freeman told him[39] 'If you can do anything to keep our case in the forefront and to obtain for us the maximum . . . number of heavy bombers, we shall indeed be grateful'.[40]

Hopkins knew the austerities of rationed food in Britain, and having mentioned that 'some lemons' for Freeman had come with the President's entourage, his gift turned out to be a huge carton of food 'luxuries' unobtainable in wartime Britain, together with a letter which gave Freeman '. . . grounds for new hope:'[41] Freeman and he were now on first name terms, their mutual trust was absolute, and Hopkins not only understood the implications of Freeman's views and proposals, but had been convinced that they were in the best interests of the USA as well as Britain. He proved thereafter to be the perfect guide to their presentation and acceptance in America.

After his return to Britain, Freeman tried to persuade the Americans to put the Lancaster into production in the USA,[42] but Hopkins was shown figures which indicated that it would be no better that the Liberator.* Freeman was more successful with his instructions to Harris to stress the advantages of turbo-superchargers for the Allison engines of the Lightning, and drop tanks for the Airacobra '. . . in a casual way . . . to induce them to accept these ideas for themselves . . .'.[43]†

As hopes of receiving increased heavy bomber allocations from the United States faded, Freeman switched his efforts back to ensuring that British production of heavy bombers was sharply increased. He was soon deeply involved in the preparation of a joint MAP/Air Ministry memorandum to Churchill about aircraft production policy which emphasised the seriousness of the output shortfall and the need for 'a sustained drive for the increased production of heavy bomber' aircraft and engines .[44]

Despite the vital help from the USA with aircraft, destroyers, and massive supplies of oil products and raw materials, Britain's strategy had to be based on the assumption of American neutrality until December 1941. The planners envisaged that whatever happened in Russia, Britain would be mobilised for war to the fullest possible degree, while a neutral America supplied enough munitions and other essential goods to enable Britain to continue, and ultimately

---

* Hopkins was told that the performance of the B-24 and the Lancaster were roughly similar. In fact the Lancaster carried 14,000lb of bombs, the B-24, 8,000lb.

† Freeman of course knew that American engine makers had been working on 'exhaust turbo-chargers' for some time, but feared that their development might not be getting adequate priority, because of serious technical difficulties. Turbo-chargers were installed on P-38s, P-47s, B-17s and B-24s, with great success.

win, the struggle with Germany. Throughout 1941 Freeman worked on these assumptions. Britain's ultimate hope was that America would somehow be drawn into the war, – a 'benevolent neutrality' strategy was not ideal – but Freeman realised that once America was drawn into the conflict, her own forces would absorb most of the output of her munitions industry, and that US supplies to Britain would have to be reduced.

Within four months of the Placentia Bay conference, America had indeed entered the war, and Britain's fundamental hopes were realised. But her previous strategic assumptions had then to be completely revised, since the earlier proposals to equip new RAF units with American aircraft were effectively made redundant by the planned deployment of American forces in Britain and a variety of other theatres. The next formal agreement between Britain and the United States, the so-called Arnold-Portal Agreement, therefore stated that allocations of American aircraft to Britain would be determined by the need to maintain combined strength in any theatre. If USAAF units could not be substituted, America would go on allocating aircraft to Britain to equip and maintain existing and projected squadrons of the RAF and Dominion air forces.[45] Freeman recommended Portal to accept these terms provided that there was sufficient and worldwide substitution.

The Placentia Bay meeting was by no means fruitless. Apart from discussing the key issue of American assistance to Britain, Freeman was able to agree plans with Arnold for sending Tomahawk and Hurricane fighters to Russia. Arnold was helped to make the case for the heavy bomber in America and to resist the attempts of the US Army and Navy to shift resources away from heavy bomber production, and Freeman gained a vital insight into the workings of the American government and high command. This insight was of incalculable value as the war progressed, especially in late 1942, when Freeman realised that massive increases in the planned production of the P-51B fighter and its Packard Merlin engine, were absolutely essential.

More generally, the conference greatly improved relations between the British and American governments and armed services, and increased the scope for effective co-operation in the future. Freeman realised, for example, that there were organisational weaknesses in the military and procurement apparatus in the United States, and that changes in the staffing of the British Military Mission in Washington would be necessary.[46]* If the British party returned from Placentia Bay disappointed by their failure to obtain more aircraft, they could only have been reassured by the US government's will-ingness to co-operate in many other spheres of policy and by the mounting evidence that America would soon enter the war.

---

* Freeman realised that the top British representative in Washington must be of a standing to be trusted by all the Anglo-American Chiefs of Staff. Dill proved to be the perfect choice.

CHAPTER 14

The triumph of the Mustang

THREE MONTHS AFTER the 'Riviera' meeting, the first North American Mustang for the RAF, was delivered in Liverpool. Tested on its arrival in Britain, the Mustang was recognized to be an excellent aeroplane, the fastest American fighter at the time, with a speed of 382mph. At first it was assigned to squadrons involved in low-level, tactical operations, because the limitations of the single-stage supercharger on its Allison engine meant that it climbed slowly, and that its performance above 15,000ft was poor.[1] When the RAF's Air Fighter Development Unit (AFDU) tested it at higher altitudes on 29 April 1942, however, Wing Commander Campbell-Orde, who ran the AFDU, immediately realised that it was the best American low and medium altitude fighter to reach Britain since the beginning of the war.[2] He was so impressed by its manoeuvrability and speed that he invited Ronnie Harker, a pilot from Rolls-Royce's Flight Test establishment at Hucknall, to come over and fly it.[3]

Harker had been flying prototypes of the Spitfire IX, with two-stage Merlin 61 engines, and after testing the Allison Mustang on 30 April, he was equally impressed, telling Campbell-Orde that a two-stage engine was bound to improve its performance. The AFDU quickly arranged two more tests, comparing a

The Allison-engined Mustang, AG422 flown by Ronnie Harker of the Rolls-Royce Flight Test establishment on 30 April 1942. He told Hives that its performance would be outstanding with a two-stage Merlin 61 instead of an Allison, and as soon as Freeman heard this from Hives, a Mustang was sent to Hucknall for conversion.

Spitfire VB first against a Spitfire Mk.IX,[4] and then against the Mustang.[5] The second test showed Harker and Campbell-Orde that the Mustang airframe had exceptionally low 'drag', since, at the same power settings, it was 30–35mph faster than the Spitfire VB at all heights, whilst the first test raised the rosy prospect of a phenomenal improvement in the Mustang's performance, if it was re-engined with a Merlin 61. The news soon reached Hives, with the recommendation that a Mustang should be sent to Hucknall for conversion, and Hives immediately telephoned Freeman.[6]

As VCAS, Freeman had no official right to get involved in planning such a hybrid aircraft, but he had ordered both the Mustang and the Merlin 61 before he left MAP, and he promptly got things moving. Arrangements were made for Lappin, Hives' assistant, to meet Bottomley and Sorley, two of the most senior 'technical assistants' to the CAS, with the aim of installing one of the new Merlin 61 engines in a Mustang as soon as possible.[7] An Allison Mustang was promptly delivered to Hucknall, with the details of Boscombe Down tests on a similar aircraft.[8]

Winant, the US Ambassador, was also brought into the process. In company with his Assistant Air Attaché, Tommy Hitchcock, he discussed the estimated figures with Portal, Douglas and Linnell from the RAF, Llewellin from MAP, General Lyons, chief technical officer for the USAAF in Britain, and with senior staff from Rolls-Royce and the North American Company.[9]

Winant cabled Arnold via Hopkins on 5 June 1942.

> ... with the [single-stage] American Merlin 28 ... the performance of the Mustang would be ... far better than ... the Airacobra at all altitudes and 20mph faster than the Spitfire V ... the plane the British suggested for [our] use in this theatre ...

The possibility of Packard making Merlin 61s was also raised,[10] and Winant's letter ended with Freeman's own, often repeated, declaration:

> The Battle of Britain was won over larger numbers because of the quality of the British fighters.[11]

Meanwhile, Witold Challier, an exiled Polish performance engineer of exceptional ability on the staff of Rolls-Royce, calculated the effect of fitting a Merlin 61[12] into a Mustang airframe, and came up with sensational figures. Challier estimated that with a Merlin 61, the performance of the converted Mustang would be improved in every respect, and that with a top speed of 441mph at 25,600ft, it would be much faster than any other piston-engined fighter likely to come into service within the next eighteen months.[13] Arnold, who happened to be in Britain, and got the AFDU test reports about the Mustang in May, before Challier's estimates were available, was sceptical at first about their forecasts. But Freeman knew that estimates such as these from Rolls-Royce would be reliable and, having initiated the conversion of the first aircraft at Hucknall, he started a relentless campaign to have large orders for the hybrid aircraft placed as soon as possible.

Challier's 1942 graph accurately forecast that a Mustang with a two-stage Merlin would have a top speed of 441 mph at 25,600 ft. Comparative curves for a Spifire VB, tested in 1941 gave 371 mph at 20,000 ft, and for a Spitfire HF IX, with a two-stage Merlin, tested in 1944, a maximum of only 405 mph at 25,400 ft. The performance curve of a P-47 Thunderbolt tested in 1943 has been included for comparison.

Key

1	1941 Spitfire V	6450 lb
2	1942 Spitfire IX	7480 lb
3	1943 P47 Thunderbolt	12700 lb
4	1944 Mustang III	8740 lb

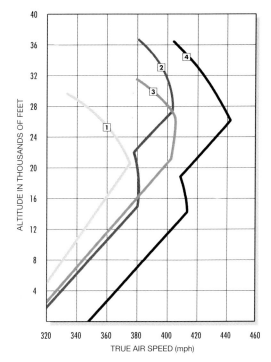

But the sheer momentum of the American rearmament process made this extremely difficult. The first 600 Allison Mustangs for the US AAF 'A-36 Invaders' had been equipped with dive-brakes, and ordered as 'ground attack aircraft' in May 1942, because the 1942 US day fighter programme had been full.[14] For 1943, large numbers of Republican P-47s and Lockheed P-38s had been ordered as standard day-fighters by the US Army Air Corps, and there were huge outstanding orders for other obsolete or undeveloped fighters all to be powered by the V12 Allison.* A decision to mass-produce the Merlin Mustang would therefore depend on the Americans being willing both to accept it as third component of their own fighter squadrons, and to make massive cuts in orders for obsolete aircraft. Strong opposition to orders for the Mustang as a third new fighter aircraft in the 1943 procurement plan was thus inevitable.

Freeman had been warned by Hopkins that extreme tact would be required if a major change in US aircraft procurement policy was to be effected *on British advice.†* So Freeman knew that the potential of the Merlin Mustang

---

* Obsolete US fighters on the order books in September 1942 included 2,500 P-40 Kittyhawks, 8,800 P-39 Airacobras. The P-63 Kingcobra awaited development of a two-stage Allison but 11,000 had been ordered.

† Tongue in cheek, Hopkins explained that most American citizens believed that: (1) American fighters were better than British ones; (2) American pilots were better than RAF pilots; (3) Aircraft designed and built in America will perform 30 per cent better when flown by an American pilot, and that (4) RAF pilots were incapable of flying the high-class Airacobra.

would have to be fed to the US Army Air Corps in a way that engaged their support without upsetting their natural desire to produce a better fighter in an ' all American' way.

He began by telling Slessor,* then in Washington, that tests at Boscombe Down showed that, with a Merlin 61, the speed and rate of climb of the Mustang would be far superior *at all heights* to the Spitfire IX. Slessor was warned that Arnold,

> does not favour the continuation of Mustang orders because it is not built to USAF specification, and is banking [all] on the P-47. To force continuation of the Mustang fitted with … a British engine would probably meet with strong opposition from Arnold … even though Americans in this country are … strongly in favour of it. … you should discuss [it] with Arnold, and if possible arrange to put forward the proposition as his own.[15]

Evill was also in Washington, and the next day, Freeman told him to help Winant to press for continued Mustang production, adding that:

> [Winant] does not know that we are working on Arnold. … the Airacobra … should go out of production and the firms concerned should jig and tool up for Mustang/Merlin 61s … I know the frightful difficulties of vested interests which will have to be overcome. One can imagine how … difficult it will be to get the US to recognize that a General Motors Allison engine is inferior to a Rolls-Royce.[†16]

Two days later, Slessor was able to report that Lt.-Gen. Carl A. Spaatz (in charge of US bombers in Europe) seemed enthusiastic about the Mustang. Spaatz had hoped that the Allies would opt for the P-47 as their only new fighter, but Slessor felt that the Mustang would [win on] the time factor, and agreed to let Spaatz try to sell the aircraft to Arnold in the first instance.[17] Freeman was delighted.

> Glad you have communicated enthusiasm for Mustang project to Spaatz, and hope he will convince Arnold. Mustang with Merlin 61 should be a far better aircraft than the P-47, and on present showing Americans would be well advised to go for it in quantity.[18]

He had an almost uncanny perception of the potential of the Mustang, when powered with a Merlin 61, and did not hedge his bets.

Rolls-Royce kept Freeman so closely informed about the progress of the first Merlin Mustang that it is obvious that he was the driving force behind its rapid development. When Hives told him that three machines were being converted at Hucknall, Freeman asked for six; when Hives asked for 250 sets of conversion parts, Freeman sought 500.[19] He also arranged for two of the five Mustangs being re-engined at Hucknall to be handed over to Spaatz for

---

* All British telegrams to the RAF delegation in Washington were marked 'from CAS', although many, including this one, were clearly from Freeman.
† The US Army had sponsored development of the Allison.

trials and evaluation by the US 8th Air Force in Britain.[20] Linnell, also hard at work demonstrating the Mustang's exceptional potential, attached a small American contingent to Boscombe Down* so that they could see the Merlin Mustang tests at first hand. Whatever happened in Washington, Freeman was making sure that the excellence of the Merlin Mustang would be recognized by those in charge of, or actually fighting, the air war in Europe.

The initial breakthrough came in August 1942, when General Oliver P. Echols, the head of Arnold's Materiel Division, visited Hucknall to see a Merlin Mustang for himself.[21] Echols had steered Freeman to North American in 1940, and had helped in the rapid development of the Mustang airframe by encouraging North American to buy from Curtiss the wind-tunnel data for their undeveloped prototype XP-46†, and once again he proved to be a worthy supporter. On 26 August 1942, the Air Corps placed an order for 400 Merlin Mustangs, soon followed by another for 1,350 on 8 October.[22] By then, Merlins were already being installed in Mustangs in the USA as well as in Britain, and the once-sceptical Arnold could tell the President: 'Tests indicate that [it] will be a highly satisfactory pursuit plane for 1943'.

Although the news from Hives about the potential of the Merlin Mustang had reached Freeman in May 1942, and Challier's figures three weeks later, he welcomed it at first, because it was obviously going to be a very high-performance day fighter. It was faster than the Spitfire IX, and would be available sooner than the partially redesigned Spitfire VIII, and long before the even newer Spitfire XIV with its Griffon 61 engine. He naturally wanted Merlin Mustangs for the RAF, and knew that the Mustang's internal tanks held nearly twice as much fuel as the Spitfire IX, giving it a much greater operational range. But the Mustang's potential as an escort fighter was not lost on him; his concern for extending the range over which American day bombers could be escorted is well documented, and Hives warned him that 'if the Merlin Mustang is too successful the AAF will collar them'.[23]

Early in 1942, the USAAF had started planning to operate no fewer than 4,000 heavy bombers from England by August 1943. The aircraft were to be used in daylight operations and, once beyond the range of their escorting day fighters, would have to rely for their defence upon high-altitude, close-formation flying, and defensive armament.[24] The British Air Staff had always been sceptical of this approach,‡[25] and warned them that losses would rise to levels that were unacceptable, once targets were chosen beyond the short range of the escorting Spitfire Vs and IXs, which alone could match the German day fighters at the time.[26] But nothing deterred the Americans from their plans for a daylight bombing offensive.

---

* Boscombe Down, the British equivalent of the US Wright Field, was where RAF acceptance and development trials of new or modified aircraft were done.

† Roger Freeman was told by Ed Schmued of North American that they derived little benefit from the Curtiss wind tunnel data.

‡ Bufton had warned Harry Berliner, a member of Hansell's team, early in 1942 that the Fortresses would need fighter escorts.

Long before the bomber formations had penetrated beyond the care of escorting fighters during the summer of 1942, the inherent shortcomings of the American 8th Air Force's tactics were becoming increasingly clear to the British Air Staff, and Freeman realised that the potential of the Merlin Mustang would greatly extend the radius of action over which escort was possible. Trenchard's rejection of the very concept of a long-range fighter,[27] and Portal's flat denial of its feasibility,*[28] simply had to be challenged.

Having been instrumental in persuading the Americans to build huge fleets of heavy bombers, Freeman knew that they flatly refused to operate at night. Unless the problem of an escort fighter could be solved, the enormous industrial effort now going into making heavy bombers in America might be wasted.

The fact that the USAAF had ordered Merlin Mustangs was a good start, but the existing production capacity at the Inglewood factory was clearly inadequate. Output of two-stage Merlins at Packard would not begin until June 1943 and production of Merlin Mustangs would reach a maximum of only 200 a month a year later. With three years experience of the 'wastage rates' of war Freeman knew that this was not enough.

As early as August 1942, therefore, two months before the first flight of the re-engined aircraft, Freeman began a sustained effort to persuade the Americans to produce Mustangs and Packard Merlins in vastly greater numbers.[29] Apart from the inherent difficulty of changing an established program, the extent to which America's aircraft production plans were politically sensitive was a serious obstacle, despite the low quality of many of the aircraft involved. Roosevelt had ordered the industry to produce 100,000 aircraft in 1943,[30] and Freeman knew from his struggles with Beaverbrook that such a total would only be achieved by freezing development, and churning out aircraft of standardised design, many of which already were, or soon would be, obsolescent.[31] Freeman warned Churchill about the 1942 American program:

> The effect . . . has been to freeze types already in production as [otherwise] production will fall and . . . concentrate on making fighters which were easy. Of 1,300 fighters scheduled for December 1943, only 150 of them have any chance of being superior. . . . The production of unusable aircraft must be stopped.'

The British leaders must somehow persuade the American government to adopt a more selective attitude, to think less of target numbers than of producing high-quality designs, above all the Merlin Mustang.[32]

Freeman's solution, as always, was to bring the facts inescapably before the key American decision makers, but politics was now involved and only

---

* On 8 June, 1941, after the air-borne attack on Crete, Churchill asked Portal to consider the use of long-range fighters. He replied; 'the long-range fighter, whether built as such or given long-range tanks will [always] be at a disadvantage compared with short-range, high performance fighters' and when Churchill queried this Portal repeated '. . . long-range fighters [are] suitable only where they will not be opposed by short-range fighters'.

The first Merlin-engined Mustang, AL975/G, flew on 13 October 1942.

A P-51B, of the US 8th Air Force Fighter Command, the first production version of the Merlin Mustang.

One of the P-51Ds supplied to the RAF and RAAF in 1944/45 under Lend-Lease. Its bubble canopy and cut-down rear fuselage greatly improved visibility for the pilot.

Churchill could intervene at this level. Freeman emphasised that the American bombers had not so far:

> ... gone beyond the limits of strong British fighter escort. They will probably experience a heavy disaster when they do. We ought to press [them] to adopt a highly selective attitude; [to] think less of target numbers than [of] producing right designs ... the Mustang with the right engine: – better 70,000 of right designs than 100,000 others.

Churchill found this 'All very alarming. I am wondering how to put it to the President; I think through Hopkins'[33] Harriman agreed, but asked to see drafts of all such messages, warning Churchill never to mention quantities except by implication from the quality aspects. After carefully consulting Hopkins and

Harriman, Churchill broached the subject with Roosevelt on 16 September 1942, to emphasise that 'the Fortress and the long range fighter are indispensable ... we suggest special emphasis on heavy bombers and pursuit aircraft'.[34]

A major increase in production of Mustangs with Packard Merlins would compete with other British requirements from the USA. Demand would rise rapidly and, if the decision to phase out Stirlings in favour of extra Lancasters went through, Britain would need 1,500 Packard Merlins a month by 1943 instead of a mere 800: the possibility of fitting Mustang airframes with Rolls-Royce Merlin 61s *in Britain* was seriously considered.

Churchill accepted that his intervention would need the utmost tact. An exceptionally convincing case would be essential. Vested interests in the USA would be strongly opposed to the replacement of the Mustang's Allison by the Packard Merlin* and, even as late as March 1943, Eaker, having allocated all the Allison-engined Mustangs to the 9th Tactical AAF, claimed that the Merlin was too heavy for performance at height.[†]

Cabling Roosevelt again on 4 October, Churchill tactfully referred only to:

> certain features of our combined programme which if not altered must lead to a misdirection of resources of materials and capacity in 1943 which we can ill afford.[35]

but he told Hopkins that he was 'deeply concerned about the layout for 1943. There are things that I can only say to you. If you can't come to Britain I will send Lyttelton over'[36]

After an unexpected query from Hopkins as to why there was a need for 8th AAF fighters in Europe, and a telegram from Dill about the US air program, Churchill again asked Hopkins to come to Britain, adding:

> Joint review of Combined Air Programmes highly desirable to ensure that expansion directed to production of types most suitable to requirements of future operations.[37]

Once he realised that there was no possibility of a visit by Hopkins, Churchill began to stress the urgent need to increase production of the Mustang fighter with the Merlin 61, to protect the B-17s and B-24s.

> If not [successful] much of your vast future production of these types may be unsuitable for the decisive European theatre for which the highest possible performance in fighters is also necessary. The dangers will increase terribly once outside fighter protection, as the range [of daylight raids] lengthens in 1943 and 1944.

* Since 1935, the Allison V.12 engine had been developed for the US Army Air Force, on the orders of their Research and Development organisation at Wright Field, and they were reluctant to acknowledge the superiority of the Merlin, even though the Merlins for the new P.-51B would be made by Packard.

† Without extra tanks their weights and radius of action were: P-38, 17,500lb, 290 miles; P-47, 14,500lb, 280 miles; P-51, 9,800lb, 350 miles.

Churchill's cable added '... I will therefore send Lyttelton ... armed with precise figures and ... *Portal* or *Freeman* [to discuss] air policy.'[38] He thereby confirmed the supreme importance, to him and to the two airmen, of changing the American aircraft and engine procurement plans.

But the pressure of other events was inexorable and final decisions were delayed. Freeman had returned to the MAP on 23 October, and Tedder, his chosen successor as VCAS, could not be released immediately from his role as AOC-in-C, Mediterranean area because the Torch* operation was imminent. Medhurst had taken over from Freeman as acting VCAS, but Portal could not leave him in sole charge because he was too inexperienced. The decision to cancel Freeman's trip had not, however, been taken by the time Oliver Lyttelton, the Minister of Production, arrived in the USA on 6 November.[†39]

Lyttelton was a member of the US War Production Board, (WPB), and had to discuss a broad range of vital supply issues with the American government. But one of his most important tasks was to persuade Roosevelt (through Hopkins) to ensure that both the military and the WPB rethought the balance of their fighter programme without losing confidence in the prospects of their day bombing plans[‡] and reduced the US aircraft production targets so that fewer, better aircraft could be made.[40] Once Freeman's visit was cancelled, John Jewkes from MAP was sent out to join Lyttelton, with instructions from Freeman to concentrate on Mustang and Merlin problems.[41]

Despite opposition from supporters of other, obsolete or unproven American fighters,[42] Lyttelton's information, the incontrovertible facts about the unique qualities of the Mustang, and the invaluable – and patient – help of the well briefed Roosevelt, convinced the US Chiefs of Staff and other authorities that there must be a massive increase in the capacity to make, and orders for, Packard Merlin engines and P-51 Merlin Mustangs. The capacity of the North American plant at Inglewood was greatly increased and part of their factory at Dallas was switched to Mustangs. Output of Allison-engined Mustangs was to cease when production of the two-stage Packard Merlin 68 began, and all such engines would be installed in Mustangs. After three months of delicate, but relentless lobbying directed by Freeman, the Merlin Mustang had at last been given the urgent production priorities it needed. By mid-1944, the monthly output of Mustangs would increase from 200 to 700, and of Packard Merlins from 1,400 to 2,400 – later 2,700.[§43]

USAAF bombing strategy was still controlled by Eaker, and based on the unshakeable conviction that close formations of their high-flying, heavily

* The Anglo-American invasion of North Africa.
† Lyttelton had had a difficult journey; his first aircraft had to turn back due to storms.
‡ Lyttelton cabled Churchill to advise against inviting Marshall or King to Britain until he had had his talk with Roosevelt. He obviously feared that British doubts about the feasibility of deep penetration, unescorted day raids, and the disastrous casualties that would be suffered, might shake the confidence of the American Chiefs of Staff, and lead to withdrawal of the 8th AAF from Europe.
§ Despite these changes, the production priority of the P-47 Thunderbolt remained higher than that of the Mustang until July 1943.

armed bombers could carry out unescorted, deep penetration raids into Germany. In 1943 the 8th Air Force had started a series of such raids.

By then the German Air Force had rearmed their day fighters. Rifle calibre guns and even 20mm cannons were replaced by new 30mm cannons which fired an 11-ounce shell: a larger 50mm cannon with a muzzle velocity of 3,000ft/second, firing a 3.5lb shell was also used.* The absence of escorting fighters meant that 'wolf packs' of heavily armed German fighters could form up, unmolested, ahead or abreast of the bomber formations and make massed attacks, often head-on, against which the defensive armament of the bombers was minimal at that time.

The 8th Air Force raids were carried out with the greatest courage and iron determination, but bomber casualties rose steadily as the German fighters discovered the tactics which exploited the weak points in the defences of the B-17s and B-24s.

Date	Target	Attacking	Numbers missing	Damaged	Percentage unscathed
14/5	Kiel	126	8	36	65
17/5	Lorient	118	6	27	72
21/5	Wilhelmshaven & Kiel	123	12	33	63
13/6	Bremen & Kiel	182	26	54	58
25/7	Hamburg	100	15	67	18
26/7	Hanover	96	16	NA	
28/7	Ochersleben	120	16	64	33[44]

By August 1943, the forecast 21 months had elapsed since America mobilised, and on 17 August 1943, badly planned attacks were made on factories at Schweinfurt and Regensburg, well beyond the range of the 8th Air Force fighters.[45] Casualties were appalling. Undaunted, re-equipped, and reinforced, General Eaker mounted three more unescorted deep penetration raids in October, with even more appalling casualties. After the last – another attack on Schweinfurt – unescorted attacks, at the end of deep penetration flights over German territory, virtually stopped.

Date	Target	Attacking	Numbers missing	Damaged	Percentage unscathed
17/8	Schweinfurt & Regensburg	315	60	168	29
8/10	Bremen	357	30	236	25
10/10	Munster	119	29	56	29
14/10	Schweinfurt	229	60	138	14[46]

The first production P-51B had flown in May 1943, the first P-51C in August.[†] There were airframe teething troubles, but it was soon obvious that the Merlin Mustang was not only faster than any of the contemporary German

* The magnificent new Mauser cannon, firing 7.4oz shells at 3,300ft/sec at the rate of 1,200/minute, was too late to be used in action.

† The airframes were the same; Cs were made at Dallas, Bs at Inglewood.

Lieutenant-General Ira C. Eaker Commander of the US Army 8th Air Force and Air Chief Marshal Sir Arthur Harris at an operational training airfield built by the US Army Corps of Engineers for the RAF. Their characters had much in common, for, despite rising evidence of unsustainable losses, Eaker remained ruthlessly convinced that, given enough aircraft and crews, his heavily armed and armoured, but unescorted, day-bombers would eventually be able to fight their way to targets deep into Germany, without excessive casualties.

piston-engined fighter aircraft, but just as manoeuvrable, and that it had a potential radius of action so outstanding as to transform the air war. In terms of US gallons, its normal *internal* fuel tanks held 183 (269 with a full rear tank) compared with 99 for the Spitfire, and it consumed an average of 64 gallons per hour compared with 144 for the P-38 and 140 for the P-47. With full internal tanks, including an 86 gallon rear fuselage tank, and two 108 gallon drop-tanks, its combat radius was 750 miles.[47]*

Eaker's prejudice against the Merlin Mustang was proof at first against its remarkable qualities, and none of the first 145 aircraft to reach Britain for the 8th AAF came as long range fighters. As late as 30 October 1943, 493 of the 673 P-51Bs and P-51Cs due to be delivered to Britain in 1943 were for roles other than escort.[48]

* This radius of action allowed for 10 minutes warm-up to take-off, a climb to 10,000ft on course, at 220mph, drop externals on reaching target area, 5 minutes combat at emergency power and 15 minutes at military power, return at 230mph plus 30 minutes reserve.

Arnold now intervened decisively, insisting that the 8th Air Force got absolute priority for P-51s for the last three months of 1943. The Mustangs which Eaker had sent to the 9th Air Force were transferred back to 8th AAF Fighter Command: Spaatz was appointed head of the US Strategic Air Forces in Europe, and Doolittle and Kepner took over command of the 8th AAF bomber and fighter forces. Eaker moved out to the Mediterranean to replace Doolittle as head of the 15th AAF. All US pilots qualified to fly Mustangs were ordered to join the 8th Air Force fighter groups, regardless of rank or postings, and to fly on every mission.[49] An extra fuselage tank was installed behind the cockpit of the P-51, despite the effect of a full tank on the way the aircraft handled, and drop tanks were urgently developed. By February 1944 more than 100 9th Air Force Merlin Mustangs were escorting 8th Air Force bombers, destroying three to five times as many German fighters per sortie as the more numerous P-47s between January and March. Before the end of March Doolittle asked for all his P-47s and P-38s to be replaced by Mustangs as soon as possible.[*50]

Tactics were changed under Doolittle and Kepner, fighters were freed from their former close escort role and staff work was flexible and responsive.[51] Their new escort system, whereby groups of fighers joined the bomber groups in relays as they penetrated further and further into Germany, was effective only as long as none of the bomber groups were separated from the main force and left without escort. Realising that the German fighters promptly concentrated on any such unescorted formations, Doolittle's staff changed their policy and directed some of the relay groups to patrol successive areas along the bomber's route which could be continually swept clear of German fighters, a change made even more effective as the number of 8th AAF long range fighters increased. Spitfires could handle the early stages, and Thunderbolts as far as 350–400 miles, each of the latter, and the Mustang groups forming the later relay units, starting with higher fuel loads.[52†]

The conundrum of the long-range fighter had been solved once it was realised that the performance of the aircraft whilst in transit to the combat area was irrelevant. As long as a high performance day fighter had enough fuel for fighting in the combat zone and for its return to base, the fact that it was overloaded with fuel from take-off to the starting position of their escort duty was not important: if not attacked, the first two or three hours flying was simply a 'ferry trip'.

* Colonel H. Zemke, who operated with all three, considered the P-51 by far the best air to air fighter below 25,000 ft: above that, he thought the P-47 Thunderbolt slightly better, despite its high fuel consumption. The P-38 Lightning's combat effectiveness was severely restricted by its maximum diving speed of 375 mph IAS: German fighter pilots soon learnt to dive away out of its reach. The critical mach numbers – the percentage of the speed of sound at which handling becomes very difficult – were: Spitfire .88, Mustang .80, P-47 .74 and P-38 .70. The speed of sound varies with temperature.

† The other two fighters were fast at height, and had longer ranges than the Spitfire, but the P-38, with turbo-charged Allisons had structural limitations. P-47 pilots were warned not to chase German fighters below 15,000 ft. until the short term boost of water injection was available.

Major-General James Doolittle (*centre*) who took over from Eaker, with Lieutenant-General Carl Spaatz, Commanding General of the US Strategic Air Forces in Europe (*left*) and Brig.-Gen. James Hodges (*right*). Arnold's decision to give Spaatz overall control of American Army Air Forces in Europe in October 1943 was crucial, for he was a man of absolute integrity, and his conduct and decisions were motivated by common sense. By appointing Doolittle, a brilliant pilot, to command the 8th Air Force, he placed at its head a man with the flying experience to see the vital necessity of long-range fighter escorts, and the way to make the best of them. It was Doolittle's good fortune that due to the decision taken in November 1942 at Freeman's behest, hundreds of vital Merlin Mustangs were coming into service.

Major General William Kepner, Commanding General of the US 8th Air Force Fighter Command (*right*) with Colonel Don Blakeslee. Encouraged by Doolittle, Kepner commanded his fighters with admirable initiative, freeing them from the bonds of close escort, and turning loose each escort relay group, after they had been relieved, to roam the German air space as Sherman's cavalry had ravaged Georgia, 80 years before. Early in March 1944, Blakeslee had led the first P-51 Mustang Groups to escort B-17s as far as Berlin.

Handled with growing confidence by superb leaders like Blakeslee and Zemke, the magnificent performance of the Merlin Mustang fighters which, through Freeman's foresight and relentless support, were now available in the nick of time, not only rescued the 8th Air Force from a near-disastrous tactical 'cul-de-sac', but exerted a decisive impact upon the course of the European war. Without air supremacy over the beachheads of Normandy in June 1944, the 'Overlord' invasion would have been seriously endangered.

'The advent of the long-range fighter in the spring [of 1944] was fatal for the Germans.'[53] Deep penetration raids, far into Germany by 800 or 900 bombers devastated key strategic targets too effectively to be ignored. But as the Luftwaffe fighters congregated to intercept the American heavy bombers, they were now confronted by ever increasing numbers of P-47s and then Mustangs with the range, speed and manoeuvrability *at all altitudes*, to hunt them relentlessly all over Germany, destroying many of them on the ground.*

* They were the aerial equivalent of the fourteenth-century Mongol hordes. Despite their range, the Mustangs were much faster and more nimble at all heights than the Me 109s and FW 190s that opposed them, and had the endurance to chase them all over Germany. There was no longer a safe area.

The performance of the German twin-engined fighters was never adequate against day fighters, but the speed and manoeuvrability of the modified FW 190s and Me 109s had been impaired by the weight of their new guns and armour. Until the D-9 version of the former was available, belatedly re-engined with Jumo 213, they could not compete with the Mustang. Monthly

Colonel Hubert Zemke (*left*) congratulating Captain Robert S. Johnson, one of his most successful fighter pilots, after shooting down his twenty-seventh German plane. Zemke, the only man to command Mustang, Thunderbolt and Lightning units in combat, described the P-51 as 'by far the best air-to-air fighter aircraft of the three below 25,000 feet'.

This is a carefully posed publicity view of a Mustang with drop tanks in a B-17
formation, but operational nonsense. Apart from the danger from 'friendly fire'
when escorting as close as this, defending fighters had to operate at the much
higher speeds which would enable them to seek out and prevent Messerschmitts
and Focke-Wulfs from attaining an attacking position – and then catch and
destroy any they found.

losses, which included most of the experienced German fighter pilots, *averaged* 450 in the first five months of 1944; by the end of May, 2,262 had been killed. By 24 May 1944, only 246 of Germany's single-engined day fighters remained operational.[54]

In the 'Battle of Germany', despite their very courageous resistance, the Luftwaffe had been shot out of the sky by 8th Air Force fighters. The superb qualities of the Mustang had won air *supremacy* for the Allies.

The magnificent achievements of the 8th Air Force, over the twelve months to 31 July 1944, have never been adequately recognized in Britain. But one British contribution to their victory was vital, for it was due to Freeman that the Mustangs were there and available in sufficient quantities. Apart from ordering the aircraft in April 1940, and starting the negotiations which led to the contract for the Packard Merlin factory two months later, he was the driving force behind the decision to re-engine the Mustang with the two-stage Merlin in the summer of 1942. And when, between August and November 1942, its forward production orders were limited to 200 per month as far ahead as July 1944, it was Freeman again who pressed Churchill to have this vital matter reconsidered, and ultimately altered, by Roosevelt himself. Because of the decisions taken in November/December 1942, adequate numbers of Mustangs were available to support the vital deep penetration raids in the spring of 1944.

The air battles that gained air supremacy over Europe for the Allies by June 1944, were vital to the success of Overlord, and when Iwo Jima island, in the Pacific, was captured by the American Marine Corps in March 1945,

A **P-51B Mustang** with drop-tanks. Even this early version of the supreme escort fighter shows the clean lines which helped to bring the whole of Germany within range.

and the main Japanese islands came within range of Mustang escort fighters, their influence on that air war was also profound.

The timely decision to mass produce the Merlin Mustang, Freeman's vital contribution to the triumph of the Allied air forces in the Second World War, is certainly the least known, but ultimately one of the most significant, of all his achievements. The Mustang effected a revolution in the air war, and rescued the American bomber forces from the disastrous technical 'cul-de-sac' into which the determination of the American Army Air Force to build and operate a force of self-defending, long-range day bombers was heading. By June 1944, AAF fighters had effectively destroyed the Luftwaffe, just when air supremacy was essential for the Allied invasion of Europe.

In November 1939 Freeman had warned:

> The experience of the last war showed that air superiority to a great extent depended on the relative performance and efficiency of the aircraft on each side, and that the introduction into service of a new type, with superior performance to that possessed by the current enemy type, was a potent factor towards securing air superiority. As a result, it is essential to continue the development of new types, even though it may be two years or more before they come into service. The introduction of new types, of high performance, may well prove a decisive factor in the final stages of the war.[55]

Seldom has foresight been so precisely and so triumphantly vindicated.

CHAPTER 15

Chaos at the Ministry of Aircraft Production: Freeman's return

AVING LOST EXECUTIVE CONTROL of aircraft production in May 1940, and left the Ministry of Aircraft Production in November 1940, when he became Vice-Chief of the Air Staff, Freeman returned as Chief Executive in October 1942. During his absence, aircraft development and production policy had stagnated. The last high level Service link between the RAF as user and the MAP as producer was severed when Tedder also left the ministry in November 1940. Beaverbrook, who knew nothing about industry, and deliberately dispensed with organisation and planning, tried to run it by 'force and fear ... threats [were] the very essence of its direction'.[*][1] By his ignorant meddling in production planning he upset many of the administrative procedures established by the Air Ministry, destroyed the team spirit between the departments of the former AMDP organisation, and poisoned relations between the MAP, the industry and the Air Ministry. The attempt to use Sir Henry Tizard as a link between the Air Staff and the MAP also failed, and Freeman asked for Tizard's powers to be transferred to Linnell in May 1941.

Craven returned to the MAP as Controller-General, after Beaverbrook's resignation in April 1941, but he was a sick man and ill health often kept him away from his office. His senior staff, infected by Beaverbrook's obsession with numbers, recoiled from the responsibility of taking any decisions which caused even a temporary fall in output.

Although such production plans as survived were seriously affected by Beaverbrook's dispersal policy, production recovered well once plants were re-located, and the dispersal reduced the effects of the heavy bombing raids in 1941. In some cases, output actually benefitted from the extra plant put in to 'balance' production. But the 'carrot and stick' system of production planning[†] continued to fail, and the higher the over-estimates of each successive MAP programme, the greater the apparent drop in numbers that would have followed reversion to a more realistic production target. The same fears inhibited the design changes needed to maintain a steady improvement in the quality and performance of aircraft and engines: they too were often deferred on the pretext that consequential falls in output were politically unacceptable.[2]

The ministry needed to be run by someone who could take a realistic view

---

[*] A letter from Tedder to Sir Archibald Sinclair, the Secretary of State for Air, in November 1940, explained the vicious incompetence with which Beaverbrook muddled the well ordered affairs of the aircraft development and production departments. Beaverbrook obviously saw it and vindictively denigrated Tedder thereafter.

[†] Producers were set excessive output targets to encourage greater output, and rewarded for success by increases in orders, or vice versa.

as to the potential of new products, and of when they were likely to be available. It had to be someone with the experience and authority to take long-
term decisions about the use of industrial capacity and the technical developments that would give the RAF the aircraft they would need in the future,
and with the status and standing necessary to carry the support of the Air
Ministry and the War Cabinet. Craven, Hives and many others knew that
Wilfrid Freeman was the only man with these qualifications.

The possibility that Freeman might return had been under discussion for
almost a year before he actually went back to the MAP. As early as December
1941 he had considered leaving the Air Ministry because of mounting friction
with Churchill. In April 1942, after a definite proposal that he should again
take charge of aircraft production, Churchill vetoed the decision. Throughout
the spring and summer of 1942 Freeman had to continue as VCAS in a state of
acute uncertainty which told on his health. Finally, in September, Churchill
had to accept that drastic reforms were needed at the MAP and that only
Freeman could be counted on to implement them effectively.

Among the Chiefs of Staff, Freeman was by no means unique in experiencing difficulties with Churchill in the later months of 1941. Military successes were rare, and the Prime Minister faced rising political criticism, and a
barrage of abrasive requests for help from Stalin. His position worsened when
Beaverbrook, his erstwhile ally, launched a vociferous and highly critical campaign in support of Soviet demands for British aid. Churchill believed that he
desperately needed a victory or two to bolster his political position and, despite
Britain's military weakness, was all too inclined to press the service leaders to
take risks which they were not prepared to countenance.

Freeman's relations with Churchill had been relatively cordial at the time
of the Riviera conference, but a marked deterioration subsequently occurred.
The Butt Report in September shook Churchill's confidence in the ability of
the Royal Air Force to make proper use of the vast fleets of bombers they had
ordered, opening a rift between the Prime Minister and the Air Staff which
went to the very heart of British strategy. Freeman had then been appalled
by Churchill's ruthless attempt to remove Tedder from Middle East Command
in October, and had subsequently done what he could to resist the politically
motivated decision to send 200 fighters per month to Russia, leaving the Far
East and Middle East short of aircraft.

By December, Freeman had seen Churchill at his best and worst: 'as a leader
full of courage and high sounding patriotism, he's pre-eminent, but as a thought-
ful strategist he is ludicrous',[3] and he distrusted the Prime Minister's reliance
on Beaverbrook. Alarmed that he had begun to share the obloquy that Churchill
heaped on those who disagreed with him, he even considered relinquishing the
post of VCAS. 'It seems to me that I must go', he wrote.

> Peter* cannot possibly go on keeping [the Prime Minister and me] apart
> because this strain on him is terrific. I think if it was possible, Peter would

* Portal, the CAS.

give me a command, but my age is against that . . . If I say anything to him he will reply as he has done before, 'Oh you can't leave me', but he doesn't really in his heart of hearts mean that. I want to do what's right and feel that by remaining on I may be doing what's wrong.[4]

That Churchill's regard for Freeman was basically unaffected was obvious when Japan's attack on Pearl Harbor brought the United States into the war two days later. Churchill immediately left Britain for the so-called 'Arcadia' conference with Roosevelt, taking with him Beaverbrook, Portal and Pound. Brooke, who had just become Chief of the Imperial General Staff, stayed in Britain, thereby allowing Dill, whom he succeeded, to go with Churchill. In Portal's absence, Freeman spent the next five weeks as acting CAS, coping with a huge variety of extra responsibilities, including the urgent problem of reinforcing RAF units in the Far East. Churchill obviously trusted him.

Freeman, however, was sceptical about Churchill's journey, grumbling to Elizabeth:

There is the day to day work to do, as well as the big decisions to take', he complained. 'While [the Prime Minister] is away the Empire bleeds and that it does so is entirely due to Winston; his policy is dictated solely by opportunism and nothing else.'[5]

His doubts about Churchill and his 'cronies' were so grave that even military setbacks, such as the loss of HMS *Barham*, and the damage to HMS *Valiant* and *Queen Elizabeth*, (all still unknown to the enemy), were greeted with wry satisfaction. 'Recent disasters', he wrote to Elizabeth, 'have a future press and publicity value and therefore are to be welcomed. The House of Commons show an uneasiness, and in a month they may bare their fangs'.[6]

Overworked and irritable at the end of 1941, Freeman probably exaggerated his difficulties with Churchill, for their worst differences soon assumed a lesser importance: Churchill's month-long absence in the USA allowed tempers to cool. Freeman had his show-down with the Cabinet over the dispatch of aircraft to Russia, while he was acting CAS, but Churchill and Portal were overseas, and there was never any question of him resigning over the matter. The fact that America was now fighting alongside Britain obviously led to a general relaxation of tension in the upper echelons of British government, and the most serious disputes between the Air Ministry and Downing Street over resource allocations simmered down.

Whatever the truth, Freeman remained VCAS, but the uncertainty surrounding his position did not abate. During the first few months of 1942 it became increasingly clear that the MAP was failing to produce the flow of the new and better aircraft on which the future capability of the Royal Air Force depended. Had Craven been fit, he might have rectified the ministry's many shortcomings, but his health was failing, and he began to lobby hard for Freeman's return.

Freeman knew this, but he also knew that Churchill was planning to create a new Ministry of War Production with Beaverbrook in charge, an appointment actually made on 4 February 1942. Luckily for Britain, Beaverbrook quickly upset Churchill and his coalition colleagues, Attlee and Bevin, and resigned from his new position after only twelve days. Even then Churchill tried to keep him in his Cabinet by offering him other posts, among them the Air Ministry and the Ministry of Aircraft Production, and for the next twelve months Freeman remained uneasily aware that if Beaverbrook remained in favour, Churchill might bring him back into his government at any time. The experience of working with Beaverbrook in 1940 made Freeman dread the thought he might return to the MAP and disorganise it all over again.

By April 1942, Craven started becoming insistent. He had already told his ministers, Moore-Brabazon and Llewellin, that Freeman, alone, was capable of taking over his job; he now tackled Portal. 'I can quite understand how you feel about giving him up', Craven wrote,

> but ... do you fully appreciate the terrible danger to the [aircraft production] programme if the wrong man is chosen? With the right man in charge you will get roughly what you want. It would be wonderful for you to have a man like Freeman [running MAP], who you trust so implicitly.[7]

The CAS was not immediately convinced and replied to Craven:

> Everyone knows Freeman's ability and what this would mean to the war effort to have him as your successor. Not nearly so many realise that to find a replacement for him here would be almost, if not quite, as difficult as it evidently is to replace you.[8]

Portal was nevertheless prepared to consider Freeman's transfer, and it was Churchill himself who vetoed the proposal outright. The Prime Minister may have believed that Portal really wanted to retain Freeman as VCAS, but it may also be, as Ralph Freeman wrote to Elizabeth, that 'to permit Wilfrid to return to MAP is to confess failure there since he left'.[9]

Freeman frankly stated that 'MAP appear to be barren of ideas and it is true to say that never before in the history of aviation has so large a staff done so little for technical advancement',[10] and he must have found Churchill's ruling and the extra delay deeply frustrating. The further production and development fell behind at the MAP, the greater the danger to all the future plans for the bombing campaign, the qualitative superiority of British aircraft – and aircrew losses. The ministry's problems required immediate attention, and by deferring a decision on Craven's replacement, Churchill and Portal were mortgaging the future for a temporary respite and jeopardising the long-term operational efficiency of the RAF. Churchill continued, nevertheless, to postpone acceptance of Craven's resignation in the hope that his health would recover. When he finally resigned in July 1942, he was replaced by his deputy, Alexander Dunbar, a capable industrialist, but lacking the self-confidence and technical knowledge to tackle essential reforms at the MAP.*

* Craven warned Portal that Dunbar was not capable of replacing him.

The continuing indecision about Freeman's position caused him intense personal anxiety. Despite the frustrations of being VCAS, he remained his usual decisive and encouraging self at work, but in private he began to show dangerous, and to his family very obvious, signs that the cumulative strains of six years of overwork and uncertainty were beginning to have their effects.[11] Diana Richmond observed in April 1942 that 'poor Wilfrid is now working from about 9 a.m. to 2 a.m. every day, and is so nervy he cannot bear anyone near him, not even Liz . . .'[12]

Elizabeth herself eventually wrote to Portal about Freeman's condition, warning that he was 'heading straight for a nervous breakdown' and she asked that he should be ordered on leave soon. 'He . . . is intensely worried as to which way his duty lies', she wrote, 'to continue as Vice-Chief or to go to MAP.'

> I believe he really thinks he could best serve the country by returning to MAP, but is reluctant to do so, both because he vastly prefers working with you to being mixed up once more with politicians and Civil Servants and because he feels too exhausted, both mentally and physically, to pick up the threats of his old job . . . to try once more to make order out of chaos.[13]*

He became pessimistic, telling Elizabeth:[14]

> I . . . feel that unless there is a radical change in the outlook of the country as a whole we neither deserve nor will win. . . . my thoughts . . . have been as to whether . . . I should . . . go on a bomb raid. . . . Baldwin† would let me go without saying a word, the trouble of course is Peter . . . [who] would forbid me to go saying that I would only be a nuisance and in the way. But going would ease my conscience . . .

The US bomber production programme, the focus of so much of Freeman's attention since his appointment as VCAS, had been reviewed and increased in 1941. By May 1942, however, when the US had been at war with Germany and Japan for six months, Freeman learned of American proposals to reallocate to the US Army Air Corps half the total US aircraft output in June 1942, three-quarters of it in July, and virtually the whole of US production thereafter, in order to create a front-line force of 16,000 aircraft, and to meet commitments to the Soviet Union.[15] Thereafter, Britain would receive only enough aircraft to maintain squadrons already operating US types.[16]

Since there was no possibility of procuring enough aircraft to supply a 4,000 bomber force without US help, the Target Force 'F' plan had to be revised. Different aircraft would be required by the RAF for the Japanese war, and the production programme for the heavy bomber force would therefore have to be changed. When published, the new programme still listed the

---

* After Portal's return, Freeman took a few days leave. Before he left Murtle, 'he stood at the drawing room window for some minutes . . . looking across the frozen dam, to the bare snow touched trees beyond while filling a pipe, taking a sort of farewell look . . .'
† AOC No. 3 Group, equipped with Stirlings.

requirement of heavy bombers as 250 squadrons, 4,000 aircraft – because the Air Staff feared that the USA might reduce supplies to Britain if a smaller programme was disclosed – but the target date for reaching a first line force of 4,000 aircraft was put back to December 1944. The target for September 1943 was lowered to 150 squadrons, 2,400 aircraft.[17]

The new Target Force 'G', for a total of 144 medium and heavy bomber squadrons, was reviewed by the Air Council on 19 August 1942. Accepting that most of the American heavy bombers sent to Britain would be for the US Army Air Corps, it was recognized that Scheme G would only be achieved if production exceeded the MAP's programme.[18]

The MAP's record in the previous twelve months gave the Air Council little grounds for optimism about achieving this: production targets had been continuously revised, and forecasts bore no relation to actual output.

In September, Sinclair made what he described as his 'clarion call' on the MAP – a demand for greater bomber output and for a firm estimate of the number of heavy and medium bombers to be delivered in September, October and November.[19] Three weeks later, after forecasting production of 868 heavy bombers for this period, Llewellin, the Minister, lowered his estimate to 781,[20] and Sinclair, totally exasperated by the incompetence of these continual changes, complained to Churchill,[21] who accepted at last that a decision about the MAP's future management could no longer be postponed.

On 2 September Churchill wrote tersely to the Minister of Production, Oliver Lyttelton, about the MAP:

> All their forecasts have been several times written down, and all their performances fall short of their reduced forecasts ... The non-expansion of MAP output is really very grave. What do you propose?[22]

Lyttelton replied that alterations in the top structure of the MAP were essential. His solution effectively went back to the AMDP system proposed by Weir in 1938, whereby responsibility for production, research and development were united under a common executive head. For this post he recommended Freeman.*[23] 'Freeman has all the qualities and experience necessary for the top post', he told Churchill, 'and would carry the confidence of the Royal Air Force and the industry.'[24]

* Lyttelton regretted that he had previously been against Freeman's appointment; 'I feared weakness in production control'.

As the production targets drifted down during the summer, Freeman realised that his return to the MAP was becoming increasingly likely, and sensibly
started assembling the support and defining the powers he was determined
to secure before he would consent to go back. The Air Council agreed to ask
Churchill for unlimited priority for the bomber programme, and a memorandum was prepared showing the minimum aircraft requirements necessary to
enable the RAF to fulfil its strategic obligations, which firmly stressed that
this minimum represented more than 100 per cent of the current MAP programme. A new programme was therefore necessary, and since RAF resources
and manpower would be allocated in accordance with this programme, there
would be serious waste if the programme was not achieved.

Freeman then persuaded Sinclair to ask for what amounted to a blank
cheque. The Cabinet's Defence Committee was asked to stipulate that the
MAP *must* fulfil its programme, and that the ministry should be given such
priorities for labour and machine tools as were necessary for that purpose.
Extra capacity for development of new types was also essential, if qualitative
superiority was to be maintained. It was a bold gambit by Freeman, a provocative pre-emptive bid, made through the proper channels by the Air Minister,
and certain to be resisted by the other two services, and by the Ministries of
Supply and Production. But it focused Churchill's mind on the measures that
were essential, if the MAP was to be reorganised.[25]

Having pitched the Air Ministry's demands as high as he could, Freeman
then set about ensuring that he would have the executive powers and political
and industrial support that he would need when he returned to the MAP. Air
Ministry policy was controlled and executed by Service officers, helped by the
Civil Servants in the Air Ministry's administrative posts, whereas the MAP was
a civilian ministry, to which serving officers like Linnell or Banks, or Freeman
himself after May 1940, were seconded to advise on specialist aspects – without executive powers. If Freeman was to have executive control of development
and production at the MAP, he would have to retire from the RAF and become
a Civil Servant, a move which he viewed with suspicion and some regret.

Top Civil Servants are notoriously reluctant to allow 'outsiders' to have
executive powers, and Freeman suspected that they would know exactly how
to block his appointment, whilst making it appear that he, the outsider, was
being unreasonable. But he had learned how to deal with senior Civil Servants
whilst in the Air Ministry, and during his six months at the MAP in 1940.
He had seen enough of Rowlands, the Permanent Secretary, to know that he
must establish the executive status and terms of service he would need for
his new and tremendously responsible job, *before* he left the RAF.

He subtly overcame these potential difficulties by informing the head of his
own service, Portal, in writing, that he wished to remain at the Air Ministry.[26]
This was not, of course, the truth. Freeman knew that his return to the MAP
was a vital necessity, and he had often told Elizabeth of his private loathing of
his work at the Air Ministry, and of the frustrations of his position as VCAS.
But the implications of that letter must have been obvious to the senior

politicians and Civil Servants who could determine his future: Freeman would only move to the MAP on his own terms. Portal could now negotiate on his behalf, and procure him the full executive powers he would need to reorganise the ministry, and the salary level which he believed appropriate for the chief executive of the biggest and most important supply department in Britain.

He got what he wanted. Describing Freeman's new position in November 1942, the air correspondent of the *Daily Mail* wrote:

> I understand that Sir Wilfred (*sic*) Freeman, the former Vice Chief of Air Staff has been given virtually complete control of the Ministry of Aircraft Production. The Minister, Colonel Llewellin of course remains the political head of department.
>
> The relation between the two has been made similar to that which exists between the Service head and the political head in a defence department: Sir Wilfred becomes in effect Chief of Staff in the aircraft factory front. His transfer to the Ministry attracted little attention when it was announced recently, but it now appears that it was one of the most important moves made in Whitehall for some time. It restores a direct and powerful Service influence to aircraft production. There had been increasing fears in many circles that without this influence, British aircraft might lose the vital technical superiority they possessed at the beginning of the war. . . .

Churchill seems to have had no reservations about giving Freeman such powers, and he thereby freed himself from ministerial interference. He would be able to tell the industry what to do, without Civil Servants postponing every decision until all its implications had been examined in exhaustive detail.

Freeman returned to the MAP as Chief Executive on 19 October 1942, after nearly two years as VCAS, resuming much the same role as he performed between 1938 and 1940, but with wider powers over a larger ministry. His appointment was confirmation that Churchill's criticism of the Air Ministry's Development and Production department* had been unjust and unfounded, and that the appointment of Beaverbrook as Minister of Aircraft Production, which thereby terminated Freeman's executive control of aircraft development and production, had been a serious, long-term mistake. Freeman was the obvious man to gather up the reins of the industry he knew so well, and the fact that he returned to his old job with the full support of the Government, the Air Ministry, and the aircraft industry, must have been deeply satisfying.

Hives, like all the members of the SBAC, was ecstatic at the news that once again there was an experienced airman at the helm. 'I saw your Minister last night', he wrote, 'and he confirmed the joyful news'.[27]

But the long delay, due to Churchill's indecision, had been a great strain, and Freeman himself was far from well.

---

* In June 1940, Churchill had described the state of aircraft production as 'a muddle and a scandal'.

CHAPTER 16

A Herculean task

FREEMAN RETURNED as Chief Executive of the Ministry of Aircraft Production on 19 October 1942, '... as a civilian much to his regret ... there could be no better way of quitting the service than being the only man, after six months, who can fill the post. He leaves on a foreign mission, I believe, in the near future ... Liz has been taking down some civilian clothes, unworn for years.'[1]*

As the extent of the formidable range of unresolved problems at the Ministry became clear, he persuaded Churchill that he could not spare the time for a visit to America. A huge backlog of deferred decisions had been built up under Beaverbrook and his successors Moore-Brabazon and Llewellin, who were competent politicians but lacked executive knowledge and experience on production matters.

Moore-Brabazon was a jovial and well-connected pioneer airman, with a life-long involvement in aviation matters, amongst them the post of Assessor for the R.101 enquiry, which did not disclose the full facts behind the cause of that disaster.† Appointed Minister of Transport in 1940, he took over as Minister of Aircraft Production in April 1941, when Beaverbrook resigned, and resigned himself ten months later, at Churchill's request, after an indiscrete comment about his Russian allies.

Llewellin was also politically well connected, indeed between 1939 and 1945, he held no less than seven different ministerial posts, amongst them that of Parliamentary Secretary to Beaverbrook at MAP. He succeeded Moore-Brabazon as Minister of Transport in April 1941, and as Minister of Aircraft Production in February 1942.

As the new Chief Executive Freeman had to take over full control of the Ministry's research, development and production department, devise a realistic aircraft production programme and cope with the backlog.

The development and production difficulties affecting the Sabre and Whittle engines had to be resolved as soon as possible, and a decision taken as to the future of the Stirling bomber. Production of the Halifax could not be stopped – too many aircraft would be 'lost' before the factories could be reorganised to make Lancasters – so the performance of the Halifax had somehow to be improved. Lancaster output had to be increased, and some of the factories producing Wellingtons and Warwicks had either to be re-equipped to make new Vickers geodetic aircraft, or switched to Lancasters. Finally, the management of com-

---

* The possibility that Churchill might send him to the USA to persuade the Americans to a major increase in Mustang production hung over him.

† *Slide rule*, Neville Shute's autobiography, gives an interesting account of the design differences betwen the successful R.100, and the R.101.

panies such as Short Brothers, Fairey, and Boulton Paul, had to be reviewed, and their boards of directors strengthened by experienced industrialists appointed and approved by the MAP.

Moreover, all of this had to be achieved quickly. Churchill was impatient, and the spectre of Beaverbrook was in the background – all too likely to reappear if there was any delay in putting the affairs of the Ministry to rights.[2] The final stage of the Alamein offensive, and the invasion of Morocco and Algeria only came in November 1942, and despite the pressure from Beaverbrook's newspapers for a 'Second Front now', Churchill still hankered for the reassurance of Beaverbrook's support. Freeman could not discount the very real possibility that many more months of meticulous and gruelling hard work at MAP, might once again be wrecked by ignorant meddling for the sake of showy but ephemeral gains.

> It is difficult to put right in a day what's been allowed to drift for so long. The general idea is that I'll be given time to get things right, and that Lord B. will once again step in, squeeze the orange, crush it under foot and go.[3]

THE MINISTRY OF AIRCRAFT PRODUCTION

Setting Dunbar to work on a new production programme, Freeman concentrated at first on the organisation of MAP, and discovered to his horror that there had been a fundamental change in the attitude of the staff since 1940. The legacy of Beaverbrook's methods was a corrosive mixture of inadequate planning, distrust and secrecy which disrupted the Ministry's internal functioning and soured its relations with the aircraft industry. A young economist, Alec Cairncross,* who was working there as a lowly 'propeller planner', had been brought in by Professor Jewkes, who kept him well informed. He realised that:

> ... spheres of responsibility in the Ministry were imprecise: decisions taken at one level or department sometimes failed to reach the officers responsible for implementing them, or those who were most affected. Conflicts which should have been resolved by a competent and decisive leader were all too often ignored or disregarded: the vital liaison between producer and user had broken down.[4]

Fearing intervention, aircraft contractors concealed their production problems – and any surplus material – from MAP officials. Difficulties were tackled on an *ad hoc* basis as and when they arose, long after a shortfall in output could be prevented.[5]

By then, many of the departments at the MAP were run by people that Freeman hardly knew, and who had yet to earn his confidence. Civil Servants, businessmen, engineers, scientists and RAF officers of varying qualities had been transferred to the Ministry as it expanded. Not only were they unused to

---

* The late Sir Alec Cairncross, KCMG, a former head of the Government Economic Service, and Master of St Peter's College, Oxford, who generously made his unpublished wartime diaries available to the author.

working with each other, but many of them were unwilling to take decisions or disclose problems for fear of being blamed for them: it was safer to do nothing. Decisions on matters as uncontroversial as factory extensions were sometimes avoided. Hives complained bitterly that capital expenditure proposals which were properly presented and uncontentious would, if approved at all, be agreed only 'in principle'; the aura of uncertainty was quite unnecessary.[6] When, in September 1941, Moore-Brabazon, the Minister, asked for news of Rolls-Royce's plans to increase production, Hives explained to Craven, the Chief Executive, that proposals had been sitting at the MAP, unanswered, for seven or eight weeks: 'I raised this point at our July meeting ... again at the August meeting and ... [it is] on the Agenda for September'.[7]

The MAP's production directors had difficulty co-ordinating their programmes to cope with rapid advances in technology. Production was constantly disrupted by Service demands for modifications and for the introduction of new marks of airframe and aero-engine. Programme changes of this nature always resulted in a loss of output, but there was no scientific basis for predicting how great that loss would be.[8]

It proved equally difficult to forecast RAF requirements for spare parts: requisitions from the RAF were often based on inadequate records. In 1940, Beaverbrook had reduced spares production to the bare minimum, in order to increase the output of complete aircraft, and production runs had to be interrupted whenever spares were insufficient: the frequent changes reduced overall output. Spares would have to be properly planned and monitored or further shortfalls in the aircraft programme would be inevitable.

When VCAS, Freeman had been outspoken in his criticism of Llewellin's regime, and once his Chief Executive status was established, he was careful to make sure that Llewellin understood that his role was now limited to being MAP's *political* chief. Llewellin would have to answer for his decisions to the Government, but the backlog of work was too great for hesitation, and he was soon by-passing his Minister. 'Yesterday I sent Llewellin a list of projects I had put in hand without his knowledge', he told Elizabeth. 'He will probably have a fit and say he should have been consulted, to which I will reply that I will stop any of them he doesn't like; of course he will want them to go on, and so why on earth should I consult him?[9]

Beaverbrook had taken all the decisions when he was Minister of Aircraft Production – for better or for worse – but the roles of Chief Executive under Moore-Brabazon and Llewellin had been filled by Craven, whose health by then was very precarious, and then by Dunbar, who was knowledgeable but lacked leadership qualities. Between May 1941 and October 1942, most of the key decisions were probably taken on the advice of Craven or Rowlands, the clever but devious Permanent Under-Secretary at the MAP, and the administrative head of the civilian ministry. He had been transferred to it from the Treasury in May 1940, and although Craven had returned as Chief Executive after Beaverbrook left in April 1941, he was frequently unwell; Rowlands made arrangements to ensure that all information about aircraft production matters came to

Sir Charles Craven, the Controller-General of the Ministry of Aircraft Production, who advised Churchill and Portal to appoint Freeman, not Dunbar, to succeed him as Chief Executive.

him and that he was consulted on important decisions.[10] Craven had advised against appointing Dunbar in his place when he retired, but that mistake was made, and Rowlands' influence was not thereby diminished. But his experience as a Civil Servant was not an ideal training as a decision maker, and he lacked experience on technical and industrial matters.

Knowing that he would have difficulties with Rowlands, Freeman had made sure that his status as Chief Executive was equal to Rowlands' in most departments, and superior to his in others, before he accepted the job. The Secretariat and finance departments remained under Rowland's control,* but Freeman had sole responsibility for research, development and production. Half way through December, he was furious to discover that Rowlands was trying to remain the focus of all MAP information, and questioning development and production staff behind his back. He pulled him up sharply, insisting that his questions must be addressed to him in future, not to his staff.[11]

Deeply depressed by his distrust of Rowlands, Freeman wanted to have a senior Assistant Under-Secretary he could trust, and asked Portal if he would

---

* Robert Hall, (later Lord Roberthall) economist and Rhodes Scholar who worked in the Ministry of Supply from 1939–46 and was later Economic Adviser to the Government from 1953–61, found it 'incomprehensible' that the heads of these departments, chosen by Rowlands, should have got such responsibilities.

release Maurice Dean, the Assistant Under-Secretary at the Air Ministry, who he admired and respected, instead of Calder. He had planned for some time to have Dean moved to MAP if he went back there, and warned Portal that Rowlands would object, that Street at the Air Ministry would also resist the move and that Dean himself might not want to get involved. In the event the transfer did not take place.[12]

Planning at the MAP had restarted in May 1941 after Beaverbrook resigned, when Rowlands had sensibly invited Professor John Jewkes, then head of the Economic Section of the War Cabinet Office, to spend a few months examining the need for planning at the Ministry.* Jewkes accepted appointment as head of a new MAP planning department, and staffed it with able young economists such as Alec Cairncross and Ely Devons. The MAP production records were so inadequate that most of the initial work of the planning department involved the compilation of statistics. Cairncross recorded much that he was told of the many problems that Jewkes discovered, so his diary entries were well informed, and, despite his inexperience, it was his lasting impression that accurate information was seldom available.

> ... information was not freely yielded; each department liked to keep its secrets, since secret information was a prime source of power... There were many different requirements to be met; many different voices urging them, and some voices that remained silent too long, or were hard to hear. Above all, requirements were constantly changing because of advances in what was technically possible, fresh operational experience, changes in the theatre of war, or in what appealed to the Air Ministry. We were wrestling all the time with uncertainties on every side. Our information at MAP Planning had to be more up to date than anybody else's, but it was inevitably incomplete, often suspect, derived perhaps from hearsay and contradicted by others who might or might not be trustworthy. We had to listen carefully to the gossip and sift it for new developments.[13]

Another 'inexperienced' young assistant was Edwin Plowden (later Lord Plowden), whose wife was a first cousin of Elizabeth Freeman. Plowden was concerned initially with aluminium supplies, from which he progressed to materials in general, and finally to engines, a task which he performed so well that Freeman nominated him as his successor three years later. Plowden confirmed the difficulty of getting accurate information from the manufacturers, and explained his success:

> I chose some very able assistants, the 'Plowden Gestapo', and they had such charm and were so reliable and nice that all the firms they visited told them what was going on, so I was properly informed and could plan effectively.[14]

Freeman valued the work of Jewkes' directorate, for he relied on his staff for information in the same way as he depended on the development and

---

* Jewkes had been Professor of Economics at Manchester before the war and held the same job at Oxford after it.

production directorates to implement his policies. Nevertheless, he soon made the same change of emphasis of the Ministry's contribution to aircraft production, as Speer had done in Germany eight months before.[15] From the moment he returned as CEO, he used the information and advice which he obtained from his staff, not as evidence on which to base instructions to the aircraft makers, but as a guide to what he must do to help and encourage the manufacturing companies. The Ministry's directorates, and their representatives at the aircraft factories, may have thought that they knew more about aircraft production than the manufacturing firms: Freeman had no such illusions.

By the end of 1942, the aircraft industry was the largest single industry in Britain: the number of workers employed had increased from 866,000 in September 1940 to 1,654,000 in March 1943. The task of directing such a huge and complex undertaking was truly daunting. To reassert his authority over the industry, Freeman naturally had to delegate many tasks to his directors. But, given his intimate knowledge of the aircraft firms, it was inevitable that he should also have sought to work with them directly, and they were all eager to discuss their affairs with him personally. Two weeks into his new job, Freeman told Elizabeth, 'My weekend is going west gradually'.

> People are encroaching into Saturday and ... Sunday. It is no good [refusing to see them so] I fix a time to get to the end of the essential interviews. They are essential, for after all they build the aeroplanes, engines, instruments, guns and whatever, and it is my business ... to tell them what to make and in what quantity and to make it possible and even easy for them to do so ...' That's all my job can ever be .. it all comes down to the fact that I am prepared to say 'yes' or 'no' ...[16]

Many of the key decision makers, of course, had maintained regular contact with Freeman since November 1940, but they all clamoured for an audience with him following his reappointment to the MAP. A typical week is described in his private correspondence:

> Next week I must work off Spriggs of Hawkers; Handley Page; Greenley whom I haven't seen for a month and twice put off; Nelson, English Electric; Mitman, aluminium; Devereux, aluminium; Aberconway, John Brown; McColl, Mobil Oil; Godber, Shell; Viyella; ... Trinidad Leaseholds; Kilner, Vickers; Reggie Rootes...; Black, Standards; Wilks, Rover; B[ruce]-G[ardner]; Hives and Sidgreaves, Rolls-Royce; Scott, Chairman of Rolls-Royce; Spaatz, G.O.C. of American Air Force; Biddle, and so on...[17]

In redirecting the activities of the Ministry, Freeman was undoubtedly correct to exploit his direct links with the aircraft industry – the industrialists themselves gave him no alternative. Nevertheless, the masterful way in which he picked up the reins of his old job contrasted sharply with 'Ministerial' approaches of Moore-Brabazon and Llewellin, his immediate predecessors, who knew relatively little about the complicated inter-relationships between the RAF and its suppliers, and Freeman occasionally ignored the 'proper channels'. This was partly because the organisation which he and Lemon had created in 1938 had changed in the two years since he left, and he was unfamiliar with the new system, but mainly due to the urgent need to clear up the enormous backlog of 'indecision'. His initial approach to his new appointment unsettled the cosy routine of departmental minutes and lengthy, and indecisive meetings. There were misunderstandings in the Ministry which probably could have been avoided; they complicated his work and sometimes upset his staff.

He was so preoccupied, so conscious of the mountain of deferred work ahead of him, that he was understandably reluctant to attend large MAP meetings: any gatherings that he attended had to be kept as small and short as possible. He once discouraged Fraser, Director General of Aircraft Production, from attending an informal discussion about the new aircraft programme, saying with a mischievous glint in his eye, 'This wouldn't interest you at all DGAP, you would just be wasting your time'.[18] The disrespectful attitude he took to the formalities of his position irritated Llewellin, while Jewkes, who had given up an important job to come to the MAP, was both furious that Freeman had so little respect for many of the other directors in the Ministry, and disgruntled that he, as a Deputy Director, had not yet attained their status.

What is quite astonishing is that neither Jewkes nor his department seems to have understood why Freeman had been given such extensive new powers at the MAP.* During his last months as Vice Chief of the Air Staff, Freeman had criticised the MAP programmes in a manner which Jewkes must have resented, and, before Freeman returned to MAP, Jewkes described him as 'neurotic, disposed to self-justification and a trifle querulous'.[19] Freeman's subsequent insistence on a complete revision of the basis of production planning probably accentuated the negative initial response from his Deputy Director.

Freeman had quickly recognised Jewkes' experience and ability, and in less than a month had chosen him for the vitally important mission to America, when he helped Lyttelton to persuade the US government to revise the Merlin and Mustang production programmes. Freeman was equally happy to make use of Jewkes' statistical ability to develop a more reliable aircraft programme. But for Jewkes this was not enough: he wanted to be appointed Director General of Programmes, with direct access to Freeman. When Freeman refused to make time throughout December 1942 and early January 1943, for the long private talk which Jewkes was impatiently demanding, he seriously contemplated resignation.[20] Rowlands too had thoughts of resigning, although, in the event, they both remained at the Ministry, and Jewkes received his promotion to Director General in June 1943. Freeman found

---

* It is clear from the Cairncross diaries that neither he nor Jewkes had any idea of Freeman's pre-eminent achievements in aircraft development and production at the Air Ministry between 1936 and 1940, and were equally unaware of his unceasing efforts as VCAS to maintain the quality of Service aircraft.

him pompous, a fault he seldom wholly forgave, and it was only when the brilliant Ely Devons became head of the planning department that a close and easy atmosphere of friendship and mutual respect developed: Devons became one of Freeman's greatest admirers.*

If Freeman had been willing to have a circular prepared and sent round his Ministry in October, clearly describing the full scope of his executive responsibilities, and listing the record of his planning and production achievements since 1936 (which were obviously unknown to many of his staff), the undercurrent of unease might soon have ended. But he was reluctant to blow his own trumpet, and, rather than blow it for him, Rowlands stirred the dissent.[21]

Despite his executive freedom, Freeman found the lack of willing co-operation at the Ministry utterly depressing, and began to think about leaving the MAP: he said as much to Portal and Sinclair, complaining of 'the foul atmosphere of intrigue, of disloyalty, [and] back-biting', and of his many difficulties with Rowlands. They, in turn, pleaded with him to stay, and the respect he soon developed for Stafford Cripps, his new Minister, clearly helped.[22]

After serving successfully as British Ambassador to Russia in 1941, and leading an unsuccessful mission to the Indian Congress Party as Lord Privy Seal in 1942, Cripps had agreed to become leader of the Commons, an uncongenial role supporting the policy of the Conservative dominated coalition government. Matters came to a head when Churchill refused to accept his advice, and Cripps was relieved to be offered the Ministry of Aircraft Production instead, taking over from Llewellin at the end of November.† Freeman found him difficult and unapproachable at first, full of preconceived views of what was wrong with aircraft production, and prepared to use his position to further political objectives in a way which made Freeman uneasy. But although Freeman considered Cripps' political views absurd,‡ they soon came to admire and like each other. Cripps fell for Freeman's charm and wit, and appreciated his tact and experience, and Freeman soon realised that he now had a punctual, hard working and very intelligent Minister who read his papers properly at lightning speed. Freeman trusted his advice on matters concerning the Government, and Cripps was soon willing to throw his full support behind the recommendations of his Chief Executive. Where intervention was necessary, Cripps acted sensibly, unlike Beaverbrook, using carefully chosen experts from the City and industry to implement the Ministry's plans.

* Devons was somewhat scruffy, and inclined to talk with a cigarette in his mouth, a sharp contrast to his always immaculate boss, but Freeman admired his brilliant mind, enjoyed his ruthless objectivity, played truant with him from the office in the summer sunshine, and offered him a job at Courtaulds after the war – which he refused.

† Cripps had become leader of the House of Commons in the wartime coalition, but disliked the role under Churchill's dictatorial leadership, and would have resigned if he had not been offered the MAP.

‡ Cripps still opposed the pre-war rearmament programme as late as 1938, and told a political audience at Stockport a year or so before the war that 'It would not be a bad thing for the British working classes if Germany did defeat us. It would be for the profit-makers and capitalists, but not necessarily for the working classes.' 'Russia was defeated in the last war, yet her working classes benefited most from the war'.

By February 1943, however, Freeman was having doubts. Whenever Cripps visited aircraft factories, he insisted on addressing the workers – and he always greeted them as 'Comrades'. He was laudably keen to encourage the workforce to contribute intelligent ideas and suggestions for improvements in production, but he was too active and ardent a socialist to miss the opportunity to promote his political ideas. There are few records of what he actually said in his factory speeches. But when addressing students at Aberdeen University in February 1943, he stressed how important it was for young people to stake their claim immediately, in the middle of the war, to the sort of improvements they wished to see in the post-war world; they should not wait until the wartime emergency was over. Freeman wryly repeated Stalin's comment that Cripps (who had been British Ambassador in Moscow) would be 'a charming man if he would only stop talking about Communism!'[23]

Freeman became so uneasy about these activities that he decided that he must offer Cripps his resignation. 'I either work for him or against him', he told Elizabeth. 'My conscience will not let me work with him, neither . . . allow me to work against him behind his back. You cannot and shouldn't try these experiments in war time . . .'[24] Cripps was appalled when he did so, realising that Freeman's departure would place him in an impossible position,* and having asked him to hold off for twenty-four hours, he gave way, and stopped pressing his political views on the aircraft workers. The two men remained at the head of MAP, and worked on together in mutual harmony and growing respect.

SABRE AND WHITTLE ENGINE PROBLEMS

The two worst technical problems which awaited Freeman's return to the MAP concerned the Napier Sabre and the Whittle jet engines, for the delays over their development were seriously impeding production planning. The long-term prospects of both engines had seemed promising in 1940: the hand-made, pre-production Sabres from the Acton factory ran well, but two years later Napier were still unable to deliver reliable mass-produced versions of their complicated 24-cylinder, twin-crankshaft, sleeve-valve engines, whilst the early reverse-flow Whittle engines made by Rover could not be made to give adequate power. The Typhoon was the only service aircraft to use the Sabre at the time, and the engine was so unreliable that there was talk of taking the Typhoon out of service. The first information about the German progress on jets was received in 1942, so a jet fighter had also become a definite requirement.

Freeman tackled the problems of these two engines immediately. The solu-

* WRF quoted Cripps:'[My] position would be impossible'. Cripps had actually been expelled from the Labour Party before the war, for his Communist views. He was now a senior Minister in a coalition government dominated by the Conservative Party, which was still deeply suspicious of Communist policies, and the resignation, for well recorded reasons, of a chief executive with Freeman's unique record and ability, would not only damage the war effort, but damage both the coalition and Cripps' political future, and reopen the rift between Cripps and his Labour Party colleagues.

tion to the manufacture of sleeves for the Sabre had been established by Rod Banks before Freeman's return to the MAP.[25]* But Banks also realised that the Sabre shadow factory built at Netherton, near Liverpool, and run by Standard Motors, was badly managed and that it's management should be transferred to another company.† Freeman knew that George Nelson, the Chairman of English Electric, wanted his firm to be allowed to resume the design and manufacture of aircraft after the war, so asked him to consider taking on the Netherton plant. Nelson visited the works, and told Freeman that he could help, but that he 'was not prepared to run somebody else's company'‡: English Electric must be allowed to take over the Napier group. Napier by then was deeply in debt to the MAP, so there was a good financial case for a take-over, and an English Electric offer for Napier's share capital was accepted by more than 80 per cent of the shareholders before the end of December 1942.

Freeman also decided that all responsibility for research and development at Napier must be taken away from Bulman. He had far too much work in any case, and had failed to recognize the extent to which production management faults were behind the company's problems – and the urgent need for drastic remedies. Rod Banks took over as Director of Research and Development at Napier, and, working closely with young George Nelson, who was put in as works manager at Napier, their reforms sharply improved the quality of new engines from Netherton. Banks insisted that Napier should refuse to deliver engines which had not been modified. When Fighter Command put pressure on Napier to ignore this, and Banks refused, Nelson complained to Freeman, who called in Banks. 'There you are,' he laughingly told Banks, 'we have just persuaded English Electric to take on Napier and you have messed it up' – and then gave Banks his full support.[26] Bulman was deeply mortified by Banks' appointment, and never really forgave Freeman,[27] but he loyally supported the decision in the Ministry. Years later, he displayed great integrity and generosity of spirit, by his evocative tribute to Freeman and his management of the pre-war rearmament programme, in his hitherto unpublished memoirs.

A somewhat similar solution was employed for the Whittle engine. Freeman brought in the industrial expertise of a more experienced manufacturer – in this case Rolls-Royce and made new appointments at the MAP to supervise the development of gas-turbine engines. He had realised the potential of Whittle's engine as early as 1936 and, despite the discouraging assessments from Griffith and other technical advisers at the Royal Aircraft Establishment, had funded Whittle's research with Air Ministry grants.

Details of British progress with gas turbines had reached America by May

---

* Bristol and its suppliers had discovered the metallurgical and production technology for mass-producing sleeves by 1939. MAP insisted that full information about their processes and materials was disclosed to Napier and used for the Sabre.

† Swarf is said to have been found inside completed production engines, evidence of careless workshop practises, and inadequate management.

‡ Author's talks with 2nd Lord Nelson of Stafford, 1992. His father told Freeman that he was not prepared to pay a fancy price for Napier.

1941. Several British aero-engine makers were also given access to technical drawings and design data about the Whittle engine: de Havilland and Metro-Vick had started design work on their own gas-turbines. By October 1941, a Whittle W.1X engine and a set of W.2B drawings were in the USA, and GEC was building Whittle-type engines. Rolls-Royce had been helping Whittle's company, Power Jets, and had also started research of their own.

As soon as he returned to MAP, Freeman told Linnell, the CRD to prepare a report on gas-turbine development, which he completed before the end of November. Linnell reported that despite Power Jets' theoretical brilliance and long experience in gas-turbine development, the company had little general engineering knowledge and virtually no production expertise or facilities. Rover, the company responsible for series production of Whittle's engine, had been working closely with Power Jets for two and a half years but still lacked basic experience in the field of aero-engine design, and had failed to test their development in an adequate manner. Rolls-Royce, however, despite their out-standing experience and superb resources for development, production and testing, lacked a practical engine design on which to work.*

Linnell recommended that Rolls-Royce and Power Jets should merge, and that Rover should cease the production of jets altogether, once they had completed the batch of relatively low-powered W.2B engines on which they were working. He also suggested that future development of gas-turbines should be controlled by a separate Gas Turbine Engine Development Directorate at the MAP.[28] Acting on this advice, Freeman sent Hives to visit the Power Jets factory at Whetstone and the two Rover 'jet' factories at Barnoldswick and Clitheroe. Hives warned Whittle that Rolls-Royce were going to start making gas-turbines and that they were interested in making his W.2/500 design, for which extra production facilities would be required. Having mentioned Linnell's suggestion that, with Power Jets' consent, Rolls-Royce should assume control of the Whetstone factory, Hives and Whittle sensibly agreed that Rover's Barnoldswick factory would be a much better alternative.[29]

A lot of preparatory work had therefore been done by the time Freeman summoned Whittle to meet him and Linnell on 11 December 1942. The suggestion that Rolls-Royce should assume control of the development and production of Whittle's engine by taking over the Rover factories, and, possibly, the Power Jets factory at Whetstone, had almost certainly been discussed with Hives by then,[30] since Freeman had the highest regard for Rolls-Royce, and knew how quickly they could set to work on new ideas.

Freeman spent the first part of the meeting trying to persuade Whittle to accept the logic of throwing in his lot with Rolls-Royce as their jet-engine designer, but although Whittle was delighted at the thought of Rolls-Royce taking over the Rover factories and advancing the development of his engine designs, he obviously hated the very idea of R-R taking over his company.

---

* Rolls-Royce was making an experimental reverse-flow multi-stage, axial gas turbine to Griffith's design, in which each stage revolved in opposite directions, the inner portion forming the compressor, the outer, the turbine. It did not work.

The Welland I: 'Whittle-designed' reverse-flow engine, properly made by Rolls-Royce, which developed 1,600 lb thrust and powered the 415 mph Gloster Meteor I.

The Derwent I engine. This was basically the same engine as the Welland I, but was a 'straight-through' version redesigned by Rolls-Royce and it achieved 2,000 lb thrust, which gave the Meteor III a top speed of 470 mph, enough to catch Flying Bombs.

Apart from his prejudice against the established aero-engine industry, there were three other likely reasons for Whittle's resistance to a formal association between the two companies.*

Firstly, Power Jets was both his 'command' in the RAF and the *'fons et origo'* of all British gas-turbine invention: jet-powered flight had been achieved with his engine, and his later designs were full of promise. He wanted to be given space, machinery and labour to originate new engine designs, to make the first batches of each new engine, and to continue to be the designer, developer, *and* most of all, the *Chief-Engineer* of the enterprise. Secondly, acquisition by Rolls-Royce would leave no role for three other Power Jets directors, Johnson, Williams and Tinling, who had given valuable, non-technical, help to Whittle since 1936, and to whom he was staunchly loyal.

Thirdly, there is little doubt that Whittle's own mind was more than a little unbalanced by this time, for he had become addicted to the frequent use of 'benzedrine' inhalers, which could then be purchased from any chemist. The amphetamine sulphate constituent of the drug was not then recognized to be addictive, but the side effects are now known to cause insomnia and feelings of tension, anxiety and, at times, paranoia.[31]†

Conscious that decisions taken without Whittle's support might 'dry up' the flow of his invaluable ideas, Freeman did his best to reassure him, but he eventually decided not to force the issue and continued to support Power Jets as an independent company. Rolls-Royce took over Rover's Barnoldswick and Clitheroe factories, and progress with jet-engine development was thereafter rapid:‡ Rover received compensation in the form of Rolls-Royce's Meteor tank engine shadow factory and its contracts. Work on turbine engines within the general framework of the MAP's engine development directorate was given to a separate department, run by Dr Roxbee Cox, later Lord Kings Norton, and Whittle was allowed to expand his company. The number of staff at the Whetstone factory increased to more than 600. But output was not satisfactory, and later in the war, against Freeman's advice, Cripps nationalized Power Jets, a move which Whittle had suggested to him in another context in April 1943.

---

* These conclusions are those of the author, but the first two are based on talks with Dr Feilden, who was working for Whittle at Power Jets, during the war.

† Bulman's memoirs explained that Whittle became increasingly suspicious and unreasonable as a colleague during the period, 1940–2.

‡ The slim drive-shafts of the early jet engines whirled (bending outwards in the middle), unless kept very short, and Whittle's early designs reversed the flow of the air *twice* in order to keep the shaft as short as possible. The precise engineering problems of a third, centre, bearing did not worry R-R, and whilst their version of the Whittle W2B/23 – the Welland – was reverse-flow, they focused development on Rover's 'straight-through' version of this engine and produced the W2B/37, Derwent 1. Most of Whittle's basic concepts succeeded, but R-R had the resources to test a range of turbines with blades of varying degrees of twist; the one that worked better than the others was then used for all other early experiments, redesign following when other problems had been solved.

THE REALISTIC HEAVY BOMBER PROGRAMME

As soon as Freeman's appointment as Chief Executive became effective, he bluntly informed Llewellin that the bomber programme could not be achieved, and launched a scathing attack on the 'carrot and stick' policy of making over-optimistic production forecasts which had been adopted by Beaverbrook and continued by his successors. In Freeman's opinion, the system actually restricted production, since there were industrial sectors which faced short-ages of key resources such as machine tools, labour, and floor space, because these had been allocated to support aircraft production in accordance with output plans that could not possibly be realised. Aircraft components, EL equipment and raw materials were being misallocated for precisely the same reason. Moreover, when production targets were not achieved, the Air Ministry aircrew training programmes were under-employed: unnecessary aero-dromes were built, and instructors and aircraft which might have otherwise been employed in the front line, were over-allocated to Training Command.[32]

There was a strong case to be made for allocating more resources to air-craft production, provided that the programme targets were realistic. 'Unless we are given the labour, machine tools and equipment to enable us to reach the programme, we must reduce it', Freeman wrote. 'If we are given the labour and equipment, we should achieve it ... We must have the labour that we want *now*, if we are to get our programme in six months time ... We must have the machine tools we want *now*.' Instead of awaiting sanction from the Ministry of Supply, Freeman proposed that a directive be obtained from the Prime Minister himself: bombers would be given priority over all other munitions for the next six months. 'The effect on other suppliers will be small, Freeman concluded, 'but the psychological effect will be immense and you will get your programme.'[33]

The reorganisation of production planning was no simple task. At the end of 1942 the War Cabinet had decided to remove the blanket screening of the aircraft industry from military conscription, and this made it necessary to be selective about the factories which would be required to expand output in future: there could be no further general expansion of capacity. Firms making important aircraft required in the greatest possible numbers would hardly be affected, but conscription and ordinary wastage would cut the labour forces at second category firms, making less important types. Third category firms, making types which the Air Staff were prepared to forgo, would be the main source of labour to supplement those in the first category.[34]

In these circumstances, Cripps soon warned Freeman that MAP would have to state its requirements accurately: the Ministry must specify the precise quantity of labour and machinery needed for each different factory. 'This will no doubt be difficult', Cripps acknowledged, 'but I expect you have the facts and figures at your disposal.'[35] Freeman accepted this from Cripps.

Changing military requirements further complicated Freeman's work. A complete production programme for the MAP could not be prepared without a clear statement by the Air Ministry of all the aircraft required by the RAF over the next eighteen months, and this in turn depended on the progress of the war. Two previous programmes had come to grief when Courtney objected to cuts in the supply of advanced training aircraft, and Freeman told Cripps that he was afraid it would be impossible to get out a new programme by the deadline of 1 January 1943 because there was insufficient information from the Air Staff.

> What we can do and what really matters is to get out a realistic Heavy and Medium Bomber programme, for we can take it for granted that the Air Ministry will want all the Heavy Bombers we can get. I will try and do this by the end of the year, but even this will need considerable discussion with the Works Managers of all the main factories.[36]

Over the next ten days Freeman had direct discussions with the top management of the firms concerned, to assess their prospective capacity. Ever since May 1940, they had complained of shortages of raw materials and EL equipment, and he recommended that these inputs should be delivered in excess of programme to enable them to exceed production forecasts.[37]

The programme which finally emerged was based on current actual production, expanded as fast as available industrial resources would allow, and represented a minimum average output for the year. Provision was made for spares production, and raw material deliveries were to be increased to make it possible for firms to exceed the programme by 10 per cent if their productivity rose sufficiently. An allowance was also made for holiday periods: the failure of the previous programme to make adequate allowances for holidays accounted for one-third of the difference between the programmes.

The draft of the new 'realistic' programme was sent to Freeman while he was on leave at Murtle, and he appended to it an introduction which read:

> This aircraft programme has taken into account all those factors which can possibly affect normal production [and] ... therefore represents a minimum for operational types, and every endeavour should be made to exceed the programme, though not at the expense of spares which are of the utmost importance if the Royal Air Force and Fleet Air Arm are to obtain a minimum serviceable front line strength.[38]

One of the greatest problems facing the aircraft firms concerned the scheduling and progressing of raw materials, aircraft components and EL equipment. He helped by directing that those responsible for planning and supplying these inputs for operational aircraft should allow an additional month's lead time:

> Thus where the present arrangement is to provide raw material seven months ahead of aircraft delivery, an eight months lead should now be built up as quickly as possible. If formerly a month's lead was allowed for engines in the aircraft factories, now allow two months.[39]

Recognizing that his initial attempt to finalise a realistic programme might not be entirely successful, he also stipulated that the whole production plan should be reviewed every quarter and that similar reviews of any type or firm must be conducted whenever necessary.[40] Finally, remembering Hives' complaints about the excessive number of MAP personnel at factories, their overlapping duties and their reluctance to act on their own initiative, he appointed the existing factory overseers as the principal Ministry representatives. He gave them authority over all other Ministry personnel and power to take decisions without referring back to the development and production directorates.

The new programme involved a reduction in the projected output for 1943 which was bound to disappoint Churchill, so efforts were made to ensure that the new delivery targets looked encouraging. The new programme forecast a total output of 22,581 combat aircraft, including spares, which represented an increase of 27 per cent over the 17,730 combat aircraft *actually delivered* in 1942. The monthly comparisons looked equally impressive: the *actual* increase of less than 20 per cent between January and *December* 1942 (December was always a short-working, holiday month) was compared with a forecast gain of 31 per cent between January and *November* 1943.[41]* Freeman insisted on distributing the new programme to all the MAP staff involved in its implementation, and ensured that each firm received a copy of the portion with which it was concerned, together with a covering letter reiterating the need for the delivery of spare parts.[42]

Writing to Trenchard in February 1943, Freeman explained the ideas which lay behind the new programme:

> The two alternative theories are: (1) to give aircraft constructors a programme admittedly in excess of capacity available, and (2) to give constructors a programme related to the available capacity. The first of these leads to a scramble for components among contractors. Far from exceeding its scheduled programme, each firm will fail ... The alternative system which I advocate is to give each firm a target of monthly output based on measured capacity ... If it should be found that the capacity available will in fact give a larger output ... the programme for the firms will be raised.[43]

While the draft Realistic Programme was being prepared for Freeman, Dunbar toured the aircraft factories and reported on the relative efficiency of the aircraft firms involved and on the quality of their management. He also arranged a programme of visits by a new labour efficiency inspection team, the Production Efficiency Board. He quickly realised that the management problems at Short Brothers and Fairey were particularly serious and required immediate action, since a substantial proportion of the shortfall in heavy bomber production in the later months of 1942 was due to their deficiencies.

Cripps had taken powers under Defence Regulations, shortly after his appointment as Minister, to appoint directors to companies. These were to be

* Jewkes' skill with statistics is evident.

simple appointments: MAP-appointed directors would not have special powers of voting or veto and would not constitute a majority on the boards concerned. Cripps hoped that men with industrial experience would be accepted by existing boards, but he obtained compulsory powers to appoint controllers, in case they were not. Sir George Scheuster* visited Short Brothers at the end of 1942 and reported in January 1943 that their directors were incapable of managing such a large and dispersed industrial undertaking; the MAP also found itself in dispute with the company over future production plans. The board of Shorts fiercely resisted the Ministry's wish to stop producing the unsatisfactory Stirling bomber, and switch as much factory capacity as possible to the Lancaster. Such were the doubts as to whether Shorts were *capable* of switching production to another type of aircraft that, in the end, they continued to make the transport version of the Stirling when bomber production stopped.

Under extreme pressure from the Ministry, H.G. Short eventually resigned as chairman to make way for Sir Frederick Heaton, of the engineering firm Tilling Stevens; he was appointed by the original board with the support of Cripps and Freeman. Unfortunately, Heaton's efforts to reorganise Short Brothers were opposed by the remaining directors, and Cripps quickly became convinced that there would be no improvement in the company's position unless Heaton was granted a free hand. Taking full advantage of the powers he had acquired under Defence Regulations, he appointed a controller and nationalised the company. Heaton's authority as chairman was confirmed and an entirely new board was established.

Freeman's views about the nationalisation of Short Brothers are not recorded in the documents, but Cripps would hardly have taken such an extreme measure without the full support of his Chief Executive.

The firm was nationalised to allow measures to promote industrial efficiency and to improve Short's contribution to the war effort, not for political reasons. Although the plan for them to produce Lancasters was eventually abandoned, the change of ownership and control soon proved very successful, for the Short's company increased production by 65 per cent in the following twelve months without employing any more workers.[44] Moreover the example was an effective warning to the industry, and several other 'problem' aircraft companies, fearing similar treatment, soon agreed to reorganise their systems. On Scheuster's advice and, again, with Freeman's support, controllers were appointed to Boulton Paul and to General Aircraft, and changes were forced on the management of Fairey Aviation. No other established aircraft manufacturer was brought into state ownership during the Second World War.

Vickers' contribution to the Realistic Programme was also reviewed. They were still producing only the Wellington and Warwick bombers, but they hoped to be allowed to put a 4-engined geodetic bomber, the B.3/42 – later

---

* Scheuster, a former merchant banker, was a member of the Council of the British Institute of Management, and on the Government's Committee on industrial production.

named the Windsor – into production, rather than stop making the geodetic structures for which all their factories were equipped.[45] Freeman, however, was interested in a new version of the Lancaster, the Mark IV, with Merlin 61 engines and a longer wing span, and thought Avro's performance estimates for this aircraft more likely to be reliable than Vickers' predictions for an aircraft which had not yet been built.[46] The Cabinet agreed to defer a decision on production orders until March 1943, and hedged against delays by ordering jigs and tools for both of them.[47] Eventually, after one of the Windsor prototypes had crashed, the decision went against the Windsor, in part because remotely controlled 20mm cannons in the rear of the engine nacelles of the flexible geodetic airframe, could not be aimed with accuracy.

Output of Lancasters started at Castle Bromwich in the last quarter of 1943 and 300 emerged before the end of the war. A total of 235 Lancasters was eventually built at the Vickers factory near Chester, and 330 were delivered by Austin by the third quarter of 1944.[48]

*   *   *

Churchill allowed Freeman to return to the MAP in October 1942, because the qualitative superiority of the RAF's aircraft was steadily being eroded, and the shortfall between forecasts and deliveries had remained too wide for too long. There were few if any doubts within the upper echelons of British government that the Ministry had been, and was being badly managed. The Service and the aircraft industry had become deeply discouraged by the way that all the production programmes had failed. Forecasts which did not allow for the drop in production during holiday periods were clearly irresponsible: the whole information system needed to be overhauled, and the Ministry's role as overall 'Controller' reduced, so that it reverted to guidance and support.

Churchill had tolerated Beaverbrook's pernicious emphasis on quantity at the expense of quality for so long that MAP's rejection of any decision which might reduce output, even temporarily, dominated ministerial thinking.

Freeman was well known to, and greatly respected by, the whole of the aircraft industry,* and he had the full support of the Royal Air Force, which was longing for more and better aircraft. He alone had the qualifications and experience to undertake the massive job of putting the whole business of aircraft production back on to the rails, and political support for his return could no longer be withheld. Having tried all the alternatives without success, Churchill eventually gave him a free hand. Only the Ministry opposed him.

Small wonder that Freeman was utterly depressed by the resentment and disloyalty he met from so many of the existing staff – from the Permanent Under-Secretary downwards – most of whom had not the slightest idea that the whole development and production organisation which was the basis of the Ministry, had actually been set up under Freeman himself in 1938. It is possible, indeed likely, that some of these tensions were exacerbated by

---

* Fedden, who thought that Freeman was prejudiced against Bristol engines, had left the Bristol engine company by November 1942.

Freeman's own, barely concealed, disrespect for Llewellin and a number of his senior staff, and for many of the established procedures. But production and development were stagnating: the need for action and decisions was urgent, and a Chief Executive who solved the Ministry's problems by taking decisions, was bound to confront, and upset, the officials who were responsible for them.

Freeman's work transformed the entire administration of the MAP. Directives could be issued, and were, without the sanction of Llewellin, who had lost his executive authority. Rowlands activities were restricted, and he was stripped of all involvement in development and production matters. The basis of MAP planning was overturned by the introduction of the 'Realistic Programme', and Freeman radically changed the role of the Ministry's production directors in ways which drastically reduced their authority. He re-established his direct contacts with the aircraft manufacturers, taking them into his confidence and allowing the best of them much more influence on production planning and policy. He remembered Hives' complaints about the number of MAP representatives at factories, and made the overseers the principal MAP representative at each plant, with authority over other MAP staff, and the right to make decisions. Finally, as a last resort in the struggle for better productivity, he created the new Production Efficiency Board, and backed this, in collaboration with Cripps, by appointing controllers to the most inefficient firms.

Key aero-engine projects were removed from Bulman's supervision, and placed under newly appointed directors like Banks and Roxbee Cox. By drawing on the outstanding engineering expertise of Rolls-Royce and English Electric, Freeman ensured that the development problems which had dogged the Whittle and Sabre engines, had massive resources and the attention of experienced production engineers devoted to them, and were quickly overcome.

None of Freeman's many outstanding achievements in the rearmament and wartime years was more remarkable than his comprehensive reorganisation of the Ministry of Aircraft production between October 1942 and May 1943. In little more than six months he firmly reimposed his authority over aircraft production, and cleared the backlog of deferred decisions which had accumulated since 1940, reorientating the direction of MAP in three ways. He stopped his officials issuing directions *to* industry, so that the Ministry reverted to their fruitful, pre-war systems and their proper role of support and guidance. Where previously there had been drift and indecision, Freeman now insisted on immediate action, and where target programming had been based on incompetent data and ignorant optimism, he insisted on ruthless realism.

CHAPTER 17

MAP: the climax of the war

REEMAN HAD MADE most of the immediate, essential, changes at the Ministry of Aircraft Production by May 1943 and, after several months of upheaval, the ministry was settling into a new, and much more efficient, routine. The military situation had improved, so Churchill interfered less frequently in production matters, and the baleful influence of Beaverbrook had waned at last. Fears that the Ministries of Supply or Production might attempt to take over the MAP's functions had proved unjustified. Indeed, Freeman admired the Minister of Production, Oliver Lyttelton, for the discreet way he used his powers to co-ordinate the activities of the various supply departments.

Industrial co-operation had been transformed by an unofficial association of executive heads, Freeman among them, self-named the 'Boiler Makers', which met regularly, but informally, for lunch at the Carlton. Members took it in turn to pay for lunch, choosing the more expensive dishes when it was the turn of the Chancellor of the Exchequer. They discussed industrial problems frankly and with absolute discretion at these meetings, taking a broad view of their obligations to supply the nation and its armed services, readily assisting one another by sharing their resources, and forming an unofficial, but highly respected 'court of appeal' on industrial matters. To have been a 'Boiler Maker' was to have achieved the highest possible status as a director of wartime industry.[1]* The contrast between the dedicated impartiality with which they handled their responsibilities, and the rapacious brigandage of Beaverbrook, could hardly have been greater.

Freeman's influential role in the higher direction of the RAF was not ended by his return to MAP, for despite his formal retirement, Portal continued to consult him over the most senior Air Force appointments.[2] Indeed, Portal's esteem was such that he offered to put Freeman's name up for appointment as commander of the Allied Air Forces for Operation Overlord. Freeman was sorely tempted, but eventually refused, partly because he was in great pain from rheumatism in one arm,[3]† but primarily because Cripps had been in poor health. 'It would be tough on Cripps', Freeman wrote,

> if I left just as he is warned to take things easy or face the chance of being down and out for life. . . . I should rather welcome the chance to get back to the RAF, but after a great deal of thought I have come to the conclusion that you should not forward my name . . . Why not Bert, [Harris] and give Sholto [Douglas] Bomber Command? I am of course not qualified operationally.[4]

* A.K.McCosh, a key member of the wartime Iron and Steel Control, at Ashorne, wistfully told the author in May, 1953, 'I wish I had known that your uncle was a 'Boiler Maker'.
† His rheumatism was cured by a Christian Scientist.

Cripps' heart trouble was much worse than anyone realised in the summer of 1943, but Freeman himself was also far from well. He was leaving his office as early as 6.30 pm at this time, and working at home, usually in bed. A brief period of leave in August allowed him to recuperate. As always, he went to Murtle, where he was joined by Elizabeth, now a Flight Officer in the WAAF, and Leigh-Mallory, AOC-in-C of Fighter Command, for whom she was working as secretary. Leigh-Mallory and Elizabeth returned early to Fighter Command leaving Freeman happy in the company of Ralph and Diana, who recorded:

> Wilfrid was just his old self at the end of the leave. I have seldom seen him happier. He was also looking extremely fit and well, good colour, anxious to do things, but not with the feverish activity of overwork. I found him more and more admirable.[5]

PRODUCTION

During his first six months as Chief Executive of the MAP, Freeman had taken a series of vital production decisions which had been deferred for many months by his predecessors – actions which brought about a substantial increase in British aircraft production in the later years of the war. A distinction must be drawn, however, between production problems which affected individual products or firms, and those which affected the aircraft industry as a whole. The former could normally be solved without undue difficulty; the latter, inevitably, proved far more intractable.

Wilfrid and Elizabeth Freeman on a rare joint visit to an RAF balloon unit.

The principal constraint on aircraft production by the end of 1942 was the shortage of labour. 'In a year's time, provided I can have the labour I can get things O.K.', Freeman told Elizabeth, 'but can I get the labour, that's the problem?'[6] The Ministry of Aircraft Production still retained its high priority for labour – although by 1943 the limits of British manpower had nearly been reached – and was promised 503,000 of the 603,000 extra workers requested by Freeman in December 1942, an allocation which was then *halved* eight months later. By December 1943, MAP not only had to forego the further allocation of 50,000 workers required for 1944, but was obliged to accept a 100,000 reduction in the labour force. Targets for deliveries to the RAF had to be reduced accordingly: when a new Realistic Programme was prepared in September 1943, the Air Force's plans were reduced by 57 squadrons, and a further cut of 89 squadrons followed the appearance of the 'Manpower' programme at the end of the year. There would now be fourteen fewer heavy bomber squadrons than planned in 1943, and nineteen fewer by mid-1944.[7]

Such was the priority given to heavy bombers, however, that the intake of extra workers for their production actually exceeded allocations until July 1944. Freeman cancelled or reduced programmes for a number of aircraft with limited potential, concentrated labour resources on Tempests, Lancasters, Mosquitoes, Meteors and the later marks of Spitfire,[8] and scaled down or halted production of several other designs. But manpower problems mounted, becoming ever more acute. The majority of new workers were now unskilled, with little or no experience of manufacturing industry, and even the labour transferred to key 'designated' types, from less important models, needed time to master new tasks. By 1943 Freeman's statisticians were anticipating a six-month delay before labour intake was reflected in extra output.[9] Freeman insisted on an unanswerable case before agreeing to any increases in the programme, but, nevertheless, Bomber Command asked for 100 extra Lancasters per month in 1944, and peak wartime production of 520 heavy bombers was achieved in March of that year.[10]

If labour supply was one of the problems facing Freeman in 1943 and 1944, the supply of aero-engines was the other. Early in 1942, Jewkes had written:

> The engine programme should lie at the very centre of all our planning. Everything else must run from our views as to how many engines we are likely to produce. I take this view because the supply of engines is less flexible than the supply of other equipment; capacity for engines is more difficult to expand and the problems of finding skilled labour and critical machine tools greater than in the case of other equipment.[11]

By the following year the entire aircraft programme was being controlled by the availability of engines. Capacity for Rolls-Royce engines would have been much greater had the company's designs remained standardised, but the switch from the single-stage to the two-stage Merlin and the introduction of the Griffon caused enormous difficulties. Until the flow of Packard Merlins increased in 1944, deliveries sometimes failed to keep pace with installation

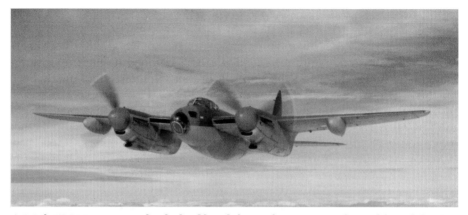

A B.Mk XVI Mosquito with a bulged bomb-bay. Alterations to the width and depth of the Mosquito's bomb bay allowed it to enclose the short, large diameter, 4,000lb 'blast bomb', but bulged the lower side of the fuselage, and gave a 'pregnant' appearance to its normally sleek lines.

requirements.[12] British output of two-stage Merlins, reached 160 per month for the first time in January 1943. The single-stage Griffon II entered service in small numbers in 1942, but monthly deliveries of the two-stage Griffon 61 exceeded seven for the first time in December 1943, and 100 in August 1944.[13] Virtually all of them were installed in Spitfires, but the first Mark XIV was only delivered in October 1943.

Freeman's insistence that the new Spitfires got priority allocations of the two-stage Merlins, delayed the production of other new aircraft. The prototype PR VIII Mosquito with two-stage Merlins had its first flight in October 1942, and achieved a top speed of 437mph at 29,000 feet, faster than most contemporary fighters, but only five were produced. The first production PR IX, with two-stage Merlins, was airborne in April 1943, and the first PR XVI, with a pressure cabin, was delivered in August 1943.[14]

Cancellation of the Sabre Mosquito freed de Havilland's design staff to work on a larger 'bulged' bomb bay for the standard Mosquito, which enabled it to carry a 4,000lb bomb. Freeman approved this modification at a meeting with Geoffrey de Havilland on 14 November 1942,[15] and thereby probably ensured the future of this version, since, three weeks later, he was told to stop all production of Mosquito bombers. Forewarned by Courtney that Harris and the Air Ministry's technical experts, had won over Portal as soon as Freeman was no longer VCAS,[16] he kept the bomber photo-reconnaissance production lines going by telling the firms concerned to make nearly all of them the PR version. Harris had based his decision on the light bomb load, and the 10 per cent casualty rate of the two Mosquito *day bomber* squadrons,[17]* but once he

---

* ADFU tests showed that if the Mosquito operated at height in daylight, and at high speed, their immunity from interception was greatly improved. Enemy fighters climbed much more slowly, and needed a lot of advanced warning to be able to intercept. This was confirmed by Galland: the bomber versions were not used in this way at first.

realised the relative immunity of Mosquitoes carrying a 4,000lb bomb and operating at night, he changed his mind and wanted all the Mosquito bombers he could get. By October 1943, it was obvious that their performance was outstanding, and the Mark B.IX aircraft in service and the production lines of the Mark B.XVI (with two-stage Merlins), were modified to carry 4,000lb bombs. Two-stage Merlins were so scarce,* however, that only 451 B.IX and B.XVI Mosquitoes were produced but, fortunately, the Canadian factory went on making bombers with Packard Merlins; more than 950 of these reached Britain before June 1945.[18]

Although the Merlin had dominated British production planning for high powered engines in the early years of the war, the Bristol Hercules assumed great importance after 1942.† Production of the Mark VI engines virtually ended in May, but Hercules output rose by 53 per cent in 1943, most of them XVIs and XVIIs, and by a further 16 per cent in 1944, 22.9 per cent of them the low level XVIIs and XVIIIs.[19] Production of Hercules 100s incorporating the long delayed turbine-entry supercharger and improved timing started in 1944, but formed only 10.4 per cent of 1944 deliveries.[20] Their installation raised the ceiling of the Halifax very significantly and transformed its performance at altitude.[21]

The Hercules 100 fourteen-cylinder sleeve-valve radial engine, incorporating the long delayed 'turbine-entry' supercharger and design features influenced by the big BMW radial from a captured German aircraft.

The new management at Napier brought about a steady improvement in the quality of Sabre engines for the Typhoon and the Tempest, and average monthly production increased by more than 130 per cent between 1942 and 1944.[22] Output of Typhoons continued at just over 1,000 a year, and although the aircraft was no match for the best German fighters at altitude, it was fast enough to catch FW 190s on low-level 'tip and run' raids. Armed with bombs, and later, rockets, and its normal armament of four 20mm cannons, the Typhoon had a formidable ground-attack capability. Despite its failure in the

* Output of two-stage Merlins grew very slowly. Out of the total of more than 17,000 two-stage Merlins produced by 31 July 1945, only about 25 per cent were allocated to Mosquitoes, and fewer than 2,000 Mosquitoes with two-stage Merlins had been delivered by 31 December 1945. Demand for all Mosquito variants grew steadily from 1943 onwards. From UK production, more than 2,500 were eventually completed as fighter-bombers, 1400 as night fighters, 670 as PR and only 930 as bombers.

† Rowbotham, who had been in charge of engine production at Bristol since 1934, took over control of engine design and development from Sir Roy Fedden in October 1942. Work on the unsuccessful two-stage Hercules VIII and the exhaust-turbo alternative was discontinued, and development of the turbine-entry supercharger, resulted in the excellent Hercules 100 series.

The Hawker Tempest V with Napier Sabre engines entered service in April 1944. With thinner wings and a longer fuselage than the Typhoon, it was very fast at low level and was successful against the flying bombs as well as in its tactical fighter/bomber role.

role of 'combat fighter', Freeman had solved the engine's problem in time for it to be available in quantity – just when fast, tactical fighter bombers were most needed for operations in Europe. After protracted delays the Sabre-Tempest V, with much better handling qualities, finally entered service in 1944, as a medium altitude fighter/bomber.

Jet engines now had a high priority. Gloster installed two de Havilland H1s in a prototype Meteor for its first flight in March 1943, and de Havilland's Vampire jet fighter with the H1 engine was airborne on 29 September 1943: production prototypes of the Vampire were flying before the end of the war. Output of jet fighters was slow to increase, however. The W.2B reverse-flow jet engines made by Rover failed to develop sufficient power for the Gloster Meteor I, and Freeman restricted production to 200, to be used for ground training. A production order for the Meteor airframe was not confirmed until April 1943, when the Rolls-Royce version of the reverse-flow, W.2B engine, named the Welland, came into production.[23]

The first German jet and rocket fighters appeared in the summer of 1944 – the best of which, by far, was the 520mph Messerschmitt Me262 – and Churchill asked for news of the Meteor.[24] A single flight of Meteor Is was rushed into service in July 1944, powered by the Welland, which gave them a top speed of only 410mph. But Rolls-Royce soon produced a 'straight-through' version of the same engine, known as the Derwent I, which raised the top speed of the Meteor III to 460mph. As usual, Freeman urged Hives to improve engine deliveries, and asked for 40 more Meteor Is in 1944, and a total output of 100 Meteor IIIs in the first four months of 1945. By then there was a shortage of airframes,[25] and although he asked the Air Ministry to forego improvements such as drop-tanks, pressure cabins and gyro-sights, to get more jets into the air, the increase in production at Gloster was very slow.

Mention must also be made of the two deep penetration bombs, the 12,000lb Tallboy and the 22,000lb Grand Slam. Barnes Wallis had wanted these made early in the war because he knew that an exceptionally heavy bomb with a perfect aerodynamic shape could be aimed with great accuracy. If given a steel casing of sufficient strength and dropped from a great height, they would penetrate deep into the ground before exploding with an 'earthquake' effect. Freeman could only authorise this expensive novelty after he returned to MAP, but then did so. In the hands of an 'elite' squadron like 617, the bombs performed notable feats, including the final destruction of the *Tirpitz*.

POSTWAR PLANNING

As the end of the war loomed, Freeman received conflicting planning messages from the Government. He complained to Cripps that while still implementing the policies initiated in September 1943, he was also being asked to plan for maximum production in 1944, to plan the industry for war with Japan after the defeat of Germany, and to plan for aircraft production in peacetime. 'Planning ... will become chaotic if we receive any further instructions from higher authority', he wrote. 'The differences between these programmes are very considerable and it is only with the greatest difficulty that those responsible can get the several factors absolutely clear.'[26]

The volume of postwar aircraft production would be primarily controlled by the availability of manpower. Consulted by Portal about minimum postwar manpower requirements for the RAF, Freeman warned that the labour force available to the entire armaments industry would probably be limited to

The 22,000lb Grand Slam bomb, which could be carried only by specially equipped Lancasters, was used successfully against the Bielefeld canal viaduct in March 1945. It was a larger version of the 12,000lb – actually 14,000lb – Tallboy, first used in February 1944. If released at the right height, a Tallboy could displace a million cubic feet of earth, making a crater which needed 5,000 *tons* of earth to fill.

500,000 workers, and that the RAF and Fleet Air Arm would account for 150,000 and 50,000 respectively. He reckoned that the RAF total could be reduced to 126,000, plus labour employed on orders for civil and export aircraft, and advised Portal to agree such a minimum as soon as possible – and then 'fight to the last ditch' to protect it.[27]

As for the choice of aircraft, Freeman thought that Meteor and Vampire production should continue, and that the Napier Sabre should be retained, together with the Tempest fighter. Supermarine should continue work on the latest Spitfires, or on Spitefuls, and production of Avro's latest Lancaster, renamed the Lincoln, would be fixed at four per month.[28]

Planning for the requirements of both wartime and postwar developments posed particular problems. As long as the war continued, Freeman could not justify the diversion of scarce resources to long-term projects unlikely to influence the outcome of hostilities. With the Far Eastern campaign in mind, he authorised production of de Havilland's Hornet long-range fighter.[29] But he had doubts about the development of a super heavy bomber to re-equip Bomber Command, eventually concluding that it would be much more profitable from a military standpoint to concentrate all efforts on improving existing designs. Types like the Lancaster IV, and possibly the Windsor, were the only British bombers likely to enter service before the war came to an end.[30]

By the end of the war, most British aircraft companies were still building aeroplanes originally designed in the late 1930s. Freeman knew that Britain might not be able to sustain her position as a leading aeronautical power in the postwar world, if long-term development was ignored altogether. No one recognized more clearly than he did the critical importance of planning aircraft development several years in advance, but whilst he was 'doing time' as VCAS, between 1940 and 1942, MAP's interest in practical new projects had been lukewarm. Planning ahead was essential.

His starting point was, of course, the aero-engine, and he had made a vital contribution to postwar aircraft design by reorganising the support for gas-turbine development and production at the end of 1942. Although large-scale production of jet aircraft did not commence until 1945 – and early models did not offer a significant improvement in performance over the most modern piston-engined designs – jet engine technology had been advancing rapidly under the umbrella of the Gas Turbine Collaboration Committee. Freeman's support was formalised when the separate MAP Directorate for gas turbines was formed under Dr Roxbee Cox.

The active involvement of Rolls-Royce gave new impetus to the emergence of practical engines and, by October 1944, the company was running the B 41, or 'Nene', engine – the first jet engine in the world to give 5,000lb of thrust. A scaled-down 3,500lb version, known as the Derwent V, was subsequently installed into the Meteor IV, giving the aircraft a substantial advantage in speed over conventional types. A Meteor IV took the world speed record at 606 mph in November 1945.[31]

Having settled jet engine development, Freeman turned his attention to wider issues, and asked Sorley to undertake an extensive study of future air-frame requirements, and make recommendations about a future procurement programme. In his first memorandum [32] Sorley confirmed that the supply of aircraft engineers and draughtsmen in Britain was totally inadequate, a conclusion which Cripps found so convincing that he immediately began the establishment of Cranfield Aeronautical College.

Sorley's second memorandum outlined an ambitious five-year programme of prototype development which provided continuity of work on essential projects for the firms likely to comprise the postwar aircraft industry. 'We must increase considerably our development after the war if we are to retain our technical superiority,' he wrote. 'We require at least two designs for each type, possibly three, and each firm must build a minimum of three aircraft.' [33] His plan provided for a total of nearly fifty prototypes, covering a very wide range of specialised designs.

Work on most of these aircraft was halted by the need for a drastic reduction in defence expenditure soon after the end of the war, but one specification which survived, was for a high-speed jet bomber. Design work had been started by Edward Petter, Chief Designer at Westland, but progress was threatened when Petter quarrelled with the Westland Board. Freeman rescued the project by arranging for Petter to join the new English Electric aircraft team, as Chief Designer. With Westland's agreement, Petter took his embryo bomber design to English Electric, whence it eventually emerged as the highly successful Can-berra, the PR version of which remains in service with the RAF to this day. [34]

As the war approached its conclusion, Freeman began planning his retirement from the MAP. Corresponding with Portal about the selection of his successor, he expressed once again his concern over the age profile of the RAF's senior officers. The preponderance of older officers, in his view, was such as to threaten not only the operational efficiency of the Service, but also the standard of its aircraft. By 1944 the ten most senior officers were, on average, 15 years older than their counterparts of 1918. In those days, Freeman recalled, 'we were led by men who were young, virile and receptive to new ideas', whereas in 1944 the RAF 'was run by grandfathers' and in danger of losing its greatest advantage over the other armed services. The Royal Air Force was better equipped ... than the Army or the Navy [because of the] vigour and adaptability of those controlling it. [35]

Worried that he might by succeeded at the MAP by old administrators and technical Civil Servants, and that 'Service personnel will gradually be squeezed out of the higher posts if it remains a separate Ministry', he was equally concerned about what would happen if MAP again became part of the Air Ministry. The senior posts could easily go to RAF officers who had 'never had the least contact with industry, and lacked any technical or scientific know-ledge ... officers who are out of touch with the Service and whose outlook has become useless, stagnant and ... dangerous'. [36]

By January 1945 he had arranged for the 38-year-old Edwin Plowden to succeed him as Chief Executive at the MAP. Considering the qualities required

English Electric Canberras. The agreement of the Westland company that Petter should join English Electric so that his jet bomber design could be developed, allowed Freeman to meet George Nelson's hopes of continuing to produce aircraft after the war. It was the first jet bomber of the RAF.

by Plowden's RAF assistant he listed among the necessary qualifications for the post 'a strong will and a natural interest in aircraft technology.... He should carry the confidence of the CAS and the RAF, [and] have operational experience as a Commander, or as a Staff officer in close contact with such work', Freeman wrote. 'I don't think you will find a man with all these qualities and I make no claim to them myself.'[37]

Air Vice-Marshal Sir William Elliot, aged 49, was eventually selected*.

IN RETROSPECT

The record of Freeman's administration of aircraft production after October 1942 when he resumed effective control of development and production, merits review. His first task was to bring the aircraft production programmes into line with reality. Although closer to actual production than all earlier plans since Freeman's 'Harrogate' version, his first Realistic Programme was not achieved, and had to be revised in April 1943 and again in September 1943.[38]

Certain categories of aircraft caused particular problems – particularly Fleet Air Arm aircraft – but Freeman knew that these shortages would be made up by superior American aircraft like the Hellcat, Corsair and Avenger, supplied

* Elliot was near the top of Freeman's list.

under Lend-Lease. The main reason why the first Realistic Programme was unrealised was the need to take account of the impact of technical change. Aircraft production was, as already noted, extensively reorganised during 1943 and 1944: resources were transferred from obsolescent aircraft like the older medium bombers to designated ones, notably the Lancaster. Halifax IIIs and VIs were introduced, and advanced versions of the Hercules, giving much greater power at height, eventually emerged. Spitfires and Mosquitoes with two-stage Merlins entered production; there was even a belated effort to boost the production of naval designs. Such plans involved a very high proportion of the British aircraft industry's capacity.

Had aircraft design and development been frozen, and no modifications or replacements been allowed to interfere with production, the output figures would have been far higher[39] – indeed, the first Realistic Programme might even have been realised. But Freeman cared too passionately about maintaining the quality of Service aircraft to impose such restrictions on technical development. Whilst he recognized that some loss of production would occur when factories were switched to another model, or a substantially modified one, he may, initially, have underestimated the effects on production.

Although production fell short of expectations, the impact of technical change was moderated to some extent by the way that Freeman reorganised aircraft production into a 'two-tier' industry. The burden of design and development was shouldered by the professional aircraft firms, where high costs were accepted in return for high quality. The most successful designs were then selected in consultation with the Air Staff, allocated to mass-production factories, and manufactured in large quantities in long and relatively stable production runs which brought substantial economies. The 'design' firms rarely achieved their programmes because there was no scientific basis for predicting the cost of, and time taken to introduce, technical changes. 'Production' firms, on the other hand, consistently matched the MAP's performance targets, and not infrequently exceeded them.[40]

There are many examples of Freeman's 'two-tier' organisation. In May 1944, production at Supermarine's main factory was divided between four variants of the Spitfire, whereas Castle Bromwich was producing only the Mark IX, and later the Packard Merlin version, Mk XVI; labour productivity at Castle Bromwich was double that of Supermarine. Similarly, Handley Page built seven different marks of their Halifax bomber between 1941 and 1945, while English Electric produced just three in much larger quantities. English Electric cut the airframe's price to £15,350; Handley Page's price never fell below £19,500.[41] De Havilland was eventually producing *eight* variants of the Mosquito at the same time on three 16-stage assembly lines. By contrast, Freeman gave Standard Motors the far simpler task of building just one mark of Mosquito at Canley. In short, Freeman achieved a balance which maintained both the quantity and quality of Service aircraft throughout the Second World War.[42]

Given that earlier MAP programmers always failed to predict the impact of technical change on production with any accuracy, the results of Freeman's production policies should not be gauged simply by the shortfalls in numbers of the Realistic Programme. Other indicators all present a much more positive picture of his achievements. Between June 1942 and December 1943, per capita output in the aircraft industry increased by 24 per cent – in spite of the deteriorating quality of the labour force, and the extensive transfer of workers from one type or mark of aircraft to another. Much of this improvement can be accounted for by simple economies of scale. By June 1944, through the group production system created by Freeman before the outbreak of war, 50 per cent of total MAP manpower (800,000 workers) were focused on the production of Lancasters, Halifaxes and Wellingtons.[43] Only Germany achieved a comparable degree of product specialisation.

British aircraft production, computed in structure weight, remained comfortably ahead of German production, yet, by 1941, Germany was employing more labour in the aircraft industry than Britain employed at any time during the war.[44] In 1943, whereas Germany produced aircraft weighing only 142 million lb, the structure weight of British built aircraft totalled 185 million; the comparable 1944 figures were 175 and 208 million lb.[45]

In another very important respect, the official production record understates Freeman's true achievement, for it makes no allowance for the output of spare parts.[46] In his blatant pursuit of numbers, Beaverbrook had raised the output of complete aircraft in 1940 by sacrificing spares production; in 1944 German aircraft output was boosted in exactly the same way. Freeman, on the other hand, insisted on producing spares in adequate numbers, and when the Realistic Programme was issued in January 1943, the importance of spares for the RAF and for the repairs organisation was emphasised.[47] Although the Lancaster had an over-riding priority – and Freeman did not object when production exceeded the programme – he always insisted that the increase should not be at the expense of spares. Sir Frederick Handley Page was sharply criticised for over-producing the Halifax, and was bluntly told to raise the output of spares and build fewer complete airframes.[48]

Freeman's stance resulted in a steady shift of resources from complete aircraft to spares from 1942 onwards. By 1944 18 per cent of British airframe labour was engaged in the production of spare parts: in terms of complete aircraft, spares production accounted for over 110 Spitfires and 20 Lancasters per month in 1944. In June 1942, 6.8 per cent of all aircraft serving with the RAF's Home Commands were awaiting spares; by June 1944 this figure was down to a remarkable 2.5 per cent,[49] whilst the proportion of aircraft awaiting spares in Bomber Command fell from 5.4 per cent in December 1942 to 1.4 per cent in June 1944.[50] The output of the repairs organisation increased from 16,636 aircraft in 1942 to 18,400 in 1944.

The rising output of complete aircraft and spares was particularly pronounced where heavy bombers were concerned. On 14 February 1944, although his figures revealed that deliveries were exceeding the January 1943 forecasts, Freeman sent Portal his amended Lancaster programme with some misgivings, warning him that unless extra labour became available, it might not be met. The actual figures, completed for the two years to end December 1944, and compared against the various forecasts show:

	ALL HEAVY BOMBERS (per quarter) PROGRAMME FORECASTS				LANCASTERS (per quarter)	
	January '43 Realistic Programme	September '43 Realistic Programme	March '44 Manpower reduction	ACTUAL output	TOTAL output	%
1943						
to end Mar.	911			984	381	38.7
to end Jun.	1119			1198	426	35.6
to end Sept.	1254			1151	471	40.9
to end Dec.	1440	1411		1282	570	44.5
Total 1943	4824			4615	1848	40.0
1944						
to end Mar.	1598	1501		1447	681	47.1
to end Jun.	1598	1601	1432	1447	746	51.7
to end Sep.	1638	1674	1422	1382	780	56.4
To end Dec.	1746	1829	1541	1236	726	58.7
Total 1944	6480	6605		5506	2933	53.3

The proportion of Lancasters was expected to rise from 39 per cent of total heavy bomber production in the first quarter of 1943, to 47 per cent a year later, and actually reached over 60 per cent in December 1944.[51] The repairs organisation had returned only 711 heavy bombers to RAF squadrons in 1942, but in 1944 the total was 3,285.[52] Freeman had done what was necessary.

But losses scythed down the bomber force almost as fast as he supplied it. There were 642 heavy bombers in units on 2 February 1943, and although a further 5,700 were produced in the fourteen months to 1 April 1944, and many more came from repair units, only 974 of them remained available for operations on 31 March 1944.[53] The worst period was the six month 'Battle of Berlin', when Harris, who *knew* that the US 8th Air Force could not, at that time, participate by day, allowed his aircrews to suffer devastating losses on frequent and ineffective raids, well beyond the range of most electronic aids. The figures speak for themselves.

Month	New aircraft	Missing	Damaged	Total casualties
October 1943	439	159	318	477
November 1943	423	162	556	718
December 1943	420	170	396	566
January 1944	478	314	416	730
February 1944	449	199	264	463
March 1944	520	283	402	685
Total: 6 months	2729	1287	2352	3699

The heavy casualties suffered by the Command between October 1943 and March 1944 – culminating in the badly planned and disastrous Nuremberg raid, in which more than 100 aircraft were destroyed – were mercifully halted when Bomber Command was diverted to targets in France and Belgium, as part of the preparation for 'Overlord'. Their casualty rate fell sharply, and it fell further still during the spring and summer, as the Luftwaffe's operational capability declined catastrophically under the scourge of the American Air Force's Mustangs. Facing a dwindling German night-fighter force, and finally allowed to make precision raids by day as well as night, Bomber Command began to develop the devastating potential Freeman had envisaged six years before. The capture of bases in France and Belgium extended the range of the *Oboe* navigation aid. Late in 1944 Harris eventually allowed his Pathfinders to use the even more effective *G-H*, which had been promptly withdrawn after its first use in 1943 and, by March 1945 no fewer than 70 heavy bomber squadrons were operational, comprising nearly 1,700 aircraft, including 1,237 Lancasters.[54]

The bomber force which Freeman developed and produced made three vital contributions to victory in the later years of the war.

Firstly, bombing significantly reduced German armaments production. As well as devastating many urban areas and reducing worker morale, bombing forced Germany to disperse her armaments factories. Dispersal caused a substantial loss of output and the vulnerability of her industries was increased by the Allied assault on her transportation network during 1944. In Professor Overy's words, bombing placed a ceiling on German industrial production in the later years of the war. The Reich Ministry of Armaments calculated that in 1944 bombing had cost Germany 31 per cent of her aircraft production, 35 per cent of her tank production, and 42 per cent of her lorry production.[55]

Secondly, bombing forced Germany into a defensive cul-de-sac from which she could not escape. By 1943 her air defence was absorbing a colossal military and industrial effort, diverting huge quantities of manpower and material from the front line. In 1944, although German aircraft production was overwhelmingly devoted to fighters, the Allies gained air supremacy: by midsummer, 'Germany was without a roof'. Once the invasion had succeeded, Allied bombers returned to the attack, and finally struck at a target system which was soon to cripple the whole German war machine.

This third and really devastating blow to the German war machine was the attack on her oil production plants. The Luftwaffe used 5,200 tons of aviation spirit in April 1944. Production was 5,850 tons in April, but it then fell steadily: to 1,766 tons in June, 935 in July, 387 in August and 313 in September.[56] The shortfall ate up the reserves, and as they dwindled, the vicious circle of inadequate flying training, heavy pilot casualties, and even worse, trained replacements, intensified. The last version of the FW190, the 453 mph D-9s, could hold their own against Mustangs, but fuel was so short that they were always heavily outnumbered. When 150 of them were delivered in April 1945, the Luftwaffe's JG 6 had only enough fuel to fly four aircraft.[57]

March 1942. Lubeck was illuminated with flares dropped by ten selected crews using *Gee*. The main force bombed from a low height using incendiaries and high explosives [HE]. Most of the damage was done by fire.

April 1942. Rostock was beyond the range of *Gee*. Of the four separate raids, the last, from below 6,000ft was the most accurate.

285

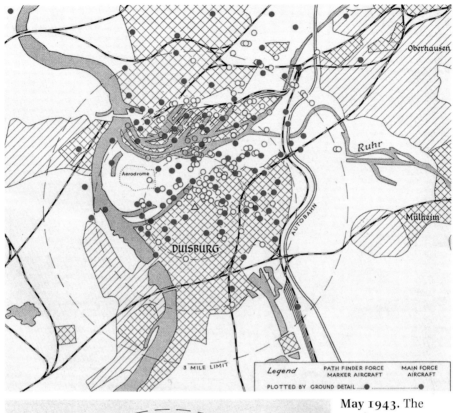

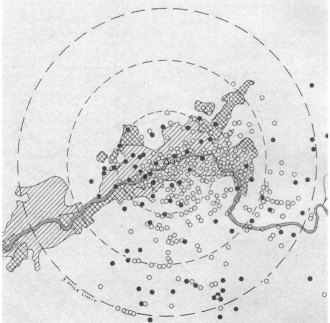

May 1943. The Duisburg aiming point was marked by nine Path Finder Mosquitoes. 80% of the markers fell within 2 miles of the AP, and 84% of the main forces attack within 3 miles.

May 1943. The accuracy of the markers dropped by the first two *Oboe* Mosquitoes, and the skill of the 'backers up' made the BARMEN-WUPPERTAL attack one of the most effective to that date.

April 1944. The marshalling yard at Juvisy, before and after. Marked by PFF Mosquitoes from 28,000ft, using *Oboe*, the main force attacked from 7,500ft.

March 1945: (*top*) Politz near Stettin. Speer reported that the extraordinary accuracy of the night attacks by the RAF, and the heavy bombs they carried, were much more damaging than the day raids of the American 8th Army Air Force.

March 1945: (*bottom*) The Bielefeld railway viaduct. Marked by PFF Mosquitoes, the earthquake effect of the eleven 'Tallboy' and one 'Grand Slam' deep penetration bombs dropped from 12,000 ft, shook down the arches, leaving massive craters.

The Luftwaffe also lost its offensive capability. Their long term production policy, and the misuse of their resources under the incompetent hands of Goering and Udet, had been a 'Strategy for defeat'. The highly competent Milch and Speer came to power too late to rescue their air force.

Freeman's insistence on developing several different heavy bombers had ensured that their technical failures, temporary or long term, did not jeopardise the entire bombing offensive. His counterparts in Germany made the disastrous mistake of placing all their eggs in one basket – the He.177 – and when it proved unsatisfactory, German plans for a renewed bombing offensive against Britain were abandoned.[58]

In equipping the RAF, Freeman's ruthless quest for quality succeeded. By the end of the war, most of Bomber Command's squadrons were equipped with the Lancasters which he had ordered, and the rest with Halifaxes. The performance of the final version of the Halifax, with Hercules 100 engines, had improved to 'near Lancaster' standard.[59]* The elegant Mosquito fulfilled a wide range of roles with exceptional invulnerability, while a succession of new Spitfires maintained the superiority they had held almost throughout the war. They were supported by Freeman's other favourite, the Merlin Mustang, which rescued the American air offensive in the nick of time. Typhoons and Tempests came into their own as low-level and tactical fighters, each of them carrying, with their eight rockets, the broadside of a 6-inch cruiser.

Most of his engines were also successful. The Napier Sabre eventually gave good service, albeit three years later than he originally anticipated. Much was hoped of Bristol's 36-litre Hercules which, built in greater numbers than any other British engine except the Merlin, eventually developed adequate power at height, after management changes and the belated modification of the supercharger. The Merlin was, however, by far the most important engine for the RAF, for it powered not only the best combat fighters, but also the Mosquito and the Lancaster. More than 160,000 Merlins were produced, 55,000 of them in the USA. Despite the formidable production problems involved, Rolls-Royce and Packard gave the RAF (and the USAAF) a steadily improving supply of increasingly powerful engines throughout the war, meeting every challenge with brilliantly effective modifications which kept the aircraft they powered ahead of their German opposition.

Freeman was all too well aware of the many occasions on which the RAF had been saved from technical inferiority by the latest variant of the Merlin, and he knew who was responsible. In 1945 he asked Portal to write a line to Ernest Hives on behalf of the RAF, declaring:

> In the whole world of industry, he stands out head and shoulders above them all. His only interest is the service and their equipment. He is the only man that deserves an Air Council dinner.[60]

This was a fitting tribute, but a typically modest one; for it was Freeman who

---

* During the Nuremberg Raid in March 1944, a brand new Halifax reached 26,000ft 'at which height they flew on in complete safety'. Their con-trails ceased.

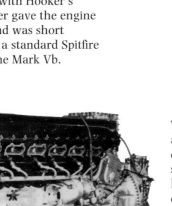

The Merlin 56, which was very similar to the Merlin 45. Even the single-speed version of the Merlin with Hooker's improved supercharger gave the engine much more power, and was short enough to be fitted to a standard Spitfire airframe, becoming the Mark Vb.

The Merlin 60 series. The axial entry ducts, doubled casing for the two-stage supercharger, and the square housing for the integral 'after-cooler' can be clearly seen in this rear view. The two-stage engine was significantly longer than the Merlin 45.

chose the Merlin for many of the aircraft, masterminded the expansion of Rolls-Royce aero-engine capacity and obtained the capital which made it possible. It was Freeman who brought in Ford to mass-produce the Merlin in 1939, and who set up the proposal for a Packard Merlin factory in the United States in 1940. It was Freeman who decided to develop a four-Merlin heavy bomber as early as 1937, Freeman who chose the four-Merlin variant of the Manchester – which became the Lancaster – in 1940, and Freeman, too, who persuaded the Air Ministry to order the twin-Merlin Mosquito. Freeman's doubts about the ill-fated Vulture led him to order the Griffon in 1939, and his awareness of the vital importance of power at height, meant that as soon as the potential of the two-stage Merlin became clear, he threw every ounce of his authority and influence behind the development of aircraft into which it could be installed. In 1944, North American Mustangs, with their two-stage Packard Merlins, inflicted an irreversible defeat on the Luftwaffe. No one did more to ensure the successful design, development and production of that superb aeroplane than Wilfrid Freeman.

CHAPTER 18

Peace: glimpses of
a great industrialist

UNLIKE THE CHIEFS OF STAFF, and those with operational commands, such as Dowding, Tedder or Harris, Freeman had been out of the limelight of publicity for most of the war. Nevertheless, his contribution to the achievements of the RAF, and of the USAAF, had been unique and outstanding. Apart from serving the RAF as Air Member for Research and Development and Air Member for Development and Production between April 1936 and May 1940, he had kept the aircraft industry on an even keel during Beaverbrook's reckless interregnum, and had pressed it forward despite the aimless drift of his successors. He had supported the inexperienced Portal after his appointment as Chief of the Air Staff, with discretion and tact, and had forced the pig-headed Harris to accept the Pathfinder force. When he returned to the Ministry of Aircraft Production he put it back on the rails in a six-month whirlwind of work. As for his American colleagues, the authority of his achievements, the practised charm and wit of his character, and personal contacts with Hopkins, Winant, and Harriman on the political and diplomatic side, and Arnold, Spaatz, Doolittle and Hitchcock among the Air Corps officers, had greatly influenced both the vital American heavy bomber programme – and the even more important production program of the Mustang fighter.

The *Daily Mail*'s reference to Freeman as a 'Chief of Staff on the aircraft factory front', while clearly an unofficial description of his status at the MAP, truly reflected the Government's trust in him, and its reliance on his ability to run the largest industry in Britain. It seems, therefore, highly appropriate that when the three Chiefs of Staff were first offered peerages in 1945, he was apparently also offered a peerage, months before such honours were bestowed on well-known Commanders in Chief like Montgomery, Tovey and Tedder. The fact that the three Service heads accepted and that Freeman was allowed to refuse, accepting a baronetcy instead, in no way diminishes the exceptional, indeed unique, honour of being recognized as one of the four most important controllers of the British war effort.*

Some years later he told his daughter Anne that he had refused a peerage because, at the age of 57, his RAF pension, abated by acceptance of a cash

---

* Careful enquiry has established that no records are kept in the papers of the Honours Secretariat of offers that were refused. Given Freeman's proven distaste for pomposity, and the complete integrity of his character, the fact that he told his eldest daughter, Anne, must surely be accepted. The first unofficial intimations of the proposal to honour the three Chiefs of Staff were presumably also made in June 1945 when his baronetcy was announced. He had tried to refuse that too, opting for the OM which Cripps mentioned as a possible alternative.

commutation, would not be sufficient to maintain his standard of living and pay for the education of two young daughters. His private means, eroded by the divorce settlement, would not make up the shortfall. He realised that he would have to go on working, and would not be able to spare time to attend the House of Lords, and he was also conscious of the pernicious influence that hereditary titles sometimes have on the lives of future generations.

But he could not refuse an offer from Hives to present Elizabeth with his portrait, and his only stipulation was that it should be painted by Dugdale.[1] Eileen, Max's wife, saw the portrait when it was nearly finished, and was delighted with it, but she unwisely said to Dugdale: 'Oh! You've caught his twinkle', his inimitable glance which somehow conveyed that he and the person he was looking at were sharing a private joke. Dugdale obviously thought it inappropriate that a portrait of an Air Chief Marshal should give that impression and, sadly, altered it.[2]

Having made up his mind to leave the MAP towards the end of 1944, Freeman was asked to become a director of Courtaulds in January 1945; he accepted the offer in March, and was appointed in April. He refused the opportunity to become Deputy Chairman of AEI, but joined Babcock & Wilcox as a part-time Director. Personal taxation had by then been raised to 19s 6d in the pound (97.5 per cent) on income over £20,000, so that an additional £2,000 per annum might only have yielded just £50 net; this probably explains why he only accepted two positions.

The Courtaulds Board was patrician in character, and until 1946 was dominated by Samuel Courtauld IV, who had become Managing Director at the age of 41, and Chairman at the age of 45; it was Courtauld who invited Freeman to join the company. In May 1946, he became seriously ill and retired as Chairman, to be succeeded by Sir John Hanbury-Williams, who had been Managing Director from 1935 to 1943 and Deputy Chairman thereafter. It was not an ideal choice since Hanbury-Williams had relatively little knowledge of production processes and was ill at ease with his technicians. But he was well aware of the vital importance of research, and fully supported Courtauld's quest for 'outsiders' – such as Freeman – and scientists, to strengthen his Board.

While Freeman was a director more than 80 per cent of Courtaulds' profits came from rayon, made by converting wood-pulp into viscose yarn, but they also made fibre and acetate yarn, and had textile mills and a chemical division. Company taxes were extremely high in the post-war years, accounting for 70 per cent of profits in 1947/48. Gross returns on net assets were under ten per cent.

The company's historian recorded that 'Freeman joined the Board with a roving brief to investigate Courtaulds' whole organisation':

> The result, whatever it did for the Company, was an historian's delight, for he wrote numerous pungent and uninhibited memoranda about what he saw. Whether in the long run his remarkable talent brought any major,

Sir Wilfrid Freeman. The portrait by Dugdale was given to Elizabeth by Rolls-Royce.

immediate improvements at Courtaulds is questionable, for although he became a Deputy Chairman in 1949, and looked like coming to exercise considerable power, he died in 1953 at the age of 64. But while he was active he was probably the most outstanding man of experience and proven administrative ability on the board, and his critical forthrightness can hardly have been anything but beneficial to an organisation which, as he described it in December 1946, 'was like a big empire on the decline'.[3]

Freeman quickly developed a poor opinion of Courtaulds' senior management. Well before he joined the company, the Board had been considering the appointment of a scientist as director of research and development. After the refusal or rejection of several candidates, A.H.Wilson, a mathematical physicist, was appointed, a decision which brought to a head a simmering dispute between the Board – most of whom lacked a technical background – and the company's chemical technicians based at Coventry. Glover, the former chief chemist, and other senior members of the Coventry staff decided to refuse all co-operation, and eventually the Board had to dismiss him and the most vociferous of his colleagues.[4]

Freeman was appalled by the disagreements between the Coventry staff and the London Board, and told the Chairman that the friction was something 'which everybody recognizes, [and] everyone ignores, and will certainly grow if it is not forcibly tackled and speedily stamped out.' If, in the process, some of the directors left the company, this had to be accepted.[5] He also told Samuel Courtauld before his death that 'there was not one man of outstanding ability among the managers' of the yarn factories, and that working conditions there were of a low standard.[6] He complained of board procedures, such as the way Hanbury-Williams allowed time to be wasted over trivia and tolerated ill-digested and badly presented papers and memoranda. In the company as a whole, he alleged, there had been a failure to decentralise operations: directors simply did not know how to delegate their responsibilities.

Years of easy money had made the company spineless and slack. Faults and mistakes tended to be covered up rather than exposed and punished. The company was astonishingly easy going, and far too many of its members put their own interest and convenience before that of the company. Too much detail was still dealt with at board level, to the detriment of consideration of major problems. There was an unhealthy 'resistance to change mentality', and the company was probably over-staffed.[7] As late as January 1951 he assessed Courtauld's as 'over-centralised, constipated and stagnant'.[8]

Brought in as a trouble-shooter, he lacked the executive power necessary to effect radical reforms. For example, eight development and management committees had been established at Courtaulds in 1943. Freeman doubted the value of their work and, echoing his criticisms of the Air Ministry in 1937, declared that they had become 'technical debating societies' instead of local boards. He urged their chairmen to delegate authority whenever possible,[9] but, while regrouping was agreed in principle, the 1952 recession halted progress.[10]

It proved no easier to solve the problem of over-centralisation. Freeman believed that different activities should be 'hived off' into separate divisions. He pointed out that this strategy, now standard practice in large corporations, had been successfully pursued by ICI and Unilever in Britain, and Standard Oil in America.[11] Courtaulds' chemical and textile branches were to be turned into quasi-independent companies, the former with a divisional board chaired by Wilson. However, there were numerous complications, and when Freeman advocated the same treatment for the fibre division, he encountered opposition from two other directors, J.E. Pedder and H.L. Johnson, who were responsible for yarn production. Wilson had, in Freeman's view, 'made a mess of the chemical division' and wished 'everyone to believe that the business of hiving-off gave rise to insurmountable difficulties.'[12] As for Pedder and Johnson, Freeman told the Chairman:

> Mr Johnson is a reactionary who likes to pretend that the present organ-isation of the yarn side is the result of a carefully planned scheme, rather than what it is – a hotch-potch, grafted onto an antiquated system. He has been consistently lobbied and persuaded by Pedder, who has lobbied steadily and energetically against the hiving off of any division, for the sole reason that he deprecates any curtailment of his empire.[13]

A proposal subsequently made by the chief accountant that Courtaulds should be grouped as share-holdings in legally separate, subsidiary operating com-panies, was rejected by the Board. Finance and general purposes committees were created, and the concept of separate divisions within the company en-dorsed, but these changes were not effective, and the 'hiving off' idea was eventually abandoned.[14]

But Freeman knew that Courtaulds was over-centralised, and he consis-tently rebuked the company's senior managers because of their failure to dele-gate responsibility. Moreover, he soon realised that many of the production processes employed in many of Courtaulds' factories were inefficient. The com-pany was wedded to out-dated techniques and extremely reluctant to invest in the latest foreign technology. A visit to the American Viscose Company (AVC) in June 1946 revealed a significant and worrying divergence between British and American practice which was, to Freeman, quite baffling. 'I find it difficult to understand how Pedder, having seen the continuous spinning of tyre yarn, did not immediately take steps to have this method introduced into our fac-tories', he wrote.[15] Nevertheless, when it was proposed that advanced German and American processes should be installed at a new fibre plant in Mobile, Alabama, there was a marked reluctance to accept the superiority of the new foreign processes by the chemical division in Coventry.[16]

Freeman had no time for this chauvinistic attitude. 'To assume that Coventry is always right, and that any idea emanating from AVC is wrong, is danger-ous and typical of our company', he complained, and he pointed out that a failure to adopt American processes in previous years would have resulted in stagnation at one major plant as well as the construction of a new and entirely unnecessary factory near Dundee.[17] Managerial conservatism lay at the heart of the problem. Unlike some of his fellow directors, Freeman had the self-confidence and experience to recruit, encourage and delegate work to younger executives such as Tony Hepper and Ted Knight. It was Ted Knight who successfully introduced foreign production processes at the Mobile fibre plant.[18]

One of the most influential historians of British business in recent years is the American professor, Alfred Chandler, and he has expressed views which help to evaluate Freeman's criticisms of Courtaulds. In an attempt to explain the poor performance of British manufacturing industry in the mid-twentieth century, Chandler argues that British business clung for too long to what he terms 'personal capitalism', by which he means family ownership. He associated personal capitalism with excessive centralisation and a failure to invest in new managerial structures, most notably the multi-divisional or 'M' form of corporate organisation. Inadequate investment in management was also closely linked to other problems, in particular an attachment to backward technology and a reluctance to embrace modern production processes.[19]

The similarity between Chandler's critique of British industry, and Freeman's uncomplimentary assessment of Courtaulds is striking. Coming from a Service ministry background, Freeman was thoroughly familiar with multi-divisional organisational structures. Through his training and experience of staff work he understood how to delegate authority and avoid over-centralisation; through his work with the aircraft industry he had come to appreciate the importance of investing in the latest production techniques. Courtaulds was in the fourth generation of family ownership when Freeman joined the Board in 1945, and he accurately perceived how this had inhibited its development and reduced its competitiveness. Drawing on examples of 'best practice' provided by the United States and Germany, as well as leading British manufacturers, he recommended a number of constructive and realistic reforms.

As well as studying Courtauld's organisation, Freeman closely scrutinised new appointments to the Board, offering the same candid assessments to Hanbury-Williams that he had provided for Portal during the war. Of one new director, he commented that 'he was unlikely to contribute much at board level, and if he could do so, I doubt if anyone would listen to him'. He was appointed, and they didn't![20]

Other remarks were equally percipient. Frank Kearton joined Courtauld's in 1946 to head chemical engineering research. Freeman described him as:

> Very able, quick thinking – and probably quick tempered; immense ability for hard work, constructive thought ... He thinks clearly and can express himself well on paper and in speech ... may be over ambitious – apt to jump to conclusions on subjects on which he is ill informed without taking trouble to ascertain the facts ... [but] I believe his worst failings will disappear when he finds his opinions subjected to critical analysis at Board level.[21]

Such assessments were always carefully considered, and based on Freeman's personal experience of the individuals concerned; he was never critical without good reason. In October 1947, he flew to Australia with Tom Davies, who had been appointed to the Courtauld's Board at the age of only 31, to consider the possibility of establishing a new factory there. They found that the labour supply in Australia was completely inadequate, and because of this, despite their guarded approval of the concept, progress was minimal for the next five years. A majority of the Board eventually agreed to set up an Australian plant – Freeman abstained – but it never made significant profits, and was closed in the 1970s.[22]

Freeman enjoyed Davies's company, and they agreed on matters of principle. But Davies undoubtedly felt that his initiative had been cramped by the presence of an older, more experienced, man, and Freeman soon concluded that Davies was a 'chancer' who lacked the ability to think through a problem systematically. 'He will plunge in and strike out on all sides with all his limbs', Freeman wrote.[23] The accuracy of this appraisal was proved all too clearly four or five years later when Courtaulds conducted an investigation into the early problems of their Canadian cellophane subsidiary: it emerged that the document submitted to the Board by Davies to support his proposal to establish the company did not 'in many instances reflect exactly the data prepared by the team which visited Canada'.[24]

Freeman's life was dominated by work, and the burden of his professional responsibilities left him with little time to devote to his family. Even after his move from Murtle Den to Victoria Road, Kensington, he remained far too deeply immersed in Courtaulds business to see very much of Joan and Susan, his younger daughters. They were often away at school, and although they enjoyed his company the age gap was too wide: the intimacies of the wider family and shared experiences were lacking; they were too young to appreciate his high standards. As they grew up, his failing health restricted their contact, and they never achieved the easy, mutual confidence he had enjoyed with Anne.

He knew that this was so. Looking in at the Courtaulds office one Saturday morning, Freeman found Arthur Knight* trying to finish some task, accompanied by his two small daughters, who had been allowed to come with him on condition that they amused themselves quietly with paper and pencil while he worked. They talked, and as he left Freeman remarked on how rewarding children were at that stage, conscious, perhaps, that he had expected too much of all his family, and, that he had failed to give his younger daughters the attention and understanding they needed as they grew up.[25]

Although Keith greatly admired him, although he flew with the RAF, naming his Mosquito 'Freeman's Folly' – and was accepted as a Courtaulds management trainee when he left the Service and worked successfully in senior management – he never really managed to achieve an easy relationship with his father. Anne married during the war, but the marriage did not last,

* Knight then subsequently became a director and become Chairman in 1975.

and if Freeman was in no position to criticise her divorce, it still distressed him. When she contracted polio in 1945, however, he took over at once, moving her into a private hospital room. Anne's two-year-old daughter, Joanna, was added to the nursery with his own young daughters, and he drove her down to see her mother every Sunday. Anne convalesced with them, until she could manage on her own again.

He remained as kind and generous as ever to his family, nephews and nieces, rewarding an ecstatic letter of thanks for a Christmas present with an extra tip, and his wit and sparkle always emerged for a visitor, especially if she was a pretty girl. He had been reconciled to Elizabeth's father during the war, and visited her parents.

In the last years of his life Freeman kept going by spending virtually every weekend in bed, resting his strained heart. Holidays were rare: he took a few weeks in Rosbeg in County Donegal in the early 1950s, and made use of the Babcock and Wilcox convalescent home on the west coast of Scotland, where he was occasionally joined by his brother Ralph. Ralph had helped his farmer nephew to buy a farm at Patna, in the bleak hills above Ayr, and after the office Bentley had been eased up the 'river bed' of an access road, the uncles demonstrated its 'windscreen washer', boyishly pleased with a new gadget.

The end came on 15 May 1953. After an argument with Elizabeth on a trivial family matter, Freeman suffered a heart attack and died, in his 65th year. An old friend wrote an almost perfect obituary four days later:

> It is almost impossible to believe that Wilfrid Freeman is dead. There was a certain ageless quality about him. In one sense he never grew up – never outlived his sometimes preposterous irreverence for pomp and circumstance. One never knew what Wilfrid would say next, except that one could be reasonably certain that it would be something entirely unexpected.
>
> He could be critical, cynical, intolerant – yet never unkind and always with a twinkle in his eye at his own extravagances. He gave his friendship sparingly, but when he gave it, it was beyond price. Incapable of suffering fools gladly, he yet inspired affection more than most people I have known – an affection sometimes tinged with amused indignation at the outrageous judgments he was liable to pass, deliberately outrageous in order to provoke argument. Of his services to his country history will some day tell. He was a great man – one of the few who deserve that overworked word 'brilliant' – whether as Chief Executive of the Ministry of Aircraft Production or as Vice-Chief of Air Staff to Portal. Caring nothing for honours and hating publicity he made a massive contribution to victory. He was a great Air Force officer, an enchanting personality, and the most loyal of friends.[26]

Abbreviated extracts from Memorandum on Aircraft Development Policy

Freeman for the Air Council, 9 November 1939

REVISED POLICY FOR RESEARCH AND DEVELOPMENT PROGRAMME

... Provision has to be made for the design and development of approved types which can be brought in to service in a later stage of the war. The experience of the last war showed that air superiority to a great extent depended on the relative performances and efficiency of the aircraft on each side and that the introduction into service of a new type, with superior performance to that possessed by the current enemy type, was a potent factor towards securing air superiority. Consequently, it is essential to continue the development of new types, even though it may be two years or more before they come into service. The introduction of a new type, of high performance, may well prove a decisive factor in the final stages of the war. Consequently it is essential to continue the long range projects in so far as (a) some aspects of these projects may be of practical application in service during the war, and (b) the potentialities of the projects of the whole are so great that the development should not be stopped even though general application in the present war may be problematical.

We must therefore keep the design staffs of firms active ... the compilation of a revised programme for 39/40 is now submitted for approval ...

Three examples which typify the three categories mentioned above:
1. High speed photographic reconnaissance aircraft. War experience has shown the need for a very fast unarmed aircraft for reconnaissance and photographic duties at high altitude.' This ... may only be achieved by a departure from orthodox designs [We propose] to place orders with three firms for two prototypes, each on a special priority basis...'
2. Large bombers. B.1/39 ... essentially a normal replacement of the Stirling, Manchester and Halifax class. The decision ... to concentrate on the production of the Halifax as the standard aircraft for the bomber striking force in no way lessens the need to press on with this improved type.... It is expected that this type will be greatly in advance of the Halifax in its defensive armament, being the first bomber designed to outgun contemporary fighter aircraft, and that its superior range and greater offensive power would enable economy to be effected in personnel, material and effort.

3. The Whittle aircraft – this is a long term project of great potential value. In essence it is jet propulsion with the consequent elimination of the power plant as at present envisaged. It is revolutionary and may fail, **but if it succeeds it is likely to mark a stage in the development of aviation, both military and civil which even the experience of war will not surpass.**

The effects of technical difficulties and new operational requirements on production of new aircraft

A summary of Freeman's briefing notes for Sir Samuel Hoare, who became Air Minister on 3 April 1940.

1. The first important date is the arrival on the unit of 20 aircraft declared for operational use. Prior delays are due to

   – under-estimated design and building times,
   – development difficulties,
   – the demands of new operational and technical requirements during development, and
   – production difficulties.

   The longer the design period the more technical and new operational requirements arise. Development flying of prototypes at the maker's works and our own [RAF] testing stations is absolutely essential.

2. The main problems with the Beaufort centred round the inadequate cooling of the Taurus engine; the engine rating had to be reduced and the supercharger changed. In the 8 months after the delivery of the first 12 aircraft to an A.&.A.E.E., only 250 hours flying had been achieved and 3 of them had crashed. Single engine performance was inadequate, cabin heating, and torpedo-dropping was unsatisfactory. New operational requirements included self-sealing tanks, extra armour, extra gun in turret, under-gun mounting, windscreen wipers.

3. Problems on other aircraft included;

   (a) Albacore; engine cooling, airscrew and the middle oscillation;
   (b) Beaufighter; engine cooling, armament, single engine flying;
   (c) Beaufort; [Taurus engine] stability unsatisfactory, poor performance single engine flying, turret operation.
   (d) Hereford; faulty factory organisation; [Shorts, Belfast]
   (e) Wellington; factory coming in later than expected caused a shortage;
   (f) Whirlwind; change in policy.

4. The main new requirements during development were self-sealing tanks and armour.

Replying to questions from Hoare on 15 April 1940, Freeman answered:

Every prototype has its development difficulties ... [none] has come into service without having to undergo changes. In the case of the Stirling the undercarriage was faulty, the tailplane had to be changed. The Manchester ... had considerable trouble ... with the flap and undercarriage operating gear, and the tailplane was also wrong. The Halifax swung violently if one engine cut out and the rear end of the fuselage is still subject to violent oscillations.... we expected at least one of the big bombers to be so seriously wrong that it would never be taken into service, [so] we chose three of them.

War experience meant changes in operational requirements. The number of guns have had to be increased, new turrets of great, but necessary, complication have been installed; armour plating, self-sealing tanks; de-icing [and] wire cutting equipment, and there have been great changes in the layout of wireless and kindred equipment.

The supply of materials is generally speaking the governing factor in production at the moment ... each design firm and experiemental establishment maintain[s] duplicate sets of drawings [are kept] in a suitably protected place. ... there are at least two prototypes, [of each aircraft] and at least two early production aircraft are allotted for development work.

... the first [Wellington] broke up in the air while undergoing its trials [due to an over-balanced rudder]. The incorporation of a mid turret entailed very extensive re-design ... and a new type of tail turret with increased armament was found necessary after the first fifteen machines had been delivered.

We order a large number of types; some have had to be duplicated as we didn't dare run the risk of a 'type' failure. I seriously considered adopting only one type of heavy bomber as a technical committee of S.B.A.C. recommended, but when the matter was gone into I found that we would lose no less than 700 aeroplanes of the heavy bomber type before the summer of 1942. The main reason for ordering three types is reinsurance against the possibility of failure. Operational requirements come into it however, since if we design a machine which can do all types of work it would be such a jack of all trades as to be operationally inefficient.

Freeman's letters to Beaverbrook

10 August 1940

... you showed me a graphic layout of your proposed organisation [of the MAP] and asked for my comments. In my opinion there should be as few people as possible at the top of the organisation directly responsible to the Minister. This should not be difficult because the organisation falls naturally into certain definite sections viz:

Parliamentary matters;

finance and contracts;

research, development and production, and, possibly, materials.

I notice that in your layout the production of equipment for aircraft and engines is separated from the production of aircraft and engines. This I think is fundamentally unsound, since the equipment must be brought forward to match the production of aircraft and engines and therefore it should be one man's responsibility to see that these items all come forward at the same time.

As regards repairs; the spares required for repairs must always be in competition with new production and therefore again one man should be finally responsible for both repairs and new production and he can allocate capacity so that maximum production is achieved. There is a growing tendency to think that repaired engines, or repaired aircraft are inferior to new ones of the same type. Generally speaking this is not so, and, as regards engines, it is more often than not the case that a repaired engine is superior to the new one.

It is your intention that I should now confine my responsibilities to Research and Development. Four and a half years ago, Research and Development were my responsibility, but more than two years ago I was also given the additional responsibility for Production. When I took over the Production side in addition to my other duties, it consisted of a small section which was built up in two years to the present organisation, and Production became my main pre-occupation.

Since war broke out, all long distance research work has been dropped, while development has not only been narrowed, but responsibility for certain aspects of development has been allocated to newcomers in the Ministry. It is a fact therefore that this branch of the Ministry's work could be better controlled by Air Vice-Marshal Tedder who has been in constant touch with it for more than two years and by Air Vice-Marshal Hill who has been Director of Technical Development for two years and D.D.G.R.D. for the last two and a half months. It certainly doesn't require control by an officer of Air Marshal rank. I therefore formally ask that I may return to the Air Ministry for duty with the Royal Air Force.

I would not like you to think that I am complaining. It is obvious that when the Ministry of Aircraft Production was formed, many of my former duties would be taken over by the Minister, and I am sure that the time has now come when I can be better employed elsewhere than in this Ministry. One final point. I feel very strongly that definite spheres of responsibility should be laid down as soon as possible, for as things are at present there is a considerable overlap and consequent waste of energy'.

6 September 1940
Minister. A month ago I asked if you would allow me to leave the Ministry and return to the Air Ministry and you said I could do so if the Air Ministry would give me a post suitable to my rank. I now ask that I may go without any such condition. My reasons for making this request are first that your recent paper to the Prime Minister in which you urge the formation of an Army Air Force is so fundamentally opposed to what I believe to be right that my position as the senior Air Force Officer in your Ministry is unbearable.

Secondly I disagree with you on so many other points of policy that it would be preferable, I believe, if someone who is more in line with your views should hold this position . . .

Thirdly I am gravely disturbed at the quarrels which seem to take place incessantly between the Ministry of Aircraft Production and the Air Ministry, many of which I feel are provoked by this Ministry rather than the Air Ministry. I do not understand your policy of non-co-operation with the Air Ministry. As the senior Air Officer in the Ministry of Aircraft Production I have done my best to prevent these quarrels but have been powerless to do so. I feel that these quarrels and lack of co-operation are doing great harm and may seriously prejudice the proper conduct of the war.

7 September 1940
You have made a proposal to the Prime Minister for setting up a separate Air Force for the Army. I feel I must record my considered view that this would be a most dangerous and retrograde step which would seriously prejudice our chances of victory. I think it would be generally regarded, except by the War office, Mr Hore-Belisha and Colonel Moore-Brabazon, as an inexplicable and wholly unnecessary dispersion of effort, particularly at the present time when the bulk of our land forces are immobilised in this country by the threat of invasion and are not participating in any war of movement.

I believe that if the Army had possessed its own Air Force in peace time we might already have lost the war. Until quite recently the number of air squadrons that we could form was wholly dependent on the output of the aircraft industry which was the limiting factor in all our air expansion programmes. If the Army had possessed its own Air Force, the War Office would have insisted on the provision in peace time of a large number of squadrons of specialised types of aircraft intended for co-operation with the Army, in a hypothetical war of movement and unsuitable for long range bombing or air defence. This force would subsequently have been dissipated in France in an attempt to redress the numerical inferiority of our Army to the German forces by which they were opposed. What remained of the force might have been brought back at the time of the evacuation from Dunkirk, but it would not have been trained or equipped to defend this country against air attack or to take part in long range bomb raids against objectives on the continent.

The inevitable result would have been that instead of having the minimum number of suitable types to defend this country and carry the air war in to Germany, as we have now, the number of such machines would have been insufficient. In such circumstances Germany would have been able to establish complete air superiority and the war might by now have been lost.

The present position is that the number of pilots and aircraft crews that we can train, rather than the number of aircraft that we can produce or purchase from America, looks like being the factor which will principally limit our air expansion, but this is by no means certain. For example we may find that production in this country is seriously affected by enemy action and nearly all the aircraft that we hope to obtain from America are inferior operational types to those already possessed by ourselves or by Germany, and the difficulties we are experiencing in bringing new types into production without adversely affecting the output of present types may lead to our losing the qualitative superiority which we now possess.

Even if it was certain that trained pilots and crews, rather than machines, would henceforth be the bottle-neck, the creation of a separate Army Air Force would provide no solution but would merely aggravate the situation. We should have to provide the Army with all those training establishments, aerodromes, instructors and training aircraft of which we are already so deficient; and when we had done so the Army would not train their men to take part in the air defence of this country and the air attack against Germany, but would merely begin to train a force of army co-operation and close reconniassance pilots destined to assist the Army at some later stage in the war when it may be thought practicable to send another expeditionary force to the continent.

I can imagine no more dangerous dispersion of effort and nothing more calculated to prevent us achieving some measure of air superiority than wasting our limited resources in an attempt to satisfy the demands of a few Army officers for a separate Air Force of their own.

The truth is we need to husband our resources and to concentrate first and foremost on building up an Air Force equal to that of Germany, if we are to avert defeat, let alone win the war. These objects cannot be achieved if we continue to believe that we can defeat the German Air Force with the British Air Force which is now inferior in quantity and may become inferior in quality if we don't make great efforts.

I believe in co-operation between the three Services, not in regarding each Service as an entirely separate arm which must have the ancillary weapons which it might conceivably need. The Air Force must be trained and equipped to co-operate with the Navy or the Army as required, or to act on its own. So far, we have not been able to provide one Air Force strong enough for our essential needs. I see no prospect of having three Air Forces, each strong enough to take on the centralised Air Forces of the Axis Powers, which are not sub-divided amongst their Armies and Navies.

The Shell-Mex House saga

THE 'BEAVERBROOK METHOD'

Soon after his appointment, Beaverbrook decided that Shell-Mex House on the Strand would be suitable for his new Ministry, and tried to requisition it. But it was occupied by the Petroleum Board, the joint body acting under the Board of Trade for the five major oil distributors, which had been given a monopoly of oil distribution in Britain. Sir Andrew Agnew, the Chairman of the Petroleum Board, a former Managing Director of Shell and later President of the Institute of Petroleum, was an experienced man 'of courage and determination', and in preparation for war and the vital work of the Petroleum Board, he had spent the previous two years perfecting its communications. A superb teleprinter network had been installed, with duplicate cables entering the building from both the Strand and the Embankment, and a duplicate set of teleprinters, one in a bomb-proof basement, with

Sir Andrew Agnew, CBE. Executive head of the Petroleum Board 1939–45. He personally planned and had installed the control systems between 1937 and 1939.

access to all the main teleprinter networks. An average of 5,000 messages a day went out to all regional offices and installations, handling the detailed control of cargo arrivals at all the West Coast ports, raising the discharge rate from 100 tons per hour to more than 450tph, and controlling even the routes of rail tanker cars. In the summer of 1940, Agnew moved the ancillary departments such as accounts, out of Shell-Mex House, leaving only those sections of the Board needed for executive operational control, a unit which could not be split if the organization was to function properly.

Agnew was not afraid of Beaverbrook, and refused to move, making the Board of Trade support him when he was overruled. When a furious Beaverbrook then persuaded Churchill to overrule the Board of Trade, Agnew circulated a detailed five-page memorandum to the Service Ministries and to the Home Office explaining the vital importance to the nation of the Board's perfect communications, and let it be known that if the Board had to move, he would retire as Chairman. Agnew had already proved his abilities; the Board was running smoothly, indeed the American armed forces in Britain were quite happy to leave the responsibility for their supplies in his hands from 1942 onwards – and under the combined pressure of the other Ministries, Churchill gave way and told Beaverbrook to look elsewhere.

A few months later Agnew met Beaverbrook, and said that it had come to his knowledge that two reporters from *The Daily Express* had been travelling round the world in BOAC aircraft, visiting the Shell oilfields and refineries at which Agnew had worked during his career, asking questions about his character, ability and record – in the hope of discovering something discreditable. Agnew asked what they had discovered. Without dissembling, Beaverbrook told him; 'Nothing of any use. You are said to be ruthless but fair', to which Agnew contemptuously replied; 'I don't mind having that said about me'.

When Britain was fighting alone against Germany and Italy, Beaverbrook's reporters had been sent overseas by air at Ministry expense, in pursuit of a petty and vindictive grudge against an able and upright man who was controlling a vital national supply system with great success. No wonder Sinclair, Freeman and their colleagues 'handled Beaverbrook with care'.

Freeman's comments on Trenchard's criticisms of a paper circulated by Beaverbrook

*Text of undated paper – probably 1941 – from Freeman to Arthur Street, Permanent Under Secretary, Air Ministry**

1. The essence of production is careful planning, followed up by 'chasing' in a helpful spirit to see that every producing firm has got the tools, equipment, floor space, labour and raw materials to enable them to carry out their plans.
2. Careful planning can only be worked out by an efficient organization who know their job. On Lord Beaverbrook's arrival planning ceased and instead of the manufacturers being helped in every possible way to achieve their plans they were bullied to produce aircraft without being given the raw materials to enable them to fulfil their job.
3. By a method of expediency ... production for a time forged ahead, firms lived on the fat they had collected in the way of raw materials, whilst raw materials hitherto destined for new types, and more especially the new heavy bomber types, were diverted to those in actual production, as a temporary expedient. There was something to be said for this but it was carried too far with the result that we see today that the Air Force is starved of the new heavy bombers which should be coming along in great numbers, and the new fighters.
4. Lord Beaverbrook has stated frequently that he does not believe in organization. He believes that personality and drive are alone required for efficient production.
5. How was Lord Beaverbrook able to produce those machines suddenly? The principal reason was that the Air Force accepted them without their full equipment.
6. Lord Trenchard is right when he says that quality will count for more than quantity and how well the truth of this dictum was proved in the Battle of Britain which took place last summer. The Germans were vastly superior in numbers – we were superior in quality. The success of Lord Beaverbrook's regime will be judged not on quantity but on quality. I would ask this question – are the bombers which are now flying to Germany new types superior to those which were flying at this time last year? Are our fighters merely fighters of the old type brought up to date, or are they new types planned years ago which should now be coming into production?

* PRO. AIR 20/2828.

7. It is impossible for Lord Trenchard to probe the whole matter by listening to reports received from people in the industry and more especially from disgruntled people in the industry. What is required is a panel of really efficient production men and business men who have hitherto had little or nothing to do with aircraft production to enquire into the whole matter. A panel such as that set up under the late Prime Minister under the Chairmanship of Colonel Greenly is the sort of body which should do the work.

8. So much for the general criticism of the paper. I cover some of the ground already covered by Lord Trenchard but in a slightly different form. Now some of the detail.

9. The real trouble was that people were introduced that knew nothing of their job, who were given work to do for which they were utterly incompetent. Mr Bickell a mining magnate from Canada was introduced into the Ministry of Aircraft Production. His first job was to put a drive behind a certain type of aeroplane, secondly he was given the job of putting a drive behind castings, thirdly he was given the job of managing the ferry pool organization responsible for the delivery of aircraft from manufacturers. Mr Bickell wisely refused to do the first job. He has tried to do the others without any marked success.

10. Senator Elliot was brought from Australia. I believe he is a newspaper man. He is a very charming man but is he competent to advise firms or even help firms on production matters? What knowledge has Sir Robert Renwick of production to enable him to carry out his functions at the Ministry of Aircraft Production?

11. Lord Beaverbrook may boast of the increased production. Did we not get a sudden increase in production and then a gradual fall? If he had never arrived at all would we now be where we stood with an organized show, rather than an upset one with all the possibilities of falling off in production?

12. What about American production? Is this up to date or has it gone back? Would it not be better if Lord Beaverbrook had left our business in America to be run by Mr Purvis who has done it so ably, without introducing his own agent into that country? Has he built up an organization in America of efficient technicians from this country who can tell the Americans what they want and enable them to benefit from our experience, or has our representation in American been starved? Has he built up an organization for flying aircraft to this country or America, or has he had to call on the Air Force to help him out? Soon we will be expecting a great flow of American aircraft to reach this country, perhaps even hundreds a month. Are there hundreds of pilots ready in America waiting to fly aircraft to this country so that each aircraft as it is produced is flown from the American factory straight over to Great Britain?

13. If I knew that Lord Beaverbrook had laid down many more new factories so as to provided additional floor space I would feel happy. Has he done this or is he just making use of the magnificent work done by former

Secretaries of State for Air? Has he vastly increased our ability to produce and fabricate aluminium and its alloys, or is he content to make use of what has been done in the past while at the same time he takes credit due to others? Finally does he perceive it to be his job as indeed it should be to be a servant of the Air Ministry to produce what they want, when they want, or does he say 'this is what I will produce, you must make use of it?' If it is the latter then he has completely wrong ideas of his proper function. Has he made the work of the Air Ministry easier or more difficult?

14. Those arguments which are advanced for keeping the Admiralty supply side within the Admiralty hold good as regards the Air Ministry. Users knowledge is what is required in the Ministry of Aircraft Production. There is no objection to the separation provided the Ministry of Aircraft Production realise the importance of users knowledge and the importance of delivering to the Air Force what they want. Fighters can be produced more easily than bombers; destroyers can be produced more easily than battleships; are the Admiralty to be told therefore that they will only get destroyers and not battleships or cruisers? Are the Air Force to be told that they will be given – what they don't want, or what they do want?

15. Lord Beaverbrook has always been an isolationist. He believes in playing a lone hand. Has he co-operated with the other supply departments, or has his policy been one of non-cooperation?

Freeman's letter to Portal on bombing policy

I think this is very interesting so I am giving it to you in full.

1. Your Minute of 28 September, suggests that it may be possible over the winter months to obtain a greater effect from our bombing attacks by a policy of dispersal than by a policy of concentration.

2. I have the gravest doubts as to the wisdom of such a change and would ask you to consider the following points: under two headings, Material Damage; Morale Damage.

3. The matter can be considered.

MATERIAL DAMAGE

4. The lesson of German air attacks on this country is that material damage is achieved by concentration. To quote from the recent analysis of Blitz attacks, 'had the Germans achieved greater concentration, the industrial effect of the Blitzes considered would have been severalfold greater'. It suggested that the pressure on the population of the United Kingdom would have been increased in the same ratio, perhaps to breaking point. The watchword for Blitzing seems therefore to be concentration.'

5. This statement conforms with general experience. Compare for example the extreme lack of results consequent on the scattered night attacks of July and August 1940.

6. The fact that less than 25% of our bombs dropped in Germany fall within 5 miles of the target does not seem to me to afford an argument in favour of dispersal. On good nights evidence derived from German attacks shows that maximum material damage will follow from concentration, on bad nights when bombing on ETA (estimated time of arrival) is common, material damage will be negligible, whether the attacks are concentrated or dispersed. This I think is clear from the [Butt] report on night photography.

7. So far as the material factor is concerned therefore the available evidence is strongly against dispersion.

MORALE DAMAGE

8. Once again the report on the Blitz action is illuminating. This report suggests that material and morale damage are closely linked. Morale is in danger when the civilian population can no longer depend on a secure base; when rest and food cannot be brought safely to the Blitz population. Light attacks tend to condition the population, and populations which have been subjected to gradually increasing raids take heavy raids better than those who experience a sudden heavy raid without conditioning.

9. This generalisation also accords with experience. The scattered attacks of July and August 1940 seemed on the whole to stimulate morale. A few months later, absenteeism following heavy raids was a major concern of the MAP. Even from the standpoint of morale therefore the evidence is strongly in favour of concentration.

BRITISH AND GERMAN MORALE

10. The above arguments rest on the assumption that it is possible to generalise from German raids on Britain to British raids on Germany. So far as the material factor is concerned this must be broadly true. Where the morale factor is concerned I realise there is an important section of opinion which believes German morale is of a different calibre and quality from British morale and should be attacked by different methods.

11. Nevertheless I find it difficult to believe that the British and German morale are so basically dissimilar that whereas maximum concentration of attack is needed to affect British morale, maximum dilution will be effective against German morale.

    A policy of widespread bombing is bound to entail both a reduction in total damage and a minimum in density of damage throughout Germany. It follows that the policy of widespread bombing must rely, not upon actual damage, but on the threat of attack and moreover that the efficiency of this threat must not diminish as warning follows warning without actual attack.

12. It may be that the German character is so radically different from our own that this is a sound basis for a bombing policy, but the assumption seems to me a risky one and I should feel our policy was more securely founded if we relied on straightforward deduction from our own experience. On such a basis, if it should prove that we have over-rated German morale, the consequence will be that the German collapse will come sooner than we suppose. If we merely assume that the German morale can be undermined by the mere shadow of attack, we shall achieve no more than Germany did in the abortive night attacks of July and August 1940.

13. To my mind the difficulty of attacking Germany effectively with our present equipment during a dark and cloudy period points to a different direction. I believe that our present attacks delivered under such conditions achieve very little and that they are unduly wasteful in aircraft. It is true that loss from enemy action in moonless nights and attacks in bad weather is usually small, but total loss including crashes on landing is often high.

14. If aircraft availability is the limiting factor, as it is at the moment, the loss of an aircraft from whatever cause and whether or not the crew escape, reacts directly on effort. We can only afford to lose a certain number of aircraft each month, whether we expend them on profitable attacks on good nights or attacks of little value on bad ones.

CONCLUSION

15. Lord Trenchard's theory, for he is the principal protagonist of these ideas, depends on a basis which is fundamentally unsound. Material damage would be negligible, the enemy's morale if not stimulated would certainly be strengthened in a very short time. Alternatively it is recommended on fine nights our bombers must attack specific targets with the greatest weight possible and since the effect of bombing is cumulative they should continue these attacks for as long as possible.

On the dark nights we should send a few aircraft to bomb certain areas, say 20, 15 of which should be concentrated on one target within the area, while the remaining 5 aim merely at creating a disturbance without hoping to achieve any great material results. This would mean that the effort of most of the bomber force would be conserved for employment under conditions where their bombing would be more effective. Greater efforts could well be spent in training and learning to use the latest types to enable them in future to carry out concentrated bombing on individual targets as well in the dark as they can in the light. When the fine weather comes the bomber force should, so long as it persists, work at maximum strength even though it means pilots going out two or even three nights in succession.

I apologise for writing so much on this subject, but I feel very strongly about it.

Bufton's secret and personal letter to Harris

*8 May 1942**

Thank you for returning the documents and for your letter which accompanied them. In it you say that you still have a fairly open mind on the subject of a target finding force but that you are not yet convinced by the arguments which have so far been advanced. I hope you will not mind my accepting this as an invitation to express further arguments or comment.

I drafted this letter while I was on leave but have not had time to complete it until now. On my return the Director said that you had referred to my having spoken to an MP on the subject of a TFF. The subject has not of course been discussed with any MP or outside the Air Ministry so I don't know how this idea arose. I have in fact, in view of your invitation, made a point of putting my arguments to you in full confidence that you would appreciate them, and, if convinced, form a TFF and that this would be the quickest way of accomplishing the step which I know in my heart will immediately treble or quadruple the effective hitting power of the Bomber Force and which is such a vital and urgent matter that I have had it constantly in my mind for some months past. My greatest difficulty is that nobody seems to want to quadruple our hitting power or realize that we can do it now.

In your letter you raise two points about the general success of our bombing. Firstly, that over the last few weeks the progressive development of our TR1335 [Gee] technique has led to the majority of our bombs landing usefully in built up areas in the Ruhr, reasonably close to the intended target and that our present methods are proving reasonably satisfactory. I will quote three recent examples to illustrate how far we are falling short of what we can achieve: Essen, a heavily defended area; Rostock, lightly defended but deep inside Germany and Gennevilliers, lightly defended and easy to locate at short range.

An analysis of the 122 plotted photographs taken on the eight raids on Essen between 8th March and 12th April shows that two were on the target, two within one mile, eight between one and five miles, 104 between five and twenty-five miles and six between twenty-five and one hundred miles from the target. 90% of the aircraft bomb points between five and a hundred miles from the target. I think you will agree that such dispersal shows our present methods fail entirely to achieve the aim in a highly defended area, despite the assistance derived from TR1335 which was being employed on its most favourable line of shoot. Subsequent photographic cover confirms this fact.

* PRO. AIR 14/3523

In the Rostock raids conditions were perfect and defences negligible. Yet on the first night most of the effort was dissipated away from the target because our methods permitted initial fires to be started elsewhere. Of seventy-two successful photos reported to be of Rostock, only sixteen or 22% in fact were. 78% of our effort as far as the aim was concerned was wasted. Correct tactics would have more than quadrupled the effect of this raid.

Gennevilliers represented the ideal operational conditions; short distance; easy to locate; light; unpractised and not fully organized defences and perfect weather with full moon. Here again the same basic defects were noted and fires away from the target were bombed. The eighty-five aircraft claiming to have attacked took ninety successfully plotted photographs of which only eleven, or 12%, were of the works. The actual results achieved confirm that the raid was only about 12% effective as suggested by the photographs. This raid proves that even under ideal conditions when the target can be clearly seen leadership and a focus is essential.

These three examples, embracing weather conditions better than we can normally expect are indicative of the results obtainable with our present tactical methods. I do not think that there can be any progressive development with them apart from the initial improvement conferred by TR1335. The basic need is the initial unmistakable conflagration. This can never be achieved when second class crews are mixed with first class ones in the initial phase of the attack. Even the first class crews will not be successful unless they are co-ordinated in one body and develop a specialized technique. We want not a 'corps d'élite' as such but a force expert in achieving this essential part of any large scale operation.

Secondly you suggest that in heavily defended areas such as the Ruhr it is physically impossible to see the pinpoint and bomb it in the face of the search-lights. If this is the case we should surely admit defeat and change our aim. Searchlights, however, only affect seriously those aircraft that are focused on. I have no doubt that the most experienced crews can locate these targets if given the opportunity to work together in a co-ordinated and specially orga-nized body, and all those I have come into contact with are enthusiastically anxious to be given this opportunity.

You refer in your letter to the very serious disadvantages of a 'corps d'élite'. The main ones I believe are possible effects on morale and promotion. With regard to the effect on morale the unanimous opinion of operational per-sonnel with whom I have come into contact is that a TFF would improve morale. Crews would always be assured of a successful show. They would not feel out of the picture because crews chosen from their own squadron would be in the TFF and would thus give them a personal interest in it. Moreover it would be their ambition to be chosen for it themselves. In this connection we should not I think lose sight of the general lowering of morale of the Command as a whole which has resulted from the inability of crews, either singly or collectively, to find and bomb heavily defended targets under average weather conditions with our present methods.

To suggest that the possibility of slower promotion would be an adverse factor is I think to do an injustice to the spirit and idealism of the crews. Promotion means little to them compared with winning or shortening the War. The majority hold temporary commissions and have no RAF career to worry about, but above all during the five or six months of their operational tour crews do not know from one day to the next which will be their last. Promotion does not therefore enter largely into their calculations, only proving themselves to themselves and achieving results.

The system which has now been introduced, while at first sight appearing to be a step towards the establishment of a TFF, does, I suggest, miss the basic and all important principles of the scheme. The main points that occur to me are:

1. The selected squadrons may have a few exceptionally good crews, but their efforts in marking the target are likely to be entirely vitiated by the less efficient crews marking places other than the target. This will immediately lead to dispersion of the main force as we know so well from our experience.

2. If the leading squadrons do achieve their aim of starting an unmistakable conflagration the task of the following, and not so good squadrons will be comparatively simple and thus for the ensuing months an inferior squadron is likely to be chosen to lead the raids. This is a fundamental defect in the scheme.

3. As only two or three crews in each of the squadrons will be first class the aggregate of first class crews in the TFF squadrons will be of the order sixteen to twenty, which is barely enough to illuminate the target let alone cause the essential conflagration with heavy concentration of incendiaries.

4. Owing to the lack of cohesion through geographical separation and the frequent change of role, there will be no development and organic growth of tactical method and technique.

5. By reason of the competitive nature of the scheme the raid leaders will not gain the confidence of the following squadrons in their ability to loate and mark the target. Such confidence would, however, be engendered in a co-ordinated force of able and reliable crews supplied from all squadrons provided it had specialized in the work of target location and marking.

6. An outstanding feature of the TFF scheme, the establishment alongside it of a development and scientific unit, will not be possible.

7. When TR1335 is jammed we will be back where we started.

There seems to be some magic inherent in the phrase 'corps d'élite' which immediately conjures up battalions of vague and nebulous antagonisms. In peace conditions I would admit them; it would be the only way to progress to disperse the best throughout the whole and encourage development by competition. No one however would dream of trying to defeat the rival school by [not] turning out the best house team, and that is what we are doing now. It is essential to put the best men in the first team and even that is not enough; they must train and co-ordinate their tactics as a team. Until we do this we cannot start to beat the enemy defences.

It is difficult to realize that the Groups, in turning down this one solution to the problem, appreciate fully the vital urgency of the present situation; that our efforts against highly defended targets are falling so short of the mark; and that it is within our power to inflict decisive damage on them. In this connection I wonder whether the issue was put to Station Commanders impartially and fully, with all emphasis on our inability to achieve our aim, and in the light of the overwhelming importance of doing decisive damage now if we are to save thousands of lives by shortening the War, and incidentally to prevent the partial disruption of the Bomber Force. In the shadow of such momentous factors the objections which have been raised surely count but little. I wonder further, whether the majority of the operational Station Commanders were opposed to the scheme. I suggest that the real test would be to call these together, explain to them fully and fairly the scheme and the background, and accept their verdict on this purely operational issue.

In conclusion I would like to raise one further matter. Since embarking on this discussion it appears that the arguments raised in it are a manifestation of a much wider issue – a conflict of ideas between the older officers of much general experience and the ever growing body of younger ones who have been actively engaged in operations. It has often been said that this is a young man's war, and this is true to the extent that only the young men have the quick reactions needed to fight our modern weapons. To fight these weapons efficiently they must be directed efficiently, and this can only be done by those who have, or who utilize, a complete knowledge of their possibilities and limitations. Only the young men have this knowledge. Here the difficulty arises. The older officers who, through the years have assumed an increasing responsibility, may perhaps be reluctant to share it, or fully to accept and apply the advice of the younger ones whom they often benevolently regard as inexperienced. This attitude is crystallized in the phrase which you have underlined in your letter – 'their own comparatively narrow spheres'. It indicates that through the years administration and organization have become the broad spheres and operational the narrow. Such an attitude is bound to cramp and frustrate imagination and development in the sphere which is after all the be-all and end-all of Bomber Command. It is this attitude, I feel, which now prevents the formation of the Target Finding Force.

This conflict need never arise. If we could marry, at all levels of command, the mature judgement and wide experience of the older officers with the imagination, drive and operational knowledge of the younger, then I think we should achieve the highest possible standard of morale and achievement throughout Bomber Command.

To bring this about I suggest we need at all Stations a Group Captain (Operations) who would be entirely responsible to the A.O.C. for the operational activities of the Station such as the Ops Room, the Ops/Intelligence Staff, aerodrome control, briefing of crews, control of operations, and supervision and development of tactics. The present duties of a Station Commander are such that he cannot give his best to either the administrative or the operational matters, and therefore there should in addition be a Station Commander of wide experience whose duties would be the running of the base from the purely administrative point of view. This is the German system and it is obviously a sound one and one calculated to extract the utmost efficiency from the operational units.

At Groups similarly, there should be a S.A.S.O. who has wide experience on operations. Here again he should be relieved of all responsibilities which are not purely operational by an older officer who might fill the post of S.A.S.O.(Air).

A similar principle should be applied at Command Headquarters.

In this way the officers conducting operations would be relieved of the grievous administrative burdens which now absorb most of their energies and make it almost impossible for them to analyze results and develop and improve our methods. There would be established, too, that which is now lacking in our organization – an unobstructed and receptive channel for the ebb and flow of new operational ideas from the squadrons to yourself.

In contrast, under the present system, a new idea which might be of extreme value reaches Command, possibly through a non-operational Station Commander, a non-operational S.A.S.O., and the A.O.C., and on the way it is possible its real implications or the supporting arguments are lost and, like so many, the idea is still-born. Under the above scheme too, when a Group Commanders conference is called to decide some tactical question, it might well be advantageous for the Group Commanders to be accompanied by their operational advisors, the S.A.S.O.s (Ops). I was particularly impressed, at the conference which we were invited to attend, by the fact that the basic tactics for the Command were discussed and determined with no reference to any person of operational experience in this War, and I feel the system here might be improved.

I believe that these measures would confer on the Bomber Force an increased hitting power and brilliancy by unleashing the full potentialities of the operational personnel which at the moment tend to be segregated, unappreciated and hence frustrated.

In conclusion and in spite of Lubecks, Augsbergs and Rostocks, I hope you will not take objection to the frankness of these views which are born only of a very great concern for the success of the bomber force. They may prove of interest either in confirmation of ideas which you have already formed, or in the light of subsequent events. In either case I believe this letter will have been justified.

Yours sincerely,
S.O.BUFTON

The essentials of the heavy bomber programme

Programme 'L', agreed in October 1938, planned the delivery of 3,500 heavy bombers, to the B.12/36 and P.13/36 specifications, by April 1942. Until the four prototypes had been flown, tested and evaluated, Freeman held out against SBAC pressure to concentrate on one standard type, such as the Halifax. Development of the two Supermarine B.12/36 prototypes was retarded by Mitchell's death, and terminated by their destruction in September 1940, but a new specification, B.1/39, had meanwhile been prepared in November 1939, for a larger 'ideal bomber' with an all-up weight of 90,000lb, capable of carrying up to 20-25,000lb of bombs, with cannons or 0.5in. guns in its turrets, to replace the B.12/36 and P.13/36 designs, two or three years later. But for the events of 1940, the Bristol type 159 and the Handley Page HP.60 designs might have been accepted, each with low profile four-cannon turrets amidships, and as much structural interchangeabilty as possible.[1]

Output of the original heavy bombers was severely checked when Beaverbrook focused on the 'big five', dispersed the aircraft factories and cancelled 90 per cent of the heavy bomber orders: work on the B.1/39 designs, and on the factory to make 0.5in. guns, stopped. Deliveries in 1940 were 13 Stirlings, 22 Manchesters and 6 Halifaxes, all with serious airframe or engine problems.

Early in 1941, Churchill approved Portal and Freeman's plan for a heavy bomber force of 4,000 aircraft, to be completed by April 1943,[2] and Craven, back as chief executive after Beaverbrook resigned, was supportive when this was discussed with Moore-Brabazon, the new Minister at MAP.[3] But Freeman soon discovered that Courtney had made no provision in the new Target Programme for heavy bombers to equip the Operational Training Units (OTUs), which would train pilots for the additional 200 to 250 bomber squadrons, and he insisted that the overall balance must be recalculated.[4] When Churchill saw the revised figures, he complained that, over the next twelve months, there would be very little increase in either the numbers of aircraft produced or the weight of bombs which the bombers would be able to carry.[5]

Knowing that the MAP would argue that the 3,500 heavy bombers, to be produced by 1 July 1943, should consist entirely or mainly of Wellingtons, and that a Wellington would be cheaper to construct than a Lancaster, Freeman pointed out that one Lancaster would carry the same load as three Wellingtons to Berlin and that, even on the shorter range targets, they would carry the load of two and two-thirds Wellingtons.[6] War experience had already confirmed all the pre-war calculations that to deliver the same tonnage of bombs to Germany, the heavy bomber gave decisive advantage in every respect: they cost less to construct in terms of materials and labour, required fewer men to maintain and operate them, and made less demands on the training system.[7]

He told Craven: 'It should be our aim to use ... [fewer] crews to drop the same weight, because thereby we can economise on our training organisation, and a smaller number of pilots will be used on non-operational work. The effects of having better machines with less pilots will mean that there will be proportionately fewer casualties and our pilots will be better trained, which will again mean fewer casualties. Thus we get increasingly better value from the bigger machines. ... In our view, therefore, it is imperative that we should aim to produce the greatest possible number of heavies within the new quota laid down by the Prime Minister [the 4,000 front line force]. We are still ahead of the Germans in the quality of our aircraft and equipment and it is quality which tells in wartime. We must maintain our lead, ... we shall do so [if we concentrate on] improvement in design, and ... research in any promising direction which new tactics, scientific study, or inventive ingenuity may suggest'.[8] Craven agreed, but warned that the number of operational aircraft produced would actually fall as the factories were re-equipped for larger aircraft. '... I appreciate ... that the Wellington to the Lancaster is a tramp to a battleship, but if ... I should stop the production of Wellingtons at Chester and Blackpool and turn over to Lancasters ... you will receive no Lancasters [from those factories] by the Prime Minister's target date.'[9]

When the ORC re-examined the pre-war 'ideal bomber' specification, they confirmed the inadequacy of the Wellington, concluding that the bomber force should consist of aircraft with an all-up weight of at least 50,000lb, carrying a bomb load of 8,000lb, (16 per cent of its gross weight). They also confirmed the obvious advantages of operating the current heavy bomber designs; aircraft weighing 60,000lb, carrying an 11,000lb bomb load, 18 per cent of all-up weight.[10]

Output of heavy bombers rose very slowly. Production doubled or trebled during 1941, but total deliveries were only 498, comprising 153 Stirlings, 165 Manchesters, 162 Halifaxes and 18 Lancasters, compared with 2,774 Whitleys, Wellingtons, and Hampdens. MAP claimed that there was virtually no idle productive capacity in the UK and that the introduction of a new product often involved labour being made idle. They actually stressed the danger that idle capacity and labour would be seized by the Ministry of Supply, then run by Beaverbrook![11]

THE LANCASTER: THE BEST OF THE HEAVY BOMBERS

By the time Freeman returned to the MAP in October 1942, it was apparent that the Lancaster was the best of the three heavy bombers. The performance of the early Halifaxes should have been roughly the same, but they had less range, and could hardly reach 17,000ft with a full load: their effective ceiling was 13,000ft. The Stirling was heavier and, until 1943, apart from 300 Lancaster IIs, was the only one in service to be powered with Hercules engines. Although its wing loading was less than the Lancaster's, its power:weight ratio was significantly lower, and not only was the range of the Stirling even less than the Halifax, but its fully loaded ceiling barely exceeded 14,000ft.

The inadequate power output of the Mark VI Hercules at altitude was, undoubtedly, partly to blame. Goaded by Harris, MAP, the Government and the RAF, Freeman agreed to accept the unpalatable side-effects of reducing the output of Stirlings, Wellingtons and Warwicks, so as to use their facilities to make more Lancasters, and a decision to switch capacity from Stirlings to Lancasters at Swindon and at the Austin factory was taken in September 1942, just before Freeman returned to MAP. Plans were also made to produce Lancasters at Chester and Castle Bromwich, despite the forecast delay before new jigs and tools could be installed for Lancaster production. Oliver Lyttelton was asked to help by negotiating for extra Liberator bombers from America, to make up for the 300 Stirlings 'not produced' during the change-over period. 287 Liberators were promised from Lend-Lease.

Although Freeman believed the Lancaster to be 'good vintage', likely to be 'further improved', he thought at first that any improvements to the Halifax would only put it on level terms with the existing Lancaster, with no further potential. When the old type Hercules VI engines were fitted to the first Halifax III, however, its initial performance figures were unexpectedly better than the Merlin versions. Freeman was sceptical, and warned Portal not to publicise them until they had been confirmed.

The 36-litre Hercules should have performed better than the 27-litre Merlin, and repositioning the engines lower and further forward helped, but when the Hercules 100 came into service, with a turbine-entry supercharger, on the later Halifax VIs, many crews found them '. . . second to none; [they] could easily outclimb the great Lancaster'[12] – a well-deserved tribute to the later, long delayed, but much improved, Hercules, and vindication for the Halifax.

DEFENSIVE TURRETS

Power-operated turrets, armed with two or four .303in. machine-guns, and fitted in nose, dorsal and tail, but not ventral positions, were a deterrent, and fairly effective for daylight defence. But the range of the .303in. guns was inadequate, and the bullets were too light to penetrate armour plate, whilst turrets armed with 20mm cannon were too heavy to replace .303in. guns in the nose or tail of existing airframes. The ideal weapon, the 0.5in. machine-gun, was not made in Britain,* but towards the end of the war, some Lancasters were fitted with American 0.5in. guns in twin-gun tail turrets made by Rose Bros.[13] 'Under defence' ventral turrets made by Preston Green, with one 0.5in. gun, were fitted in Halifax IIIs for a time, whilst H2S sets were in short supply.[14] Until they were fitted, there was a blind spot directly below all the heavy bombers, and the Luftwaffe installed 'upward facing' cannon, code named 'Schrage Musik' in their night fighters to exploit this. They climbed up within the blind area until they were close enough to aim at one of the wings, and set fire to the fuel tanks, rather than the bomb load.[15]†

* In 1940, Beaverbrook cancelled Freeman's plan to produce 0.5 machine-gun turrets in Britain.
† One German night fighter with 'Schrage Musik' shot down six bombers within an hour.

Aero-engine development and performance 1936 to 1945

The performance of piston aero-engines is governed by the rule;

Engine power is proportional to the weight of air consumed

The amount of air/fuel mixture used by an engine can be increased by:

1. enlarging the swept volume (cubic capacity) of the engine,
2. increasing the permissable limits of revolution of the engine, and
3. forcing more air into it with superchargers, and/or the 'ram' effect of high speed on a forward-facing air-intake.

Air pressure falls with altitude, and aero-engine designers compensated for this, by using a gear ratio for their superchargers which increased to sea level pressure, the air density at a chosen operational height. By using a second gear, third gear, or fully variable gears, optimum power within the limitations of the engine and its fuel could be obtained over a wider range of altitudes. At heights above 15,000 ft, single-stage superchargers were less adequate, and a second stage was required to maintain full power. Integral superchargers were built as part of the engine assembly, but separate 'auxiliary' units could be geared to the engine or driven by the exhaust gases (turbo-chargers). An extra radiator (inter-cooler or after-cooler), could be fitted to reduce the temperature, and increase the density of supercharged air before it entered the engine, and this allowed higher boost pressure to be used, leading to even greater power.

The development of variable-pitch propellers, and constant-speed units meant that, within certain limits, engine revolutions (revs) and the power demanded (boost) could be controlled independently.

The success of all such developments depended on the avoidance of 'detonation',* the likelihood of which generally rises with the compression ratio and with the pressure of the incoming fuel/air mixture. It is thus particularly dangerous and destructive to highly supercharged aero-engines. The special fuels used for the Schneider Trophy racing engines were very inefficient, but fuels with high octane qualities, especially those based on crude oils from regions like California and Borneo, and specially refined, could be used at high pressures without detonation, properties which were enhanced by the addition of minute quantities of tetraethyl lead.

* The uncontrolled explosion of an over-compressed fuel-air mixture.

From 1936 to 1940, the RAF used 87 octane fuel. Supplies of 100 octane began to increase in 1939, and, although these were barely adequate, the decision to switch the aircraft of Fighter Command to 100 octane was made in March 1940.[1] Bomber Command aircraft followed in 1941 after Lend Lease gave access to American refinery resources. The use of 100 octane allowed the combat rating of the single-stage Merlins in fighters to be raised progressively from 1,030 shp in 1939, to 1,440 shp (at maximum boost) by early 1942. Even higher boost was made possible by additives; such fuels were referred to as 130/150 grade.

FUNDAMENTAL DESIGN DIFFERENCES

After 1938, the rearmament of the RAF was planned on the basis that orders for most of the more powerful aero-engines would be shared equally between Bristol and Rolls-Royce, both well established producers of reliable engines. The only Rolls-Royce aero-engine in series production in 1936, was the 21-litre, liquid-cooled, V-12 Kestrel, designed in 1927, but a new 27-litre V-12 was running in 1933, emerging as the Merlin II by 1937. The Merlin was a conventional poppet-valve, liquid-cooled design, logically developed from the first Rolls-Royce Eagle of 1916, and although R-R experimented with air-cooling, all their production piston engines were liquid-cooled

Production of Bristol's air-cooled radials was much greater than the output of Rolls-Royce in 1936, but output was focused on the Mercury and the Pegasus, both of them single-row engines with four poppet-valves [PVs] per cylinder, designed in 1927 and 1933 respectively. By 1931, however, it was clear that two-row engines would be needed and Roy Fedden, the brilliant and dynamic head of the Bristol engine division, with the consent of the Bristol directors and the Air Ministry, made a policy decision that all their new engines would have 'sleeve-valves'[SVs], and ceased to develop PV engines.* Unlike the reciprocating PVs, the sleeve-valve system chosen by Bristol had an extra cylindrical sleeve between each piston and its cylinder, and by making this twist as well as rise and fall, it was possible to arrange that openings in the sides of the sleeve and the cylinder coincided, allowing the ingress of the fuel/air mixture or the release of the exhaust. The mechanical ingenuity of the sleeve-actuating mechanisms and the design of the three-bearing crankshaft may be glimpsed by three illustrations from the Hercules manual.

Examples of Bristol's, single-row SV Perseus were running successfully as early as 1933, and the first (and for some time, only) two-row, SV Hercules in January 1936, but they were all hand made, because the metallurgical and machining problems of mass producing sleeves proved to be extremely difficult.[2] The sleeves had to be *thin* for heat dissipation, *hard* to stand the abrasion of their own cycloidal movements within the aluminium cylinder, and that of the

* Fedden realised that greater power would require two-row radials, and was reluctant to revert to single inlet and exhaust poppet-valves on each cylinder. The difficulties of actuating four PVs per cylinder on a two-row radial would be so severe that the use of sleeve valves, long promoted by Ricardo, looked an attractive alternative.

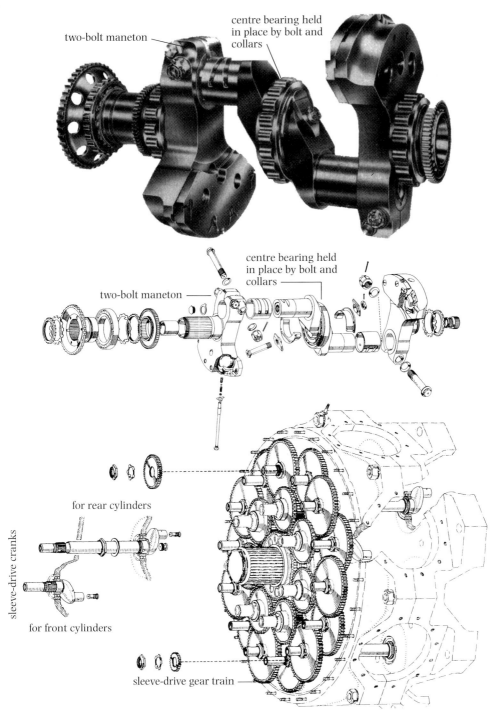

two-bolt maneton

centre bearing held
in place by bolt and
collars

two-bolt maneton

centre bearing held
in place by bolt and
collars

for rear cylinders

sleeve-drive cranks

for front cylinders

sleeve-drive gear train

The Hercules/Centaurus crankshaft and sleeve-drive assembly. The centre bearing of the
two row crankshaft had to be fitted before attaching the manetons.

piston as it moved up and down inside the sleeve, and *perfectly cylindrical* because although they were the tubes within which the piston reciprocated, they were also required to slide up and down, and turn within the light alloy cylinders, without jamming. Moreover the coefficient of expansion of the alloy steel sleeves had roughly to match those of the aluminium pistons and cylinders between which they had to be able to move freely, whether the engine was hot or cold, and this compounded the difficulties. The effort of mastering the new sleeve technology seriously aggravated Bristol's development difficulties.

The only other firm to be given substantial orders for high powered engines was Napier, whose 12-cylinder Lion engine had been a success between the wars. Napier's horizontally-opposed, 24-cylinder, sleeve-valve, liquid-cooled, twin-crankshaft Sabre engine was compact and potentially powerful, but very difficult to make, and its eventual success was ensured by invaluable help from Bristol, on sleeves.

TIME AND RELENTLESS TESTING NEEDED FOR RELIABLE HIGH PERFORMANCE

Despite the skills and experience of the Allied and Axis aero-engine companies, it usually took four or five years to bring a new engine to the point at which it could deliver high power reliably. New British engines had to pass the demanding RAF 'type test' of running at high power for 100 continuous hours, before a production order could be given. But rapid development was greatly helped by Freeman's decision to order several of each experimental engine and up to twelve of the pre-production versions, so that testing did not have to stop when one of the experimental engines failed. Even when hand-made engines passed such a test, however, the type could not safely be put into production until methods of mass-producing all its components had been successfully established. Production engines, assembled from such components, were also run for long periods on test rigs to prove their reliability. Flight testing was also very important, since the way engines and their cowlings, air-intakes, radiators, etc., were positioned and installed on the airframe could vitally affect the cooling and performance of the engine and of the aircraft concerned.

FACTORY MANAGEMENT

Bristol had encouraged overseas production of their Jupiter engines under license in the 1920s and 1930s. It readily agreed plans for shadow factories to make their engines in Britain, six in 1936 and another four in 1939, nine of them to be run by motor companies for the Air Ministry, under guidance from Bristol. Output of the PV engines grew successfully, but Bristol's management problems were greatly increased. Bristol had separated engine research and development from production as soon as rearmament started, placing the latter under Norman Rowbotham so that Fedden could concentrate the whole of his time and energy on developing and perfecting the new engines. But the consequent lack of a general works manager of the whole engine division undoubtedly had adverse side effects. Nevertheless, compared with Rolls-

Royce, twice as many Bristol engines were delivered in the second half of 1939 and roughly 35 per cent more in 1940, most of them PV types. Technical development of the new sleeve-valve engines was perhaps hampered by the need to keep Bomber Command supplied with PV engines, until the long delayed four-engined bomber airframes emerged.

Encouraged by the Air Ministry many firms made optimistic forecasts about progress, and new designs of engines and airframes were frequently put into production prematurely, output of the Hercules being specially affected. Although satisfactory ways of mass producing sleeves were not discovered until late in 1938, Fedden had assured Swinton and Weir, in March 1936, that 'he was quite definite that the problem of production [of the sleeve valve] had been solved, and that all production drawings would be cleared by October 1936'.[3] He told the Bristol board in May 1937 that further development of PV engines was not necessary. By May 1939, the Hercules production programme was ahead of design clearance, and a large number of modifications were needed for production engines. Fedden's plans for a separate plant for experimental testing, costing £300/400,000 were refused,[4] and as late as January 1940, the Chairman is on record as having '... thought it inadvisable as a matter of policy to create additional experimental plant at Government expense'.*

With only half as many development staff as Rolls-Royce,[5] the need to go on making the PV engines whilst they were trying to develop the Perseus, Hercules, Taurus and Centaurus SV engines – and put them all into production – imposed an excessive load on the Bristol development staff.† Facilities at Filton for flight testing of engines were inadequate, and Bristol was allocated the Yatesbury airfield in 1940,[6] but after visiting Rolls-Royce in March 1940, Rowbotham reported that Bristol's test facilities were in fact better than those at Derby and Crewe.[7]

The whole concept of allowing their engines to be made in shadow factories had been resisted by Rolls-Royce at first and, although this policy was changed in 1938, they were allowed to build and run the first two new factories themselves, at Crewe and Hillington. Once war began, they also agreed that Merlins should be made by Ford at Trafford Park, and Packard in Detroit. It must be emphasised that for the first few years, all four of the new factories made only the well developed and reliable Merlin.

DEVELOPMENT AND PRODUCTION POLICY: BRISTOL AND ROLLS-ROYCE

The Rolls-Royce Merlin was the most important British engine of the Second World War. Design started in 1932 and the engine flew for the first time three years later, its early development having been beset with problems, requiring major redesign in several areas.

* Both Bristol and Rolls-Royce were seriously concerned, first that allowing the Government to pay for development facilities might improve the case for nationalisation and, secondly that in the event of a cut back, future Government orders might be directed to factories constructed at Government expense, and thus starve privately financed factories of further work.
† Work on the design of the 64-litre Orion also started in August 1942.

Although the Merlin 'E' failed to complete a 100-hour test in March 1936, Freeman ordered the interim Merlin I version into limited production, to permit development of the new aircraft already committed to use the engine, including the Hurricane, Spitfire, Battle and Defiant. The first satisfactory Merlin, the Mark II, was delivered in August 1937, and rated at 1030 shp, and the Mark III for the new fighters in July 1938. The Merlin X with a two-speed supercharger, for bombers like the Whitley, Halifax and Wellington II, was first delivered in December 1938.

*   *   *

The 27-litre Merlin was relatively small and, but for the brilliance of the engineers in charge of supercharger development at Rolls-Royce, might have been superseded by larger engines such as the Vulture or the Sabre, as Freeman expected. However the huge, and relatively inefficient superchargers, designed by Ellor, and fitted to the 'R' engines of the Schnieder Trophy racing seaplanes, had shown that engine power could be increased almost exponentially with appropriate fuels, and the primitive supercharger design of their early Kestrels with its spiral airflow entry duct and fully shrouded impeller was soon modified with unrestricted airflow, turbine entry and a single-sided impeller. Developments of these were used on the later Kestrels, and the Vulture, Peregrine and early Merlins.

Supermarine Spitfire IXs over Italy. The Mk.IX had a two-speed, two-stage Merlin engine with a four-blade propeller. The after-cooler for the second stage needed a second, large, radiator; its weight counterbalanced the longer, heavier engine.

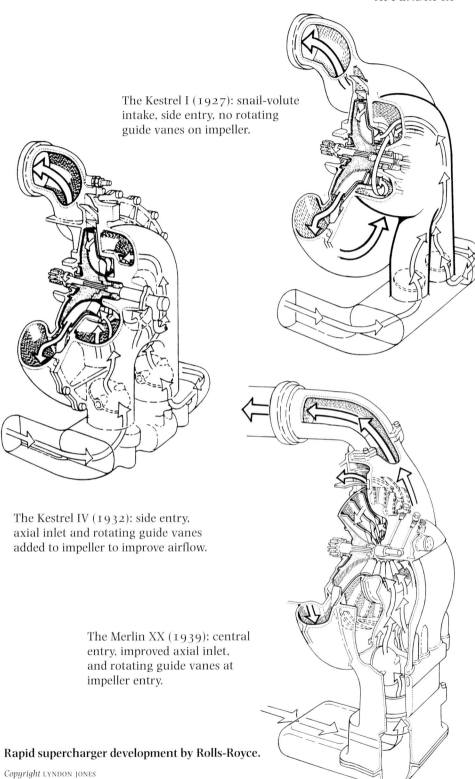

The Kestrel I (1927): snail-volute intake, side entry, no rotating guide vanes on impeller.

The Kestrel IV (1932): side entry, axial inlet and rotating guide vanes added to impeller to improve airflow.

The Merlin XX (1939): central entry, improved axial inlet, and rotating guide vanes at impeller entry.

Rapid supercharger development by Rolls-Royce.

Copyright LYNDON JONES

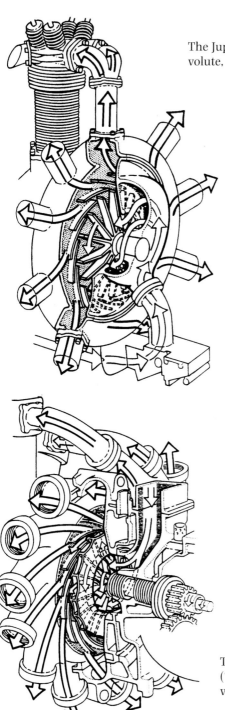

The Jupiter VII (1927): entry via snail-volute, no rotating guide vanes.

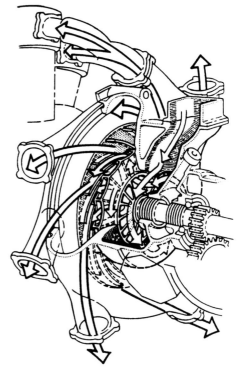

The Hercules VI (1943): entry via snail-volute, no rotating guide vanes. The basic design had remained unchanged since 1927.

The Hercules 100 (1944): axial inlet ('turbine entry') and rotating guide vanes added to impeller entry.

Very slow supercharger development at Bristol. *Copyright* LYNDON JONES

But in 1938, Hives had engaged Stanley Hooker, a brilliant young flow-dynamicist, who promptly recognised the importance of recent research by Ellor's assistant, 'Prof' Allen, and convinced Hives and Ellor that the design of even the latest supercharger on the Merlin was inefficient, and must be modified. Hives was alert and responsive, and the first Merlin with Hooker's new supercharger was running in October 1939.* Production of the Merlin XX, a two-speed version for the Hurricane II had started by June 1940, and it was chosen for the Halifax and Lancaster in December 1940. By January 1941, a shorter version, the single speed Merlin 45, was in use for the Spitfire V.

*   *   *

Meanwhile, in June 1940, Hives had set Hooker to work on a scheme for an integral, two-speed, two-stage version of the Merlin, with after-cooling, to power a high altitude bomber.† The new engine had its first flight in September 1941, and production – for Spitfire IXs – began in April 1942. The high boost pressures and air mass flow achieved by Hooker's new superchargers kept the Merlin competitive with much larger engines: the two-stage engine could climb at full boost to 23,500 ft, and take-off power grew to more than 2,000 shp for special variants.‡

Rolls-Royce recognised that, by incorporating these improvements in the Merlin, *the performance of airframes that were already in production could be rapidly enhanced without expensive and time-consuming modifications to the jigs and tools of the airframe production lines.* Work on new engine designs like the two-stroke Crecy, the sleeve-valve X-24 Pennine, and the H-24 Eagle continued, but the great majority of their 3,000 development staff worked on the continuous development of the conventional V-12 Merlin and Griffon. Besides curing the problems revealed by service experience, such as camshaft drive and reduction gear failures, separate teams under Hives maintained a continuous mechanical development of all engine components, adding improvements such as a lighter, more efficient radiator, so that the power increases made possible by improved fuels and superchargers could be exploited without reducing engine reliability.§ This policy was so successful that the time between overhauls [TBO] actually increased on the later, more powerful, engines.¶

More than 105,000 Merlins were made in Britain and a further 56,000 in America. They were used for most of the RAF's high performance aircraft of the Second World War, including Spitfires, Mosquitoes and Lancasters and for most of the American Mustangs.

---

* Bristol had access to Hooker's discoveries for 'Fedden sent a team to Derby early in the war to learn the secret, which Hives freely disclosed'. Fedden seems to have made no use of the discovery.

† The pressurised high altitude Wellington was a failure but the engine made a vital contribution to fighter performance and to PRU and bomber versions of the Mosquito.

‡ Stanley Hooker thought they were two of his four greatest achievements.

§ Cyril Lovesey, the chief development engineer for the Merlin, also recognised the need to produce illustrated brochures to explain new features to the RAF, MAP and the rest of the Rolls-Royce organisation, and these hastened their acceptance.

¶ TBO in fighters grew to 300 hours and in bombers to 420 hours – short by commercial standards but few bombers survived that long.

The Bristol Hercules was the next most important engine for the RAF, and more than 60,000 were produced. Designed early in 1935, and first run in January 1936, this 14-cylinder air-cooled, sleeve-valve radial, was hurried into production for the Stirling and the Beaufighter, with inadequate development running and flight testing. The same problem applied to the Taurus, a later, smaller engine, used for the Beaufort.

The sleeve machining solution had been found, just in time, but other serious problems emerged, such as maneton bolt failures, hydraulic locking, metal fatigue of sleeve-drive cranks, inadequate lubrication and unreliable bearings, all of which had to be resolved whilst production pressure steadily increased: production of the 'definitive' 1615 shp Hercules VI was thereby delayed.

Despite his inventiveness as an engineer, Fedden was slow to give adequate attention to the importance of supercharger efficiency. In his lecture to the RAeS[10] he claimed that it was 'bad practice' to use significant positive boost except briefly on take-off, and found the snail inlet satisfactory at pressure ratios up to 2 – his Mercury VIII had a maximum pressure ratio of 2.2. Thus

The Advisory Committee to the Minister at the Royal Aeronautical Society in 1943: Arthur Gouge (Short), Sir Ralph Sorley (Controller of R&D), Capt J. Laurence Pritchard (Secretary of the Society and of the Committee), visitor Dr Theodore P. Wright (Administrator, Civil Aeronautics, USA), Sir Stafford Cripps (Minister of Aircraft Production), Sir Roy Fedden (Chairman), Sydney Camm (Hawker), Rex Pierson (Vickers), Dr Leslie Aitchison (James Booth and University of Birmingham) and C.C. Walker (de Havilland). The missing member was Roy Chadwick (Avro). Hives had resigned from the Committee in 1941.

developments of the 'snail volute' which he introduced to Bristol from the RAE in 1927 must have seemed adequate to him. Even what his staff told him of Hooker's achievements, after they had visited Rolls-Royce at Derby in the early months of the war, did not convert him to the need to adopt the unrestricting axial entry and rotating guide vanes used in Rolls-Royce engines for the previous 8 to 10 years, instead of the snail volute.

Fedden had used an extra, separate, shaft-driven supercharger when special Pegasus engines in a Bristol airframe captured the world altitude record in 1938, but when the experimental Hercules VIII was designed in this way, it suffered from incurable surging. In 1939 he sought the help of the RAE, and by 1941, Hayne Constant had firmly advised changing from the 1927 'snail volute' to a turbine-entry alternative.

Even this failed to convince Fedden – or perhaps the senior managers on whom he had begun to rely – that the technical and manufacturing upheaval involved for such radical changes to the engine, would improve its performance enough to be worth the effort, and the inevitable production delays.

It is difficult to avoid the conclusion that by 1941, just when his development team were faced with the need for a number of urgent and difficult modifications, the focus of Fedden's attention had been diverted from the further development of the Hercules, Bristol's most important engine, by his numerous other responsibilities.

Fedden had been asked, in July 1941, to become chairman of the RAeS Advisory Committee to Moore-Brabazon, the Minister of Aircraft Production, and the Bristol Board, perhaps unwisely, agreed to this prestigious but time-consuming diversion of Fedden's attention at what was obviously a critical development period of the vitally important Hercules. It is also possible that in the period before Freeman returned as Chief Executive, MAP had put Bristol under such pressure to maintain an increasing supply of Hercules engines, that their production and development staff chose to defer any type of redesign that would check production of 'finished engines'.*

The change came in the spring of 1942 when members of his middle management, having experimented without authority, went over the heads of their seniors to tell Fedden that their experiments had indicated that supercharger redesign and other changes would greatly improve the high altitude performance of the Hercules. Fedden promptly began work on redesign,† but by then the yawning gap between his insistence on total control of research and development on Bristol engines, and his actual achievements with the Hercules, had exasperated his Board. He was dismissed long before the redesign work he had put in train was finished.

Development and production of Bristol engines were combined under Rowbotham in October 1942, just before Freeman returned to MAP,[11] and

---

* The reluctance of MAP to authorize any modifications to airframes or aero-engines which would restrict production probably affected Bristol more then Rolls-Royce, because the Hercules was a later design with much technical innovation.

† This is confirmed in letters and discussions with the late Peter Ware and Dr Alex Moulton CBE.

besides the redesign of the supercharger, other measures were initiated to improve the performance and reliability of the Hercules. These included modifications to piston rings, better sleeve finish, and a more powerful oil pump which solved its lubrication problems. Preliminary tests on all these had been completed by 9 March 1943.[12] Work on Fedden's alternative proposals, such as the Hercules VIII and exhaust turbo-chargers, were then dropped.[13]

Hercules 100 engines incorporating these changes and improvements were test flown in December 1943, and in quantity production by mid-1944; the full potential of the engine was thus realised. Its performance at altitude was transformed by the changes,[14] and wheras a Hercules Mark VI gave 1,455 bhp at 12,000 ft, the Hercules 100, operated with the same boost pressure and RPM, gave 1,590 bhp at 19,500 ft:[15] 10% more power, with a vital 7,500 ft gain in altitude.

> Had this supercharger development taken place [earlier] the effectiveness of [aircraft with] Hercules engines would have been improved considerably . . .[16]

THE CENTAURUS AND THE GRIFFON

Design of the 54-litre Bristol Centaurus started in 1937 and of the 37-litre R-R Griffon I in December 1938. Beaverbrook slowed development work on both of them in 1940, and flatly rejected the offer by General Motors to make the Centaurus in America. Work on the Centaurus in Britain was resumed late in 1940, but it weighed more than 2,600 lb and was too heavy to replace either the Hercules or the Merlin[‡] unless airframes were radically altered.[17] Output of any airframe ceased for months when a factory had to be re-equipped to make a different design, and since output never satisfied the relentless demands of the Service, the need for better performance was best achieved by improvements to established engines. Very few completely new airframes were chosen for mass production after 1940. The Warwick airframe was altered to accept a Centaurus, and it could be easily substituted for the 2,450 lb Sabre, in the Tempest II, but even so, service use was long delayed by Centaurus engine cooling troubles* and the defects of the Warwick airframe.

The Griffon I had to be redesigned to save weight, and its length curtailed to simplify its installation as a Merlin replacement in a Spitfire 12, but this version of the engine lacked power at height. Following the success of the Merlin 61, development of the *two-stage* Griffon 61 involved a major redesign which lengthened it: the Spitfire airframe had then to be radically altered to 'balance' the longer, heavier engine,[†] delaying the first deliveries of the other marks of Griffon Spitfire until October 1943.

---

* Bristol's engine installation team made use of the 24 ft 'full scale' wind tunnel at Farnborough for the Buckingham's Centaurus engine nacelle tests in 1942/43, but don't seem to have made much use of it until then. Much was also learnt from a BMW radial captured on an undamaged German aircraft. The installation of which was far in advance of British practice, and showed the RAE and Bristol what could be done.

† The two-stage Griffon was 300lb heavier than the Merlin 61.

THE UNSUCCESSFUL ENGINES

Rolls-Royce asked to stop work on their single crank-shaft, 24-cylinder Vulture in 1940, because they wished to concentrate on the Merlin, and because it was overweight, and unreliable.

Reliability improved, but the fact that it developed less power than expected, and weighed over 2,400 lb meant that major increases in power output would be needed, involving significant redesign*. Production of their 21-litre Peregrine was also stopped: it was smaller than the Merlin, lacked its development potential, and Rolls-Royce wished to focus their resources on the Merlin and Griffon. Bristol stopped development of their 25-litre, single-row Perseus which was too low powered for military success, and the two-row Taurus, designed after the Hercules but in service seven months earlier. The Taurus was very unreliable, and apart from its cooling problems and its weak 'hairpin' maneton, there was a unsuspected but narrow band of engine speed at which periodic vibration was excessive, causing destructive failures.

OTHER ENGINES

Work on the underpowered two-row Armstrong Siddeley 'Tiger', and multi-row 'Deerhound' radials stopped when their factory was bombed in 1941, and the company only made small 'Cheetahs' for Ansons and Oxfords thereafter. Radial engines to Gnome-Rhône designs, made under licence by Alvis, were rejected because they were overweight and underpowered, so Alvis eventually filled their expensive new factory with sub-contract and repair work on Bristol and Rolls-Royce engines.[18] Wolseley radials from the Nuffield private venture factory, were rejected for the same reasons.

The Fairey P-24 Monarch: two crankshaft, vertically-opposed, 24-cylinder, liquid-cooled, poppet-valve engine; 51 litres, 4-speed, two-stage supercharger, 2,240hp.

Bulman probably influenced Freeman's contentious decision to accept Fairey's offer to design and produce four 51-litre, 24-cylinder H-shaped engines with two crankshafts and four-speed, two-stage superchargers, at a cost of £9,000 each,[19†] and support was also given

---

* The need to attach a master and three slave con-rods to each web of the single crank-shaft imposed a critical load on the big-end bolts. Engine power could not therefore be safely increased by running the engine at higher revs, or greater boost pressure.

† Their designer, Graham Forsythe, had left the Ministry in 1931 to work for Fairey, and after designing a twelve-cylinder V-12 engine, driving a single crankshaft, he changed to a more advanced, H-shaped 'double' engine concept, the 'Prince III' with 16 cylinders, and the 'Monarch' with 24. Each set of eight or twelve vertically opposed cylinders drove a separate crankshaft, but they were mounted on a common crankcase, to drive co-axial, contra-rotating propellers. Several of the large, 51-litre, 24-cylinder 'Monarch' engines were made, and it might have been easier to develop than the Sabre.

for the 500shp de Havilland 'Gipsy 12' for the Albatross airliner, and for Napier's other H-shaped, 24-cylinder engine, the air-cooled, 17-litre, 1000hp Napier 'Dagger', both of them designed by Major Halford. Freeman was determined to keep the Napier design and production teams going, lest some of the new engines from Rolls-Royce or Bristol were failures,[20] and the Napier Sabre eventually succeeded. Freeman had great faith in Halford's ability, and the early Sabres, hand made by the very experienced work force at Napier's Acton factory, passed their type test in 1939. But the Acton factory was too small to produce Sabres in adequate numbers, and once the engine had been ordered in quantity, a new shadow factory was set up to make it, at Walton near Liverpool. Napier, however, had only about 500 research and development staff, and the Acton management were unable to spare nearly enough managers and foremen to bring the Netherton factory into efficient production. Apart from problems with 'sleeves' as at Bristol, the early engines were often badly made,* and disastrously unreliable. Freeman was inclined to blame Halford,† (perhaps unfairly, since he was a designer not a 'works manager'), but, as late as 1942, he continued to plan the use of Sabres in many of the more advanced designs. After Rod Banks had been put in charge of the Sabre's development, and insisted on help with sleeves from Bristol, the management of the Netherton factory was transferred to English Electric, and production of reliable Sabres was eventually achieved. The Sabre Typhoon and Tempest fighters were successful additions to the Tactical Air Force.

THE PRE-EMINENCE OF ROLLS-ROYCE

Ernest Hives, the General Manger of Rolls-Royce, was one of the very few people Freeman admired without reservations. Helped by the full backing of his Board, Hives had the perception to concentrate most of the formidable resources of Rolls-Royce on two engines, which greatly simplified the expansion of production, when three new factories in Britain and one in America, (making Packard Merlins) came into production.

Although his delivery forecasts sometimes slipped, Freeman trusted Hives as he had trusted Tedder in 1938–1940, and was in turn greatly respected by Hives. Even when Freeman was VCAS, they wrote to each other frequently and frankly, and met occasionally, although it was 'against the rules', and Freeman was deeply impressed by – and immensely grateful for – the speed with which Rolls-Royce brought into production the regular improvements in engine power which culminated in the two-stage Merlin and Griffon engines. Merlins powered the Mosquito and 95 per cent of the Lancasters, and, apart from the period of about nine months before deliveries of Spitfire IXs began, when the new German FW 190 was superior to the Spitfire Vs, successive Rolls-Royce piston engines in the various marks of Spitfire, gave them a qualitative edge over the German fighters throughout the war.

* The failure of some new engines was traced to the presence of 'swarf' – the metal residue from machining operations – which meant that supervision was inadequate.
† Freeman said; 'He designed a brilliant engine but did not know how to put it together'. (Nelson tapes)

By September 1942, Freeman realised that the Spitfire VIIIs and IXs and the Merlin Mustang, (a totally unexpected rival for the Spitfire), all of them fitted with two-stage Merlin 61 types of engine, and later, the Spitfire XIV with a two-stage Griffon, were likely to meet the Allied needs for superior land-based combat fighters for the next two years, and indeed they did so. Moreover, once the major Merlin development period was over, Rolls-Royce had the resources to work on new projects. When Freeman discovered, in 1942, that Rolls-Royce was developing only their 12-cylinder, two-stroke 'Crecy', he asked them to tackle his 'shopping list' for engines.[21] This mentioned:

1. jets for the future,
2. a new 2,500hp engine with approximately the same frontal area as the Sabre, with no more than a 15 per cent increase in weight and the prospect that after development it would produce 3,000hp without an increase in weight. This resulted in the 3,500hp Rolls-Royce Eagle – which weighed nearly 3,900 lb!
3. the Merlin 61, for Spitfires and Mosquitoes, and
4. the Griffon 61 before the fighting season began in 1943.

Rolls-Royce promptly started the development of a new Eagle, (their version of the Sabre, a 24-cylinder, sleeve valve, liquid-cooled 'H' formation engine with two crankshafts) in July 1942, and an 'X' configuration, air-cooled alternative, the Pennine in June 1943. Production of two-stage Merlins and Griffons steadily increased, and once Rolls-Royce had taken over the Rover factories, they soon produced Welland reverse-flow Whittle engines of adequate power for the Meteor I in 1944, and their Derwent I, a better, 'straight-through' version of the Welland for the Meteor III. Their 'Nene', with 4,000–5,000lb thrust emerged by 1945. Freeman told Elizabeth,

> That man Hives is the best man I have ever come across for many a year. God knows where the RAF would have been without him. He cares for nothing except the defeat of Germany and he does all his work to that end, living a life of unending labour.[22]

The Rolls-Royce Nene engine – the first complete R-R design of a jet engine and the first jet engine in the world to give 5,000lb of thrust.

TOP: **The Halifax II**; two hundred of this version were ordered from English Electric because the Handley Page factories could not cope with the orders. The Mk.II had a dorsal turret and extra fuel capacity, but these modifications increased the weight and reduced operational performance.

CENTRE: **The Halifax III**, with the front turret removed and the Hercules engines positioned so that the airscrew 'boss' was well below the wing.

LEFT: **The new rear turret.** With twin 0.5 in. Brownings supplied from the USA, Rose Brothers designed a fine new rear turret which could be retro-fitted on existing Lancaster turret rings. It was first used operationally in June 1944. Only 227 were made.

The design and development of airframes for the RAF

Until 1938/39, specifications for British military aircraft were constrained by the fact that airfields were small, and lacked hard runways. It was potentially dangerous for the light, and sometimes under-powered, aircraft of that time to take off or land in any direction except 'up wind'. Specifications for new aircraft, issued prior to 1939, therefore allowed for the presence of hangers, trees or houses near or within the airfield boundaries, and included minimum take-off, and maximum landing distances, 'over a 50ft screen'. The limitations were applied to aircraft *with full load*, so that existing aerodromes could be used, and fuel and cargo need not be jettisoned.

All pre-war designs of 'leak-proof' fuel tanks failed because of the way they were tested. The most likely cause of failure in peace time was a crash, so the standard RAE test was to fill the tanks with water and drop them off a roof, on to concrete! Early combat showed that most future leaks were likely to be caused by gun-fire, and self-sealing linings were soon devised.

BOMBER AIRCRAFT

By 1936, prototypes of the twin-engined Wellington, Whitley and Hampden were being made to a 1932 specification and Vickers and Handley Page were working on a larger twin-engined aircraft to the B.1/35 specification. Most of them had stressed skin, monocoque airframes, for which the metal skin formed an essential component of the stress-bearing structure, but Vickers, advised by Barnes Wallis, designer of the Vickers R-100 airship, was making airframes on the same geodetic principles; their single-engined Wellesley was now obsolescent, but a larger twin-engined bomber was to be called the Wellington,[1] and proved to be the only pre-war bomber airframe to be kept in production throughout the war.*

Meanwhile, Freeman had issued two new specifications for even heavier bombers, the large B.12/36 with four 800–1000hp engines, and the smaller, twin-engined P.13/36, to use the new 1,800hp Rolls-Royce Vulture. Both were to be bomber-transports, and there was emphasis on multi-role performance, and size limitations. The aircraft were to have multi-gun turrets in the nose and tail, a retractable ventral turret, but no dorsal turret. The fuselages had to be large enough to accommodate twenty-four and fifteen armed troops

---

* The geodetic structures were so flexible that the airframes had to be covered with fabric, and any factory chosen to make a Wellington needed to be equipped with special machine tools, Lang lathes, rolling mills for machining the special geodetic sections, and other special milling machines for the fishplates which held the lattice-work together.[2]

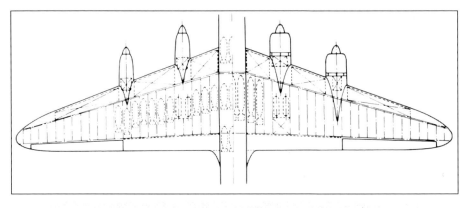

Supermarine's B.12/36 design had a single spar wing like that used for the Spitfire, and provision for storage of bombs in a single tier in the fuselage, and in the wing behind the swept-back main spar. Fuel tanks were in the leading edge of the swept-back wing, and two four-wheeled undercarriage units reduced the space necessary for retraction.

respectively, and needed level floors and 'push out' exit windows, and they had to stay afloat for several hours in the event of having to 'ditch' in the sea.

When dismantled, their components had to be small enough to fit into the packing cases used by the Air Ministry, the dimensions of which were based on standard gauge railway wagons, the wingspan was restricted to 99ft to fit existing hangers, and both types of aircraft had to be able to operate from grass airfields. The largest bombs specified were 2,000lb armour-piercing types, but aircraft to the P.13/36 design had to be able to carry torpedoes, so needed long fuselage bomb-bays. P.13/36 aircraft were expected to be lighter and easier to maintain than the B.12/36 alternatives, but both called for much greater bomb-carrying capacities than all previous RAF bombers.*

Mitchell forecast that his design for the Supermarine B.12/36 would cruise at 300mph, with 14,000lb of bombs and fuel for a range of 2,000 miles. The firm and its factory were much too small to cope with quantity production of

---

* Apart from the planned normal load of 2,000lb, an overload of 4,000lb, (and a possible load of 8,000lb which might be needed if the aircraft's take-off was 'catapult-assisted'), there was also mention of maximum permissable bomb load of 14,000lb and provision for this was made in both the B.12/36 designs which were subsequently chosen.

such a large aeroplane, but Freeman had such regard for Mitchell's genius that he pressed for its acceptance on the basis that Supermarine would construct the prototypes and the drawings and jigs that would be needed when production lines were set up elsewhere. He warned that its great size might make it necessary to involve three or four other firms in its production, each making separate parts of the aircraft.[2]* Two prototypes were ordered from Supermarine on 5 January 1937,[3] on condition that details of Supermarine's preliminary work for the F.37/35 twin-engined, cannon-gun fighter,[4]† were given to Westland.‡ The other B.12/36 prototype was ordered from Shorts;[5] Handley Page and Avro were chosen to make P.13/36 aircraft,[6] the former stopping work on their B.1/35 bomber design.

BRIEF COMMENTS ON THE MORE IMPORTANT AIRCRAFT

The Wellington prototype was too small to accept power-operated turrets, and redesign had started before the original aircraft broke-up in mid-air. The larger aircraft was a success, and its performance and ceiling was steadily improved by bigger engines, so that by 1942, the Mark X with Hercules engines could carry 4,500 lb of bombs 1,500 miles. The backbone of Bomber Command well into 1942, Wellingtons still equipped the majority of OTUs as late as March 1945. More than 11,400 were made.

The Whitley's original 'Tiger' radial engines were inadequate, but it was transformed when Merlin Xs were substituted. The Mark V could carry 8,000 lb of bombs 600 miles and 5,500 lb, 1,370 miles. Slower than the Wellington, with a lower ceiling at full load, it was not used by Bomber Command after April 1942, but 1,680 were made.

The Hampden prototype's fuselage was too slim, and the gun positions of the larger production aircraft were manually operated. Its range was 1,200 miles with 4,000 lb of bombs. Successfully adapted for minelaying and torpedo dropping, 1240 were built by 1941; the Hampden continued in operation until 1944.

The Blenheim prototype was faster than any of the RAF's fighters in 1936, but the aircraft was obsolescent by 1941: the bomb-bay carried only 1,000 lb. Production continued until designs and jigs and tool for alternative aircraft were available.

The Beaufort was an alternative to the Botha, but with Bristol Taurus engines: its comparative failure was largely due to the unreliability and inadequate

* Both prototypes of the Supermarine B.12/36 were destroyed, half built, by a German air raid in September, 1940, and further work on Mitchell's design was abandoned.

† Mitchell had, as usual, produced a superb looking design for Supermarine, with six cannon mounted in the wing roots between the engines and the fuselage, three on each side, to allow for a tricycle undercarriage. Powered by two Merlins, he estimated its top speed at 465 mph.

‡ The Operational Research Committee (ORC) of the Air Ministry was aware that 20 mm cannon could cause more damage at longer range than .303 in. machine-guns, but feared that the recoil shock of the cannons would be too great for them to be mounted in the wings of single-engined fighters, hence the 1937 specification for a cannon-fighter, as a twin-engine aircraft with the cannon mounted in or near the fuselage.

power of the engines. Carrying a torpedo, or 1,700 lb of bombs, it was used for low level day strikes against shipping, with appalling losses in that role.

The Beaufighter, the fighter version of the Beaufort with Merlin and later Hercules engines, was armed with four 20mm cannon. Unsuitable for daytime combat against the latest German day-fighters, it proved to be a good interim night-fighter, an adequate long-range escort fighter for convoy work, and an admirable 'strike' aircraft for operations against enemy shipping.

THE HEAVY BOMBERS

The B.12/36 Stirling was the first of the new heavy bombers. Its airframe was 7,000–8,000 lb heavier than the Halifax or the Lancaster, and hampered by a design fault – a three degree error in the angle at which the wing was attached to the fuselage. Rather than alter the wing root to make it possible to take off with a full load, Shorts lengthened the undercarriage! Its operational ceiling with a full load was officially only about 14,000 ft, and its 740 mile range compared badly with the Halifax's, 1,000, and the Lancaster's, 1,600. Apart from the extra weight, its Hercules VI and XVI engines did not develop adequate power at high altitudes: production of the bomber version of the Stirling ended before Hercules 100s were available.[7] 1,748 were made as bombers.

Hindsight is always 20:20. The Stirling was ordered in January 1937, had a maximum speed of 270 mph, and could carry a bomb load of 14,000 lb, but it is compared with the Lancaster, which also carried 14,000 lb, and was

The Short Stirling was the first of the new heavy bombers. A basic design fault meant that the undercarriage had to be lengthened to allow 'take-off' at full load.

ordered in August 1940, not the Harrow, maximum speed 200 mph, which was ordered in 1935, and carried 3,000 lb.

The Manchester was built to the P.13/36 specification, but as soon as it was clear that its Vulture engines were unlikely to be capable of greater power without a radical redesign, Freeman reluctantly accepted that production of the Vulture must stop.[8] Replacement by the 54-litre Centaurus was seriously considered,[9] but Fedden warned that production versions of the unproven Centaurus were unlikely to be available before mid-1942, even if the engine had no problems.[10]*

Knowing that plenty of Merlins would be available by mid-1941, and convinced by Chadwick, Avro's designer, that his factories could be switched to a four-Merlin version with little loss of time and at a minimum cost in new jigs and tools, Freeman favoured the Merlin alternative: Manchester production could continue until Lancaster output began in 1941, but only 198 Manchesters were made.

The Lancaster There was strong opposition from Farren, by then the Director of Technical Development (DTD) at MAP,[11] when Freeman chose the four Merlin variant, but the industrial logic of keeping up production at the Manchester factories was too strong, and Beaverbrook agreed to order Lancaster prototypes in August 1940. The airframe was excellent, and designed for mass production, so the prototype Lancaster was flying by January, 1941, and the first production Lancasters were being assembled at Woodford in August 1941, barely a year later. Chadwick wrote thanking Freeman for the:

> ... help and the confidence which you placed in me when you arranged a year ago that the Lancaster should be designed and built. I am sure that it must be a great satisfaction to you that this valuable addition to the strength of the RAF has been produced in so short a time. I am confident that the Lancaster will prove to be the outstanding aircraft of the war and it is, I feel, largely due to you that it has come into existence.

Chadwick claimed that it was capable of still further development, including the ability to carry a total bomb load of 15,000 lb for 1,000 miles, and be modified to load 8,000 and 12,000 lb bombs: 'the necessary strong points had already been incorporated'.[12]

By 1942, it was obvious that the Lancaster was by far the best of the heavy bombers, and once he was back in control of MAP, Freeman agreed to switch factories making Stirling bombers, and some of the Wellington factories, to Lancasters. Re-equipping English Electric's Halifax factory at Preston for Lancasters as well, would have taken at least nine months, and involved the unacceptable loss of nearly 1,200 Halifaxes, so it remained in production. 6,939 Lancasters were made by the end of 1945.

The Halifax was the first of the twin-engined P.13/36 aircraft to be altered

---

* Fedden offered eight engines by May 1941, four more by August 1941 and eight more by January 1942.

on Freeman's instructions, to a four-engine configuration,[13] and the second multi-engined aircraft to be fitted with Merlins. By 1941/42, it was obvious that the performance of the Lancaster was much better, and since they were both roughly similar in weight and wing area, and fitted with Merlin XX engines, the difference caused much concern. Service tests proved that a fully loaded Halifax I climbed slowly, had a very poor performance above 13,000 ft and could only just maintain height at 17,000ft. Evasive action, or any abrupt use of the controls resulted in immediate loss of height of at least 1000ft.[14]* Modifications were essential.

Some of the Merlin Halifax's problems were caused by the way the engines were installed by Handley Page. Avro had designed the twin-Vulture installation for the Manchester, but when the Merlin Lancaster alternative was agreed in August 1940, Avro wisely accepted the advice of Rolls-Royce† and installed the Merlins well forward and below the leading edge of the wing. The nacelles for the Merlins on the Halifax were shorter, and sited higher, bringing the propellers very close to the leading edge of the wings. The high thrust line disturbed the airflow over the wing, causing loss of lift, whilst the proximity of the propellers to the wing's leading edge interfered with the efficiency of the propeller blades, causing heavy vibration, and reduction gear failures.‡

When Rolls-Royce fitted Merlin 65s to a Halifax IV in 1943 (in Lancaster type nacelles), they raised its ceiling, and increased its top speed by 60mph to 324mph at 19,000ft,[15] but there were not enough two-stage Merlins to put this version into production. Plenty of Hercules would become available when Stirling bomber production stopped, so Hercules VI, and later Hercules XVI engines were fitted on Halifax IIIs and VIs, installed with a lower thrust line in longer nacelles. Despite the poor performance of the Hercules at height, they gave the early Halifax IIIs a better performance than the Merlin version, when the carburettor air intakes were resited.[16] The subsequent re-design of the Hercules supercharger and re-timing of the engine raised the ceiling, and maximum and cruising speeds of the later Halifax VIs significantly,§ and some crews found that they easily outclimbed Lancasters. 5,654 Halifaxes were built.

THE IMPORTANCE OF HEIGHT

Aircraft with a high operating ceiling suffered lower casualties from 'flak' and night fighters. Published data of the ceilings, ranges and capacity of the three heavy bombers seldom reflects their actual performance, but most Merlin Lancasters could be relied upon to attain a ceiling of about 22–24,000ft with a full load. A fully loaded Merlin Halifax could barely maintain 16,000ft, and even after the installation of Hercules engines, they were restricted, as late as

* Confirmed by a report from the Operational Research department about Halifax Is of No. 5 Group.
† Rolls-Royce had by then designed the Merlin engine nacelles for the Beaufighter II.
‡ Gears which linked the engine to the propeller shaft so that the propeller did not have to revolve at engine speed.
§ It is significant that Barnes quotes a ceiling of 24,000ft for both the Halifax III and VI, the latter with Hercules 100 engines, but gives no data for the Merlin Marks I, II and V.

March 1944, to carrying only incendiary bombs which were bulky, and much lighter than explosive bombs: a full load was less than half that of a Lancaster with explosive bombs.[17] Even then they were referred to as 'ground bait' for the German fighters[18]. When the Hercules 100 at last became available, their ceiling rose by some 7–8,000ft. The low ceiling of the Stirling made it so vulnerable that it was taken off main force raids in November, 1943.

OTHER GEODETIC AIRCRAFT

The Warwick, designed to a 1935 specification for Vulture or Centaurus engines, had to be fitted with Hercules or American 'Double Wasps' until reliable versions of the Centaurus became available in 1943. Until then it was underpowered; none were used as bombers. More than 800 Warwicks were made, and used by Transport and Coastal Commands.

Freeman also ordered prototypes of the **Windsor**, a new, four-engined, geodetic heavy bomber, which Vickers forecast would be faster than the Lancaster at economical-cruising speed, but carry a smaller bomb load, and have a shorter range. The innovation of fitting remote-controlled guns in the rear of the engine nacelles, which might have solved the problem of siting 20 mm cannon near the centre of lift, failed because the flexibility of the geodetic airframe made it impossible to aim them accurately. Work on the aircraft stopped after one of the Windsor prototypes crashed.

FREEMAN'S RELENTLESS QUEST FOR QUALITY

Freeman's appointment as VCAS did not distract him from the long term need for better aircraft, and within three weeks, he was asking Hives to modify Merlins to increase the operating height of PRU Spitfires,[19] and pushing for important developments like two-stage Merlin, Hercules or Griffon engines,* a pressure cabin, high altitude fighter by Westland, a twin Whittle [jet] fighter by Gloster, a faster Beaufighter and a high altitude Wellington.[20] He was loath to suggest new designs of airframes to MAP, on the grounds that anything new would take too long to mature, but he stressed that unless the RAF 'aimed high', MAP would reply that '. . . the improvement is so small that it cannot be worth while producing it'. Amongst airframe variants, his 1942 list included Mosquitoes with Merlin 61s and at least three new marks of Spitfires.[21]

FIGHTERS

Although Hawkers had anticipated an order for 1,000 Hurricanes in 1936, only four had been delivered by the end of June 1938, and production was running at three per week. The Hurricane's airframe was easier to make

* Rolls-Royce was the only British company to produce engines with successful two-stage integral superchargers. In the USA, Pratt & Witney, made a successful, integral, two-stage supercharger for their R-2800, and turbo-superchargers, driven by exhaust pressure, were added to the radial engines of the B-17 and B-24 bombers, and the Allisons of the P-38 fighter. No Allisons with integral two-stage superchargers were available during the war.

than the Spitfire's, but Hawkers were still producing fabric-covered wings as late as November 1938, and attempting to finish their contract to supply biplane Hinds to Iraq, at the expense of Hurricane production. Few changes were made to the Hurricane airframe, all improvements to the 12,754 that were produced coming from increases in engine power. Superseded in Fighter Command by the Spitfire in 1941, they were used in the Middle East and India, and as bombers, (well escorted) over Europe, until 1944. Fitted with the Merlin 22, it had a better performance at height than the Allison-powered American alternatives like the P-39 and P-40.

The Spitfire was faster, and apart from difficulties with fabric-covered ailerons at high speed, it had handled almost perfectly from the start. Mitchell's thin, single spar design for its famous elliptical wing was light, strong and most efficient aerodynamically, and could be fitted with the eight machine-guns called for by the 1934 specification, but it was desperately difficult to make, and by November 1938, there were more than 180 completed Spitfire fuselages and only twenty-one finished aeroplanes.

The initial contract for 310 should have been completed by April 1939, but the 150th aircraft was actually delivered three weeks later. Production was so bad that an order for another 1,000 placed in April 1939 was cut in June, but reinstated in July, as hopes for the Whirlwind faded. More than 300 Spitfires had been built and tested by 3 September 1939, however, and the total reached 1,000 by August 1940. The performance of Hurricanes and Spitfires was enhanced, first by 100 octane fuel and variable pitch propellers in May, 1940, and then by new engines, with better superchargers. Work on the Spitfire III airframe to accept the longer, two-speed Merlin XX slowed when MAP warned that few Merlin XXs would be available for fighters, so Supermarine compromised, and fitted the *single speed* Merlin 45, with the new supercharger*, giving an extra 300–400 hp to the interim Mark Vas and Vbs that first came into service in March, 1941. Deliveries of both Spitfire Vs and Hurricane IIs, however, were well below MAP forecasts at first.

The first batch of experimental Merlin 61 engines, with two-stage superchargers, which Freeman had ordered in 1939, had been under test for some time, also the early Griffons, and in September, 1941, Freeman must have been delighted by the news that an unarmed Spitfire III, temporarily fitted with a Merlin 61, achieved a maximum speed of 422mph on its first flight, a spectacular 45mph gain on the Mark V. The Spitfire Vc airframe, then being made at Castle Bromwich, was adapted to accept the production versions of the 'Merlin 61' engine, and designated Mark IX: it needed an extra radiator for its after-cooler and a four bladed propeller to absorb the extra power. Freeman told Hives '. . . it is vital to us to get the Spitfire IX into service at the earliest possible date. . .' , and the first production Mark IXs arrived on the

---

* The importance of Stanley Hooker's contribution to the Rolls-Royce supercharger designs cannot be overemphasised. His new two-speed, single stage 'blowers' achieved quite exceptional efficiency, whilst his two-stage version lifted the performances of Mosquitoes, Mustangs and Spitfires well above their enemy and allied rivals.

Squadrons in June 1942. It was the Merlin 61 and the Supermarine design team, which stretched Mitchell's astonishing 1935 Spitfire so that in 1942, the performance of the Mark IX more than matched the new German FW190 at height, and kept the RAF ahead.

The Griffon Spitfires. Hoping that the 36-litre RR Griffon engine would further improve the Spitfire,[22] Freeman kept this version on the programme, telling Lemon and Tedder on 27 January 1940, to plan for its introduction late in 1941, 'with six 0.5in. guns'.[23] His intuition was not mistaken, helped no doubt by the news that the first Griffon II had gone on test on 21 November 1939, by his growing respect for Hives and by the first class support he was getting from Rolls-Royce, Supermarine started work on this advanced variant of the Spitfire airframe. Despite Beaverbrook, Supermarine worked on the Griffon variant (without a contract) until Freeman left MAP in November 1940, but progress was slow because their small design team was busy with improvements to Merlin aircraft. The first Griffon Spitfire eventually flew on 27 November 1941, a low-level version, the Mark XII, with a 'single-stage' Griffon II.B, was ordered in July 1942, and reached Squadrons in March 1943, proving fast enough to catch the Luftwaffe's 'tip-and-run' FW190s on their low-level raids: Spitfires with Griffon 61s were not available until 1944.

The Spitfire airframe was aerodynamically efficient, and capable of significant development, but Freeman well knew that the brilliant engineers at Rolls-Royce had rescued the RAF– and eventually the USAAF – time and again, by producing new versions of engines for existing airframes.

THE NEW FIGHTERS

The Hurricane and the Spitfire had both been designed in 1935, but the new fighters to replace them, some under development since 1937, were not at first successful.*

The Whirlwind. To keep this fighter as small and light as possible, Petter used Peregrine engines, ducted radiators, and magnesium, (an inflammable metal normally used for incendiary bombs), for the butt-jointed skin. To cut down 'drag', he routed the exhaust pipes not only *inside* the magnesium engine cowlings,† but actually *through* the petrol tanks in the wings. Happily, when the shrouding of an exhaust pipe on the prototype failed, it merely burned through an aileron control rod without setting fire to the petrol. The prototype handled badly in the air, the rudder had to be redesigned to mitigate the consequences of its offset hinges, and the tailplane given an acorn fillet where it joined the fin. The modifications succeeded, but when production of the Peregrine stopped, the Whirlwind contract was cancelled.

---

* The Whirlwinds were cancelled, the Beaufighter was too slow and unwieldy for day-time combat in Northern Europe, and progress on the two Hawker fighters was so disappointing that before the end of 1940, Freeman knew that he must continue to rely on the Spitfire Mk.II and the Hurricane Mk.II, for at least another year.

† Most magnesium was used for incendiary bombs!

The Hawker Tornado/Typhoon/Tempest Series. When development of the Vulture ceased, Hawker's plans for their new fighter seemed to depend on the success of the Sabre-engined Typhoon which first flew in February 1940. The cockpit hood of the first Typhoon obscured the pilot's rear view and Freeman sent it back for modification, complaining to Sinclair that the Air Staff's efforts to make aircraft operationally fit were unsupported, because design and development are separated from production,

> ... under a Minister who will be judged on quantity rather than quality. ... I hope that the rear view of the Typhoon will be the last incident in which the Air Staff encounter obstruction to their requirements.[24]

Reluctant to become wholly dependant on the Sabre version, the front fuselage of a Tornado was lengthened, given the tail and wings of a Typhoon, and fitted with a Centaurus. It flew for the first time on 23 October 1941, but was 10mph slower than a Typhoon. Given a later engine and a four-bladed propeller it eventually achieved 430mph.[25] But whilst the nose of a standard Typhoon airframe was too short for a radial engine, the long-nosed Sabre Tempest airframe was able to accept one with little modification*, and, likely to be faster and handle better than the Typhoon. Freeman had ordered two Tempest airframes in November 1941, and early in 1942, he stopped work on six modified Centaurus-*Typhoon* airframes,† and ordered four more *Tempest* prototypes, two with Centaurus and two with Griffon engines.‡

Typhoon deliveries lagged in 1941 and 1942, whilst Napiers struggled with the problem of mass-producing Sabres, and Hawkers investigated, and eventually identified, the design fault which had caused the tails of some Typhoons to break off in flight.[26]§ The structural problem was cured, but the Typhoon airframe had other defects,¶ and early in 1942, full of doubts about Sabre development, and fears that Napiers would let the RAF down, Freeman told Sorley to plan for 'Centaurus' Tempests as a replacement for the Sabre-engined Typhoon,[27] and to step up Centaurus production from 250 to 950 Centaurus a month by September 1944[28].

By the time the Sabre was properly made, and the Typhoon's structural

---

• Typhoons had fuel tanks in their 'thick' wings. There was no room for large tanks in the 'thin' wings of the Tempest, so the nose was lengthened to accommodate a fuel tank in front of the cockpit.

† The Sabre Tempest I, cooled by wing radiators attained 460mph, but never went into production because the large plan area of the radiators made them vulnerable to 'flak' as a low level fighter.

‡ The Griffon Tempests were cancelled, probably because of installation problems; the Griffon was at least 600lb lighter than the Sabre or the Centaurus.

§ The elevator mass balance of the Typhoon had been specially designed so as to save weight, but at the time the causes of high frequency elevator 'flutter' were imperfectly understood. In the process of saving some 20lb, the effectiveness of the mass balance had been impaired, and the resultant vibration caused metal fatigue in the lightweight bracket supporting it. If and when this broke, the immediate aerodynamic stress was huge, and the rear fuselage fractured. The RAE helped Hawkers to identify the cause of the problem.

¶ The 'thick wing' of the Typhoon caused severe buffeting and aileron reversal at high speed. The aircraft was liable to 'flick' (due to a high speed stall), if the pilot imposed a heavy 'G' load whilst turning or recovering from a dive.

The first generation.

The effectiveness of the Hurricane (*above*) was raised by fitting 20-mm cannon, a three-bladed propeller with a CSU and the 2-speed Merlin using 100 octane. But the airframe was not altered, and the increase in maximum speed was marginal.

The performance of the Spitfires (*below*) was steadily increased throughout the war by the development of the Merlin and Griffon engines, and modifications to their airframes and propellers to absorb the extra power. This superb view of a Spitfire 22 with the twin radiators of a two-stage engine epitomises the timeless elegance of Mitchell's design.

The second generation. The failure of the Rolls-Royce Vulture left the Royal Air Force dependant on the Hawker Typhoon (*above*) and Tempest (*below*), and their combat performance was limited by the single-stage supercharger of their Sabre engines. Fighter Command and the US Air Force were rescued by the later marks of Spitfire and the Merlin Mustang while the speed of the Typhoon and Tempest at low level was ideally suited to tactical work before and after the invasion of Europe.

problems solved, a fast, low-level fighter bomber was needed to equip the Tactical Air Force for the invasion of Europe, and Typhoons proved their worth. But the Sabre-engined Tempest V was faster than the Typhoon, and handled better. Hopes of the Centaurus version nearly foundered because of the cooling problems of the Bristol engines, but the faults were cured eventually, and the Tempest II entered service before 1946. 3,315 Typhoons and 1,209 Tempests were made.

TWIN-ENGINED LIGHT BOMBERS

Deliveries of **Blenheims** totalled 4811, when production ceased in 1943, and 1,429 **Beauforts** had been made by the end of 1944. Their respective bomb loads were only 1,000 and 1,650 lb, and with a range of about 1,400 miles, a fast, new light bomber was urgently needed to replace them, and the American Bostons and Baltimores by 1942. Early marks of the Mosquito were coming into service, Bristol was working on the Centaurus-powered Buckingham, and Hawker on a Sabre-powered alternative which they hoped to get into production by January, 1944.

Freeman had wanted de Havilland to follow the Merlin Mosquito with a larger variant, powered with Griffons or Sabres as soon as the engines were available, but once he saw the estimated performance figures of a standard Mosquito, if re-engined with two-stage Merlins, he stopped worrying de Havilland about the alternatives. Putting them into production would be a longer job than changing over to Merlin 60 series and, even in 1944, output of these was comparatively slow. The Griffon version was cancelled, and he asked for the Mosquito to be re-engined with Merlin 61s as soon as possible, in the order: bomber/PRU, fighter bomber and night fighter. The Hawker bomber was cancelled and orders for the Buckingham reduced to a trickle, since the new Mosquito would outperform them all.* Thirty-two Buckinghams were delivered.†

AIRCRAFT FOR THE FLEET AIR ARM

Between 1936 and 1938, the Admiralty disregarded Freeman's advice to order a modern single-seater fighter for the Fleet Air Arm, thinking that a navigator was essential, and speed relatively unimportant. The Admiralty changed their mind in 1939, and fixed-wing Hurricanes were adapted for carrier work, entering service by July 1940: American Grumman Martlets ordered by the French were diverted to the FAA and operating from a shore base by September 1940: folding-wing Martlets, renamed Wildcats, started working from Escort carriers in August 1941. Fixed-wing Seafires were adapted to operate off carriers in the summer of 1942, and the first with folding wings, built at Westlands and at Cunliffe-Owens, replaced them in November 1943.

* Further details of the way Mosquitoes were adapted and used are given in Chapter 13.
† The Buckingham airframe had defensive armament. Despite its more powerful engines, it was slower than the Mosquito, proving that Freeman was right to have rejected that alternative in 1939.

The Fairey Barracuda was described as being 'designed by a committee'. It was so overweight because of the variety of extraneous equipment it carried that it had to be re-engined twice. These Mk.IIs were powered by Merlin 32 engines.

Development of a modern torpedo bomber had been inhibited by the fragility of the Navy's old 18in. aerial torpedo, which had to be dropped at a slow speed and a low height. The biplane Swordfish, which was said to have a maximum speed of 200mph in a vertical dive, was an ideal carrier, as was its 'saloon version', the Albacore, although the latter was powered by the unreliable Taurus. Eventually they were replaced by the Barracuda, which was so overweight that it had to be re-engined, but even this only carried these 18in. torpedoes, and so needed the appropriate flying characteristics. The American Avenger, the first carrier torpedo/bomber able to carry a modern, 21in. torpedo, came into British service in June 1943, the equipment of a FAA Squadron, operating off USS *Saratoga* during the Solomon Islands campaign, but the Barracuda was eventually re-engined a second time to carry it. For single-seater fighters, Martlets were superseded by Hellcats in July 1943, and Corsairs were operating with the FAA by April 1944, both American Lend-Lease aircraft.

Notes

ABBREVIATIONS

Anne	Letters and notes by Anne Beese, WRF's eldest daughter
Bufton	Personal papers of the late Air Vice-Marshal Bufton and tape recorded interviews;1991
CA	Churchill Archive, Churchill College.
CC	Churchill College (Cambridge)
CCC	Christ Church College (Oxford)
DR	Diana Richmond; Wartime letters from Murtle
EF	Letters from WRF to Elizabeth, his second wife
F-T	Freeman to Tedder; letters; MAP 1940
McC	McCloughry papers, IWM
Portal	Personal papers of MRAF Lord Portal.
SAOAG	*The Stategic Air Offensive against Germany*
SSPM	The S of S's Expansion Committee Progress Meetings
SSEC	The S of S's Expansion Committee (minutes)
T-F	Freeman to Tedder; letters; MAP 1940
WRF diary	Freeman's personal diary of his trip to and from the 'Riviera' meeting; August 1941.
WRF	Wilfrid Rhodes Freeman
WT	Wireless Telegraphy

CHAPTER 1

1   Lewer & Calkin, *Curiosities of Swanage*, 1975.
2   Anne (Freeman) to Author.
3   Wilfrid's letters to his second wife, Elizabeth: hereafter, EF.
4   William Freeman kept diaries, now held by Anne, Wilfrid's daughter.
5   WF's diaries.

CHAPTER 2

1   Macmillan. *Sefton Brancker*, p.35.
2   Hare, P.R. *The Royal Aircraft Factory*, p.68.
3   Macmillan, N. *Sefton Brancker*, p.26.
4   Bruce, J.M. *Aeroplanes of the RFC*, pp.346–50.
5   Macmillan, op. cit., pp.50–1.
6   William Freeman's diary, 9.5.14.
7   Ibid, 5 and 14 June 1914.
8   Macmillan, op. cit., p.55.
9   Nahum, A. *The rotary aero-engine*, p.24.
10 Macmillan, op. cit., p.71.
11 Ibid, p.75.
12 W. Freeman's diary, 10.8.14.
13 PRO, AIR 1/2162. No 2 Squadron diary.
14 Jones, H.A., *The War in the Air*, Vol. 1, pp.337–8.
15 PRO, AIR 1/2162, No. 2 Squadron's diary.
16 Ibid. No 2 Squadron diary.
17 Ibid. No 9 Squadron diary
18 WRF to Gladys, 3.11.14.
19 Extract from Max F.'s letter from France, 4.1.15.
20 PRO, AIR 1/1262, 9 Sqdn papers. Original handwritten memo, dated 13.1.15. St Omer.
21 Messenger, C. Article 'Neuve Chapelle' in *War Monthly*, April 1981.
22 Jones, H.A., op. cit., Vol. 1.
23 Fraser, D. *Alanbrooke*, p.63.
24 Letter to Gladys, 1.4.15.
25 Douglas, S. *The Years of Combat*, p.68.
26 Freeman's Egypt diary, 11 January 1916.
27 Ibid, 16 and 18 January 1916.

28 Slessor, J. *The Central Blue*, pp.16–17.
29 Egypt diary, 19, 21, 23–26 January 1916.
30 Ibid, 29 and 31 January, 2, 14 and 26 February 1916.
31 Ibid, 1 and 11 February 1916.
32 Ibid, 9 February 1916.
33 Murray's dispatch, *London Gazette*, 22.9.16.
34 Ibid.
35 Egypt diary, 20 February 1916.
36 Ibid, 5 March, 27, 28 and 29 April, and 6, 11, 20 and 29 May 1916.
37 Ibid, 24 and 29 February, 3–5 and 30 March, and 27 April 1916.
38 Ibid, 13–14 February and 8–31 March 1916.
39 Ibid, 26.3.16.
40 Family papers, including hotel bills sent to Freeman.
41 Egypt diary, 28–9 and 31.5.16.
42 Murray's dispatch, *London Gazette*, 22.9.16,
43 Egypt diary, 18–19 June 1916. Norris, G. *The RFC, a History*, pp.128–9.
44 Ibid, 19.6.16.
45 Eileen Freeman, Max's widow; Family records and hearsay.
46 Egypt diary, 25–26.6.16.
47 Jones, H.A., op. cit., Vol. VI, pp.32–8.
48 Bruce, J.M. op. cit., 1992 edition, p.436.
49 King, H.F. *Sopwith aircraft, 1912–1920*, p.521.
50 Bruce, op. cit., p.435.
51 Jones, H.A., op. cit., Vol. III, pp.322 and 333.
52 Gray and Thetford; *German Aircraft of the First World War*, p.48.
53 1st Army records. G.S.323, 17.2.17.
54 Jones, H.A., op. cit., Vol. III, p.322.
55 Bruce, op. cit., p.331–3.
56 Ibid, p.418.
57 Jones, H.A., op. cit., pp.371–2, also Air 1/2177/209/14/26: No 1 Brigade war diary, May 1917.
58 Ibid, Vol. III, pp.371–2.
59 First Army No. G.S.576, 4.5.17. Haig's handwritten comment dated 6.5.17.
60 Jones, H.A., op. cit., pp.231–47.
61 Ibid, pp.253–9.
62 PRO, AIR 1/1945. 204/247/19, 26.2.18, and 2.12.17.
63 PRO, AIR 1/1532, 204/76/7. Ninth Wing orders, including letter, 279/G from Freeman to AHQ, RFC, 29.11.17.
64 Chapter 12, pp.206–8.
65 Jones, H.A., op. cit., p.272.
66 RFC Order of Battle, 21 March 1918. Harvey, W.F.J.; article 'Germany might have won the war in 1918'. *Air Pictorial*, April 1968.
67 Jones, H.A., op. cit., pp.271–2.
68 Ibid, p.320–7.
69 Ibid.
70 Harvey, W.F.J. *Air Pictorial*, March 1968.
71 WRF to Gladys, 30.3.18.
72 Jones, H.A., op. cit., Vol. V, p.221.
73 Strange, L. *Recollections of an Airman*. Details from an extract 'cut' during editing, and given by Strange to Max Freeman in 1935.
74 Jones, H.A., op. cit., Vol. VI, p.37.
75 Bruce, op. cit., p.462–3.
76 Strange, op. cit.

CHAPTER 3

1 Joubert de la Ferté, *Fun and Games*, p.75.
2 *Hansard*, 12.5.38, p.1086.
3 Beauman, W/Cdr. E.B, *Some recollections of the first course*.
4 Richards, *Portal*, pp.79–80.
5 Roskill, S. *Naval policy between the Wars*, p.409.
6 1923. R.S.Walker to Author, 1989.
7 Taylor, J.W.R. *C.F.S. Birthplace of Air Power*, p.115.
8 Penrose, H. *The adventuring years, 1920–1929*.
9 Taylor, J.W.R. op. cit., p.110.
10 Ibid, pp.102–3.
11 Trenchard letter, 20.4.28.
12 Martin. Letter to Author, 1991.
13 Ibid.
14 OBrien, C.C. *The Siege*, (Paladin, 1988), pp.179–82.
15 EF, 8.6.42.
16 Anne (Freeman) to Author, 1996.
17 Viscount Swinton's autobiography, *I remember*, p.113.
18 Miller, C. Original letter from Freeman, 17.11.33. (IWM),
19 EF.
20 Betty Whitcome. Talks with Author, 1991.
21 Ibid, 1994.
22 Strafford papers; pocket diaries for 1932 and 1933 (IWM).
23 Betty Whitcombe, 1991.
24 Anne; notes for Author, 1996.
25 EF, '...a torrent of love swept over me'.
26 Whitcombe, B. ibid.
27 Entry in Ralph's 'birthdays book'.
28 Letter, 4.5.33, WRF after Sibyl's visit to Jerusalem.
29 Wilfrid's wartime letters to Elizabeth, his second wife; undated, but probably 1941. Such letters hereafter 'EF'
30 Miller papers; (IWM).
31 Letter, Dawson to Quill, 30.9.87.
32 Ibid.
33 Miller papers; handwritten letter from Freeman, 20.2.35; (IWM).
34 Anne to Author; 1996.
35 Gibbs, N.H. *The Grand Strategy*, Vol. 1, p.561.
36 Hyde, H.M. *Baldwin*, p.376.
37 Ibid, p.561.
38 Swinton, *I Remember*, p.113.

CHAPTER 4

1 Londonderry, *Hansard*, 12.5.38, p.1086.
2 Slessor, J. *The Tools of Victory*. A tribute to Freeman broadcast on 15 September 1953.
3 Anne. 13.6.36.
4 Anne. 21.6.36.
5 Penrose, H. *Ominous skies*, p.59.
6 Bulman, G.P. unpublished autobiography, pp.291 & 293 (RAF Museum).
7 Slessor, op. cit., p.5.
8 Gunston, B. *By Jupiter*, 1978 edition pp.68–9.
9 Jones, H.A. op. cit., Vol. VI, pp.28–56.
10 Postan, Hay & Scott; (PHS). *The Design and Development of Weapons*, p.26.
11 Secretary of State's Progress Meetings (SSPM) No.39, 12.5.36.
12 PHS, op. cit., p.100.
13 PRO, AIR 6/45. EPM 45 (36) SSPM No.38, 5.5.36.

14 Quill, J.K. *The Birth of a Legend*, p.80.
15 Quill, op. cit., pp.81–2. Also *The Times* obituary, 22.1.87.
16 PRO, AVIA 46/115.
17 Anne. 1936.
18 SSPM No. 97. 19.10.37, item 3.
19 Jarrett. *Air Enthusiast* No. 35, 'Parnall's Final Fling'; Autumn 1994.
20 PRO, AIR 20/2785.
21 EF.
22 SSPM No. 101.
23 PRO, AIR 2/2715, 7B.
24 R.RHT. Rolls-Royce bought a Heinkel 70 as a flying test bed in 1935 and senior R-R staff visited Rostock when it was being fitted with a Kestrel engine.
25 PRO, AIR 20/9. May 1937.
26 PRO, Air Ministry file S.41268. Air Staff paper concerning the Volkert proposal; 16.11.37 (encls, 13A and 13B).
27 PRO, AIR 2/2059. Air Ministry file S. 41268. WRF note; 1.8.37.
28 PRO, Minute by Freeman to Newall, CAS, 24.2.38. A.M. file No. S.41268.
29 Baldwin, in Parliament, 10. 11.32.
30 Hough and Richards; *The Battle of Britain*, p.332.
31 SSPM No. 87. 30.6.37.
32 Bulman, G.P. op. cit., pp.276–7.
33 PRO, AIR 6. SSPM No. 39. 12.5.36.
34 SSPM No. 63, 22.12.36. EPM 156(36).
35 N.Shute Norway; *Slide rule*.
36 PRO. AIR 6/48. EPM 32.
37 SSPM No. 68.
38 Slessor, op. cit., p.6.
39 PRO, AIR 6/51. EPM 155(37).
40 PRO AIR 6/51, note by AMRD, 3 December 1937.
41 SSPM 104.
42 PRO, AVIA 10/151, Note by AMRD, 14 May 1938.
43 Anne, 8 and 15.12.36.
44 R-R Archive, Nos. 6, 7 and 8.
45 Bulman, op. cit., pp.317–19.
46 Gunston, Bill. *By Jupiter*.
47 Gunston, B. op. cit., p.90.
48 Gibbs, N.H. op. cit., p.298.
49 Gibbs, *The Grand Strategy*, Vol. 1, pp.586–9.
50 Postan, M.M. *British War Production*, HMSO, p.84 and Gibbs N.H. op. cit., p.532.
51 Postan, op. cit., pp.19–20.
52 R-R files; Memo dated 21.5.38, *re* Air Ministry letter, 14.5.38.
53 Ibid.
54 Ibid. R-R quoted Freeman's remarks at a recent meeting.
55 Ibid.
56 Anne, undated, May/June 1938.
57 Reader; *Air Ministry II*, p.212.
58 Anne, 22.5.38.
59 Anne, 28.5.38.
60 Letter from Freeman, 3.6.38 (Glasgow University; Weir archive).
61 Swinton papers; Letter from Freeman, 18.5.38; (Churchill archive).
62 Swinton's autobiography, p.113.
63 Weir biography, *Architect of Air Power*, pp.291–2.
64 Ibid, p.292.
65 Slessor, J.C. BBC broadcast; *Tribute to Freeman*, 15.9.53, p.5.
66 Penrose, *Ominous skies*, p.214.

67 Richmond letters, 1941.
68 Anne; notes for Author of her teenage memories.

CHAPTER 5

1 Postan, op. cit., p.21.
2 Connolly, J.V. Chapter entitled 'Aircraft Production' in *A century of British Aviation*, R.Ae.S., p.217.
3 PRO, AIR 6/51, note by AMRD, 3 December 1937.
4 Postan, op. cit., p.21.
5 PRO, AIR 6/58, memorandum by DGP, 12 July 1939.
6 Tedder, A.W. *With Prejudice* Cassell, 1966. pp.7–8.
7 PRO, Air Ministry file 815, 13.8.38.
8 Ibid.
9 Ibid.
10 Ibid, Freeman minute to KW, 13.8.38.
11 SSPM 105, 14.12.37.
12 Gunston, op. cit., pp.85–86.
13 Bulman, op. cit.
14 PRO, SSPM No.138. 4.10.38.
15 PRO, AIR 6/57. AMDP's 21-page memo, July 1938, p.17.
16 Bulman, op. cit., p.325.
17 Gibbs, *The Grand Strategy*, Vol. I, p.551. Cabinet Papers (CP) 24(38).
18 PRO, AIR 8/257. 20-page memorandum to Air Staff, dated 22.12.38. SSPM No. 127, 21.6.38.
19 Gibbs,N.H. *The Grand Strategy*, Vol. I, p.587.
20 Ibid, pp.587–9.
21 PRO, AVIA 10/155, 2nd DUS to Hawker Siddeley, 6 October 1938; PRO AVIA 10/9, Spriggs to AMDP, 26 September 1938.
22 PRO, AVIA 10/217, Supply Committee meeting, 5 October 1938.
23 Ibid, Supply Committee meeting with Craven, 6 October 1938.
24 Ibid, Dunbar (Vickers) to Riverdale, 16 April 1940; MAP to Vickers-Armstrong, 16 July 1940.
25 PRO, AIR 6/55, EPM 176 (38).
26 PRO, AVIA 10/153. Second Lord Nelson to Author, 4 July 1991.
27 PRO, AIR 6/55. EPM 176 (38).
28 PRO, SSPM No.126/128.
29 Ibid.
30 Ibid.
31 PRO, AIR 6/56. SSPM, No. 160.
32 PRO, Air Ministry memorandum by Calder, S8, dated 3.4.39.
33 PRO, SSPM No. 160. 20.3.39. Briefing for KW before his meeting with the Chancellor of the Exchequer, 10.4.39.
34 PRO, AIR 6/56. EPMs 48 (39) and 53 (39).
35 Ibid.
36 Ibid. EPM 47 (39).
37 SSPM No.161. Air Ministry EPMs 49/(39) & 53/(39).
38 Air Ministry files; Freeman to Henry Self, 8.4.39.
39 PRO, AM file, 8.4.39.
40 Self, reporting discussions with the Treasury and Freeman, 11.4.39.
41 Self to Barlow, 20.4.39.
42 PRO, Barlow to Self, 26,4,39.
43 R-R files. Cogswell, D. Unpublished *History of Rolls-Royce in Scotland*, pp.15–16.
44 Bulman, op. cit., Chapter 43, pp.342–7.
45 Freeman's 21-page memorandum; July 1939; [possibly 13/7].
46 Bulman, op. cit., p.343.

47 R-R files, Sidgreaves to Freeman, 20.6.39.
48 Ibid; Hives memorandum for meeting with Freeman, 23.2.39.
49 Unpublished RAeS paper: 1991.
50 R-R files; Hs. memo sent to Freeman, 28.8.39.
51 PRO, AVIA 10/230. Self to KW, 12.5.39. Also Freeman to Lemon, 29.6.39.
52 Letter, Austin to AMDP, 28.9.39.
53 Freeman's 21-page memorandum, July 1939.
54 Letter from Sir Alan Barlow, PS at the Treasury to Self (DUS) at the Air Ministry, 26.4.39.
55 PRO, AIR 6/56.
56 PRO, AVIA 46/72, DGP to SofS, 28 March 1940.
57 PRO, Air Ministry memo. Self (DUS), 11.4.39.
58 PRO, AIR 6/57. EPM 127 (38) AMDP's memorandum, p.15.
59 PRO, AIR 6/54. SSPM No.135, 14.9.38.
60 PRO, AIR6/58. SSPM No.188.
61 PRO. AIR 6/54, EPM 141(38), Appendix 2.
62 Ibid, also Appendix Y.
63 Ibid.
64 PRO, AIR 6/54. SSPM 134.
65 PRO, AVIA 46/286 Official History, Table 5, p.19.
66 PRO, AVIA 46/286. Official History, Summary, Part II Policy.
67 Richards, *Portal* pp.123–4. Portal was Director of Organisation under AMSO, and '... involved in ... the formation of Maintenance Command'.
68 PRO, SSPM No. 137 27.9.38.
69 SSPM 168, 16.5.39.
70 PRO, AVIA 10/31. 21.6.39.
71 Ibid, Tedder minute to Freeman, 10.7.39.
72 Ibid. Brand minute 2A 10.7.39.
73 PRO, AIR 6/58.
74 PRO, AIR 6/57. At Air Ministry on 10.8.39, and at SSPM No. 180, 25.8.39.
75 Ibid.
76 PRO, AVIA 10/31. Bulman, (DEP), to Lemon, (DGP), 11.7.39.
77 Ibid.
78 Ibid: Freeman and Bulman met Hives in late June, 1939.
79 R-R files; Hs.7/Kw, 28.8.39.
80 Ibid, Hs.17/Kw; Hives to Freeman, 3.11.39.
81 PRO, SSPM No. 137.

CHAPTER 6
1   EF, undated.
2   EF. 3.9.39.
3   MI6 was known as 'Passport Control' in the First World War.
4   PRO, Air Ministry files. Freeman's letter to KW, 1.9.39.
5   EF.
6   EF. 5.9.39.
7   PRO, SSPM No.182.
8   PRO, SSPM No.183.
9   PRO, SSPM No.183.
10   Postan, *British War Production*, p.69.
11   PRO, SBAC Files, B–G to Freeman, 2.11.39.
12   PRO, SBAC Files, Freeman to B–G, 22.9.39.
13   PRO, AVIA 10/20. 15.10.39.
14   R-R files, Hives letter and memorandum to Freeman, 28.8.39.
15   EPM 132 (39), discussed at the Air Council meeting on 13.9.39, Folder 1243 explains the decision to cancel the Boreas (Exe) engine.
16   PRO, AIR 6/58. Also R-R files.

17 PRO, Lord Austin to Freeman, 28.9.39.
18 PRO, AVIA 15/41. Freeman to Perry, 22.10.39.
19 W. Hornby, *Factories and Plant* (HMSO and Longman, London, 1958) p.211.
20 EF, 16.10.39.
21 PRO, Cab 102/275: table by D.Stats P. 9.4.40.
22 PRO, AVIA 10/20. 15.10.39.
23 EF, 14.12.39.
24 PRO, Cab 102/275: table by D.Stats P. 4.4.40.
25 PRO AVIA 10/310, DGP meetings, 18 January, 8 February 1940.
26 Thomas, *War Industry-Society*, p.22.
27 Vickers 194, Vickers-Armstrong (Weybridge) quarterly report to September 1939.
28 PRO, AIR 6/58 Air Ministry meeting, 12 December 1939.
29 PRO, AVIA 10/169. Note by DGP Vickers reports.
30 PRO, AVIA 10/310, DGP meetings, 2 October 1939.
31 PRO, AIR 6/58. 12.12.1939. AVIA 46/72. 28.3.1940.
32 EF, 13.10.39.
33 Anne, 20.12.39.
34 EF, 25.11.39.
35 A four-page EPM to the Air Council in April 1940. Also covering letters between Freeman and Douglas, 18 and 20 April.
36 PRO, SBAC letter.
37 Details from the copy of Bristol's 'Centaurus' file held by Dr Alex Moulton.
38 Golley, J. op. cit., pp.143–5.
39 PRO, AVIA 6/58 and SSEC No. 188, EPM 149(39).
40 EF, 30.1.40.
41 PRO, AIR 46/286. Official History, 'Summary', p.9.
42 PRO, 6/58. SSPM 185, 26.9.39.
43 PRO, AVIA 46/500. 6.10.39, confirmed by AIR 6/58 SSPM 186, 10.10.39.
44 SSPM 178, mid-July '39.
45 PRO, AVIA 46/500, 6.10.39.
46 EF, 25.11.39.
47 The conclusions were minuted by Street in an Air Staff 'Office Memorandum' 56/40, dated 19.3.40.
48 PRO, AVIA 10/31, 16.12.39.
49 Air Staff memorandum A.42325/39, dated 15.3.40, by Rowlands to AMSO.
50 PRO, AVIA 10/31. 16.3.40.
51 PRO, AVIA 10/31. Brand to Freeman, 27.4.40.
52 Ibid 5.5.40. Freeman to Newall, AMDP 1545.
53 PRO, AIR 6/59. SSPM 199, 23.4.40.
54 EF, 4.5.40.
55 PRO, Air Ministry file 1558, 15.4.40.
56 PRO, Ibid.
57 'Notes for Sir Charles Craven.'
58 Ibid.
59 PRO, AIR 6/59, EPM 61/40.
60 AMDP's files, Air Ministry. A two-page memo randum. about the conclusions of the 4.5.40. meeting. It was chaired by Freeman and attended by Tedder, Bruce-Gardner, Bulman, Calder and seven others.

CHAPTER 7
1   C. Barnett, *The Audit of War*, pp.146–7
2   Slessor, op. cit., p.6.
3   PRO, AIR 2/1790, DAP to AMSO, 11 May 1936.
4   PRO, AVIA 46/114, information supplied by Hawker to the official historian in 1943.
5   PRO, AIR 2/1668, DTD to AMSR, 15 January 1935.

6   AC 70/10/67, RAFM; Handley Page to SBAC, 14 June 1938; PRO, AIR 6/51, note by AMRD, 3 December 1937.
7   PRO, AIR 6/33, S of S EPM, 5 April 1938.
8   Barnett, *Audit*, pp.141–2.
9   Handley Page archive, Production Engineer to Managing Director, 16 March 1938; PRO, AVIA 46/115, Official Historian's 'Type Biography of the Lancaster'.
10   PRO, AIR 14/251. Tedder to de Havilland, 3.10.39.
11   Ibid, Liptrot. Handwritten, three-page memo. to DD/RDT, 31.10.39, marked 14A.
12   Ibid, three-page typed memo, 14B.
13   Ibid, Minute to CAS, 47A, dated 16.11.39.
14   Ibid, Air Ministry file S.B.125. Douglas to Freeman, 20.11.39.
15   Ibid. 22.11.39.
16   PRO, AIR 14/251. Minutes of meeting at Harrogate, 22.11.39.
17   PRO, AIR 14/251, 53A, Ludlow-Hewitt to Douglas, 25.11.39.
18   Terraine, *The Right of the Line*, p.89.
19   PRO, AIR 14/251. file S.B. 125.
20   PRO, AIR 14/251, 50B, Farren memo. of discussion with de Havillands.
21   PRO, AIR 14/251. Minutes dated 12.12.39, (S.41268), and marked '12 10'.
22   PRO, AIR 14/251. memo. 57A, dated 12.12.39.
23   Ibid.
24   Ibid, Four-page memo, marked '12 10' of conference at King Charles St, 12.12.39, (S.41268).
25   Postan, Hay and Scott, *Design and Development of Weapons*, p.86; Sharp and Bowyer. *Mosquito*, p.34.
26   PRO, AIR 14/251. Air Ministry file No. S.41268. Handwritten covering note by Farren dated 22/12.
27   Connolly, J.V. FRAeS. *Aircraft production*. The RAeS, 1966 'Jubilee' issue, p.219. Also JVC's talks with author, February 1990.
28   PRO, AVIA 46/116, Official Historian's Type Biography of the Mosquito.
29   PRO, AVIA 46/116. note by de Havilland, 11 December 1941.
30   AFDU Report No.39. 27.3.42.
31   PRO, AIR 20/2889, March 1941.
32   Penrose. *Ominous skies* p.131.
33   PRO, AVIA 46/129, extract from DGRD/ACAS(T) liaison meeting, 4.9.40.
34   R-RHT, Archive No. 35. 'The flight of the nutcracker'.
35   Penrose, op. cit., p.235–6.
36   Penrose, op. cit., p.275.
37   Sir Robert Lickley to Author, 4.2.95.
38   See USSBS, Report 4, *Aircraft Division Industry Report (European Theater)*,p.96.
39   Findings of Senator Truman's Enquiry.
40   PRO, AIR 6/37, S of S EPM, 24 January 1939.
41   Postan, Hay and Scott, *Design and Development*, pp.133–8.
42   Overy, *Goering*, p.193; *Air War*, p.230.
43   Freeman,R.A. *The Mighty Eighth War Diary*.

CHAPTER 8
1   EF, 8.5.40.
2   Tedder. *With Prejudice*, pp.14–16.
3   Chisholm and Davie. *Beaverbrook*, p.377, AMDP files; 20/21 May 1940, and de Groot. *Liberal Crusader*, p.167.
4   PRO, AMDP files; Tedder to Freeman, 25.5 and 29.5.40. 7 See Chapter 6, pp.11–12.
5   Minute of meeting, 18.5.40. ?AMDP files? B12. DCMDP/421, 1(3)b 5B.
6   Dr Alex Moulton's Bristol Engine Co.'s 'Centaurus' file.
7   Meeting; 20.5.40. Transfer of CRO and responsibility for all salvage and repair to MAP. Minutes enclosed in letter; Tedder to Freeman 20.5.40.

8   EF, June, 1940.
9   Chisholm and Davie, op. cit., pp. 386/7.
10 Freddman to Tedder 20.5.40.
11 PRO, MAP files, Freeman to Tedder, 6.6.40.
12 PRO. AIR 20/4078.
13 Freeman to Tedder, 30.5.40.
14 PRO. ?AMDP? Letter from W.L. Scott at MAP. to Treasury; 16.6.40.
15 Tedder to Freeman, 5.6.40.
16 J.V.Connolly to Author, February 1990.
17 Tedder to Freeman, 29.5.40.
18 Golley. *Whittle*, p.146.
19 Colville. J. *The Churchillians*, p.75.
20 Churchill Archive, [CA] Cambridge. Churchill to Sinclair 3.6.40.
21 Chisholm and Davie. op. cit., pp.394–5.
22 Richards. *Portal*, Note, p.195.
23 MAP statistical summaries, 1939 to 1945. Table 3; Monthly average of new aircraft deliveries by types.
24 PRO, AVIA 10/219, Dunbar to AMDP, 23.11.39. Aim to raise output from 50–100 p/m.
25 29 MAP staistical summaries. Table 4; Monthly average of new aircraft deliveries by firms.
26 PRO, AIR 20/2828. Freeman to PUS [Street?]
27 MAP files. Freeman to Tedder, 8.6.40.
28 PRO.AMDP File 8/24. 23.6.40.
29 See Appendix IX.
30 Mason, F.K. *Hawker aircraft since 1920* pp.329–330.
31 Rolls-Royce Heritage Trust records.
32 Ethell, J. *Mustang*. Janes, 1981, pp.9–16.
33 R-R files, Hs5/KW. Hives to Freeman, 2.9.39. Note in Freeman's writing on his copy. 'Remind me to speak Hives sometime'.
34 R-R files, Freeman to Hives, 6.9.39. A hand written note thereon, includes: 'I liked your American scheme but we can't afford it'.
35 R-R Archive, No.22.
36 Piggott, D. *The Vulture files*, R-RHT.
37 Without a radical redesign, the power of the Vulture could only be increased by running it at higher speeds and greater boost pressure. Each of the big-ends was connected to four con-rods however, and as the big-end bolts were already overstressed, the safe potential increase was inadequate.
38 See Appendix X.
39 Freeman to Tedder; S8, 3.6.40.
40 Obituary of Louis Armandias, *The Times*.
41 Beaverbrook papers/D/22.
42 Beaverbrook papers; 11/15 June, 1940, and de Groot, p.167.
43 McCloughry papers, IWM. In the course of researches for this biography, Dr Sebastian Ritchie discovered these, and made a thorough study of McCloughry's background and his services to Beaverbrook in 1940.
44 McCloughry papers.
45 The copy of the paper 'A weak link . . .' in the Beaverbrook files, (D.328) contains several typing errors: all other copies are typographically perfect.
46 McCloughry had worked under Welsh when he was AMSO, and had then moved to the Department of War Organisation, so he was well informed.
47 EF. Letter headed 'Wednesday'; probably 3 or 10 July 1940.
48 PRO, Air Ministry, D/29 and D/35.
49 EF, July 1940.
50 Ibid.
51 McCloughry's own notes about this incident, IWM.

52 PRO, Cabinet Office file 118/11; Atlee papers; 'weaknesses in the Air Ministry; The technical direction of the RAF'. This paragraph was omitted from later drafts.

53 Beaverbrook papers, 10.8.40.

54 Ibid, 5.9.40.

55 Ibid, 6.9.40.

56 Ibid, 7.9.40.

57 Ibid, 11.9.40.

CHAPTER 9

1 Gilbert, M. *Winston S. Churchill*, Vol. 6.

2 Made by one of his ADCs, L.G.S.Payne, in May 1940, and sent by Freeman to Elizabeth. EF, 4.5.40.

3 PRO, AIR 19/572, Churchill to Sinclair, 10 July and 10 August 1940.

4 Salmond papers, Hendon; B.2638, Salmond to Trenchard, 12 September 1940. As Marshals of the Royal Air Force, neither of them had 'retired'.

5 Salmond papers, B.2638, Salmond to Trenchard, 25 September 1940.

6 Ibid.

7 Terraine, J. *The Right of the Line*: The Royal Air Force in the European War, 1939–1945 (Sceptre: London, 1988), p.98.

8 Boyle, *Trenchard*, pp.715–6.

9 Trenchard papers, RAF Museum, Hendon; fiche 467, Trenchard to Churchill, 25 September 1940.

10 Trenchard papers, Trenchard to Freeman 25.9.40. (to fix a meeting before Trenchard met Beaverbrook – on 27th or 28th September, and to 'lunch' Freeman on 30th.)

11 Salmond papers, B 2638; 4.10.40.

12 J.Colville, *The Fringes of Power. Downing Street Diaries*, 1939–1955 (Hodder and Stoughton: London, 1985), entry of 2 October 1940, p.256.

13 Portal papers; Freeman to Sinclair, 7.10.40.

14 PRO. Air 20-2795.

15 Richards, op. cit., p.141.

16 Jones, R.V. *Most Secret War*. Portal was in the Cabinet Office on 21.6.40, when the German navigational beam system was discussed, and he accepted the claims about the accuracy of the astro-navigation alternative.

17 Salmond papers, Trenchard letter to Salmond, B.2638, 4.10.40.

18 Richards, op. cit., p.157.Trenchard to Portal, 1.6.40. 'You are splendid...'

19 Trenchard papers, B.2638. two letters from Trenchard, both dated 25.9.40, one to Salmond and the other to Freeman.

20 Richards, op. cit., p.167.

21 Churchill. *The Second World War*, Cassell, Vol. 2, p.19

22 Gilbert 5, 809–31

23 Macksey K. *Armoured Crusader*, p.147.

24 Portal papers, Christ Church.

25 Ibid.

26 EF, probably September 1940.

27 PRO, AIR 19/473. 17.10.40.

28 PRO, MAP files A.234. 1.11.40.

29 Richmond, Sir John. Quoted in a letter to the Author, 19.3.87.

30 EF.

31 Beaverbrook papers; Freeman's letter 4.11.40.

32 PRO, MAP file FD.8 AMDP, 4.11.40.

CHAPTER 10

1 DR, 25.11.40.

2 EF, 27.12.40.

3 EF. Letter headed 'Wednesday'; probably end June 1942.

4   Evill papers AC/74/8/38; Mansion house speech, 12.6.46.
5   Richards D. *Portal* pp.219–220.
6   EF, 8.6.42.
7   Slessor, J. *The Central Blue*, pp.40–41.
8   Slessor, J. BBC broadcast, 15.9.53.
9   DR, undated; end Jan 1941.
10 DR, January 1941.
11   D/328. CAS, 27.1.40.
12 Jones R.V., *Most Secret War*, pp.162–7.
13 Jones, op. cit., pp.182–3.
14 Freeman to Jones, 22.1.41.
15 Jones, op. cit., p.166.
16 EF, 'Wednesday', probably end January 1942.
17 PRO, AIR 20/2776.
18 PRO, AIR 20/2776. Advice wrapped in memorable, penetrating wit.
19 EF. 19.7.41.
20 Portal papers, CCC. Freeman to Portal, 8.2.42.
21 Portal papers, CCC. Freeman memorandum to Sinclair: 6.1.42.
22 Ibid.
23 EF. 'Sunday'; probably November 1942.
24 PRO. AIR 20/2896. 10.12.40.
25 Colville, *The Churchillians*, p.140.
26 PRO, AIR 20/2785. 29.11.41. 29 PRO, AHB/II/116/14 (Manning plans and Policy);
    Appendix 3.
27 PRO, AIR 20/2864. Bomber Command expansion and re-equipment; 19.12.40.
28 PRO. AIR 8/1001. RAF future requirements and expansion; 9.40 – 8.42.
29 Ibid and AIR 2/7336. Expansion; 21.12.40.
30 PRO, AIR 8/495. The balance of the production programme; 26.12.40.
31 PRO, AIR 2/7336, 5.12.40.
32 AIR 20/2891, Operational control of Coastal Command; and Air 41/73, pp.274–5 and
    277–80.
33 Goulter, C. *A forgotten offensive*, p.142.
34 PRO, AIR 20/3028, 1.6.42.
35 PRO, AIR 20/2775, 27.9.41.
36 PRO. AIR 20/3028
37 PRO. AIR 8/634.
38 PRO. AIR 20/3028; 21.5.42.
39 PRO, AIR 20/3028. Sorley to Freeman, 23.5.42.
40 PRO, AIR 20/3028; Minute from DWO, 29.5.42.
41 PRO, AIR 20/3028. Freeman letter to Joubert, 11.6.42.
42 Ibid, 10.9.42.
43 PRO, AIR 20/2874. 14.7.41.
44 Ibid. Salmond to Freeman, 22.9.41.
45 R-R files; Freeman letter to Hives, 2.12.40.
46 PRO, AIR 20/2775, 4.12.41.
47 PRO, AIR 20/3107. 1.3.41.
48 Portal papers CCC: Peirse, A.O.C in C.India, to Freeman, 17.5.42.
49 Ibid; Freeman's reply to Peirse, May 1942.
50 Connolly J. Memorandum to Cripps, 1943.
51 PRO, AIR 8/452. 20.12.40.
52 PRO, AIR 8/252. December 1940; probably 1st week.
53 Ibid; Portal opted for 30 out of 50 as fighters. 10.12.40.
54 Sharp and Bowyer, op. cit., p.83.
55 PRO, AIR 8/452. 23.1.41.
56   Sharp and Bowyer, p.86.

57 PRO, AIR 20/2854. Freeman to Linnell; 29.4.41.
58 The superchargers of the Napier Sabre, and the R-R Vulture which powered the two Hawker fighters were not as efficient as that of the Merlin, and there was no prospect of making them 'two-stage', so their power declined above 15,000 ft.
59 Portal papers, CCC. Freeman to Portal, 3.4.41.
60 R-R files. Hives to Freeman, 24.6.41.
61 EF, end June 1942.
62 PRO, AIR 20/3072, 8.5.42.
63 Ibid, 18.5.42. and AIR 20/3065.
64 PRO, AIR 20/3072, Freeman minute to Dunbar, in reply to his of 18.4.42.
65 PRO, AIR 20/2775, AIR 20/3029 and AIR 20/3076.
66 PRO, AIR 20/3072. Freeman's draft comments on MAP's programme; 8.5.42.
67 Ibid.
68 Bristol director's committee minutes; 2.12.41.
69 Middlebrook, M. The Nuremberg raid, p.276.

CHAPTER 11
1 Portal papers, CCC. November 1940.
2 Tedder, With Prejudice, pp.32–3.
3 Tedder, op. cit., pp.49–50, and Playfair The Mediterranean and the Middle East, Vol. 2, p.236.
4 PRO, AIR 20/2837.
5 Tedder, op. cit., pp.50–51.
6 Tedder, op. cit., p.111.
7 PRO, AIR 20.2837.
8 PRO, AIR 20/2976, 12.6.41.
9 Tedder, op. cit., pp.81–2.
10 Portal papers, CCC.
11 PRO, AIR 19/211.
12 Richards, Portal, p.235.
13 Embry, Mission completed, pp.209–11.
14 Embry, op. cit.
15 Tedder, op. cit., p.181.
16 Richards, op. cit., pp.235–7.
17 Playfair, op. cit., p.292–3.
18 Richards and Saunders 2, 166–7.
19 AHB narrative on Middle East.
20 Tedder to Freeman, 16.12.41. There was no such organisation in India.
21 Tedder to Freeman, 15.1.42. 155a.
22 Tedder papers, box 'Correspondence, Papers, 1940–41, Freeman to Tedder 30 December 1941; Freeman to Courtney, 30 December 1941.
23 PRO, AIR 20/2976. Meeting on 13.6.41.
24 Official RAF narrative: Aircrew Training, 1934–1942 (Second Draft), chronology.
25 Official RAF narrative: Aircrew Training, 1934–1942 (Second Draft), p.520.
26 Official RAF narrative: Aircrew Training, 1934–1942 (Second Draft), pp.520–1.
27 PRO, AIR 20/2428. 3.2.42 and 20/2976.
28 PRO, AIR 19/211. 20.10.41.
29 Official RAF narrative: Aircrew Training, 1934–1942 (Second Draft), 522.
30 PRO, AIR 20/2837. 18.8.42.
31 Ibid.
32 PRO, Freeman to Tedder, 28.12.41. 135a.
33 PRO, Tedder to Freeman, 29.12.41. 136a.
34 Terraine, The Right of the Line, p.369.
35 PRO, AIR 20/2958.
36 PRO, AIR 20/2958.
37 PRO, AIR 20/3029 and /2958.

38   PRO, Freeman to Tedder, 30.12.41. 140.b.
39   PRO, AIR 20/2782.
40   Ibid.
41   Churchill, op. cit., Vol. IV, pp.268–9.
42   PRO, AIR 20/2428. 27.3.42.
43   EF, end June 1942.
44   Tedder to Freeman, 11.7.42. 216a.
45   Freeman to Evill; [r] Tedder. 9.7.42. 215a.
46   PRO, AIR 20/2857. Also Freeman to Tedder, 15.8.42. 228b.
47   PRO, AIR 20/2809. 14.12.40.
48   PRO, AIR 20/2946. 13.4.42.
49   PRO, AIR 20/2970. 10.5.41.
50   PRO, AIR 20/2983. Target force 'E'.
51   PRO, AIR 20/2996, & Terraine, pp.351–2, AHB Air Support Narrative, 23–31.
52   WRF letter, 30.12.41. 140.B.
53   AHB Air Support Narrative, 31.
54   PRO, AIR 20/2810. Undated, probably 14.3.42. in reply to Nye; 12.3.
55   PRO, AIR 20/2812.
56   PRO, Cipher files, Air Min. to HQ,ME Freeman to Tedder, 24.8.42, AX 229.
57   PRO, AIR 2/7336.
58   AHB Air Support Narrative, 31–2.
59   PRO, AIR 20/2812. 29.6.42.
60   AHB Air Support Narrative, 32–5.
61   Ibid., 35–6.
62   Tedder,A. With Prejudice, p.319.
63   Terraine, op. cit., p.380, quoting General Montgomery; Italy, 1943.
64   Webster and Frankland, The Strategic Air Offensive against Germany, [SAOAG] Vol. 1, p.176.

CHAPTER 12

1   21 PRO, AIR 14/43. L–H letter to Air Ministry, 10.11.37.
2   Richards, D. The hardest victory, Coronet edition, p.54, quoting Hugh Lloyd's diary.
3   PRO, AIR 6/39. SSPM 179, 4.8.39. Also Smith, Dr M. 'Ludlow-Hewitt and the expansion of Bomber Command'. RUSI Journal, March 1981, p.54.
4   Terraine, op. cit., p.105.
5   PRO, AIR 8/424. Minute; Freeman/Portal; 9.5.41; Portal's reply, 10.5.
6   Webster and Frankland, The Strategic Air Offensive against Germany, [SAOAG] Vol. 1, p.176.
7   Terraine, op. cit., pp.284–5.
8   PRO, Air 20/2921. 8.5.41.
9   PRO, AIR 20/2795. Portal to DCAS, 28.9.41.
10   PRO, AIR 8/424. Minute; Portal to Freeman, 5.10.41, replying to Freeman's long memo.,
11   Terraine, op. cit., pp.459–60.
12   Ibid. p.461: Churchill: the grand alliance, p.748.
13   SAOAG, Vol. IV, p.142. DCAS Directive to Peirse, C-in-C Bomber Cmd. 13.11.41
14   Bufton tapes. The Author taped many hours of talks with Air Vice-Marshal Bufton in October, 1991.
15   Tizard papers, IWM, T. to Bottomley, DCAS, 6.6.42.
16   SAOAG, Vol. I. p.249 Cherwell minute to WSC, 2.9.42.
17   PRO, AIR 20/4782. 20.11.41. Bufton to Baker. (DBO)
18   PRO, AIR 20/2795. Minute, Freeman to Bottomley, DCAS. 8.4.42.
19   AIR 20/2758. Freeman to Portal. 18.12.41.
20   Harris to Bufton. Bufton tapes.
21   SAOAG, Vol. I, pp.388/9.
22   PRO, AIR 20/4782.
23   PRO, AIR 20,2795, 8.4.42.
24   Jones, R.V. Most Secret War, pp.220–1.

25 PRO, AIR 20/2795, DCAS TO VCAS, 8.4.42.
26 PRO, AIR 20/2795. 27.4.42.
27 PRO, AIR 20/2795. 29.4.42.
28 PRO, AIR 20/2795. WRF to Baker, D.B.Ops. 1.5.42.
29 SAOAG, Vol. I, p.452–3.
30 PRO, AIR 20/2795, 29.5 – 3.6.42.
31 Henshaw, A. *Sigh for a Merlin*, Hamlyn edition, p.174.
32 PRO, AIR 20/2795. WRF, 3.6.42.
33 PRO, AIR 20/2795. Harris to Freeman, 1.6.42.
34 PRO, AIR 20/2795. Freeman to Harris, 3.6.42.
35 Terraine, *The Right of the Line*, p.501.
36 Portal files; Harris to Portal, June, 1942.
37 RAF. Hist. Soc. proceedings, No.6, pp.25–6.
38 RAF. Hist. Soc. proceedings, No.6, pp.25–6.
39 Bufton tapes.
40 Portal papers, CC.
41 SAOAG, Vol. I, pp.431–2.
42 Bufton Tapes.
43 SAOAG, Vol. III, pp.76–94. Whilst this account was being written, Portal was shown Frankland's draft paragraph to this effect and threatened to sue him unless it was censored.

CHAPTER 13
1   PRO, AIR 19/473. 6.10.40. Purvis to Salter (Central Office for N.American Supplies)
2   Ibid, 9.10.40. Lothian, to British Govt, (probably Air Minister).
3   Ibid, 11.10.40. Sinclair to Beaverbrook.
4   Ibid, 16.10.40. Report from Sinclair to CAS, (via their P.Ss.).
5   Ibid, 22.10.40, Sinclair to Churchill.
6   Roosevelt Museum, Hopkins papers, Jan.1941. Hopkins got Churchill to insist that Beaverbrook released the details. B's covering letter, 8.2.41.
7   Ibid. Handwritten by Scanlon.
8   PRO, AIR 2/7336. 27.2.41. Beaverbrook to Margesson; War Minister.
9   PRO, AIR 2/7336, 14.3.41. Margesson to Beaverbrook.
10 PRO, AIR 20/2905. 30.3.41. Freeman to Courtney, AMSO.
11 Ibid. 7.4.41. S.6, (for Freeman) to Director of Bomber Ops.
12 Ibid, 30.3.41. Ibid, Freeman to Courtney.
13 Ibid, 7.4.41. MAP to BAC, Washington.
14 Boyle, A. *Trenchard*, p.727. Also, Trenchard files RAFM; three page note, dated 11.6.54.
15 Trenchard papers, Hendon.
16 Hopkins papers, Roosevelt Museum. Book 3, March 1941.
17 PRO, AIR 20/2905. Air Staff Conference, 8.4, on US aircraft program.
18 Coffey, T.M. *HAP*, (biography of Arnold), p.227.
19 PRO, AIR 20/2905. Freeman to Arnold, 16.4.41.
20 Ibid.
21 Hopkins; Box 1027. 18.4.41. Arnold to US War Department.
22 Hopkins papers; FDR to Stimson, US Secretary of War.
23 Hopkins papers. FDR to Stimson, 4.5.41.
24 Winant files. Roosevelt Museum; Arnold to Winant, 29.7.41.
25 PRO, AIR 20/2689. Concern by Churchill, 12.7.41, leading to decision that Freeman approach Hopkins, 17.7.41.
26 Richmond letters.
27 Freeman's diary.
28 WRF diary, Thursday, 7.8.41.
29 PRO, AIR 8/414. 2.7.41, Harris to Portal,
30 PRO, AIR 8/591. Portal to Freeman, 8.8.41.
31 PRO, AIR 8/591. Freeman's notes; 10.8.41.

32 PRO, AIR 8/591. Freeman's notes.

33 Hopkins papers. Arnold file, Box 271, 'Additions'. Notes on Roosevelt-Churchill conference.

34 PRO, AIR 8/591. Freeman to Portal, 12.8.41.

35 PRO, CAB 80/30. Informal meeting on USS *Tuscaloosa*, 12.8.41.

36 PRO, AIR 8/591. 9.8.41. Freeman's notes.

37 WRF Diary, 10.8.41.

38 Hopkins, Arnold papers, Box 271. 11.8.41.

39 on 11 August.

40 Hopkins papers, Book 4. Letter WRF (on HMS *Prince of Wales*), to HH.

41 PRO, AIR 8/591. 11.8 and 12.8.41. Freeman's acknowledgment by an addition to his earlier letter.

42 Hopkins papers, WRF's letter dated 9.9.41.

43 PRO, AIR 8/1377. 10.9.41.

44 PRO, AIR 20/2689.

45 PRO, AIR 20/3036, AIR 8/648 and AIR 8/650.

46 CAB, 80/30. COS 504. 12.8.41.

CHAPTER 14

1 The V-12 Allison was an excellent engine, but its single stage supercharger meant that its power decreased rapidly above 10,000 ft.

2 AFDU report, 5.5.42.

3 Harker, R.W. *Rolls-Royce from the wings*, Chapter 4.

4 AFDU report No.46. 4.5.42.

5 AFDU report, dated 5.5.42.

6 Birch, *The Merlin and the Mustang*, p.11. R-RHT.

7 Ibid.

8 Ibid, p.13.

9 Ethell, J. *Mustang*, p.44.

10 Hopkins papers, From London 5.6.42, No.84.

11 Winant papers, Roosevelt Museum, Winant to Hopkins for Arnold, N. 84.

12 Birch, p.13.

13 Ibid. p.14–15.

14 Ethell, J. op. cit., p.37.

15 PRO, AIR 8/648, Webber 283; 5.6.42, 'from CAS' for Slessor.

16 PRO, AIR 8/648. Freeman to Evill in Washington, 6.6.42.

17 PRO, AIR 8/648, Marcus 136.

18 PRO, AIR 8/648 Webber 362.9 June.

19 Birch, op. cit., p.21.

20 Ibid, p.25. Linnell (CRD) to DTD, 1.7.42.

21 Ibid.

22 Ethell, op. cit., p.44.

23 Birch, op. cit., p.19.

24 Hansell, Haywood F. Jr. *The air plan that defeated Hitler*, pp.92–7, 110 and 106–7.

25 PRO, Prem 3; Draft memo by Freeman. Also Bufton Tapes.

26 Richards, *Portal* pp.308–9, and SAOAG, Vol. I, pp.357–63.

27 SAOAG, vol. I, p.54.

28 Terraine, J. *The Right of the Line*, Appendix G.

29 PRO, AVIA 15/1583, and Prem 3, 453.3 CAS 1.10.42.

30 Roosevelt Museum, FDR to Churchill. 23.10.42.

31 Hopkins papers. US War Production Board (WPB) Aircraft Branch engine summaries, 9–I for 23.2.42, 9–K for 9.9.42, and 9–L for 14.1.43, for changes in fighter production plans.

32 PRO, PREM 3. Draft memo from Freeman.

33 PRO, PREM 3, 453.3 CAS 1.10.42.

34 PRO, PREM 3 11/6 T.1229/2.

35 PRO, PREM 3 453. 3 – T.1229/2.

36 PRO, Prem 3 453. No. 6131, WSC to HH.
37 CA.Cam. Churchill to Hopkins, T. 1345/2.
38 CA, T 1345/2, 16.10.42.
39 WRF to EF. 6.11.42.
40 He cut the 1943 program from 100,000 to 83,000 aircraft.
41 Cairncross, op. cit.
42 Hopkins papers; Lovett, the US Assistant Secretary of War to Hopkins, 13.11.42.
43 Lyttelton failed to persuade the WPB to make an immediate cut in production of P-39s and P-40s, 11,000 of which were still to be delivered, but the provisional agreements that he reached, resulted in the following changes to Mustang and Merlin production policies.

    1. total output of Packard Merlins would rise from 1,400 to 2,000/month – later to 2,700/mth – by early 1944,

    2. a new factory, to be run by the Continental Engine Company, would be considered to make an extra 1,200 Packard Merlins/month.

    3. all production versions of the Packard Merlin 68s, (or V-1650-3), would be installed on the P-51Bs, [currently those] being made at Inglewood,

    4. output of P-51Bs would be increased to 380/mth at Inglewood by the end 1943, and a further 320 P-51Cs/mth would now be made at Dallas, bringing the total output to 700/mth by 1944.

44 Freeman R. *The Mighty Eighth War Diary*.
45 Middlebrook, M. *The Schweinfurt and Regensburg raids*.
46 Freeman R.A. *The Mighty Eighth War Diary*, p.126.
47 Ethell, op. cit., p.51. Air Material Command's Case History.
48 SAOAG, Vol. II, p.81.
49 McFarland S.L. 'The evolution of the American strategic fighter in Europe, 1942–1944', *Journal of Strategic Studies*, June 1987, p.193.
50 McFarland, op. cit., p.210.
51 Ibid, p.195.
52 Ibid, op. cit., pp.195–8.
53 Overy, R. *Why the Allies Won*, p.322.
54 McFarland, op. cit., p.203.
55 PRO, AIR 6/58. Memorandum on Aircraft development policy by Freeman for the Air Council; EPM 149 (39), 9.11.39.

CHAPTER 15

1   Tedder, op. cit., pp.14–16.
2   PRO, AIR 20/2689, September 1941.
3   EF, 20.12.41.
4   EF. 5.12.41.
5   EF, December 1941.
6   EF, end December 1941.
7   Portal papers, CCC. Craven to Portal, 3.4.42.
8   Portal papers, CCC. 3.4.42.
9   Letter from Ralph Freeman to Elizabeth, April/May 1941. A tactful letter which reassured EF, but clear evidence that Wilfrid confided in his brother.
10 PRO, AIR 20/3072. 8.5.42. Freeman's draft of an Air Ministry response to the latest MAP programme.
11 DR. February 1942.
12 DR, 17.4.42.
13 Portal papers; EF letter, 16 April 1942.
14 EF, 30.7.42.
15 PRO, AIR 8/647. April–June 1947.
16 PRO, AIR 8/648, and AIR 20/3036. 30.5.42 – 21.8.42. Portal/Freeman to Evill/Slessor in USA, about the revision of the Arnold/Portal agreement.
17 PRO, AIR 20/2984. Notes, 18.4.42.

18   PRO, AIR 20/2985, and AVIA 15/1583, 8.10.42.
19   PRO, AVIA 9/9. Sinclair to Llewellin, 23.9.42.
20   PRO, AIR 8/693. 1.10.42.
21   PRO, AVIA 9/9 and AIR 8/692.
22   Churchill Archive, (Churchill College, Cambridge) [CA], Prem 3/13/14 of 2.9.42. minute M 344/2.
23   CA. Prem 3/13/14.
24   CA, Prem 3/36/2, part 1.
25   PRO, AIR 20/2985. draft paper circulated by Freeman for discussion 4.9.42.
26   Portal papers, CCC, 25.9.42.
27   R-R files.

CHAPTER 16

1   DR. October 1942.
2   When Beaverbrook resigned as Minister of Production in February, 1942, Churchill offered him the Air Ministry or a return to MAP. He refused both.
3   EF, December 1942.
4   Cairncross, A. *Planning in Wartime*, p.11.
5   Ibid.
6   R-R files, Hives to Craven, 14.9.42.
7   Ibid.
8   Cairncross diaries.
9   EF, November 1942.
10   Cairncross, op. cit.
11   II EF, Letter dated 'Tuesday', probably 15.12.42.
12   Portal papers, CCC, 15.12.42.
13   Cairncross, op. cit., p.18.
14   Talks between Lord Plowden, Sebastian Cox, (AHB), and Author, July 1991.
15   Sereny, Gitta. *Albert Speer*, p.295.
16   EF, 6.11.42.
17   EF, 'Saturday', probably 5th or 12th December, 1942.
18   Cairncross op. cit., p.53.
19   Cairncross, op. cit., p.49.
20   Cairncross diaries; Dec. 42–Jan. 43. Talks between Rowlands and Jewkes.
21   EF, November 42.
22   Cairncross, op. cit., p.6. A brilliant lawyer, Cripps liked the challenge of involvement in industry, telling his economists: 'There's no limit in theory is there, to central planning?'
23   DR. WRF told this gem to DR.
24   EF, 12.2.43.
25   Gunston, Bill. *By Jupiter* pp.74–5. Banks, Rod. *I kept no diary*.
26   Banks, op. cit.
27   Bulman memoirs, p.500. RAFM.
28   PRO, AVIA 15/1708. CRD to WRF, 29.11.42.
29   Golley, J. *Whittle*, p.201.
30   Ibid p.202–3.
31   Golley, J. op. cit., pp.149–50. Benzedrine is amphetamine sulphate.
32   PRO, AVIA 9/9, Freeman to Llewellin, 3.11.42.
33   Ibid.
34   Postan, M.M. *British War Production*, HMSO, & PRO, AIR 20/1789.
35   PRO, AVIA 9/9, 26.11.42.
36   PRO, AVIA 9/44, Freeman to Cripps, 12.12.42.
37   PRO, AVIA 9/44.
38   AVIA 9/44. Telegram to MAP, 13.1.43.
39   Ibid.
40   Ibid.

41   PRO, AVIA 9/44, 4.1.43.
42   Ibid, 6.1.43.
43   Trenchard papers, Hendon; letter from Freeman, 24.2.43.
44   PRO BT87/142, Memorandum by the Ministry of Production, 17 April 1944.
45   PRO, AIR 8/714, 30.10.42. and 14.12.42. Also AIR 9/44, November 1942.
46   PRO, AIR 9/44. MAP memorandum, to Cabinet, dated 14.12.42, WP (42) 579.
47   WP (42)526 & 527.
48   AHB. Copies of MAP statistical summaries. Deliveries of aircraft by firms.
49   Fedden, who thought that Freeman was prejudiced against Bristol engines, had left the
     Bristol engine company by November, 1942.

CHAPTER 17
1   Reid, J.M. *James Lithgow, Master of Work*, pp.212–13.
2   Richards, D. *Portal*, pp.220–1.
3   Richmond letters.
4   Portal papers, CCC, Freeman to Portal, 15.7.43.
5   DR, August 1943. 'What fun they are these Freemans, and what a good start is automati-
     cally given to a family of . . . eight children.'
6   EF, undated, probably December 1942.
7   Postan, M.M., *British War Production*, pp.225–6, and 304–5.
8   Ibid, p.309.
9   AVIA 10/269, DGPS to Freeman, 29 April 1944.
10   MOD/AHB. MAP's statistical summaries.
11   PRO, AVIA 10/378, note by DDG Stats. P, 12 February 1942.
12   Rolls-Royce Archive, Hives File, 'MAP General, 1941–43', Sidgreaves to Lord Herbert
     Scott, 19 September 1943.
13   MAP statistical summaries.
14   MAP statistical summaries.
15   Sharp and Bowyer, op. cit., p.72.
16   PRO, AIR 20/2884. VCAS.5347. AMSO/45/4 Courtney to Freeman, MAP, 6.12.42.
17   AFDU report No. 39, 27.3.42.
18   Sharp & Bowyer, op. cit., and AHB: MOD statistical summaries.
19   MAP statistical summaries.
20   AHB, AVIA 10/10/311, table 10. MAP statistical summaries.
21   See Appendix IX.
22   Calculated from AVIA 10/311, table 10, UK New Engine Deliveries by Firms.
23   PRO, AVIA 15/1105, 27.4.43.
24   PRO, AVIA 15/1923. WRF to CRD, 2.8.44.
25   Ibid, 25.7.44.
26   PRO, AVIA 46/75, 15.11.43.
27   AIR 8/792, Conclusions after Portal/Freeman meeting, 7.2.45.
28   Ibid.
29   Jackson, A.J. *de Havilland aircraft since 1909*, pp.433–4.
30   PRO, AVIA 9/51. Draft to Cripps from Freeman, 10.11.43, as basis of reply to Churchill's
     minute to Cripps of 6.11.43, anxious for British V heavy bomber.
31   Harvey-Bailey, *Hives, The Quiet Tiger*, Sir Henry Royce Memorial Foundation, 59–65.
32   AVIA 9/819, 'Programme for research and design'. 18.9.44.
33   PRO, AIR 8/819. Sorley; '5 year programme for prototype aircraft', 18/9/44.
34   PRO, AVIA 15/2189, also E. Mensforth, *Family Engineers*, Ward Lock, London, p.113.
35   MFC 76/1/486. Letter, Freeman to Trenchard, 5.5.44.
36   Portal papers, CCC; letter from Freeman, 19.1.45.
37   Portal papers; letter from Freeman, 19.1.45.
38   Postan, op. cit., p.308.
39   Ibid, p.322.
40   Ritchie, *Industry and Air Power*, pp.246–7.

41　Ritchie, 'A New Audit of War', *War and Society*, Vol.12, No.1 (May 1994), p.140.
42　Ritchie, *Industry and Air Power*, p.247.
43　Ritchie, *A New Audit of War*, pp.128 & 132.
44　Overy, *Goering:The Iron Man*, p.176, & Overy, *The Air War*, p.142.
45　Ritchie, *A New Audit of War*, p.127.
46　Ibid, p.129.
47　PRO, AVIA 9/44 and telegram from Freeman to MAP, 13.1.43.
48　PRO, AVIA 46/75, Freeman to Cripps, 9.5.43.
49　Ritchie, 'A New Audit of War', p.129.
50　Postan, op. cit., p.321.
51　Ibid, pp.479–82, and MAP statistical summaries.
52　*Statistical Digest of the War*, table 133, p.154.
53　Webster and Frankland, op. cit., Vol. II, p.3.
54　Webster and Frankland, op. cit., Vol. lV, pp.416–21.
55　Overy, *War and Economy in the Third Reich*, pp.372–3; Overy, *The Air War*, p.158.
56　Webster and Frankland, op. cit. Vol. lV, Appendix 32.
57　Marshal Cavendish, *Great Aircraft of the World*, 1988 edition, p.281.
58　Overy, *Goering: The Iron Man*, 193–7, p.217.
59　Middlebrook, *The Nuremberg raid*, p.140.
60　Portal papers, CCC. Final sentence of undated letter, Freeman to Portal, probably early 1945.

CHAPTER 18
1　Rolls-Royce files; Hives correspondence, March 1945.
2　Authors talks with the late Mrs E. Freeman. 1992–3.
3　Coleman, D.C. *Courtaulds*, Vol. III, p.16.
4　Ibid, p.19.
5　Ibid, p.20.
6　Ibid, p.29.
7　Ibid, p.29, (December 49).
8　Ibid, pp.29–30.
9　Ibid, pp.32–3.
10　Ibid, p.34.
11　Ibid, p.34.
12　Ibid, p.33.
13　Ibid, pp.32–3.
14　Ibid, pp.33–4.
15　Ibid, p.50.
16　Ibid, p.50.
17　Ibid, p.50.
18　Letter from Sir Arthur Knight to Author, March 1995.
19　Alfred Chandler, *Scale and Scope*,
20　Coleman, op. cit., p.37.
21　Ibid, p.37.
22　Ibid, pp.120 and 265–6.
23　Ibid, p.135.
24　Ibid, pp.100–101.
25　Knight, A. Letter to Author.
26　*The Times*, 19.5.53.

APPENDIX VIII
1　Barnes, C.H. *Handley Page Aircraft*, p.411.
2　PRO, AIR 20/2983.
3　8 May 1941.
4　PRO, AIR 8/555.

5   PRO, AIR 20/2689.
6   PRO, AIR 20/2689.
7   PRO, AIR 20/3059. Freeman to Craven, 1941.
8   PRO, AIR 20/2689, 15 September 1941. Freeman to Craven.
9   Craven's reply, ibid, September 1941.
10   PRO, AIR 20/3059.
11   Meeting between MAP, Freeman and Courtney; December 1941.
12   Richards, D. *The hardest victory*, Coronet edition, p. 413, quoting F/O F.C.Cronshaw, DFC.
13   Clarke, R.W. *British aircraft armament* pp. 154–5.
14   Clarke, op cit, pp. 146–9.
15   Middlebrook, M, *The Nuremberg Raid*, pp. 147–8.

APPENDIX IX
1   Banks, F.R. op. cit., 1983 edition, p. 234–5.
2   Gunston, B. *By Jupiter*, 1978 edition, p. 68.
3   PRO, AIR 6/44, E.P.M. 26 (36). p. 2.
4   Bristol Directors Committee Minutes [BDCM], 2.11.37.
5   Sawyer, W.J.A. *The Bristol Aircooled Radial Engine: A technical History*, Ch. 11. Although the Air Ministry paid the costs and overheads of all development work, '...the Board had not permitted graduate recruitment on ...[the R-R scale] and the technical staff were... fully stretched'.
6   BDCM, 22.2.39.
7   Ibid, 5.3.40.
8   R-RHT, *Archive* Vol. 4, Issue 2, 1986.
9   Harvey-Bailey, *The Merlin in perspective*. R-RHT No.2 P. 40.
10   On 7 December 1933.
11   BDCM, 6.10.42.
12   Ibid, 9.3.43.
13   Ibid, 2.3.43.
14   Sawyer W. op. cit., Ch. 11, p. 4–8.
15   Ibid, Ch 11, p. 5.
16   Ibid, p. 5.
17   Lumsden, A. *British piston aero-engines*. The Merlin XX weighed 1,450lb, the Hercules 1,845, and the Centaurus, 2,695.
18   SSEC No. 45.
19   SSEC, No. 38.
20   PRO, AIR 6/48. EPM 22 (37).
21   PRO, AIR 20/3072. Freeman to Dunbar at MAP on 18 April 1942.
22   EF, 1944.

APPENDIX X
1   SSEC No. 61.
2   SSEC No. 63.
3   SSEC No. 64.
4   Andrews and Morgan, *Supermarine Aircraft*, p.331.
5   SSEC No. 84, AIR 6/49.
6   AIR 6/48.
7   PRO, AIR 20/2921.
8   MAP files. Freeman to Tedder, 3.6.40.
9   AIR 6/59. EPM 48 (40) and Bristol Director's Committee minutes, (BDCM) 8.2.40.
10   Bristol Centaurus file: meeting at MAP 21.11.40 with Bulman and Fedden.
11. Connolly.
12   PRO, AIR 20/2966.
13   Barnes, C.H. *Handley Page Aircraft since 1907*, p. 385.

14 PRO, AIR 20/2914. 15 August 1942.
15 Letter to author from Rolls-Royce Heritage Trust.
16 AIR 20/2914.
17 Middlebrook, M. *The Nuremberg Raid*, p. 99.
18 Middlebrook, op.cit., p. 38.
19 R-R files; Freeman to Hives, 2 December 1940.
20 PRO, AIR 20/2854, 24 December 1940.
21 PRO, AIR 20/3072.
22 PRO, AVIA 46/119, and AIR 20/425.
23 PRO, AMDP folder No. 1301.
24 PRO, AIR 20/2854.
25 W. Gunston Letter. 10 October 1997.
26 Talks with Sir Robert Lickley.
27 PRO, AIR 20/3018.
28 PRO, AIR 20/3065.

Bibliography

Aldrich, Nelson, W., *Tommy Hitchcock an American hero*, Fleet Street Publishing Corp., 1985

Andrews C.F. & Morgan, E.B., *Supermarine aircraft since 1914*, Putnam, 1989

Banks, Air Commander, F.R., *I kept no diary*, Airlife, 1983 edn

Barker, *The RFC in France*, 2 vols., Constable, 1994

Barnes, C.H., *Bristol aircraft since 1910*, Putnam, 1964

Barnett, Correlli, *The Audit of war*, Macmillan, 1986

Beauman W/Cdr., *Some recollections of the first course*, RAF Staff College

Bickers, *The first Great War*, Coronet edn., 1989

Birch, David, *Rolls-Royce and the Mustang*, R-RHT, 1987

Birkenhead, The Earl of, *The Prof in two worlds*, Collins, 1961

Boyle, Andrew, *Trenchard*, Collins, 1962.

Brodie, J.L.P., 'F.B.Halford', *RAeS Journal*, Vol. 63, April 1959

Brooks, David S., *Vikings at Waterloo*, R-RHT, 1997

Bruce, J.M., *Aeroplanes of the RFC*, Putnam, 1992

Cairncross, Sir A., *Planning in wartime*, Macmillan, in association with St Anthony's College, Oxford, 1991

Chandler, A., *Scale and Scope*, Harvard University Press, 1990

Chisholm and Davie, *Beaverbrook*, Hutchinson, 1992

Churchill, W.S., *The Second World War*, Cassell, 1948–54

Clarke, R.W., *British Aircraft Armament*, Patrick Stephens, 1993

Cogswell, D., *History of Rolls-Royce in Scotland*, R-R files

Coleman, *Courtaulds*, Vol 3, Oxford University Press, 1980

Colville, Sir John, *The Churchillians*, Weidenfeld & Nicolson, 1981

   The Fringes of Power; Downing Street Diaries, Hodder & Stoughton, 1985

Connolly, J.V., 'Aircraft Production', *RAeS Journal*, Vol. 70, Jan 1966

Cox, Sebastian, *The difference between White and Black*, Churchill, Imperial politics & intelligence before the 'Crusader' offensive; unpublished monograph.
   The dismissal of Air Chief Marshal Dowding from Fighter Command; November 1940

Dean, Sir Maurice, *The RAF and Two World Wars*, Cassell, 1979

De Groot, Dr, *Liberal Crusader*, a biography of Sir Archibald Sinclair, Lord Thurso, Hurst, 1993

Devons, E., *Planning in Practice*, Cambridge University Press, 1950

Douglas, Marshal of the Royal Air Force Lord, *Years of Combat*, Collins, 1963

Dundas, H, *Flying Start*, Penguin, 1988

Embry, Air Chief Marshal Sir Basil, *Mission Completed*, Methuen, 1957

Ethell, Jeffrey, *Mustang*, Jane's Publishing, 1981

Fedden, Sir Roy, 'The first 25 years of the Bristol engine department', *RAeS Journal*, Vol. 65, May 1961
   'Possible future development of air-cooled engines' (R.AeS lecture, 7 December 1933), *RAeS Journal*, March 1934

Fraser, General Sir D., *Alanbrook*, Collins, 1982

Freeman, Roger, *The Mighty Eighth war diary*, Arms & Armour, 1990 edn, 1986

Galland, Adolf, *The first and the last*, Methuen [English edn], 1955

Gibbs, N.H., *The Grand Strategy*, Vol. 1, HMSO, 1976

Gilbert, Martin, *Winston S.Churchill*, Vol. VI, Heinemann, 1983

Golley, John, *Whittle*, the true story, Airlife, 1996

Goodson, J., *Tumult in the clouds*, Arrow edn, 1986

Goulter, C.A., *A forgotten offensive*, Frank Cass, 1995

Gray and Thetford, *German aircraft of the 1st World War*, Putnam

Great Aircraft of the World, Marshall Cavendish, 1988

Gunston, W, *By Jupiter!* The life of Sir Roy Fedden, Royal Aeronautical Society, 1978
   Fedden – the life of Sir Roy Fedden, R-RHT, 1998

Hansell, Major-General H.S., *The air plan that defeated Hitler*, Atlanta, 1972

Hare, *The Royal Aircraft Factory*, Putnam

Harker, R., *Rolls-Royce from the wings*, Oxford Illustrated Press, 1976

Harvey, W.F.J., 'RFC experiences in the March and April retreats, 1918', *Air Pictorial*, April 1968

Harvey-Bailey, Alec, *The Merlin in perspective; the combat years*, R-RHT, 1983

Harvey-Bailey, Alec & Evans, Mike, *Rolls-Royce; the pursuit of excellence*, R-RHT, 1987

Harvey-Bailey, Alec & Piggott, Dave, *The Merlin 100 series*, 1993
   Rolls-Royce; the formative years, 1981
   Hives the quiet tiger, 1985

Haslam, E.B., 'How Lord Dowding came to leave Fighter Command', *Journal of Strategic Studies*, 1981

Hastings, Max., *Bomber Command*, Michael Joseph, 1979

Henshaw, Alec, *Sigh for a Merlin*, Hamlyn edn, 1981

Hooker, Sir Stanley, *Not much of an Engineer*, Airlife, 1984

Hornby W., *Factories and Plant*, HMSO, 1958

Hough and Richards, *The Battle of Britain*, Hodder & Stoughton, 1989

Hyde, F. Montgomery, *British Air Policy between the wars*, Heinemann, 1976
   Baldwin, Hart Davis Macgibbon, 1973

Jackson, A.J., *De Havilland aircraft since 1909*, Putnam, 1987

Jarrett, 'Parnalls final fling' *Air Enthusiast*, No. 35, 1994

Jones, H.A., *The War in the Air*, 6 vols, Clarendon, 1922–37

Jones, R.V., *Most Secret War*, Hamish Hamilton, 1978

Joubert de la Ferte, Air Chief Marshal Sir Philip, *Fun and Games*, Hutchinson, 1964

Keegan, John, *Churchill's Generals*, Weidenfeld & Nicolson, 1991

King, H.F., *Sopwith aircraft 1912–1920*, Putnam

Laffin, *Swifter than eagles*, [MRAF Sir J.Salmond]

Lewis, *Saggitarius rising*, Corgi edn, 1969

Macksey, *Armoured crusader*, Greenhill Books

Macmillan, Norman, *Sefton Brancker*

McFarland, 'The evolution of the stategic fighter in Europe 1942–44', *Journal of Strategic Studies*, June 1987

Marder, A.J., *From Dreadnought to Scapa Flow*, 5 vols, Oxford University Press, 1966–70

Mason, Francis K., *Hawker aircraft since 1920*, Putnam, 1991

Maynard, *Bennett and the Pathfinders*

Mensforth, E., *Family Engineers*, Ward Lock, 1981

Messenger, C., 'Neuve Chapelle', *War Monthly*, April 1981

Mets, *Master of Air Power:* Carl A. Spaatz, Presidio Press, 1997

Middlebrook, Martin, *The Schweinfurt-Regensburg Mission*, Penguin, 1985
   The Peenemunde Raid, Penguin, 1988
   The Nuremberg Raid, Penguin, 1986
   The Hamburg Raids, Penguin, 1984
   The Berlin Raids, Penguin, 1990
   Battleship, Penguin, 1986

Miller, C., Personal Papers, IWM

Mitchell, G., *Schooldays to Spitfire*, Nelson and Sanders, 1986

Morris, G., *Bloody April*
   The RFC. A History, George Allen & Unwin, 1983

Murray, Williamson, *The Luftwaffe, 1933–1945*, Nautical and Aviation Publishing Company, 1985

Nahum, A., *The rotary engine*, HMSO/Science Museum

Nahum, Foster-Pegg, Birch, *The Rolls-Royce Crecy*, R-RHT, 1994

O'Brien, C C., *The Siege*. Paladin, 1988

Orange, Vincent, *Sir Keith Park*, Methuen, 1984
   Coningham, Methuen, 1990; Center for Air Force History, 1992

Orange, Vincent & Cross, Air Chief Marshal Sir Kenneth, *Straight and Level*, Grub Street, 1993

Overy, Richard, *The Air War 1939–45*, Europa, 1981
   Goering, the iron man, Routledge and Kegan Paul, 1984
   Why the Allies won, Cape, 1995
   War and economy in the third Reich, Oxford University Press, 1995

Penrose, Harald, *Ominous skies*, HMSO, 1980
   British Aviation: The adventuring years, Putnam, 1973

Piggott, Dave, *The Vulture files*, R-RHT

Playfair, I.S.O., *The Mediterranean & the Middle East*, Vol. 2 ,1959

Postan, *British war production*, HMSO/Longmans, 1952

Postan, Hay & Scott, *The design and development of weapons*, HMSO/Longman, 1954

Price, Alfred, *World War II Fighter Conflict*, Macdonald, 1975

Quill, Jeffrey, *Spitfire*, Murray

Quill, Jeffrey & Cox, Sebastian, *The birth of a legend*, Quiller Press, 1986

Reader, *Architect of Air Power*, Collins, 1968

Reid, J.M., *James Lithgow, Master of Work*, Hutchinson, 1963

Richards, Denis, *Portal of Hungerford*, Heinemann, 1977
   The hardest victory

Richey, Paul, *Fighter pilot*, Jane's Publishing, 1980

Ritchie, Sebastian, *Industry and Air Power*, Frank Cass, 1997
   'A New Audit of War' *War & Society*, Vol. 12, May 1994
   'A political intrigue'. The downfall of Air Chief Marshal Sir Cyril Newall.
   War & Society, Vol. 16, No. 1, May 1998

Roberts, A, *Eminent Churchillians*, Weidenfeld and Nicolson, 1994

Robertson, A.J., *Lord Beaverbrook and the supply of Aircraft*, 1940–1

Roskill, Captain S.W., *Naval policy between the wars*, Collins, 1968

Rubbra, A.A., *Rolls-Royce piston aero engines*, R-RHT, 1990

Salmond, MRAF Sir John, *Report on night fighting*, September 1940

Schlaifer R. & Heron, S.D., *The development of aircraft engines and aviation fuels*, Harvard Business School, 1970 edition

Scott, John P., *Vickers; a History*, Weidenfeld and Nicolson, 1963

Sereny, Gitta, *Albert Speer*, Macmillan, 1995

Sharp, Martin and Bowyer, Michael, *Mosquito*, Faber, 1967

Shute, *Slide rule*, Heinemann, 1954

Slessor, Marshal of the RAF Sir John, *The Central Blue*, Cassell, 1956
   The Tools of Victory, BBC 3rd Programme, September 1953

Smith M., 'Sir Edgar Ludlow-Hewitt and the expansion of Bomber Command 1940/1', *RSUI Journal*, March 1981

Speer, Albert, *Inside the Third Reich*, Weidenfeld & Nicolson, 1970

Strange, Colonel Louis, *Recollections of an airman*, Greenhill, 1989

Swinton, Viscount, *I remember*, Hutchinson, 1948

Taylor, J.W., *CFS: Birthplace of Air Power*, Jane's Publishing, 1987

Tedder, Marshal of the Royal Air Force Lord, *With prejudice*, Cassell, 1966

Terraine, *The right of the line*, Hodder & Stoughton, 1985
   Douglas Haig, Hutchinson, 1963

Thetford, Owen, *British naval aircraft since 1912*, Putnam, 1991 edn

Thoms, *War, Industry & Society*, 1989

USSBS, 4; Aircraft Division Industry Report (Europe)

Villa, B.L., *Unauthorised action*, Collins, 1989

Webster, Sir Charles and Frankland, Noble, *The Strategic Air Offensive Against Germany 1939–1943*, 4 vols, HMSO, 1961

Whittle, Sir Frank, *Jet*, Frederick Muller, 1953

Yoxall, J., 'History of No 2 Squadron', *Flight*, June 1949

General index

Page numbers in *italic* type refer to picture captions.

Index of aircraft

Index of engines

Illustration credits

The publishers would like to thank the following for their assistance in providing
illustrations and for giving permission to reproduce copyright material. Every effort has
been made to locate copyright holders but in a few instances this has not been successful.

Imperial War Museum: frontispiece, pages 65, 68, 73, 107, 109(b), 123, 131(b), 139,
    149, 158, 165, 179, 181, 186, 209(a)&(b), 213, 221, 231(c), 235, 237, 238, 239,
    249(a)&(b), 276, 285(a)&(b), 287(a)&(b), 328, 338(a)&(b), 350(a), 352
RAF Museum: pages 61(a), 69, 71(a)&(b), 89, 106, 112, 130(a)&(b), 143(a), 168, 274,
    280, 338(c), 349(b)
Philip Jarrett: pages 49, 61(b)&(c), 109(a), 119, 125,(a)(b)&(c), 127, 231(a)&(b), 342,
    350(b)
J.M. Bruce/G.S. Leslie Collection: pages 25, 28, 29, 31, 32, 33, 35, 38(a)&(b), 39,
    40(a)&(b), 42, 43
National Portrait Gallery: pages 62, 63, 86, 115, 171
Rolls-Royce Heritage Trust: pages 79, 227, 290(a)&(b), 325, 337
The Institute of Petroleum: page 307
Royal Aeronautical Society: page 332
National Railway Museum: page 111
Express Newspapers: page 138
Hulton Getty: page 148
TRH Pictures: page 240
Royal Naval College 45
RAF Staff College 48